Lecture Notes in Computer Science 2376

Edited by G. Goos, J. Hartmanis, and J. van Leeuwen

Springer

Berlin
Heidelberg
New York
Barcelona
Hong Kong
London
Milan
Paris
Tokyo

Enrico Gregori   Ludmila Cherkasova
Gianpaolo Cugola   Fabio Panzieri
Gian P. Picco (Eds.)

Web Engineering and Peer-to-Peer Computing

NETWORKING 2002 Workshops
Pisa, Italy, May 19-24, 2002
Revised Papers

Springer

Series Editors

Gerhard Goos, Karlsruhe University, Germany
Juris Hartmanis, Cornell University, NY, USA
Jan van Leeuwen, Utrecht University, The Netherlands

Volume Editors

Enrico Gregori, Consiglio Nazionale delle Ricerche, Istituto IIT
Via G. Moruzzi, 1, 56124 Pisa, Italy; E-mail: enrico.gregori@iit.cnr.it

Ludmila Cherkasova, Hewlett-Packard Laboratories, 1501 Page Mill Road
MS 3U-6, 94303-1126 Palo Alto, CA, USA; E-mail: cherkasova@hpl.hp.com

Gianpaolo Cugola, Politecnico di Milano, Dipartimento di Elettronica e Informazione
Via Ponzio 34/5, 20133 Milano, Italy; E-mail: cugola@elet.polimi.it

Fabio Panzieri, University of Bologna, Via Mura Zamboni 7
40127 Bologna, Italy; E-mail: panzieri@cs.unibo.it

Gian Pietro Picco, Politecnico di Milano, Dipartimento di Elettronica e Informazione
Piazza Leonardo da Vinci, 32, 20133 Milano, Italy; E-mail: picco@elet.polimi.it

Cataloging-in-Publication Data applied for

Die Deutsche Bibliothek - CIP-Einheitsaufnahme

Web engineering and peer to peer computing : networking 2002 workshops,
Pisa, Italy, May 19 - 24, 2002 ; revised papers / Enrico Gregori ... (ed.). -
Berlin ; Heidelberg ; New York ; Barcelona ; Hong Kong ; London ; Milan ;
Paris ; Tokyo : Springer, 2002
     (Lecture notes in computer science ; Vol. 2376)
     ISBN 3-540-44177-8

CR Subject Classification (1998): C.2, C.4, D.2, H.4.3, J.2, J.1, K.6, K.4

ISSN 0302-9743
ISBN 3-540-44177-8 Springer-Verlag Berlin Heidelberg New York

Springer-Verlag Berlin Heidelberg New York
a member of BertelsmannSpringer Science+Business Media GmbH

http://www.springer.de

© Springer-Verlag Berlin Heidelberg 2002
Printed in Germany

Typesetting: Camera-ready by author, data conversion by Steingräber Satztechnik GmbH
Printed on acid-free paper   SPIN: 10870423   06/3142   5 4 3 2 1 0

Preface

This book constitutes the refereed proceedings of the two thematic workshops held jointly with Networking 2002: WEB Engineering and Peer-to-Peer Computing.

Networking 2002 was organized by the Italian National Research Council (CNR) and was sponsored by the IFIP working groups WG 6.2 (Network and Internetwork Architectures), WG 6.3 (Performance of Communication Systems), and WG 6.8 (Wireless Communications). The program of the conference covered five days and included the main conference (three days), two tutorial days, and one day of thematic workshops.

The International Workshop on Web Engineering was dedicated to the discussion of the principal issues that emerge in the design and implementation of large-scale, complex, Web-based systems. Scalability issues pose a number of challenging problems to solve for both applications and the underlying web/network infrastructure. On one hand, web services and internet applications must take into account network performance and transport protocol design, to achieve acceptable performance and robustness. On the other hand, emerging network and Web technologies are determined by the requirements of these applications.

Fifteen papers were presented that illustrated the current state of the art in this area.

In addition to the authors of these papers, the Workshop on Web Engineering was attended by about thirty participants, who contributed to the workshop by stimulating fruitful discussions at the end of each presentation. Thus, this workshop provided a excellent opportunity for researchers, from both industry and academia, to gather, exchange ideas, and discuss recent results in the development of Web-based systems and emerging Internet applications.

The aim of the International Workshop on Peer-to-Peer Computing was to bring together researchers and practitioners active in the field of peer-to-peer computing with the goal of identifying the core open research issues, and defining the research agenda for the next generation of peer-to-peer systems.

The peer-to-peer paradigm of communication is not new to researchers, who have adopted it for years. As an example, most Internet network protocols are based on this model, which results in highly adaptive systems. In the last few years, however, the peer-to-peer paradigm has gained popularity at the application level, thanks to the emergence of file sharing applications over the Internet. Napster, Gnutella, and Freenet are examples of applications that enable users to share information residing on their own machine with other connected peers by exploiting an overlay network. The interest in the opportunities opened up by this paradigm has been so great that many have already welcomed the birth of "the next Internet".

The workshop received 26 submissions from all over the world. Each paper was assigned three reviewers drawn from the Program Committee, composed of researchers actively involved in peer-to-peer computing. In the end, ten regular papers and six short/position papers were accepted. The workshop program was organized in four sessions: routing and discovery, applications, programming models, and security.

The workshops on Web Engineering and on Peer-to-Peer Computing would not have been possible without the enthusiastic and hard work of a number of colleagues. A special thanks to the TPC members, and all the referees, for their invaluable help in reviewing papers for the workshops. Finally we would like to thank all the authors that submitted their papers to this conference for their interest.

We are also indebted to our supporters. First of all CNR. CNR not only gave Enrico Gregori enough time to organize this event during the year leading up to the workshops, but also financially supported the event through sponsorship by the CNUCE and IIT institutes. A special thanks to Telecom Italia for joining us in the organization of this event. We are also indebted to our corporate sponsors (Cassa di Risparmio di Pisa, Compaq, Microsoft, Provincia di Pisa, and Softech) whose help removed much of the financial uncertainty and who also provided interesting suggestions for the program.

July 2002

Enrico Gregori
Ludmilla Cherkasova
Gianpaolo Cugola
Fabio Panzieri
Gian Pietro Picco

Organizers

Sponsoring Institutions

Networking 2002 Organization Committee

Conference Executive Committee

General Chair:
Enrico Gregori, National Research Council, Italy

General Vice-chair:
Ioannis Stavrakakis, University of Athens, Greece

Technical Program Chair:
Marco Conti, National Research Council, Italy

Special Track Chair for Networking Technologies, Services, and Protocols:
Andrew T. Campbell, Columbia University, USA

Special Track Chair for Performance of Computer and Communication Networks:
Moshe Zukerman, University of Melbourne, Australia

Special Track Chair for Mobile and Wireless Communications:
Guy Omidyar, National University of Singapore

Tutorial Program Co-chairs:
Giuseppe Anastasi, University of Pisa, Italy
Stefano Basagni, Northeastern University, USA

Workshop Chairs:

Workshop 1 — *Web Engineering*
Ludmilla Cherkasova, Hewlett Packard Labs, USA
Fabio Panzieri, University of Bologna, Italy

Workshop 2 — *Peer-to-Peer Computing*
Gianpaolo Cugola, Politecnico di Milano, Italy
Gian Pietro Picco, Politecnico di Milano, Italy

Workshop 3 — *IP over WDM*
Giancarlo Prati, Scuola Superiore S. Anna, Italy
Piero Castoldi, Scuola Superiore S. Anna, Italy

Invited Speaker Chair:
Fabrizio Davide, PhD, Telecom Italia S.p.A., Italy

Organization Chair:
Stefano Giordano, University of Pisa, Italy

Publicity Chair:
Silvia Giordano, Federal Inst. of Technology Lausanne (EPFL), Switzerland
Laura Feeney, SICS, Sweden

Steering Committee Chair:
Harry Perros, North Carolina State University, USA

Steering Committee Members:

Augusto Casaca, IST/INESC, Portugal
S. K. Das, The University of Texas at Arlington, USA
Erol Gelenbe, University of Central Florida, USA
Harry Perros, NCSU, USA (Chair)
Guy Pujolle, University of Paris 6, France
Harry Rudin, Switzerland
Jan Slavik, TESTCOM, Czech Republic
Hideaki Takagi, University of Tsukuba, Japan
Samir Thome, ENST, France
Adam Wolisz, TU–Berlin, Germany

Electronic Submission:
Alessandro Urpi, University of Pisa, Italy

Web Designer:
Patrizia Andronico, IAT–CNR, Italy

Local Organizing Committee:
Renzo Beltrame, CNUCE–CNR, Italy
Raffaele Bruno, CNUCE–CNR, Italy
Willy Lapenna, CNUCE–CNR, Italy
Gaia Maselli, CNUCE–CNR, Italy
Renata Bandelloni, CNUCE–CNR, Italy

International Workshop on Web Engineering

Co-located with Networking 2002
Pisa, Italy, May 24, 2002

Program Co-chairs:
Ludmilla Cherkasova, Hewlett Packard Labs, USA
Fabio Panzieri, University of Bologna, Italy

Technical Program Committee

Jon Crowcroft, University of Cambridge, UK
Anindya Datta, Georgia Tech, USA
Wolfgang Emmerich, University College London, UK
Rachid Gerraoui, EPFL, Lausanne, Switzerland
Vittorio Ghini, University of Bologna, Italy
Anne-Marie Kermarrec, Microsoft Research Ltd., UK
Tomas Rokicki, Instantis Corp., USA
Gianpaolo Rossi, University of Milan, Italy
Santosh Shrivastava, University of Newcastle-upon-Tyne, UK
Wenting Tang, Hewlett Packard Labs., USA
Helen Thomas, Carnegie Mellon University, USA
Amin Vahdat, Duke University, USA
Jia Wang, AT&T Labs–Research, USA
Philip S. Yu, IBM Research, USA
Willy Zwaenepoel, Rice University, USA

Referees

Tim Brecht	Harumi Kuno	Amin Vahdat
Jon Crowcroft	Mallik Mahalingam	Alistair Veitch
Anindya Datta	Elena Pagani	Jia Wang
Wolfgang Emmerich	Tomas Rokickihu	Qian Wang
Rachid Gerraoui	Gianpaolo Rossi	Haifeng Yu
Vittorio Ghini	Santosh Shrivastava	Philip S. Yu
Sven Graupner	Sharad Singhal	Willy Zwaenepoel
Magnus Karlsson	Wenting Tang	
Anne-Marie Kermarrec	Helen Thomas	

International Workshop
on Peer-to-Peer Computing

Co-located with Networking 2002
Pisa, Italy, May 24, 2002

Program Co-chairs:
Gianpaolo Cugola, Politecnico di Milano, Italy
Gian Pietro Picco, Politecnico di Milano, Italy

Technical Program Committee
Ozalp Babaoglu, Università di Bologna, Italy
Gianpaolo Cugola, Politecnico di Milano, Italy
Li Gong, Sun Microsystems, China
Manfred Hauswirth, EPFL, Lausanne, Switzerland
Jean-Pierre Hubaux, EPFL, Lausanne, Switzerland
Gian Pietro Picco, Politecnico di Milano, Italy
Robbert van Renesse, Cornell University, Ithaca, USA
Ant Rowstron, Microsoft Research, Cambridge, UK

Table of Contents

Workshop on Web Engineering

Models and Characterization of WWW Traffic

Caching Infrastructure and Content Delivery Networks

Methodologies and Tools
for Building Web-Based Systems

Web Server Performance, Testing and Benchmarking Environment

Workshop on Peer-to-Peer Computing

Routing and Discovery in Peer-to-Peer Networks

Applications

Programming Models

Security

A Parsimonious Multifractal Model for WWW Traffic*

Abdullah Balamash and Marwan Krunz

Department of Electrical & Computer Engineering
University of Arizona
T ucson, AZ 85721
{balamash,krunz}@ece.arizona.edu

Abstract. In this paper, we capture the main characteristics of WWW traffic in a stochastic model, which can be used to generate syn thetic WWW traces and assess WWW cache designs. To capture temporal and spatial localities, we use a modified version of Riedi et al.'s multifractal model [18], where we reduce the complexity of the original model from $\mathcal{O}(N)$ to $\mathcal{O}(1)$; N being the length of the synthetic trace. Our model has the attractiveness of being parsimonious and that it avoids the need to apply a transformation to a self-similar model (as often done in previously proposed models [2]), thus retaining the temporal locality of the fitted traffic. Furthermore, because of the scale-dependent nature of multifractal processes, the proposed model is more flexible than monofractal models in describing irregularities in the traffic. Trace-driven simulations are used to demonstrate the goodness of the proposed model.

keywords — WWW modeling, w eb caching, m ultifractals,stack distance, self-similarity.

1 Introduction

The ability to assess the performance of WWW caching policies hinges on the availabilit y of a represen tative workload that can be used in trace-driven simulations [5, 13]. Measured ("real") traces can be used for this purpose. However, due to the difficulty associated with capturing real traces, only a handful of such traces are available in the public domain (see [1]). This makes it hard to provide simulation results with reasonable statistical credibility. A more feasible alternativ e is to rely on synthetic traces that are derived from a stochastic model. The need for such a model is the main motivation behind our work.

In this paper, we use a modified version of the multifractal model by Riedi [18] to simultaneously capture the temporal and spatial localities in WWW traffic. Riedi's model has the attractiveness of being able to simultaneously capture the (lognormal) marginal distribution and the correlation structure of a time series.

---

* This work was supported in part by the National Science Foundation under grants CCR 9979310 and ANI 0095625.

E. Gregori et al. (Eds.): Networking 2002 Workshops, LNCS 2376, pp. 1–14, 2002.

Its main disadvantage is its complexity, which grows linearly with the size of the generated trace. We modify this model, reducing its complexity to $\mathcal{O}(1)$. The resulting (modified) model is parsimonious, in that it is characterized by four to five parameters, that represent the mean, variance, and correlation structure of the "scaled stack distance" string (see below). The popularity profile of the traffic is incorporated in the model during the trace generation phase (assuming that the popularity profiles for all documents are given beforehand). Our model is mainly intended for offline generation of the traffic demand *seen by a WWW server*. Accordingly, the popularity profiles can be easily computed from the server logs.

Two datasets were used in our study. The first one was captured at the Computer Science Department of the University of Calgary, while the second set was produced by ClarkNet, a commercial Internet Provider in Baltimore, Washington DC [1, 3]. Details of these traces can be found in [1, 3]. Note that the two traces have contrasting loads (Calgary's load is light while ClarkNet's load is very heavy). The data provide several pieces of information, including the name of host that generated the URL request, the day and time the request was recorded, the name of requested file, the HTTP reply code (explained below), and the number of transferred bytes in response to the request. Four types of HTTP reply codes were recorded: *successful, not modified, found*, and *unsuccessful*. In our analysis, we only included the requests with *successful* code, since they are the ones that result in actual data transfer from server. We also excluded dynamic files (e.g., cgi and pl files).

WWW traffic modeling has been the focus of several previous studies; examples of which are given in [15, 2, 4, 14, 8]. In these studies, the temporal locality of the traffic was represented by the marginal distribution of the stack distance string. This distribution was found to follow a lognormal-like shape. The stack distance string, which is an equivalent representation of a reference string, is obtained by transforming the reference string using the LRU stack. In [2] the authors showed that spatial locality can be captured (at least, in part) through the autocorrelation structure (ACF) of the stack distance string. They argued that the stack distance string exhibits long-range dependence (LRD) behavior. Thus, to simultaneously model the marginal distribution (temporal locality) and the correlation structure (spatial locality) of the stack distance string, they relied on the work in [12], which proved the invariance of the Hurst parameter to transformations of the marginal distribution of an LRD process. More specifically, the authors in [12] proved that under some mild assumptions, a point-by-point transformation $Y = F_y^{-1}(F_x(X))$ of a *Gaussian* self-similar process X with Hurst parameter H results in a self-similar process Y with the same Hurst parameter, where F_x and F_y are the CDFs for X and Y, respectively. It should be noted, however, that the proof of this result is valid asymptotically and only for Gaussian processes (e.g., fractional ARIMA). More importantly, while this result assures the invariance of H, it does not necessarily preserve the shape of the ACF. As an example, consider the transforming of the Gaussian distribution of a F-ARIMA model into a lognormal distribution, which adequately models the marginal distribution of the stack distance string. The resulting ACFs are shown in Figure 1, along with the A CFof the "real" traffic. The figure illustrates the t wo main drawbacks of the transformation. First, the transformation distorts the o verall shape of the ACF of the F-ARIMA process. Second, the original F-ARIMA model itself is not accurate in representing the real ACF at finite lags.

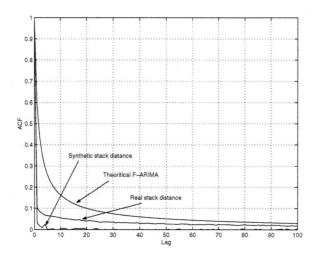

Fig. 1. Impact of transforming the distribution of a F-ARIMA model on the ACF.

T oavoid the problems stated above, w eresort to multifractal modeling to simultaneously capture the correlation structure and the marginal distribution of the stack distance string. Multifractality is a generalization of self-similarity (monofractality), whereby the Hurst parameter (the scaling exponent) is not fixed, but varies with scale. This variability makes multifractal processes more flexible than monofractal processes in describing "irregularities" in the traffic (e.g., contrasting short-term and long-term behaviors). The reader is referred to [17, 11, 18, 9, 10] and the references therein for comprehensive discussions of multifractal processes. In [18] the authors used a w avelet-basedconstruction of a multifractal process to show that the correlation behavior of a strongly correlated time series can be approximately captured b y appropriately setting the second moments of the wa velet coefficients at each scale of the multifractal generation process. This result provides the basis for modeling the ACF of the stack distance string. Combined with the fact that the above multifractal model exhibits an approximately lognormal marginal distribution, they can be used to model both the temporal and spatial localities in WWW traffic.

Relying on the observation that temporal locality is induced by both temporal correlation and long-term popularity [16], the authors in [6] introduced a new measure for temporal locality called the *scaled stack distance*. This measure represents the deviation of the stack distances from their expected values, *assuming that requests to a given document are uniformaly distribute dover the duration of the trace.* The scaled stack distance captures the impact of short-term correlation, but does not capture the spatial localit y For our WWW traffic model, w e use a similar measure with the same name, but that measures the deviation of the stack distances from their *empirical* expected values. We model the expected stack distance as a function of the popularity profile. Equally popular documents have the same expected stack distance. This scaled stack distance string was found to have a lognormal-like distribution and the same correlation structure as the original stack distance string.

We use extensive simulations to ev aluate the performance of our WWW traffic model and con trastit with the self-similar model in [2] and the model in [6], using the original (real) traces as a point of reference. Our performance measures include sample statistics of the synthetic traces (e.g., mean, variance, correlations, percentiles) as well as the cache and byte hit ratios for a trace-driven LRU (least recently used) cac he. The results indicate marked improvement in performance when using the proposed multifractal-based WWW model.

The rest of the paper is organized as follows. Section 2 gives a brief overview of Riedi et al.'s multifractal model and the modification we make to it to render it parsimonious. The proposed WWW traffic generation approach is given in Section 3, follow ed ly simulation studies in Section 4. We conclude the paper in Section 5.

2   Multifractal Analysis of WWW Traffic

As indicated earlier, multifractality is a generalization of monofractality (self-similarity), where the fixed (scale independent) H parameter of a self-similar process is now scale dependent. Certain multifractal processes, including the one considered in this paper, inherently exhibit lognormal-like marginals, in line with the shape of the marginal distribution of typical WWW traces. This conv enient feature allows us to skip the risky step of transforming the marginal distribution, leaving us with the task of fitting the ACF. In this section, w e first briefly describe Riedi et al.'s multifractal model [18]. This model uses a wavelet-based construction to approximately capture the correlation behavior of a given time series by appropriately setting the second moments of the wavelet coefficiets at each scale. We then describe how we modify this model to reduce its complexity from $\mathcal{O}(N)$ to $\mathcal{O}(1)$. We then apply the modified model in characterizing the temporal and spatial localities of WWW traffic.

2.1   Riedi et al.'s Multifractal Model

Riedi et al.'s model relies hea vilyon the discrete w avelet transform. The idea behind the wavelet transform is to express a signal (time function) $X(t)$ by an approximated (smoothed) version and a detail. The approximation process is repeated at v arious levels (scales) b y expressing the approximated signal at a given level j, say X_j, by a coarser approximation at level $j-1$, say X_{j-1}, and a detail D_{j-1}. At each scale, the approximation is performed through a scaling function $\phi(t)$, while the detail is obtained through a wavelet function $\psi(t)$. More formally, a wavelet expansion of the signal $X(t)$ is given by:

$$X(t) = \sum_k U_{J,k}\phi_{J,k}(t) + \sum_{j=J}^{\infty} \sum_k W_{j,k}\psi_{j,k}(t) \tag{1}$$

where

$$W_{j,k} \stackrel{\text{def}}{=} \int_{-\infty}^{\infty} X(t)\psi_{j,k}(t)dt \tag{2}$$

$$U_{j,k} \stackrel{\text{def}}{=} \int_{-\infty}^{\infty} X(t)\phi_{j,k}(t)dt \tag{3}$$

and $\psi_{j,k}$ and $\phi_{j,k}$, $j,k = 0,1,2,\ldots$, are *shifted* and *translated* versions of the wavelet and scaling functions $\psi(t)$ and $\phi(t)$, respectively, and are given by:

$$\psi_{j,k}(t) \stackrel{\text{def}}{=} 2^{-j/2}\psi(2^{-j}t - k) \tag{4}$$

$$\phi_{j,k}(t) \stackrel{\text{def}}{=} 2^{-j/2}\phi(2^{-j}t - k). \tag{5}$$

In (1), the index J indicates the coarsest scale (the lowest in detail). The coefficients $W_{j,k}$ and $U_{j,k}$ are called the wavelet and scale coefficients at scale j and time $2^j k$. Together, they define the discrete wavelet transform of the signal $X(t)$ (assuming that $\phi(t)$ and $\psi(t)$ are specified).

Several wavelet and scale functions have been used in the literature, giving rise to different wavelet transforms. One popular (and simple) transform is the Haar wavelet transform. This transform, which is specified by the coefficients $W_{j,k}$ and $U_{j,k}$ for all j and k, can be obtained recursively as follows (we adopt the same convention of [18], in which the higher the value of j, the better the approximation of the original signal):

$$U_{j,k} = \frac{U_{j+1,2k} + U_{j+1,2k+1}}{\sqrt{2}} \tag{6}$$

$$W_{j,k} = \frac{U_{j+1,2k} - U_{j+1,2k+1}}{\sqrt{2}} \tag{7}$$

To initialize the recursion, the values of $U_{j,k}$, $k = 0,1,\ldots,2^j - 1$, at the highest value of j are taken as the empirical trace to be modeled.

In order to generate synthetic traces with a given autocorrelation structure, the Haar transform is reversed by rewriting (6) and (7) as:

$$U_{j+1,2k} = \frac{U_{j,k} + W_{j,k}}{\sqrt{2}} \tag{8}$$

$$U_{j+1,2k+1} = \frac{U_{j,k} - W_{j,k}}{\sqrt{2}} \tag{9}$$

Now to generate nonnegative data, which in our case represent the stack distance string, w eneed to have $|W_{j,k}| \leq U_{j,k}$. T osatisfy this constraint, the w avelet coefficients can be defined as:

$$W_{j,k} = A_{j,k}U_{j,k} \tag{10}$$

where $A_{j,k}$ is a random variable (rv) defined on the interval $(-1, 1)$. Using (8), (9), and (10), the following recursion can be obtained for synthesizing the scale coefficients:

$$U_{j+1,2k} = (\frac{1 + A_{j,k}}{\sqrt{2}})U_{j,k} \tag{11}$$

$$U_{j+1,2k+1} = (\frac{1 - A_{j,k}}{\sqrt{2}})U_{j,k} \tag{12}$$

The rvs $A_{j,k}$ must also satisfy the following additional constraints [18]:

1. $A_{j,k}, k = 0, 1, ..., 2^j - 1$ are $i.i.d.$
2. For each j, the probability density function of the rvs $A_{j,k}, k = 0, 1, \ldots, 2^j-1$, is symmetric with zero mean.
3. A_j is independent of A_l for $l > j$ and is also independent of $U_{0,0}$.

The wavelet energy at a given scale is defined as the variance of the wavelet coefficients at that scale. It has been shown that the correlation structure of the signal can be approximately captured by con trolling thew avelet energy decay across scales. The ratio of the energy at scale $j - 1$ to the one at scale j (j is finer than $j - 1$) was found to be [18]:

$$\eta_j = \frac{E[W_{j-1}^2]}{E[W_j^2]} = 2\frac{E[A_{j-1}^2]}{E[A_j^2](1 - E[A_{j-1}^2])} \tag{13}$$

Assuming that $E[W_j^2]$ is given for all j, Equation (13) can be used to solve for $E[A_j^2]$, $j = 1, 2, \ldots..$ The recursion can be initialized using $E[A_0^2] = \frac{E[W_0^2]}{E[U_0^2]}$, where W_0 and U_0 are the wavelet and scale coefficients at the coarsest scale.

In [18], the authors suggested tw o different distributions for A_j. One of them is a symmetric beta distribution that has the following pdf:

$$f_{A_j}(x) = \frac{(1 + x)^{\rho_j - 1}(1 - x)^{\rho_j - 1}}{\beta(\rho_j, \rho_j)2^{2\rho_j - 1}} \tag{14}$$

where ρ_j is the parameter of the rv and $\beta(., .)$ is the beta function. The variance of this random variable is given by:

$$\text{var}[A_j] = \frac{1}{2\rho_j + 1}. \tag{15}$$

The other distribution is a point-mass distribution defined as:

$$\Pr[A_j = c_j] = \Pr[A_j = -c_j] = r_j$$
$$\Pr[A_j = 0] = 1 - 2r_j$$

In the case of a beta distributed A_j, the parameter ρ_j at each scale can be found by solving (13) and (15), resulting in:

$$\rho_j = \frac{\eta_j}{2}(\rho_{j-1} + 1) - 1/2 \qquad (16)$$

This, however, assumes that $E[W_j^2]$ is given for $j = 1, 2, 3, \ldots$. Since η_j, $j = 1, 2, \ldots$, cannot be obtained using a parametric model, it would be computed from the empirical data, which makes the number of fitted parameters in the model in the order of N; N being the trace length.

On the other hand, if A_j has a point-mass distribution, then (13) by itself is not sufficient to compute both parameters of A_j (c_j and r_j). An alternative approach to computing these parameters is to rely on the following expression for the moments of the scaling coefficients at different scales [18]:

$$\frac{E[U_j^q]}{E[U_{j-1}^q]} = 2^{-q/2} E[(1 + A_{j-1})^q], \quad q = 1, 2, \ldots \qquad (17)$$

However, to apply (17) one needs to have two moments (i.e., two values for q) for each scale j. Again, unless we can compute these values using a parametric model, we need to rely on the empirical data to do so, which makes the model more complex than if a beta distributed A_j were to be used.

It was shown in [18] that the above model (with either distribution of A_j) generates positive-valued autocorrelated data with an approximately lognormal marginal distribution.

2.2 Reducing the Number of Parameters

As shown in the previous section, whether A_j has a beta distribution or a point-mass distribution, one needs to provide the second moments of the wavelet co-efficients or two moments of the scale coefficients at each scale in order to completely determine A_j, $j = 1, 2, \ldots$. This significantly increases the complexity of the model, as the number of parameters to be computed a priori is in the order of the trace length (unless we have a parameterized model to compute these values). Moreover, the point-mass rv is not rich enough and has only three possible values.

To reduce the complexity of the model, we let A_j be a triangular rv in the range $[-c, c]$. This distribution is richer than the point-mass distribution and has only one parameter. It allows us to fit the second moment of the scale coefficients for all scales using (17), provided that we can compute the second moments analytically knowing the mean μ and the variance σ of the modeled data, as will be shown later in this section.

For a discrete time series $X = \{X_i : i = 1, 2, \ldots\}$, we define $X^{(m)} = \{X_i^{(m)} : i = 1, 2, \ldots\}$ to be the aggregated time series of X at level m:

$$X_n^{(m)} = \sum_{i=nm-m+1}^{nm} X_i, n = 1, 2, 3, \ldots, N/m \qquad (18)$$

where $m = 1, 2, 4, 8, \ldots N$; N is the length of X. Note that if the aggregation level m corresponds to scale j, then the aggregation level $2m$ corresponds to scale $j - 1$. From the definition of the Haar wavelet transform, the following holds:

$$\frac{E[(X^{(m)})^q]}{E[(X^{(2m)})^q]} = 2^{-q/2} \frac{E[U_j^q]}{E[U_{j-1}^q]}, \quad \text{for } q = 1, 2, \ldots \qquad (19)$$

From (19) and (17) we get:

$$\frac{E[(X^{(m)})^q]}{E[(X^{(2m)})^q]} = 2^{-q} E[(1 + A^{(2m)})^q] \qquad (20)$$

where $A^{(2m)} = A_{j-1}$. Let $c^{(2m)}$ be the parameter of the rv A_{j-1} at aggregation level $2m$. From (20) and the definition of the triangular random variable, we obtain the following expression for $c^{(2m)}$:

$$c^{(2m)} = \sqrt{6(4 \frac{E[(X^{(m)})^2]}{E[(X^{(2m)})^2]} - 1)} \qquad (21)$$

To reduce the number of parameters in the multifractal model, we analytically obtain the second moments of the scaling coefficients, as shown next. The variance at a given level of aggregation, $\text{var}[X^{(m)}] = V^{(m)}$, can be computed analytically as a function of the autocorrelation function of the signal [7]:

$$V^{(m)} = mv + 2v \sum_{k=1}^{m} (m - k)\rho_k \qquad (22)$$

The mean, $E[(X^{(m)})] = \mu^{(m)}$, is given by:

$$\mu^{(m)} = m\mu \qquad (23)$$

where μ and v are the mean and the variance of the original signal, respectively. The second moment of $X^{(m)}$ is then given by:

$$E[(X^{(m)})^2] = mv + 2v \sum_{k=1}^{m} (m - k)\rho_k + m^2\mu^2 \qquad (24)$$

From Equations (21) and (24), the parameter of the rv A_j can be computed for all scales $j = 1, 2, \ldots$, given μ, v, and the correlation structure of the time series being modeled. For WWW traffic stack distance strings, we found that the form $\rho_k = e^{-\beta \sqrt[n]{g(k)}}$, $k = 0, 1, \ldots$, fits the correlation structure very well, where g is a function of the lag k. For the ClarkNet trace, $g(k) = k$ produced a good fit to the empirical ACF, while for the Calgary trace, $g(k) = \log(k + 1)$ was found appropriate.

In summary, to use the multifractal model for modeling the scaled stack distance string, we only need four parameters:

- Mean of the stack distance string (μ).
- Variance of the stack distance string (v).
- Autocorrelation structure (parameterized by β, n, and g).

Using these parameters, along with (24) and (21), one can compute the parameter $c^{(m)}$ at each aggregation level (scale).

The synthesis process starts from the highest level of aggregation. At this level we can start with l data points that are normally distributed with mean $m_h \mu$ (the mean at aggregation level m_h) and variance of $\text{var}[X^{(m_h)}]$, where m_h is the highest aggregation level, which is the length of the trace that needs to be generated. After that, the process can be carried out using Equations (11) and (12).

3   Modeling WWW Traffic

In this section, we describe our approach for modeling the stream of file objects generated by a WWW server. Let U be the number of unique files (or objects) at the server and let fr_i be the fraction of times that the ith file, $i = 1, 2, ..., U$, appears in the reference string (fr_i is the popularity profile of file i). The modeling approach proceeds in three steps. First, we extract the stack distance string from the URL reference string. Then, we apply some form of scaling to capture both sources of temporal locality (temporal correlation and long-term popularity). The modified multifractal model described in the previous section is then applied to model the scaled stack distance string after computing its mean and variance and after fitting its correlation structure. Finally, we incorporate the popularity profile of the traffic during the process of generating synthetic reference strings. These main steps are described next.

3.1   Extracting the Empirical Scaled Stack String

In our model, we use the concept of stack distance to model the temporal and the spatial localities in WWW traffic. The authors in [4] extract the stack distances from the original trace assuming an arbitrary initial ordering of the stack. Whenever an object is requested, its depth (stack distance) in the stack is recorded and the object is pushed to the top of the stack. In our model we avoid making any assumptions on the initial ordering of the stack, which we have found to affect the marginal distribution and the correlation structure of the stack distance string. We start with an empty stack and process the empirical reference string in the reverse direction, starting from the last reference. If a file is referenced for the first time (in the reverse direction), it is pushed to the top of the stack but no stack distance is recorded. Otherwise, if the file has already been referenced before (hence, it is already in the stack), then it is pushed from its previous location in the stack to the top of the stack and its depth is recorded as a stack distance. Finally, the resulting trace of stack distances is reversed to get the correct stack distance string. The following example illustrates the idea. Consider the reference string [a d c b c d d a b], where each letter indicates the name of a file. If we process this string starting from the end, the first reference is to file b. Since this is the first time file b is being referenced, we push it to the top of the stack without recording any distance. The same procedure is performed for the next two references (for files a and d). The fourth reference (from the end) is for file d. Since this file has been referenced before, it gets pushed to the top of the stack and its stack depth is recorded (in this case, the stack depth for file d is one). The procedure continues until all references are processed (see Figure 2). The end result of this process is the stack distance stream [4 3 2 4 1].

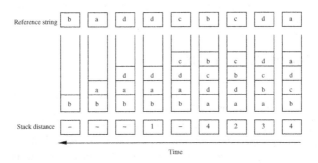

Fig. 2. Example showing our approach for extracting the stack distances from a real trace.

Temporal locality is attributed to both short-term correlations and long-term popularity [16]. Documents that have long-term popularity profiles tend to have small stack distances. Some documents are not popular but have short-term correlation profiles, which make these documents appear often within a short interval of time. As a result, these documents have small stack distances (i.e., they exhibit strong *short-term popularity*). In general, unpopular documents tend to have longer stack distances. The authors in [6] tried to model these trends by modeling the deviation of a stack distance from its expected value; assuming that the documents are uniformally distributed over the whole trace. Instead, we model the deviation of a stack distance from its *empirical expected value* (the scaled stack distance), as we found that the approach in [6] affects the correlation structure. We model the expected stack distance as a function of the popularity profile. Equally popular documents have the same expected stack distance. Figure 3 shows the relationship between the number of requests a file gets (its popularity profile) and the empirical expected stack distance. In both traces, it is observed that the expected stack distance drops exponentially with respect to the popularity profile.

The scaled stack distance string is obtained by normalizing each stack distance by its expected value. This string was found to have an approximately lognormal marginal distribution and a slowly decaying correlation structure that is almost identical to the correlation structure of the stack distance string.

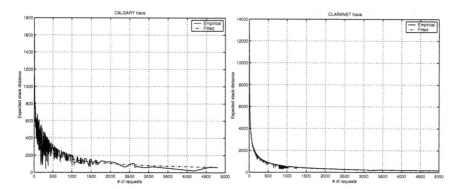

Fig. 3. Number of requests versus the expected stack distance for the two traces.

3.2   Modeling the Scaled Stack Distance String

To model the scaled stack distance string, we need to determine μ, v, β, and n. Once the values of these parameters are determined, the multifractal model described in Section 2 is used to capture the marginal distribution (temporal locality) and the correlation structure (spatial locality) of the scaled stack distance string.

3.3   Modeling Popularity and Generating Synthetic Reference Strings

To generate a synthetic WWW reference string, we first need to generate a synthetic scaled stack distance string, as shown in the previous section. The process of generating a synthetic WWW reference string starts by arranging the unique documents of the WWW server in an LRU stack. This is done by sampling from a probability distribution that is weighted by the popularity profiles of the various documents (i.e., the more popular a document is, the more likely it will be placed closer to the top of the stack). To generate a reference string of length N, we first compute the number of references a document can get according to its popularity profile. Then the top document at the LRU stack is considered as the next referenced document in the synthetic reference string. If the required number of references for this document is reached, then this document is flushed out of the stack. Otherwise, it is pushed down the stack according to the next value in the scaled stack distance string. This is done after scaling back the scaled stack distance by multiplying it by the corresponding expected stack distance for the object in hand (objects with the same popularity profile have the same expected stack distance). This process continues until the popularity profiles of all objects are satisfied (no documents are left in the LRU stack).

4   Experimental Results

In this section, we evaluate the performance of the proposed multifractal model and contrasting it with tw o other models. The first model is a self-similar (monofractal) model [2, 4], which characterizes the temporal and spatial localities in WWW traffic. This model involves transforming the Gaussian marginal distribution of a fractional ARIMA process into a more appropriate distribution (e.g., lognormal). We simply refer to this model as the LRD model. The second model was proposed by Cherkasova et al. [6], which was discussed in the introduction. The three inv estigated models were mainly designed for offline operation, with the primary purpose of generating synthetic traces for use in cache design studies. Accordingly, w ecompare these models in terms of the file and byte miss ratios seen at an LRU ca he that is drived by synthetic traces from these models. The comparison is made with reference to the cache performance seen under the real traffic (the tw ostudied traces). The results are shown in Figures 4, 5, 6, and 7.

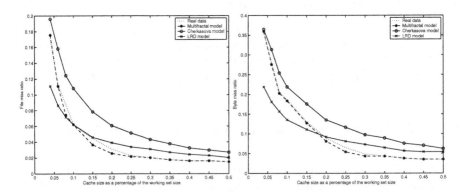

Fig. 4. File miss ratio versus cache size (CALGARY trace).   **Fig. 5.** Byte miss ratio versus cache size (CALGARY trace).

It is clear that of the three models, the proposed multifractal model produces the most accurate performance, especially for small cache sizes. The performance improvement is greater in the case of the CALGARY data. Consider, for example, the CALGARY data with a normalized cac he size of 0.3. The percentage

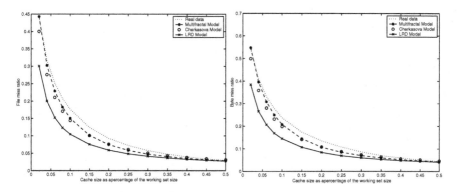

Fig. 6. File miss ratio versus cache size (CLARKNET trace). **Fig. 7.** Byte miss ratio versus cache size (CLARKNET trace).

inaccuracies in the file miss rate for the multifractal model, the LRD model, and Cherkasova et al.'s model are given by 0.5%, 53%, and 111%, respectively. In the case of the byte miss rate, the corresponding values are 4.9%, 65%, and 109%. The overall improvement in the accuracy of the file and byte miss rates due to the use of the multifractal model is significant.

5   Conclusions

In this work, we demonstrated the potential of multifractal processes as a viable approach for WWW traffic modeling. We started with the multifractal model of Riedi et al., which is capable of generating approximately lognormal variates with any desired autocorrelation structure. However, to apply this model in traffic fitting and trace generation, one needs to match as many parameters of the model as the length of the trace to be generated. To make the model parsimonious, we modified it by using a different distribution for the multiplier A_j (which relates the wavelet and scale coefficients) and by analytically expressing the parameter of A_j, $j = 1, 2, \ldots$, in terms of the mean, variance, and ACF of the modeled data. As a result, the modified multifractal model is specified by five parameters only. We fitted this model to the scaled stack distance strings of two WWW traffic traces. The proposed model captures the spatial and temporal localities of the real traffic as well as the popularity profile. Trace-drive simulations of the LRU cache policy indicates that our model gives much more accurate cache miss rates than two previously proposed WWW traffic models. Our future research will focus on designing new cache replacement and prefetching policies that exploit the characteristics of the traffic and that rely on model predictions in making file replacement and prefetching decisions.

References

1. Internet traffic archive at http://ita.ee.lbl.gov/.
2. V. Almeida, A. Bestavros, M. Crovella, and A. Oliverira. Characterizing reference locality in the WWW. In *Proceedings of the Fourth International Conference on Parallel and Distributed Information Systems (PDIS)*, pages 92–103, 1996.
3. M. Arlitt and C. Williamson. Web server workload characterization: The search for invariants. In *Proceedings of the ACM SIGMETRICS Conference*, pages 126–137, 1996.
4. P. Barford and M. Crovella. Generating representative web workloads for network and server performance evaluation. In *Proceedings of the ACM SIGMETRICS Conference*, pages 151–160, 1998.
5. P. Cao and S. Irani. Cost-aware WWW proxy caching algorithms. In *Proceedings of the 1997 USENIX Symposium on Internet Technology and System*, pages 193–206, 1997.
6. L. Cherkasova and G. Ciardo. Characterizating temporal locality and its impact on web server performance. In *Proceedings of the Ninth International Conference on Computer Communication and Networks (ICCCN)*, pages 434–441, 2000.
7. D. Cox. Long-range dependence: A review. *Statistics: An Appraisal*, pages 55–74, 1984. The Iowa State University, Ames, Iowa.
8. C. Cunha, A. Bestavros, and M. Crovella. Characteristics of WWW client-based traces. *IEEE Transactions on Networking*, 1(3):134–233, Jan 1999.
9. A. Feldman, A. Gilbert, W. Willinger, and T. Kurtz. The changing nature of network traffic: Scaling phenomena. *Communication Review*, April 1998.
10. A. Gilbert, W. Willinger, and A. Feldmann. Scaling analysis of conservative cascades, with applications to network traffic. *Special Issues of IEEE Transactions on Information Theory on Multiscale Statistical Signal analysis and its Applications*, 1999.
11. A. Gillbert and W. Willinger. Data networks as cascades: Investigating the multifractal of internet WAN traffic. *IEEE Transactions on Information Theory*, pages 971–991, 1999.
12. C. Huang, M. Devetsikiotis, I. Lambadaris, and A. R. Kays. Modeling and simulation of self-similar variable bit rate compressed video: A unified approach. In *Proceedings of the ACM SIGCOM Conference*, pages 114–125, 1995.
13. S. Jin and A. Bestavros. Popularity-aware greedy-dual size web proxy caching algorithms. In *Proceedings of the International Conference on Distributed Computing Systems (ICDCS)*, Taiwan, May 2000.
14. S. Jin and A. Bestavros. Sources and characteristics of web temporal locality. In *Proceedings of IEEE/ACM International Symposium on Modeling, Analysis and Simulation of Computer and Telecommunication Systems*, San Fransisco, CA, August 2000.
15. S. Jin and A. Bestavros. Temporal locality in web request streams. In *Proceedings of the ACM SIGMETRICS Conference*, pages 110–111, 2000.
16. S. Jin and A. Bestavros. Greedy-dual* web caching algorithm. *International Journal on Computer Communications*, 24(2):174–183, Febreuary 2001.
17. R. Riedi. Introduction to multifractals. http://www.dsp.rice.edu/publications/.
18. R. Riedi, M. Crouse, V. Ribeiro, and R. Baraniuk. A multifractal wavelet model with application to network traffic. *IEEE Transactions on Information Theory*, 45(3):992–1018, April 1999.

Characteristics of Temporal and Spatial Locality of Internet Access Patterns

Keisuke Ishibashi, Masaki Aida, and Makoto Imase

NTT Corporation, Information Sharing Platform Laboratories,
3-9-11 Midori-cho, Musashino-shi, Tokyo 180-8585, Japan
ishibashi.keisuke@lab.ntt.co.jp

Abstract. The locality of access patterns is a significant characteristic to be considered in analyzing Internet access behaviors. Previous research focused on temporal locality, which implies a high probability of the same IP address reappearing. In this paper, in addition to temporal locality we analyze spatial locality behavior, which implies a high probability of neighboring IP addresses appearing. Using actual Internet traces, we have analyzed the relationship between the number of accesses and the number of distinct elements appearing for both full addresses and address prefixes. We found that the number of distinct full addresses appearing grows much faster than the number of address prefixes, and they are related by a power law. Also, we compose a stochastic model that generates an address sequence with hierarchical structure consisting of full address and address prefix. We verify that an address sequence generated by the model shows both spatial and temporal locality behaviors similar to those of actual data.

1 Introduction

To evaluate Internet performance, it is necessary to understand and model Internet access patterns. In particular, the locality behavior of Internet access patterns is a significant characteristic that must be considered. Locality behavior was originally studied in computer memory reference models. Jain reported that Internet access behaviors also exhibit similar locality behaviors [1].

More specifically, the locality of an Internet access pattern can be classified into two categories, temporal and spatial. Temporal locality implies a high probability that a previously accessed address is again accessed in the near future. Spatial locality implies a high probability that a neighboring address is accessed in the near future.

We previously described a stochastic model for Internet access patterns [2]. This model, however, considers only temporal locality and gives no information about the probability of accessing neighboring addresses. To completely model locality behaviors, we need to characterize and model both temporal and spatial locality.

Recently, spatial locality has been investigated in the area of Web object prefetching [3], [4], [5]. Because spatial locality indicates a high probability of

E. Gregori et al. (Eds.): Networking 2002 Workshops, LNCS 2376, pp. 15–28, 2002.

accessing neighboring objects in the near future, prefetching these objects implies an increase in the hit ratio. In some previous studies [4], [5], the prediction of which page to prefetch was done based on the conditional probability matrix. The element $p[i, j]$ of the matrix denotes the conditional probability of page j access in the near future given page i accessed. The conditional probability matrix describes the spatial locality if the page j is regarded as a neighbor of j when $p[i, j]$ is high. Those modeling of locality, however, depends on the access address itself and cannot be applied to other environments. Also, these probabilities do not give macroscopic characteristics of the spatial locality.

Fang analyzed traffic patterns among Autonomous Systems (ASes) [6] and defined spatial locality as the number of hosts appeared divided by the number of ASes (networks) appeared. The value indicates the degree of concentration of hosts to the same AS, but does not describe the temporal correlation of the address sequence.

In this paper, we characterize both temporal and spatial locality in terms of IP addresses by extending our existing method of characterizing temporal locality [2]. We also propose an algorithm to generate address sequences exhibiting both temporal and spatial locality.

The rest of this paper is organized as follows. In Section 2, we introduce the characterization of address locality, and we analyze address locality by using actual data in Section 3. In Section 4, we propose the address generation algorithm to reproduce both spatial and temporal locality. We present experimental results in Section 5 and then conclude the paper in Section 6.

2   Characterization of Temporal and Spatial Locality

2.1   Temporal Locality

Temporal locality of internet access pattern is described in [2]. In this subsection, we briefly review the results presented in the previous researches.

First, we review typical Internet access models [1].

- independent reference model (IRM)
  This model assumes accesses are independent. The probability that a new access has address i is determined by the address i (and the probability is denoted as p_i). Accessed address sequence is generated by i.i.d and the distribution is p_i. Because recently accessed address do not give any information about the next accessed address, IRM can not capture temporal locality.
- least recently used (LRU) stack model
  An LRU stack is a list of addresses sorted according to the time of the most recent access. Thus, the most recently accessed address is at the top of the stack and the least recently accessed address is at the bottom. In the LRU stack model, the probability that a newly accessed address is the same as the address at the k-th position in the LRU stack is determined by position k, and its probability is denoted as a_k. Usually, a_k decreases with respect to increasing k. Because the most recently accessed address is at the top of

the LRU stack, the probability that the next accessed address is the same is high. The LRU stack model, therefore, captures temporal locality.

Next, we introduce notions used to describe the diversity of the access destinations.

- working set: $W(t, \tau)$
  The set whose elements are distinct addresses generated during a period $(t - \tau, t]$. In case for $\tau < 0$, the period is $(t, t - \tau]$. Here, the time t is incremented when an access occurs.
- working set size: $w(t, \tau)$
  Size of a working set $W(t, \tau)$, i.e., the number of elements of $W(t, \tau)$.
- Inverse Stack Growth Function (ISGF): $f(t, \tau)$
  The expectation value for the number of distinct addresses generated during a period $(t, t + \tau]$,

$$f(t, \tau) := \mathrm{E}[w(t, -\tau)]. \tag{1}$$

In addition, stack growth function (SGF), $g(t, k)$, denotes the expectation value of the number of access such that the number of distinct addresses is k, i.e.,

$$f(t, \tau) = k \leftrightarrow g(t, k) = \tau. \tag{2}$$

Note that because ISGF f is defined only on integer, SGF g cannot be defined directly. The consistent way to obtain the relation between ISGF and SGF is shown in [7]. Hereafter, we regard ISGF and SGF as functions defined on the real number with respect to τ and k, respectively.

In this paper, we assume that the ISGF is time-transition invariant as [2],

$$f(t, \tau) = f(s, \tau) \qquad (t \neq s), \tag{3}$$

and denote $f(\tau) := f(t, \tau)$. This assumption was examined in [2].

The physical meaning of the time-transition invariance (3) is a stationary condition for access patterns, that is, access behaviors are independent of the time when we start measurements.

Address generation probability
It is proved that the stochastic model of Internet access patterns is described as the LRU stack model if and only if the ISGF has time-transition invariance [2]. The probability a_k in this case is defined as

$$a_k := \{f(g(k - 1) + 1) - (k - 1)\}$$
$$-\{f(g(k) + 1) - k\}. \tag{4}$$

If an address sequence has no temporal locality, then a_k should be independent of k. Thus, temporal locality can be described with a_k, which is perfectly described with the ISGF according to (4) when the ISGF is time-transition invariant.

Here, we present the summary of the proof. First, we consider three adjacent periods A, B, and C (Fig. 1). Let the sets of distinct addresses generated in these

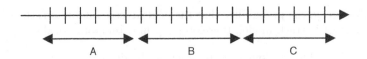

Fig. 1. Time intervals A, B and C

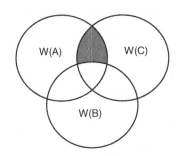

Fig. 2. Venn's diagram of working sets

periods, i.e., working sets, be $W(A)$, $W(B)$, and $W(C)$, respectively. Figure 2 denotes Venn's diagram of these working sets.

Here, we focus on the subset W^* whose elements are also elements of both $W(A)$ and $W(C)$, but are not elements of $W(B)$, i.e., hatched part in Fig. 2,

$$W^* := W(A) \cap W(C) \setminus W(B). \tag{5}$$

The size of W^* is obtained as

$$\begin{aligned}
|W^*| &= |\{W(A) \cap W(C)\} \setminus W(B)| \\
&= \{|W(B) \cup W(C)| - |W(B)|\} \\
&\quad -\{|W(A) \cup W(B) \cup W(C)| - |W(A) \cup W(B)|\}
\end{aligned} \tag{6}$$

We can choose m,n ,and 1 accesses as the periods A, B, and C, respectively (Fig. 3).

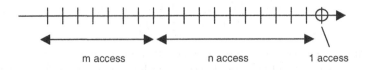

m access   n access   1 access

Fig. 3. Time intervals

Then we have

$$|W^*| = \{w(t, n+1) - w(t-1, n)\}$$
$$-\{w(t, n+m+1) - w(t-1, n+m)\}. \tag{7}$$

Applying the time-transition invariance, we have

$$E[|W^*|] = \{f(n+1) - f(n)\}$$
$$-\{f(n+m+1) - f(n+m)\}. \tag{8}$$

The physical meaning of $E[|W^*|]$ is as follows. When we denote an address generated in the period of C as X, then $|W^*|$ can be written using indicator function $\mathbf{1}\{\cdot\}$ as

$$|W^*| = \mathbf{1}\{X \notin W(B), X \in W(A)\}. \tag{9}$$

Therefore, $E[|W^*|]$ means the probability of $|W^*| = 1$;

$$E[|W^*|] = \Pr\{X \notin W(B), X \in W(A)\}. \tag{10}$$

Next, we choose n such as $f(n) = k - 1$ $(k = 1, 2, ...)$ and choose m such as $f(n+m) = k$. Substituting $n = g(k-1)$ and $n+m = g(k)$, we obtain from (8)

$$E[|W^*|] = \{f(g(k-1)+1) - (k-1)\}$$
$$-\{f(g(k)+1) - k\}. \tag{11}$$

Equation (11) means the probability that the newly accessed address, X, is identical with the k-th most recently accessed address. Furthermore, address generation probability is determined by k, thus address generation must obey the LRU stack model whose probability is (4). It is known that the reverse also holds [2].

Summarizing, we obtain that:

address generation process whose ISGF has a time-transition invariance

address generation process can be modeled as LRU stack model whose probability is (4).

2.2 Spatial Locality

Spatial locality implies a high probability of neighboring address generation. To define spatial locality, we must determine the neighbor of an address. In this paper, we define two addresses as neighboring each other if their address prefixes are the same. This definition is appropriate for performance evaluation because two addresses belonging to the same network have the same address prefix and packets are forwarded based on their address prefix.

Under this definition, we can analyze spatial locality of a full-address sequence by analyzing temporal locality of a prefix sequence, because temporal locality of a prefix sequence implies a high probability of generating addresses belonging to the same network. That is, we make an identification as follows:

Spatial locality of a full-address sequence

$\Updownarrow$

Temporal locality of an address-prefix sequence.

Here, as with a full-address sequence, we define the ISGF for an address prefix $f_p(t, \tau)$ as the expectation value of the working set for distinct address prefixes generated during a period $(t, t + \tau]$. We write the working set size as $w_p(t, -\tau)$. We define stack growth function of address prefix as $g_p(t, k)$ as well.

We assume that the ISGF for an address prefix is also time-transition invariant, which means the stationary condition for the prefix sequence. Then we can denote $f_p(\tau) := f_p(t, \tau)$. We verify the assumption by using an actual data in Sec. 3.2. Then, the stochastic process of address prefix generation is described by an LRU stack model, which has the probability a_k^p for selecting the k-th stack position in the LRU stack of address prefixes, defined as

$$a_k^p := \{f_p(g_p(k-1)+1) - (k-1)\}$$
$$-\{f_p(g_p(k)+1) - k\}. \tag{12}$$

With these concepts we can characterize spatial locality by comparing the ISGFs of an address-prefix sequence and a full-address sequence. The larger increase of $f(\tau)$ than that of $f_p(\tau)$ means more elements of distinct full addresses than that of address prefixes. Therefore, it means more addresses have the same address prefix, i.e., higher spatial locality. Therefore, when we write the relationship between $f_p(\tau)$ and $f(\tau)$ as

$$f_p(\tau) = P(f(\tau)), \tag{13}$$

then the shape of P specifies the degree of spatial locality. Note that the time-transition invariances of f and f_p, mean that P is also time-transition invariant.

3   Locality of Actual Data

We examined the locality of actual data measured for our laboratories' network. The data were measured from 15:00 to 16:00 on December 13, 2000 at the border network between our LAN and the Internet. The number of packets captured during this period was 5,993,454. From the traces, we determined the destination (out-band) address sequence of IP flows. The total number of flows was 121,103. We found that 89 % of those flows are WWW flows, which indicates the characteristics described in this paper mainly come from WWW traffic characteristics.

3.1   Temporal Locality

Previous papers [2] characterized the temporal locality of an address sequence in terms of its ISGF.

In this paper, to show the temporal locality more directly, we compare the probabilities of selecting the k-th position in the LRU stack, a_k, for the original address sequence and a sequence which is randomized the generating order of original address sequence. Note that the randomized sequence has no temporal correlation. Thus the sequence can be considered as the sequence generated by IRM model.

Figure 4 shows the a_k for both the original and randomized sequences. The original sequence had a high probability of access for small stack positions compared to the randomized sequence. This figure shows that actual access patterns exhibit strong evidence of high temporal locality.

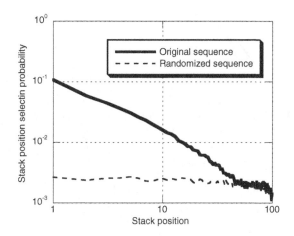

Fig. 4. Access frequency as the function of stack position

3.2 Spatial Locality

First, We evaluate the assumption of time-transition invariance for an address-prefix sequence. As preliminary study, we fixed the prefix length at 16 bits, even though it is currently distributed from around 16 to 24 bits in the Internet [8]. Figure 5 shows working set size behaviors. Each line indicates working set size of address prefix $w_p(t, -\tau)$ for $t = 3 \times 10^4, 6 \times 10^4, 9 \times 10^4$, respectively. From the law of large number, asymptotic behavior of the working set size can be related to the behavior of ISGF, as

$$w_p(t, -\tau) = f_p(t, \tau) \qquad (\tau \gg 1). \qquad (14)$$

Thus, this figure implies the time-transition invariance of ISGF, at least in the asymptotic region, $\tau \gg 1$.

Next, based on the definition of the spatial locality presented in subsection 2.2, we compared the ISGFs for both full addresses and address prefixes. Figure 6 shows the two ISGFs. The ISGF for address prefixes increased slower than that for full addresses. Both ISGFs followed asymptotic power laws, which can be written as

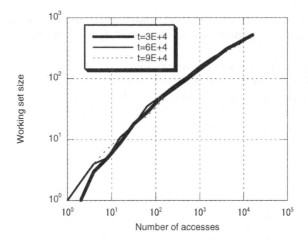

Fig. 5. Working set size behaviors for different measurement periods

$$f(\tau) \propto \tau^{\alpha} \qquad (\tau \gg 1), \tag{15}$$
$$f_p(\tau) \propto \tau^{\beta} \qquad (\tau \gg 1), \tag{16}$$

where α and β are constants and $0 < \beta \leq \alpha < 1$.

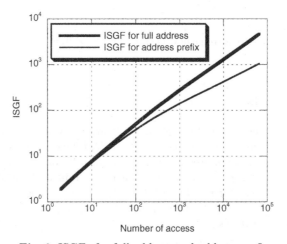

Fig. 6. ISGFs for full address and address prefix

Figure 7 plots the function P defined in (13). The plot shows an asymptotic power law between the two ISGFs. This is natural, since both ISGFs follow an asymptotic power law. We write the exponent here as γ, so that the two ISGFs obey (15) and (16), then

$$\gamma = \frac{\beta}{\alpha}. \tag{17}$$

Thus the function P is described with one parameter γ as

$$P(f(\tau)) = f(\tau)^\gamma. \tag{18}$$

If γ is one, then the address prefixes of any two distinct addresses are different. Thus, the probability of a prefix being accessed is independent of the access history of other prefixes and there is no spatial locality.

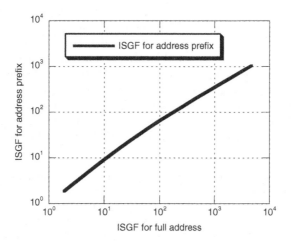

Fig. 7. The relationship between $f(\tau)$ and $f_p(\tau)$

Then, as same as examination of the temporal locality, we compare the probabilities of selecting the k-th position in the LRU stack, a_k^p, for the original prefix sequence and a sequence which is randomized the generating order of original prefix sequence. Figure 8 shows the a_k^p for both the original and randomized sequences. The original sequence had a high probability of access for small stack positions compared to the randomized sequence.

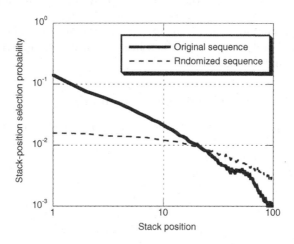

Fig. 8. Prefix selection frequency as the function of stack position

4   Address Generation Algorithm

In this section, we propose an address generation algorithm that uses the parameter γ, described in subsection 3.2, to extend the algorithm in [2].

4.1   Outline

The address generation algorithm described previously [2] gives the pseudo address sequence as a sequence of integers. Although this algorithm can take temporal locality into consideration, spatial locality is not considered. This is because a simple integer cannot represent the topology structure for an address, i.e. whether it is a neighboring address or not. To introduce the topology structure into the address expression, we use a doublet of two integers. One component of the doublet denotes a pseudo full address, while the other denotes a pseudo address prefix. An pseudo address sequence with spatial locality must satisfy following conditions:

- The sequence is stationary that is same as the time-transition invariance for both f_p and f (at least for $\tau \gg 1$).
- The sequence has both temporal and spatial locality.

An sequence generated full addresses and address prefixes independently canno satisfy these conditions, thus we propose an algorithm whose outline is as follows:

- For a full address, determine whether a new address is generated or an existing address is accessed by using the ISGF.
- If a new full address is generated, determine whether it has a new address prefix or an existing address prefix by using the parameter γ.
- If an existing full address is accessed, generate the address prefix for the address that was attached when the full address was first generated.

As this outline shows, the algorithm requires a conditional probability for which address prefix is generated, given that a new full address is generated. This conditional probability is discussed in Sec. 4.2, and the proposed algorithm based on the conditional probability is described in Sec. 4.3. We evaluate the algorithm satisfies above conditions in Sec. 5.

4.2   Calculation of the Conditional Probability

First, we define the probability that a brand-new full address (or address prefix) is generated when the stack depth of full addresses (or address prefixes) is m (or m_p), as $b(m)$ (or $b_p(m_p)$). Then,

$$b(m) = \sum_{k=m+1}^{\infty} a_k, \tag{19}$$

$$b_p(m_p) = \sum_{k=m_p+1}^{\infty} a_k^p. \tag{20}$$

We also define the conditional probability that a brand-new address prefix is generated, given that the brand-new full address is generated when the depth of the address-prefix stack is m_p, as $b_c(m_p)$.

From the observations in subsection 3.2, the depth of the full-address stack, m, can be asymptotically expressed in terms of the depth of the address-prefix stack, m_p, as

$$m \simeq (m_p)^{\frac{1}{\gamma}}, \qquad m \gg 1. \tag{21}$$

Then, for $m_p \gg 1$, because a generation of a brand-new prefix also means a generation of a full address,

$$b_c(m_p) = \frac{b_p(m_p)}{b(m)} \tag{22}$$

$$\simeq \frac{f_p(g_p(m_p) + 1) - m_p}{f(g(m)) - m}. \tag{23}$$

The equation (23) is derived from (4) and (12). Using (15) and (16),

$$b_c(m_p) \simeq \frac{(m_p^{1/\beta} + 1)^\beta - m_p}{(m^{1/\alpha} + 1)^\alpha - m}$$

$$\simeq \gamma m_p^{1-1/\gamma}, \tag{24}$$

for $m_p \gg 1$.

Next, we define the conditional probability that the stack position k in the LRU stack for an address prefix is selected when a brand-new full address appears as

$$a_k^c := \{(k-1)^{1/\gamma} + 1)^\gamma - (k-1)\} - \{(k^{1/\gamma} + 1)^\gamma - k\}. \tag{25}$$

This is similar to the forms of the probabilities defined by (4) and (12).

Since a_k^c satisfies

$$b_c(m_p) \simeq \sum_{k=m_p+1}^{\infty} a_k^c, \tag{26}$$

the conditional probability defined by(25) is consistent with (24).

4.3   Algorithm

We define the generative LRU stack vectors $\mathbf{L}(i,m)$ and $\mathbf{L_p}(i,m_p)$ as follows. At the time immediately before the i-th ($i = 0, 1, 2, \ldots$) address generation, we denote the most recently accessed full address and address prefix as x_1 and y_1, respectively, and the k-th most recently accessed address and prefix as x_k and y_k, respectively. Then,

$$\mathbf{L}(i,m) := \{x_1, x_2, \ldots, x_m\}, \tag{27}$$

$$\mathbf{L_p}(i,m_p) := \{y_1, y_2, \ldots, y_{m_p}\}. \tag{28}$$

We also define a mapping $p(\cdot)$ that picks the prefix from a full address, i.e., $y = p(x)$ when the prefix of the full address x is y. Note that this mapping is not an injection, because multiple full addresses have the same address prefixes.

Here, the numbers of components of $\mathbf{L}(i, m)$, m, and of $\mathbf{L_p}(i, m_p)$, m_p, are called the depths of $\mathbf{L}(i, m)$ and $\mathbf{L_p}(i, m_p)$, respectively. Initially, the depths of both stacks are chosen as 0, i.e., $m = n = 0$ for $\mathbf{L}(0, 0)$ and $\mathbf{L_p}(0, 0)$.

Let the doublet (X_i, Y_i) denote the full address and address prefix of the i-th access. An address sequence (X_i, Y_i), $i = 0, 1, 2, \ldots$ is generated by the following procedure.

1. Initially, choose $(X_0, Y_0) = (1, 1)$, $\mathbf{L}(1, 1) = \{1\}$, $\mathbf{L_p}(1, 1) = \{1\}$, and $i = 1$.
2. Determine the number j as a realization of an i.i.d. random variable J that obeys the distribution

$$\Pr\{J = k\} = a_k \quad (k = 1, 2, 3, \ldots), \tag{29}$$

   by using (4).
3. For the full-address depth m of $\mathbf{L}(i, m)$, if $m < j$, then assign the full address for new access as

$$X_i = m + 1. \tag{30}$$

   Else, go to the step 7.
4. Determine the number s as a realization of an i.i.d. random variable S that obeys the distribution

$$\Pr\{S = k\} = a_k^c \quad (k = 1, 2, 3, \ldots). \tag{31}$$

   Here, a_t^c is the conditional probability from (25).
5. For the address-prefix depth m_p of $\mathbf{L_p}(i, m_p)$, if $m_p < s$, then assign the address prefix for the full address $X_i = m + 1$ as

$$Y_i = m_p + 1, \tag{32}$$
$$p(x_{m+1}) = y_{m_p+1}, \tag{33}$$

   update $\mathbf{L}(i+1, m+1)$ and $\mathbf{L_p}(i+1, m_p+1)$, and increment $i \leftarrow i+1$. Return to the step 2.
6. For the depth m_p of $\mathbf{L_p}(i, m_p)$, if $m_p \geq s$, then assign the address prefix for the full address $X_i = m + 1$ as

$$Y_i = y_s, \tag{34}$$
$$p(x_{m+1}) = y_s, \tag{35}$$

   update $\mathbf{L}(i + 1, m + 1)$ and $\mathbf{L_p}(i + 1, m_p)$, and increment $i \leftarrow i + 1$. Return to the step 2.
7. For the depth m of $\mathbf{L}(i, m)$, if $m \geq j$, then assign the full address and address prefix for new access as

$$X_i = x_j, \tag{36}$$
$$Y_i = p(x_j), \tag{37}$$

   update $\mathbf{L}(i + 1, m)$ and $\mathbf{L_p}(i + 1, m_p)$, and increment $i \leftarrow i + 1$. Return to the step 2.

5   Experimental Results

We evaluate the algorithm by analyzing the sequence generated by the proposed algorithm. To generate the sequence, we fixed the parameters as $\alpha = 0.85$, $\gamma = 0.70$, and the number of addresses generated was 121,103 as for the measured sequence.

First, we evaluate the time-transition invariance for the generated sequence. Figure 9 shows working set size behaviors of address prefix for the generated address sequence. Each line indicates working set size of address prefix $u_p(t, -\tau)$ for $t = 3 \times 10^4, 6 \times 10^4, 9 \times 10^4$, respectively. It can be shown that each line shows similar behavior at least for $\tau \gg 1$, which implies the time-transition invariance of ISGF. This result indicates the address generation process of the algorithm asymptotically obeys the LRU stack model and stational for both full address and prefix sequence.

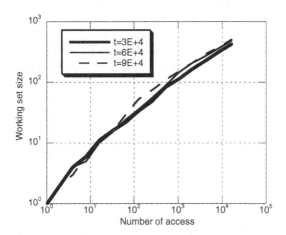

Fig. 9. Working set size behaviors for different measurement periods

We compared the ISGF behaviors of address sequences obtained from the proposed algorithm and those we measured (Fig. 10). It can be observed that the forms of the generated and measured ISGFs are similar for both full addresses and address prefixes. Thus, the sequence exhibits similar characteristics of measured one. The results indicates the sequence shows proper spatial locality which is compatible with temporal locality.

6   Conclusion

In this paper, we have characterized the spatial locality of Internet access patterns by extending the method of characterizing temporal locality presented in our previous researches [2]. Analyzing actual data measured in a LAN showed

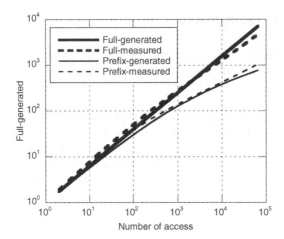

Fig. 10. Comparing the ISGFs

that the Internet access patterns exhibit spatial locality as well as temporal locality. We have also proposed an algorithm that reflects both temporal and spatial locality. The access patterns generated by this algorithm exhibit characteristic similar to those of actual data.

Acknowledgement

We would like to thank Dr. Ron Addie for his valuable comments that strengthen the proof of our paper.

References

1. R. Jain, "Characteristics of destination address locality in computer networks: A comparison of caching schemes," DEC Tech. Rep., 1990.
2. M. Aida and T. Abe, "Pseudo-address generation algorithm of packet destinations for Internet performance simulation," proc. IEEE INFOCOM 2001, April 2001.
3. V. Almeida, A. Bestavros, M. Crovella, and A. Oliveira, "Characterizing reference locality in the WWW," proc. 4th Int. Conf. on Parallel and Distributed Information Systems (PDIS '96), December 1996.
4. A. Bestavros, "Speculative data dissemination and service to reduce server load, network traffic and service time in distributed information systems," proc. 4th Int. Conf. on Data Engineering (ICDE '96), March 1996.
5. V. N. Padmanabhan and J. C. Mogul, "Using predictive prefetching to improve World Wide Web latency," proc. ACM SIGCOMM 96, 1996.
6. Wenjia Fang and Larry Peterson, "Inter-AS Traffic Patterns and Their Implications," proc. Global Internet 99, Rio, Brazil.
7. M. Kobayashi and M.H. MacDougall, "The stack growth function: Cache line reference models," IEEE Trans. Comput., vol.38, no.6, 1989.
8. Internet Performance Measurement and Analysis Project, "Internet Routing Table Statistics," http://www.merit.edu/ipma/routing table/ .

A Scalable Architecture for Cooperative Web Caching

Riccardo Lancellotti[1], Bruno Ciciani[2*], and Michele Colajanni[3]

[1] Dip. di Informatica, Sistemi e Produzione, Università di Roma "Tor Vergata"
[2] Dip. di Informatica e Sistemistica, Università di Roma "La Sapienza"
[3] Dip. di Ingegneria dell'Informazione, Università di Modena e Reggio Emilia

Abstract. Cooperative Web caching is the most common solution for augmenting the low cache hit rates due to single proxies. However, both purely hierarchical and flat architectures suffer from scalability problems due to cooperation protocol overheads. We present a new cooperative architecture that organizes cache servers in well connected clusters and implements a novel cooperation model based on a two-tier lookup process. The experimental results carried out on a working prototype show that the proposed architecture is really effective in supporting cooperative Web caching because it guarantees cache hit rates comparable to those of the most performing architectures and it reduces cooperation overhead at a small fraction of that of other protocols.

G Introduction

Web caching has evolved as the first way to deal with performance and network resource utilization issues related to the growth of popularity of the World Wide Web. The idea is quite simple. Instead of connecting to a "far" and possibly overloaded Web server, the client request reaches a *proxy server*, that hosts resources frequently requested by a set of clients in a cache server "nearer" than the origin server.

The main problem of this approach is that the cache hit rate of one proxy server can be really low. The proposed solutions aim to establish interactions among various proxies. *Global caching* or *cooperative caching* architectures are used by public organizations (e.g., IRCache [1]), Internet Service Providers (e.g., AT&T [2]), third party companies, such as Content Delivery Networks (e.g., Akamai [3], Digital Island [4]). Cooperation among Web caches has been widely studied. For some recent surveys, see [5, 6] or [7, 8]. Cooperation among cache servers can occur for several reasons, but the most important motivations are: cache content lookup (*cooperative lookup*), data placement and document removal. In this paper, we focus on cooperative lookup. The two most popular approaches for cooperative lookup refer to a hierarchy of cooperating caches

---

* Bruno Ciciani is currently Visiting Professor to the IBM Thomas J. Watson Research Center, NY

E. Gregori et al. (Eds.): Networking 2002 Workshops, LNCS 2376, pp. 29–41, 2002.

(*hierarchical architecture*) or to a flat cooperation topology (*distributed architectures*).

In hierarchical architectures a cache miss will result in looking for the resource to an upper level cache [9]. In distributed architectures every cache is supposed at the same level, and missed resources at one proxy are looked for in all cooperating cache servers. *Hybrid architectures* have been studied as well [6]. In this paper we refer to distributed architectures.

Any cooperation among a set of distributed servers has to decide a protocol and an implementation technique for exchanging some local state information which, in the case of cooperative lookup, basically refers to cache content (although other information can be useful, such as network and/or server load conditions). The two opposite approaches for sharing state information are well defined in literature: *on-demand protocols* in which state information exchanges occur only in response to a client request, and the family of *informed protocols* in which state information is exchanged periodically or when (significant) state modifications occur. ICP [10] and Summary Cache [11] are examples of the former and latter protocols, respectively.

The main drawback of any pure approach to Web caching cooperation is its lack of scalability because lookup latency and/or amount of data exchanges for cooperation augment dramatically for higher numbers of cooperating nodes. For example, *on-demand protocols* require a query/response message to/from each cache server for every local miss, moreover they risk that state information from "far" cooperative cache servers is received well beyond the chosen threshold (e.g., 2 seconds is the default limit for ICP). On the other hand, periodic exchanges of state information among all cache servers are impracticable when the number of cooperative nodes is high or there are many "far" nodes. In these instances, to limit protocol overheads, state refreshments should occur sporadically, but this would affect the nature itself of an *informed protocol* because of high risks of distributing stale state information.

The main claim of this paper, also validated through extensive simulations in [12], is that a better scalability for caching cooperation can be achieved only by architectures that use hybrid protocols. Indeed, each protocol has some tradeoff and its pros can be exploited by taking into consideration the network characteristics of the geographically distributed system. A multi-tier architecture may allow the cooperation of more cache servers with a potential increase of hit rate or permit a better usage of network resources by reducing the lookup time or the bandwidth overheads for coordination among cache servers. A two-tier architecture is the simplest form of a multi-tier architecture, where the basic concept is that cache servers can be distinguished between "near" (that is, well connected nodes) and "far" (that is, nodes connected through multiple network hops and/or through possibly highly loaded links). The two-tier approach aims at being more flexible and scalable than other cooperation mechanisms: first-level lookup cooperation occurs only among limited sets of "near" cache servers with the goal of minimizing lookup latency; second-level lookup cooperation involves only some representative "far" cache servers with the goal of minimizing amount of exchanged information needed for cooperation.

Another advantage of two-tier cooperation derives from the logical distinction maintained between the two levels. In such a way, integration of existing distributed caches (e.g., a group of proxies cooperating with CRISP [13]) into a two-tier infrastructure becomes easier because such a group of cooperating caches can become a first tier cluster with little modifications.

The contribution of this paper is twofold. We propose the architecture of a new prototype of cooperative cache servers where the nodes are organized in clusters (intra-cluster and inter-cluster cooperation protocols has been implemented by modifying the Squid software [14]). Moreover, we present a set of experimental results showing that the proposed prototype offers a good hit rate with a cooperation overhead significatively lower than that of other cooperation mechanisms.

The rest of this paper is organized as following. Section 2 describes the intra-cluster and inter-cluster cooperation protocols that are modified versions of the 2TC protocol proposed in [12]. Section 3 discusses the architecture of the prototype by evidencing main modifications made in Squid. Section 4 describes the experiments and compares the results with those of other cooperative and non-cooperative protocols. Section 5 contains an overview of existing approaches to cooperation. Section 6 summarizes the results of this paper.

2   Two-Tier Web Caching Architecture

The problem of lookup cooperation between proxy servers is essentially a problem of state information exchange within the components of a distributed system where the nodes are connected through heterogeneous links.

Let us consider an initial set S of proxy servers $\{P_1, \ldots, P_n\}$. Let C_i be a subset of S such that $\bigcup_{i=1}^{n} C_i = S$.

The number of cache servers inside C_i is chosen to allow cooperation without incurring in performance penalties caused by scalability issues. Moreover, consider that this clustering is done in a way such that cache servers inside the same cluster are "near", whereas cache servers belonging to different clusters are "far". The distance between nodes can be calculated by considering static (e.g., number of hops) or dynamic information (e.g., Round-Trip Time), although the concept of Internet vicinity is still an open issue. Figure 1 shows an example of clustering, where grouping corresponds to a *partition* of the set S. This is not a requirement for the proposed architecture because some overlapping is acceptable. However, for the sake of simplicity, in this paper we assume that the clusterization phase gives a partition of the available cache servers. The problem of finding an optimal clustering is out of the scope of this paper. It can be easily solved by management motivations (e.g., because the organization can find more convenient to place sets of cache servers in specific regions and none in others), by geographical considerations at different levels of granularity (for example, a coarse grain choice could be to consider four partitions of cache servers: East US,

West US, Asia, and Europe) or by more sophisticated optimization algorithms
(e.g., the Goemans-Williamson algorithm [15]).

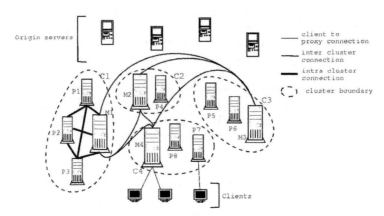

Fig. 1. Clustering of proxy server.

Intra-cluster cooperation is the most used mechanism, so it should be done
through a protocol that offers a fast lookup, to keep the latency at acceptable
levels. Assuming that the cache servers in the same cluster are well interconnected, the cost of frequent data exchanges occurring "off-line" is affordable.
This makes the use of an informed protocol appealing because it offers a lookup
extremely fast (if not false hits occur), typically done on some sort of hash table
structure kept in RAM.

Inter-cluster cooperation occurs among "far" cache servers that are possibly
connected through congested and limited bandwidth links. Hence, it is important
to use cooperation protocols that limit the waste of network resources. An on-
demand protocol could be a good choice because it is activated only consequently
to a client request. Unlike an informed protocol, it works "on-line" and exchanges
state information only when necessary. The drawback is that this choice tends
to increase the latency time of an inter-cluster lookup.

In the following subsections we describe the intra-cluster and inter-cluster
protocols implemented in the proposed two-tier Web caching architecture.

2.1   Intra-cluster Cooperation

Intra-cluster cooperation is implemented through the Cache Digests protocol.
This means that each cache server is informed about the resources stored in any
other cache of the cluster.

A local miss in the first contacted cache server activates a lookup process that
scans the local information about cooperating caches to check whether another
node has the required resource. This cluster lookup phase can result in a *cluster*

hit or in a *cluster miss*. A cluster miss activates the inter-cluster cooperation. A cluster hit allows the retrieval of the object from another cache server of the same cluster. Figure 2 shows this process: the cache lookup on P_2 (step 1) returns a cache digest hit (step 2) and the resource is retrieved from cache P_3 through an HTTP connection (step 3).

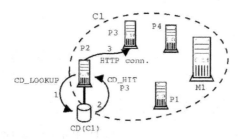

Fig. 2. Two-tier architecture: cluster hit.

In fact, the cluster lookup phase process can lead also to *false hit* or *false miss* because of stale state information or digest inaccuracy. To limit hit rate loss due to false positive or false negative, it is possible to augment the frequency of information exchanged among the caches of the cluster, and the precision (and the size) of exchanged digests. Anyway, the common rule is that the closer is the cooperation, the lesser nodes should be in the cluster.

In the case of false hit, the resource is fetched directly from the origin server to reduce latency time.

2.2   Inter-cluster Cooperation

A cluster miss activates the inter-cluster cooperation. An on-demand protocol is used to contact cache servers belonging to other clusters. In the architecture described in this paper, inter-cluster cooperation occurs only among special cache servers, called *master caches*.

The reference architecture for two-tier cooperation is a mesh of peer cache servers: there are no parent nodes with respect to the retrieval of documents. A master cache acts as a parent for on-demand protocols: when a query must be sent to a cache server not belonging to the same cluster, the query is sent to the master cache of the cluster and the duty of contacting other clusters is left to it. This approach allows an easier configuration of the system of cooperative clusters: cache servers inside each cluster need to know only which caches belongs to the same cluster and which of them is the master. The master cache needs only one more information about which are the masters of the other clusters.

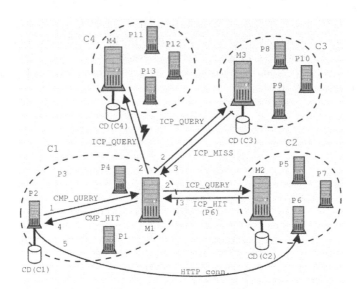

Fig. 3. Master proxy in the 2TC implementation

Figure 3 shows how a master proxy works: P_2 needs to use the second tier of 2TC because lookup in cluster cache digests returned a cluster miss. P_2 knows nothing about other clusters. Its only duty is to send a query to its master M_1 using CMP (Cache-to-Master Protocol, described in section 3.2) as shown in step 1. The master cache sends a query to all other masters through the ICP protocol (step 2). The masters of the other clusters check in their cache digests if the required resource is present in some cache server of its cluster and then returns a response (step 3) of hit (M_2) or miss (M_3). ICP uses a timeout mechanism to detect message loss (as for the one sent by M_4). The information is then sent back to the first proxy using CMP (step 4). In the case of global hit, the resource is retrieved through a normal HTTP connection (step 5).

Each master is informed about the content of the caches in its cluster because of the informed-based protocol used at the first cooperation level, so it can immediately return a message of cluster hit or miss. In the case of cache hit, the master returns also the address of the cache server that holds a valid copy of the requested document (in Figure 3 M_2 returns the address of P_6). It should be noted that the inter-cluster cooperation too is subject to false hit and false miss, because it relies on the informed cooperation protocol at the cluster level.

In summary, for each client request we can have one of the following four scenarios.

- **Local hit** when a valid copy of the requested resource is inside the first contacted cache server. The document is sent to the client and no cooperation is necessary.
- **Cluster hit** when the requested resource is found in the cache server of the same cluster ($P_j \in C_i$) to which the first contacted node belongs to. The intra-cluster cooperation protocol does not require message exchanges among caches during the lookup phase.
- **Global hit** when the resource is retrieved from a proxy $P_k \notin C_i$. As the intra-cluster cooperation determines a cluster miss, the inter-cluster cooperation protocol is activated. The hit is due to a cache server not belonging to the first contacted cluster.
- **Global miss** when the resource must be retrieved from the original server. Both cooperation levels fails in finding a valid copy of the resource in other cooperative cache servers or the first level incurred in a false hit.

3 Prototype Implementation of the Two-Tier Architecture

The two-tier cooperation architecture was implemented by modifying Squid 2.4 [14], a well known and widely used proxy server. The main modifications to the Squid software are localized in the modules called *peer selection* and *neighbors* [16]. The *peer selection* module contains the routines that selects a cache that may hold the requested resource and is used in the phase called *cooperation* in Figure 4. This phase is activated by a client request that results in a local miss or in a local hit with a stale file. The peer selection module uses other modules that implement some cooperation protocols, such as ICP and CMP.

The *neighbors* module contains the data-structure definitions and the routines to manage the database of cooperating proxies and the statistics about their state.

We also created a quite new module to support the Cache-to-Master protocol described in Section 3.2.

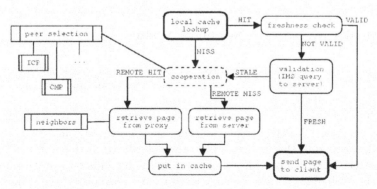

Fig. 4. Service of a client request by Squid.

3.1 Modifications to the Peer Selection Module

The default Squid behavior for the cooperation phase shown in Figure 4 carries out a one-step lookup over the known active cooperating caches. This step can be done through multiple protocols such as ICP [10], HTCP [17], CRISP [18], depending on the compile-time options and on the configuration of the caches.

The main modification of our cooperative Web caching architecture makes this operation a two-step process: if the normal lookup fails (in the case of cluster-miss) a second step is activated, and the CMP protocol is used for inter-cluster lookup.

3.2 Cache-to-Master Protocol

The Cache-to-Master Protocol (CMP) is used to manage the intercommunication between the two levels of the two-tier architecture. CMP is essentially a modified version of ICP, designed to be lighter and simpler than the original ICP protocol.

Both ICP and CMP have a *sender address* field. However, its use is quite different. In ICP this field is considered untrusted, and the information is usually taken from the lower level protocols. In our prototype architecture, a master proxy can report a hit referred to another cache. Hence, in both CMP and ICP responses the sender address contains the IP address of the cache holding the requested document. This approach was preferred to that based on the ICP_OP_MISS_POINTER opcode. There are two motivations for this choice. The opcode is still experimental, and our choice kept our prototype simpler without disrupting its ability to cooperate with existing proxy servers. For example, hit referring to other caches are discarded by the standard ICP implementation as malformed messages, thus preserving the original ICP behavior.

The use of a master proxy to communicate with other clusters is a two-way process: both queries and replies pass through the master. This is necessary to avoid the risk of *cache poisoning*: cache hit in unknown proxies are trusted only if signalled by the cluster master, which is trusted.

3.3 Modifications to the Neighbors Module

The implementation of CMP required a modification of the *neighbors* module. For security reasons, Squid does not fetch resources from unknown proxies, but this would not allow inter-cluster cooperation.

Each proxy knows only the caches belonging to its cluster. With the modified module, when a CMP_HIT reply pointing to a previously unknown proxy is received, the module that manages this protocol calls a function in the neighbors module that dynamically adds a new entry to the list of known proxies. In such a way, the Web objects are always retrieved from known peers even if they come from caches of other clusters.

4   Experimental Results

4.1   System Configuration

The prototype of the cooperative Web caching architecture was tested on a cluster of nine PCs running Linux. Eight PCs hosted a proxy server and an HTTP workload generator. The nineth PC hosted an HTTP server. We used Web-Polygraph version 2.5 [19] as a workload generator. The results were collected from the Squid logs and do not refer to latency times. The proxies were configured in order to implement four cooperation mechanisms, namely *no cooperation*, Cache Digests, ICP and 2TC. The first was used as a comparison for the other scenarios. For Cache Digests and ICP the proxies were configured to let each cache cooperate with each other, while for the last architecture we organized the cache servers in two clusters each composed of four nodes.

To emulate a steady-state initial cache population, all experiments were done twice and collected information referred only to the last one.

4.2   Workload Model

The workload model was based on that used in the second cache-off promoted by IRCache. We used a mix of content types made as following: images 65%, HTML documents 15%, binary data 0.5%, others 19.5%. Table 1 reports minimum, maximum and mean size for each type of object.

10% of requests were referred to *hot* resources. The hot set was 1% of the working set. Only 50% of the requests of each client was taken from a public set of pages, common to all clients. Each client was configured to visit more than once only 80% of the URLs. HTML resources could contain embedded objects.

Each proxy served requests coming from 5 clients. The working set of each cache was 47MB, corresponding to about 4250 URLs. It changed over time during the experiment, so that the global working set was 157 MB for each cache, corresponding to nearly 14200 URLs. The whole system of cooperating caches dealt with a 180.5 MB of documents, that generated over time a global working set of 601.8 MB. The caches were configured to hold no more than 30 MB of data each, so that each cache server could keep 5% of the global working set.

Table 1. Hit Rate

Type	Min size (KB)	Max size (KB)	Mean size (KB)
images	0.5	49	4.5
html	0.5	77.5	8.5
binary data	24	1577	300
other	7.5	89	25

4.3   Performance Results

The experiments were focused on obtaining two performance indices, that is: *object hit rate*, and *protocol overheads* due to cooperation. It is worth to observe that no latency measure was collected, hence it was not a problem to use cache servers belonging to the same local network.

Figure 5(a) reports same indices contained in Table 2. The *object hit rate* (HR) was divided into *local HR* (clients requests that were served without any cooperation), *cluster HR* (when a cache server belonging to the same cluster provided the object), and *global HR* (when a cache server belonging to other cluster provided the object). Of course, cluster HR has no meaning for ICP and Cache Digests architectures because their cache servers are not organized in clusters. We found that the differences in the local hit rate were induced by changes in the access locality caused by the cooperation.

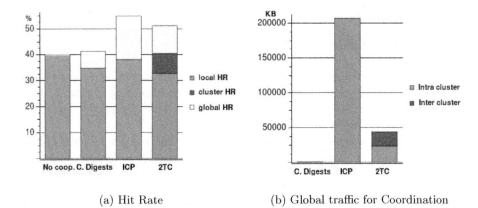

(a) Hit Rate   (b) Global traffic for Coordination

Fig. 5. Experimental results

Table 2. Hit Rate

Coordination	Local HR	Cluster HR	Global HR
No Cooperation	39.84	n/a	**39.84**
Cache Digests	35.57	n/a	**42.09**
ICP	37.99	n/a	**54.89**
2TC	35.28	42.83	**53.63**

The protocol overhead was measured both as an absolute value and as a per-request overhead. In Table 3, column 2 and in Figure 5(b), we reported the traffic generated for coordination purposes. The traffic produced by 2TC was composed of traffic generated by Cache Digests exchange (3331.65 KB), CMP queries and replies (20259.35 KB) and ICP messages (20907.80 KB). In column 3 of Table 3, we compared how many bytes for each request were necessary for cooperation among cache servers. Considering that the request size was between 500 bytes and 1.5 MB, with a mean of 11 KB, the cooperation overhead for ICP seems acceptable in a well connected network environment but can be intolerable for a geographic environment.

Table 3. Traffic for coordination

Coordination	KB for coord.	Bytes for coordination per request
No Cooperation	0	0
Cache Digests	790	3
ICP	207064	811
2TC	44499	140

Our experiments show that the proposed cooperative Web caching architecture offers high hit rates, slightly lower than that of ICP, which gave the best hit rate in our test-bed scenarios. It is even remarkable that the proposed architecture introduces much less traffic (i.e., less than 20%) for cooperation than that needed by ICP.

These results demonstrate that the proposed cooperation protocol reaches its goal because it offers high cache hit rate with an overhead much lower than that of other approaches. This positive combination is the first step to guarantee scalability of the architecture when the number of cooperative cache servers augments significantly.

5   Related Work

The issues related to cooperative cache lookup have been addressed in many ways, but the main philosophy behind them, except for a few exceptions, are two: on-demand protocols and informed-based protocols.

On-demand protocols are activated at lookup-time. They are typically designed to be fast and lightweight, usually relying on UDP messages. The most important of those protocol is ICP [10]. It was proposed as a part of the Harvest project and then adopted in many other proxy servers, such as Squid and NetCache. UDP is not a reliable protocol, so it can happen that a message is lost. ICP uses a timeout mechanism to detect packet loss and not well connected proxies.

ICP scales poorly: increasing the number of cooperating proxies leads to a quadratic increment of coordination traffic and increases the probability of packet loss (proportional to $1 - (1 - P_{err1})^N$ [20]), thus increasing the latency time because of more requests being served only after the timeout has expired. Additionally, ICP does not support HTTP/1.1 caching directive semantics, so it is subject to false hit and false miss due to different freshness parameters among caches.

This last ICP problem was addressed by the HTCP protocol [17], which is more expressive, although more complicated than its predecessor. Scalability issues remains similarl to those that affect ICP.

Informed-based protocols uses a completely different approach to cooperation: information exchange occurs *before* the lookup phase, that in such a way becomes much faster than that of on-demand protocols. Information exchange can be periodic or synchronous. This latter form requires some message exchange at the occurrence of any new event and guarantees strong consistency. Nevertheless, it introduces big overheads, so that state information is usually exchanged in an asynchronous way, through some form of compression, even if this form of cooperation may cause stale state information. Particularly useful is a lossy compression called Bloom filters [21] used by Summary Cache [11] and Cache Digests [22]. There is a well known trade-off between cooperation effectiveness and scalability of informed-based protocols: to increase the first it is necessary to exchange state information more frequently and to use more accurate description of cache contents. This increases network resource usage and leads to scalability problems.

Pure versions of on-demand and informed-based protocols have one trait in common: both them performs the cooperation as a *one-step* process. A different scheme is proposed by CARP [23, 24] that uses an implicit cooperation that does not need any message exchange among the cache servers. The main drawback of CARP is its static nature, that makes this protocol not suitable when cache servers are geographically distributed and network status is subject to variations, as it is the typical case of Internet.

A hybrid cooperation protocol that is more related to the 2TC protocol is CRISP by Chase et al. [13, 18]. Similarly to 2TC, CRISP combines an informed protocol with a query approach to build a scalable cooperation mechanism. Unlike the cooperative Web caching architecture discussed in this paper, CRISP relies on a centralized directory that makes this architecture not scalable in a geographic network environment, as observed by the same authors [25].

F   Conclusions

This paper presents a novel architecture for cooperative Web caching based on a two-tier cluster-based lookup process. The prototype has been implemented by modifying the Squid proxy server. Experiments carried out through an artificial workload based on Polygraph show that the proposed architecture guarantees better scalability because its object hit rates are comparable to those of ICP, the best performing protocol (about 50%), but its overhead due to cooperation is much lower (140 bytes per request vs. 811 bytes).

References

[1] IRCache: Ircache project (1995) – http://www.ircache.net.
[2] AT&T: At&t (2002) – http://www.att.com.
[3] Akamai: Akamai inc. (2002) – http://www.akamai.com.
[4] DigitalIsland: Digital island inc. (2002) – http://www.digitalisland.com.
[5] Wang, J.: A survey of web caching schemes for the internet. ACM Computer Communication Review **29** (1999)
[6] Rodriguez, P., Spanner, C., Biersack, E.: Web caching architectures: hierarchical and distributed caching. In: Proc. of Web Caching Workshop (WCW'99). (1999)
[7] Rabinovich, M., Spatscheck, O.: Web Caching and Replication. Addison Wesley (2002)
[8] Wessels, D.: Web Caching. O'Reilly (2001)
[9] Yu, P.S., MacNair, E.A.: Performance study of a collaborative method for hierarchical caching in proxy servers. Computer Networks and ISDN Systems (1998) 215–224
[10] Wessels, D., Claffy, K.: Internet cache protocol (icp), version 2 (1997) RFC 2186.
[11] Fan, L., Cao, P., Almeida, J., Broder, A.Z.: Summary cache: A scalable wide-area web cache sharing protocol. IEEE/ACM Transactions on Networking **8** (2000) 281–293
[12] Santoro, A., Ciciani, B., Colajanni, M., Quaglia, F.: Two-tier cooperation: A scalable protocol for web cache sharing. In: Proc. of IEEE International Symposium on Network Computing and Applications, Cambridge, MA (2002)
[13] Gadde, S., Rabinovich, M., Chase, J.: An approach to building large internet caches. In: Proc. Sixth Workshop on Hot Topics in Operating Systems (HotOS-VI). (1997)
[14] Collins, R., Nordstrom, H., Russkov, A., Wessels, D.: Squid web proxy cache (2002) – http://www.squid-cache.org.
[15] Goemans, M.X., Williamson, D.P.: A general approximation technique for constrained forest problems. In: Proc. of ACM-SIAM Symposium on Discrete Algorithms. (1992)
[16] Wessels, D.: Squid Programmers Guide. (2002)
[17] Vixie, P., Wessels, D.: Hyper text caching protocol (htcp/0.0) (2000) RFC 2756.
[18] Gadde, S., Chase, J., Rabinovich, M.: A taste of crispy squid. In: Proc. of Workshop on Internet Server Performance (WISP'98). (1998)
[19] Russkov, A., Wessels, D.: Web polygraph (2000) – http://www.web-polygraph.org.
[20] Papoulis, A., Pillai, S.U.: Probability, Random Variables and Stochastic Processes. McGraw-Hill (2001)
[21] Bloom, B.: Space/time trade-offs in hash coding with allowable errors. Communications of the ACM **13** (1970) 422–426
[22] Rousskov, A., Wessels, D.: Cache digests. Computer Networks and ISDN Systems **30** (1998)
[23] Valloppillil, V., Ross, K.: Cache array routing protocol v1.0 (1998)
[24] Ross, K.W.: Hash-routing for collections of shared web caches. IEEE Network Magazine (1997)
[25] Rabinovich, M., Chase, J., Gadde, S.: Not all hits are created equal: Cooperative proxy caching over a wide-area network. In: Proc. of Third International WWW Caching Workshop. (1998)

Caching Web Services:
Aspect Orientation to the Rescue

Marc Ségura-Devillechaise and Jean-Marc Menaud

EMN, La Chantrerie, 4, rue Alfred Kastler. B.P. 20722,
F-44307 NANTES Cedex 3, France,
Phone: (+33) (0) 2 51 85 81 00
Fax: (+33) (0) 2 51 85 81 99
{msegura,jmenaud}@emn.fr

Abstract. Web caches are a software answer to the growing demand of bandwidth on the Internet. But the increasing number of dynamic Web objects like Web services decreases caches performances. This paper proposes to adapt dynamically caches to the cached objects. The required adaption is often dynamic, motivated by a variability that programmers could not anticipate before runtime. This paper discusses the possibility to use aspect orientation to achieve dynamic adaptation. While aspects are appearing as a suitable tool, dynamic adaptation adds some requirements to the aspect system that could be used. The purpose of this paper is to reach a clear and explicit understanding of these requirements.

Keywords: web caching, dynamic adaptation, aspect orientation, dynamic weaving, web services.

1   Introduction

The ever-increasing popularity of the Internet creates an urgent need to reduce the resulting traffic congestion. The problem is to improve the average response time. Researchers have explored two types of solutions. The first one consist in increasing the bandwidth of the network links. This raises a number of financial and technical problems. The second is to use caches over the Internet to replicate the most frequently accessed data. Although the latter is more affordable than the former, the actual benefit of using caches to improve response time over the Internet still remains negligible.

The maturation of Web-caching infrastructures raises hopes that clients and servers will both become more cache-friendly, for example, by using some H.T.T.P. and H.T.M.L. tags. This could increase both the fraction of Web content that is cacheable, and the fraction of Web content served through caches (rather than trough originating servers). Unfortunately, the World Wide Web is growing and changing rapidly. As shown in [1], the dynamic nature of Web data poses a

E. Gregori et al. (Eds.): Networking 2002 Workshops, LNCS 2376, pp. 42–52, 2002.

generic problem to information systems that either cache, summarize or index the Web.

Two key factors explain the growing number of dynamic objects on the Web. The first is a direct consequence of the web page lifecycle. More than 40% of pages in the .com domain change every day [2, 3]. Professionals maintaining commercial pages, update them frequently to provide timely information and attract more customers. The second source of dynamism is provided by the use of C.G.I.[1] scripts. Our study [4] on Internet traces shows that 45% of the different requests contain a question mark character ("?") characteristic of these scripts. These particular requests are directly sent to C.G.I. scripts. Then, the script generates a dynamic H.T.M.L. response. Whatever the reasons, dynamicity decreases Web caching performance.

However, a new trend is emerging. Traditionally, the algorithms involved in the dynamic pages generation remains buried in the information system, in the Web server back-end. But now, the wide-spreading Web services are externalizing their algorithms in one or several components. Therefore, contrary to C.G.I. scripts, the generating components; Web services, are identified. This identification is done both in terms of server localization and semantic description of the offered functionalities. An appropriate answer is to apply caching techniques to Web services.

Unfortunately, caching Web services sounds difficult. First, downloading an entire Web service might outweigh the gain. This is a size problem. Secondly, most Web services are strongly coupled to the information systems they came from. Typically, they are interacting with the information system databases and potentially with other Web services. A cached Web service still requires these interactions. It is unclear if the gain in caching the Web service will not be outweighed by the amount of data exchanged during these interactions. These two problems lead to the idea that information systems should be responsible to provide specialized caches meeting their specific constraints.

Still, as shown in section 2, the previous idea is not easy. A cache remains a complex piece of software. As for Web services, the size of a specialized cache might prevent it to be downloaded. A solution, then, is to cope only with the specific parts of the specialized cache. The goal then is to download only these specific parts and to adapt a generic cache.

However, the practical experiments described in section 2 show that traditional modularization approaches are insufficient to allow this type of adaptation. The roots of the problem is that the alterations to tailor the cache to the information system are generally crosscutting the generic cache modularization. Section 3 proposes to use aspect-orientation to solve this problem. Section 4

---

[1] Common Gateway Interface

analyses how this technique can support dynamic adaptation. Section 5 presents future work and discusses research tools that might be suitable. Finally, section 6 concludes.

2   Motivations: Modifying a Cache

This section summarizes the problems we encountered while implementing a Web caching system. First, an overview of the different subsystems is given. It allows us to describe the issues arising while augmenting an existing cache; Squid, with a new cooperation protocol. Finally, the last subsection provides an abstract view of the described problems.

2.1   Web Caches

Basically, a cache is a software that stores commonly accessed data elements on disk. The cache management policy drives data replacement to keep in the cache only the elements that are likely to be reaccessed. Considering network topology, the idea of making network caches cooperate has emerged.

The hierarchical approach to network cache cooperation is a pioneering idea. The idea was suggested by a study on Internet traffic in the United-States [5]. It concludes that Internet traffic can be a priori reduced by 30% by introducing a cache on every network node. The cache system's hierarchical structure is mapped on the national network hierarchical organization. In this type of system, a missing object is located by propagating the request to the upper level in the cache hierarchy. This process is iterated until either the object is found or the root cache is reached; it might ultimately involve contacting the object's server. While returned to the client, the object is then copied in all the contacted caches. A transversal system refines the hierarchy concept by grouping, at each level, in sets of caches roughly having the same latency time. In these systems, on a cache miss, a cache not only contacts its ancestral cache but also the other caches in its sets, its siblings.

For different reasons, detailed in [6], a transversal approach is ineffective: it introduces a significant augmentation of bandwidth consummation. Based on the aforementioned evaluation of transversal systems, we designed a new protocol for transversal cooperation combining their benefits while having negligible network and machine overhead, hence providing a scalable solution. The principle is to fairly distribute knowledge among the caches composing the transversal system. We described the integrated protocol in previous publications [6, 7].

2.2   Technical Introspection

We integrated our work with the most successful free cache software : Squid. This cache integrates directly the transversal cooperative protocol previously described, named I.C.P. [8]. Squid is the basis for our prototype: it provides the base cache management and a first hierarchical cooperative protocol. The purpose here is not to describe technically and precisely how the Squid cache version 1.2.22 is designed but only to give an intuition on how and what was modified to build our prototype.

Squid is a Web cache developed by the National Laboratory for Applied Network Research and members of the Web community. Squid implements only one unblocking process based on a main loop. This process handles all requests. For portability reasons, Squid do not use the thread programming paradigm. To manage different simultaneous requests Squid use a sequence of "functions handlers" invoked on I/O operations. Thus the code is difficult to understand. Moreover, the source is not commented and variables names are not explicit.

Moreover, the Squid main features are split in different modules. We classified these different modules in four essentials functionalities: client treatment (authorization, request parsing etc), server treatment (contact, fetching etc), store manager (hash table etc), and communication (protocol cooperation). In fact, in version 1.2.22, 17 modules are clearly separated. These modules can be roughly grouped in five groups as follow:

Client treatments client_side, icp, acl and url
Server treatments http, gopher, wais, ssl, pass and proto
Storage management store, store_clean, disk, stmem and hash
Communication management comm and neighbors
Misc. (mainly for statistic) debug, objcache and stat

To integrate our cooperation protocol we believed naively that only a couple of modules should be modified : comm and perhaps neighbors. Unfortunately, the final implementation altered seven modules: icp, http, store, comm, neighbors, url, and client_side. Acknowledging only the main alterations that we have committed, the replacement of the Squid cooperation protocol - protocol already localized in two modules (roughly 10% of the code) - required in practice the alteration of seven modules representing roughly 40% of the code.

Moreover, we did not simply add functions and mask others: we added variables, inserted hooks into some functions, modified some structures, and spread enumerate variables. We did not succeed to modularize the modifications on the original software. We experienced the same difficulties when inserting a new cache policy management in our prototype.

2.3   Discussion

In the previous experiment, the modification of a particular strategy (cooperative protocol or cache policy), required an in-depth analysis and the modification of more than 40 % of the source code, while the cache was designed in a modular way. Actually the Squid modularization was not exactly reflecting what we needed to change. Unfortunately, this kind of problem; variability mismatching the original program modularization, is not an isolated case.

For instance, in the Active Cache research prototype [9], information servers supply applets attached with documents. On cache hits, the cache invokes these applets. They provide the necessary processing without contacting the information server they came from. We understand Active Cache as a relatively generic cache specialized by applets techniques. More precisely, variability is modularized and parameterized through applets. In Active Cache, the interface through which applets and the cache are interacting is focused on file management. This design decision is motivated by security and performance concerns. Nevertheless, this interface constrains the huge variability anticipated by this kind of modular architecture. For example, the introduction of a new cooperative protocol requires a complete rewriting of all the applets: only the file manager can be reused. In Active Cache, the adaptation interface does not anticipate variability of the file management system.

These examples highlight the fact that the alterations to tailor the cache to the information system are generally crosscutting the generic cache modularization. As described before, this was the case with Squid, it is the case with Active Cache. It is even likely that it is always the case with traditional modularization techniques.

3   Towards a Solution

The previous section shows that a good modularization is not sufficient to support the adaptation needed in section 1. Thus, we wonder if existing adaptation techniques could not allow us to tailor a generic cache for a specific information system. The first subsection 3.1 will show that aspect-orientation offers this potential. This technique will be described in subsection 3.2.

3.1   Adaptation Techniques

As seen previously, the required adaptation is dynamic and motivated by a variability that can not be anticipated. Unexpected variability, or in other words, unanticipated changes in how the computation has to be done, puts a strong requirement on the adaptation technology. Typical applications anticipates variability through configuration files: most applications can now reload them at runtime. An advanced technique like reflection [10] supposes that variability occurs at the language level. For example, reflection has been used in OpenCorba [11] to build an adaptable object broker. Typically in these approaches, variability is modelled through meta-classes. Open Implementation [12, 13] requires the application developer to anticipate the changes to offer an adaptation interface. Using these techniques to support dynamic adaptation seems difficult because they anticipate variability prior to runtime.

At runtime, to support dynamic adaptation, the program has to change "how" it is doing its computation. As shown before, there is a potential mismatch between this change and the activities promoted by the original decomposition of the program: the required changes potentially crosscut the compositional structure of the original program. In this context, because variability can not be predicted in advance, adaptation appears as a dynamic cross cutting concern. We propose to use Aspect Oriented Programming (A.O.P.) [14, 15] to support dynamic adaptation. We characterize dynamic adaptation as an alteration of how the program performs its computation motivated by the occurrence of a variability, unanticipated by the program. According to this definition, supporting adaptation means re-composing how the computation is done by the original program so that the resulting program anticipates the encountered variability.

3.2 An Overview of Aspect Orientation

Because aspect orientation is still a young fertile research domain, it is relatively difficult to define. We propose a description based on the operational model described in [16] using AspectJ [17] terminology. Typically *advices* are used to incrementally modify "how" the computation is done by the program. More precisely, an advice specifies an action to be taken whenever some condition arises during the execution of the program. The events by which advices may be triggered are called *join points*. The process of executing the relevant advice at each join point is named *weaving*. The condition is specified using a predicate language over the join points. These predicates are known as *point cuts*.

Thus, compared to other adaptation techniques, aspect-orientation appears as having the potential to support dynamic adaptation. The choice of an appropriate aspect-language should be based on: the join point model, the point cut language, and the advice model. The first element designs which events the weaver can observed. The second element covers how the information from the events are communicated to the advice. Finally, the advice model describes how advices are composed. Composition is twofold: first the advice has to be composed with the program but the composition of advices together is an important issue too.

4   From Dynamic Adaptation to A.O.P.

Considering the A.O.P. key elements described previously and the character-ization of dynamic adaptation given in section 3, we can propose a mapping between the two. Point cuts describe the occurrence of variability that advices are addressing. The advice model defines how the computation performed by the program will be re-composed. Join points defines where variability could be ob-served in the original program. Dynamic adaptation puts specific constraints on each of these elements. To move from tailor-made to ready-to-wear, the reusabil-ity of adaptation code is a key issue.

4.1   Dynamic Adaptation and the Join Point Model

The join point model actually limits the scope of the variability that the point cuts can address. The generic cache cannot anticipate all the information system it may encounter. Consequently, because "what has to be changed" can not be anticipated previously, point cuts need to be able to describe an occurrence of variability at any point during the execution of the program. Therefore, to fully support dynamic adaptation, the join point model should cover the entire exe-cution of the program. It should not only be dynamic: each action performed at runtime should be a potential join points. Furthermore, runtime monitors could also be used as join point, allowing, for example, an aspect to be woven when the bandwidth drops under a certain value. However this could lead to poor run-time performance. But, we believe that observing only the relevant part[2] of the program through dynamically inserted probes, combined with the use of partial evaluation can lead to an acceptable overhead.

4.2   Dynamic Adaptation and the Advice Model

The advice model merging aspects with the original program corresponds to the program recomposition in the characterization of dynamic adaptation. In most A.O.P. systems, composing advices together is not easy. It means that composing different adaptations on the same program using A.O.P. can be po-tentially difficult. However it is very desirable to be able to compose different dynamic adaptation together: a Web cache is intended to meet several different information systems. Most problems arising in composing advices together occur because of a static weaving process[3] and because it is unclear if once weaved, the advice is observed by the join points. Thus an advice model to support dynamic adaptation should allow dynamic weaving and ensure that woven advices are observed by join points.

---

[2] That is the one referenced by the point cut.

[3] I.e. performed before load time

4.3   Dynamic Adaptation and the Point Cut Language

To describe the variability, a declarative language seems an appropriate choice: information systems are not interested into "programming" they would rather "declare" the changes. This task however can be complex, the point cut language must be expressive enough.

Because the point cut language intends to describe something: a change in the original program, it raises the problem of the desirable coupling degree between point cuts and the program. What level of coupling between the advice and the program should the point cut language allow to express? Coupling entails that the advice (or the program, or both the program and the advice) knows of the program (of the advice or of each other respectively). To support dynamic adaptation, the program simply can not make assumptions about the woven advices: from the program viewpoint, weaving must occur transparently. Therefore, an appropriate point cut model should only allow advices to assume, through the point cuts triggering the weaving, where they are woven. To support the adaptation required by web caching, the program should never know about advices.

4.4   Dynamic Adaptation Code Reusability

In the mapping defined between dynamic adaptation and A.O.P. in section 4, the reusability of the code achieving dynamic adaptation corresponds to the aspect reusability. The less an aspect assumes where it will be woven, the more it becomes reusable. This is another side of the question expressed previously: what level of coupling between the advice and the program should the point cut language allow to express? This section rephrases this question in: should the point cut language forbid coupling between the advices and program to ease aspects reusability? Aspect-oriented development case studies, like for example Kersten and Murphy [18], stress that complete decoupling occurs rarely. It is likely that this is the case in dynamic adaptation as well. An aspect adapting the storage management strategy in an a Web cache must know about the program it is adapting: it needs to know at least that the program described by the join points is a Web cache.

Thus, assuming that few adaptation concerns are truly orthogonal to the adapted program appears as a reasonable hypothesis. Consequently the advice must be aware of the program. Therefore, the declarativness of the point cut language should grant that a programmer can start by writing advices assuming completely their weaving location. And its expressiveness should grant that ad hoc advices can be incrementally refined to reach the other side of the spectrum: the full decoupling of an aspect from the program it is adapting. More precisely, it should be possible to write an ad hoc aspect for a specific program encountering a given variability and to refine this advice incrementally so it can adapt almost any program encountering this variability. Technically, the point cuts of the ad hoc aspect version refer to class and method names while the generic advice version analyzes the context, through the state of the runtime, and the actions taken by the program. While fully decoupled aspects open exciting perspective like aspect-on-the-shelf, it still makes sense to write aspects assuming their weaving positions. This kind of aspects are not reusable but they still localize the adaptation code.

5 Future Work

We are currently writing the cache sketched in the introduction to test our ideas. This requires to dispose of an adequate A.O.P. system. It is likely that we shall write one from scratch. From an implementation viewpoint, join points are often reduced to positions of syntactic elements appearing in the source code. This restriction allows the weaving to be performed entirely before the program execution. While this approach avoids the introduction of overhead at runtime, it fails to handle dynamic concerns. But we are still reviewing the recent work of Kris Gybels [19]. This work supports dynamic cross cutting concerns and follows Kris de Volder [20] idea of using a logic programming language as point cut language. Kris Gybels tool is an aspect system for Smalltalk with a Prolog system named SOUL on top. SOUL is used as a point cut langauge. Another alternative PROSE [21, 22] allows dynamic aspect weaving and unweaving. It stands for PROgrammable extenSion of sEervices. PROSE uses a Java API as predicate language over the join points. Technically PROSE is based on the Java Virtual Machine Debugger Interface (JVMDI).

6 Conclusion and Future Works

Caching techniques are a software answer to the growing demand of bandwidth on the Web. But the Web is becoming increasingly dynamic. New dynamic objects like Web Services are emerging. This identification is done both in terms of server localization and semantic description of the offered functionality. It is therefore possible to cache them. Still, Web services are strongly coupled to their information systems. Typically they need databases connections, access to other application servers, etc This paper advocates that information systems should tailor a cache to their needs. Our practical experiments shows that the required adaption is dynamic, motivated by a variability that could not be anticipated before. We suggested to understand dynamic adaptation as a dynamic cross cutting concern. Therefore, we believe that aspect orientation has the potential to support dynamic adaptation. However, as explained previously, dynamic adaptation puts some specific constraints on the aspect system that can be used. First, the join point model should cover every action performed at runtime by the program. Secondly, the point cut language should be declarative, expressive, and minimizing the coupling between advices. Finally, the weaving process should be dynamic and advices once woven should be observed by join points. Our on-going work is focusing on validating our ideas through the implementation of a Web cache achieving the scenario sketched in the introduction.

Moving to a conceptual point of view, Aspect Oriented Programming tries to provide tools allowing *"the modularity of a system to reflect the way "we think about it" rather the way the language or others tools force us to think about it"* [17]. Because the program authors and the program users are different, the code achieving a particular adaptation should be a concern separated from the program. From a software engineering point of view, because different users have different and diverging adaptation needs, it is desirable to separate the adaptation code from the original program.

Another way to understand our proposition is to say that we would like to use A.O.P. re-modularization capabilities to solve the potential mismatch between the original program modularization and what dynamic adaptation needs to alter in it. We use aspects to dynamically separate the concern that have to be adapted from the original program.

As a proof of concept of our ideas, we currently prototype a Web cache supporting dynamic adaptation. We are paying attention to security (code verification, code validation, ...) and to performance.

References

[1] Lawrence, S., Giles, C.L.: Accessibility of information on the web. Nature 400 (1999)
[2] Cho, J., Garcia-Molina, H.: The evolution of the web and implications for an incremental crawler. In: The VLDB Journal. (2000) 200–209
[3] Lim, L., Wang, M., Padmanabhan, S., Vitter, J.S., Agarwal, R.C.: Characterizing web document change. In: Web-Age Information Management. (2001) 133–144
[4] Menaud, J.M.: Cooperative Caches System for Large Scale Distributed Information System. PhD thesis, IRISA/INRIA Rennes France (2000)
[5] P. Danzig, R.S.H., Schwartz, M.F.: A case for caching file object inside internetworks. In: Proceedings of ACM Sigcomm'93. (1993) 239–248
[6] Menaud, J.M., Issarny, V., Banâtre, M.: A new protocol for efficient cooperative transversal web caching. In: International Symposium on Distributed Computing. (1998) 288–302
[7] Jean-Marc Menaud, Valrie Issarny, M.B.: A scalable and efficient cooperative system for web caches. In: IEEE Concurrency. (2000)
[8] Wessels, D.: Configuring hierarchical squid caches. Squid/Hierarchy-Tutorial (1997)
[9] Cao, P., Zhang, J., Beach, K.: Active cache: Caching dynamic contents on the web. In: Proceedings of IFIP International Conference on Distributed Systems Platforms and Open Distributed Processing (Middleware '98). (1998) 373–388

[10] Smith, B.: Reflection and semantics in Lisp. In: Proceedings of the Symposium on Principles of Programming Languages, ACM Press (1984) 23–35

[11] Ledoux, T.: OpenCorba: A reflective open broker. Lecture Notes in Computer Science **1616** (1999) 197–215

[12] Kiczales, G., Lamping, J., Lopes, C., Maeda, C., Mendhekar, A., Murphy, G.: Open implementation design guidelines. In: International Conference on Software Engineering. (1997) 481–490

[13] Rao, R.: Implementational reflection in Silica. In: ECOOP. (1991) 251–267

[14] Lopes, C., Hursch, W.: Separation of concerns. Technical Report NU-CCS-95-03, Northeastern University (1995)

[15] Kiczales, G., Lamping, J., Menhdhekar, A., Maeda, C., Lopes, C., Loingtier, J.M., Irwin, J.: Aspect-oriented programming. In Akşit, M., Matsuoka, S., eds.: ECOOP. Volume 1241. Springer-Verlag, New York, NY (1997) 220–242

[16] Douence, R., Motelet, O., Südholt, M.: A formal definition of crosscuts. In: Proceedings of the 3rd International Conference on Reflection and Crosscutting Concerns. Volume 2192 of LNCS., Springer Verlag (2001)

[17] Kiczales, G., Hilsdale, E., Hugunin, J., Kersten, M., Palm, J., Griswold, W.G.: An overview of AspectJ. In: ECOOP. (2001) 327–353

[18] Kersten, M., Murphy, G.C.: Atlas: a case study in building a Web-based learning environment using aspect-oriented programming. ACM SIGPLAN Notices **34** (1999) 340–352

[19] Gybels, K.: Using a logic language to express cross-cutting through dynamic joinpoints (2002)

[20] Volder, K.D., D'Hondt, T.: Aspect-oriented logic meta programming. Volume Proceedings of Meta-Level Architectures and Reflection, Second International Conference, Reflection'99. (1999) 250–272

[21] A. Popovici, T. Gross, W.B.: Dynamic homogenous AOP with PROSE. Technical report, ETH Zürich Department of Computer Science Institute of Information Systems (2001)

[22] A. Popovici, G. Alonso, T.: AOP support for mobile systems. OOPSLA 2001 Workshop: Advanced Separation of Concerns in Object-Oriented Systems (2001)

Replicated Web Services: A Comparative Analysis of Client-Based Content Delivery Policies

Marco Conti, Enrico Gregori, and Willy Lapenna

CNUCE Institute, C.N.R, Via G. Moruzzi, 1, 56100 Pisa, Italy
{Marco.Conti, Enrico.Gregori, Willy.Lapenna}@cnuce.cnr.it

Abstract. The increase of the Internet users and web applications leads to the need for more reliable and faster Web services. Different techniques were developed to address this issue and to provide a better QoS for the Internet users. Among them, an important role is played by the replication of Web services. Replication of Web services is obtained by implementing a Web service with several Web servers. This replication can be deployed either locally (e.g. by a cluster of computers) or geographically (e.g. servers distributed sparsely in the Internet). In this paper we deal with geographical replication. Two main approaches are currently used for geographical replication: client-side and server-side approach. We focused our analysis on the client-side approach. We classified and contrasted, qualitatively and quantitatively (via simulation), different client side techniques to find the pro and cons of each approach with the aim to identify the best solutions for content-delivery systems.

1 Introduction

Currently, a large fraction of users accesses network resources through web clients/browsers. The Quality of Service (QoS) perceived by users is thus becoming a dominant factor for the success of an Internet based Web service. The principal QoS attributes that users perceive include those related to the service "responsiveness", i.e. the service availability and timeliness. The performance perceived by the users of a Web service depends on the performance of the protocols that operate between web clients and servers. The main issue is to minimize the User Response Time (URT), i.e. the elapsed time between the generation of a request from a browser, for the retrieval of a Web page, and the rendering of that page at that browser's site. Hence, the URT includes both the communication and the processing delays involved in servicing a browser request. Solutions currently investigated in the literature range from new protocols to enhance the network QoS (e.g. differentiated services) to mechanisms running into the end systems to enhance the QoS perceived by the users (e.g. caching, prefetching, Web servers' replication, etc.). While, in the medium-term,

This work is partially founded by MIUR in the framework of the project "SP 1: Strumenti, ambienti e applicazioni innovative per la società dell'informazione".

it is envisaged that Internet evolves to a universal transport service that will be able to provide (when it is required) a delivery of the traffic with QoS guarantees, currently, an IP network provides a best effort service. Hence, in the short term, the middleware must cope with the network insufficient bandwidth and high latency. The issues that need to be addressed to improve the QoS are: i) the decrease of the document retrieval latency, ii) the increase of data availability, for example, through replication of the information, iii) the reduction of the amount of data to transfer, and iv) the redistribution of network accesses to avoid network congestion.

Several techniques have been developed to meet the demand for faster and more efficient access to Internet. These techniques include caching, prefetching and pushing. However they are only a partial solution to introduce QoS in Web services. The more advanced approach of autonomous data replication has been recently introduced to attack the problem ([1], [2], [3], [4], [7], [8], [9], [10], [11], [12], [19], [20], [21], [22]). The primary aim of replication is to increase data availability and to reduce the load on a server by balancing the service accesses among the Replicated Web Servers (RWSs). As the Web access is prevalently timing zone dependent, the Service Replication may help to a better use of available resources to provide a QoS improvement. The main Internet feature that is exploited by the Service Replication is that at a fixed time there is a different amount of requests to the same Web service coming from different geographical areas. In this paper we analyze and contrast the most promising client-side solutions for achieving QoS improvement in Web servers' replication. Our target is to identify the effect of several choices for an optimal strategy that has to be adopted by clients to reach a QoS improvement.

This paper is structured as follows. In the next section we present an overview on the Web Service Replication. In Section 3 we contrast qualitatively the most interesting client-side solutions presented in literature. In Section 4 we quantitatively compare (via simulation) under different conditions the analyzed client-side approaches.

2 Web Service Replication

The common Internet scenario is shown in Fig. 1 and it references to the centralized server model. In this model there is only one server, named origin server, and a multitude of users accessing to this Web server via their own Internet Service Provider (ISP). The user fetches all requested data from the origin server. In the centralized server model several elements affect the URT. Specifically, the two main elements are: the Web server performance issues and the Network infrastructure issues. We focus our attention on these two aspects to improve the URT.

Web sever performance are generally concerned with the capacity of the servers to process more and more client's requests. On the other hand, in the connection between the server and the client 4 types of bottlenecks can be identified in the Internet infrastructure (see Fig. 2) ([1], [13]). These issues are:

The first mile. The first mile problem takes into account the limited bandwidth that is available to connect the server to the Internet. More bandwidth is needed with the growth of users that access to the same Web Service.

The peering points. With peering point we consider the points of interconnection (i.e. routers) between different Autonomous Systems (AS). Traffic generated in an AS is easily managed inside the same AS. This traffic is in competition with traffic of other AS when it crosses a peering point. This competition, when these peering points became overloaded, may determine packets' losses with consequent data retransmissions ([13]).

The backbone capacity. Backbone capacity is the available network capacity. It varies from a Network Provider to another one. Backbone capacity depends on routers' and cables' capacity. While the latter is not a problem, the routers' capacity (i.e. software and hardware capacity to forward packets) is heavily limited by the current technology. The amount of the Internet traffic that crosses the backbones overcomes the capacity of backbone bandwidth available. This gap is subjected to grow with the increase of Web service requests ([1]).

The last mile. Finally last mile problem directly concerns the limited client connectivity to the Internet. Clients are generally connected to their own ISP via a modem connection. This connection may be a great bottleneck in transferring data.

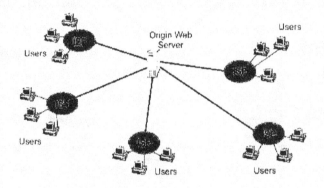

Fig. 1. The centralized server model [IGP99]

A very interesting approach to tackle the described issues (in term of Web server performance and Internet infrastructure) consists of adopting the Replication model. In this model we have more than a single server that may satisfy the users' requests. Respect to the centralized model, with the Replication model we have more resources availability. The vast majority of the load distribution strategies for RWSs assume that these WSs are replicated within a cluster of resources, and the access to them is governed by the cluster DNS server. These strategies aim to maximize the WSs throughput, rather than minimizing the User Response Time, and pay little attention to such issues as client latency time over the Internet. While this approach is oriented prevalently to tackle the Web server performance issue it doesn't consider the previously mentioned Internet infrastructure bottlenecks. A more general approach that tackles both issues has been proposed. It i s based on the geographical distribution of the information to increase both the service availability and the timeliness. This approach is based on the implementation of a Web service, by replicating Web servers at distinct sites distributed across the Internet (see Fig. 2), rather than within a single cluster, and ensuring that each client (or browser) takes advantages of this replication. In the geographical replication we have RWSs that are spread in the whole Internet, in multiple locations. This approach leads to a distribution of the user's requests among the several RWSs. Geographical replication is a new and promising area both from a research and industrial standpoint. Akamai, Nortel and Cisco products are only examples of appliances deployed in the common market to address this problem (see [9] and [10]). When we consider replicated Web servers we intend that all the content of a server is exactly present at the other replicas. This may introduce consistency problems. Hereafter we will not consider the data consistency problem introduced by replication.

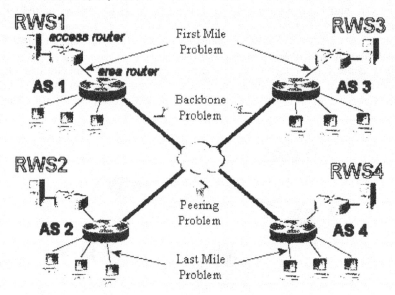

Fig. 2. Internet Bottlenecks

It is worth noting that combining the paradigms of caching, prefetching and replication promises to be a synergetic way to provide QoS guarantees to Web-based applications. When we have several RWSs we need to define a policy to bind the client that makes a request to one or more of these servers. This selection policy can be implemented at two different places. According to this location we can define two main approaches: i) server-side approach and ii) client-side approach. The client-side and server-side approaches are distinguished by the place in which the choice to bind the client is taken. If it is taken at the client, i.e. close to the client (e.g. into the client browser, client-side proxy, etc.) we have a client-side solution, otherwise we are speaking about a server-side solution. A client-based approach has the advantage that the client-side solution has an overall network vision (in term of congestion of the links involved in the data transfer between server and client) that coincides with that observed by the browser. Another advantage of this approach is that it seems appropriate when the group of server is heterogeneous or widely dispersed across the network [11]. This approach makes the assumption, easily achievable, that when the browser makes a DNS request to obtain an URL resolution, it obtains all the available IP addresses of the RWSs [6]. In this paper we focus our attention on the client-side techniques, for further information on server-side solutions and a comparison between client-side and server-side, please refer to [9] and [10].

3 Client-Side Approaches: Analysis of Existing Solutions

In the literature we can find several client-side techniques to face the problem of improving the QoS in a geographically distributed RWSs environment. A classification of the several client-side techniques can be found in [9]. The approaches currently proposed in the literature to access a replicated Web service are substantially two: i) the client downloads data from all available servers; ii) the client downloads data from only one server. If all servers are used to download data, the attention is on the way the replicas are used ([2], [19], [12]), i.e., on the portion of data requested to each replica. By using all RWSs the server(s) selection algorithm that may be critical is not deployed. Two significant techniques belong to this class ([19], [12]). In the technique presented in [19] "the client polls the servers using a HTTP request". The client downloads portion of data from all the RWSs simultaneously. Data to download are divided in blocks of fixed size and their size is defined a priori ([19]). The great advantage of the technique of Rodriguez et al. is related to its simplicity: when a server is faster than the others, it automatically receives more block requests. From the client overhead standpoint this approach seems to be convenient. In this technique the state information is small because the requests to the servers are made automatically without monitoring the connections' state. We have to note that [19] technique was tested adequately only for large documents of several hundreds of Kbytes, while a common Web page size has an average size about 32 KB [16]. Among the others techniques that download data in parallel from all servers, the conceptually closest to [19] is the C^2LD presented in [12]. The most important difference with the [19] approach is that with C^2LD mechanism the data block size varies dynamically. Specifically, the data block size is proportional to the measured throughput for every client-server connection. Hereafter we don't evaluate the [12] strategy because it involves a greater number with respect to [19] of parameters to be evaluated and this makes the comparison difficult. Hence hereafter, we focus on the [19] as representative approach for all-RWS strategies. When the client downloads data from only one server the goal is to define an algorithm ensuring that each client (or browser) gets bound to the "most convenient" RWS for the whole download time ([3], [4] , [7], [8], [11], [20], [21], [22]). In this case the main issue in the server replication is the algorithm to select the best server that will be used for downloading data. We selected the QoS based approach ([8]) like the representative of the single server techniques. In the QoS-based strategy the client browser (after receiving from the DNS all the RWSs IP addresses), initially probes each RWS. This probing is made by sending a dummy request that provides an estimation of the URT that each replica can guarantee. This dummy request involves few server' processing but is indicative of the server load. In addition, the RTT of the dummy request is indicative of the network status. Based on this probing phase the browser decides from which server it downloads all the requested data. The only-one-server approach has many advantages with respect to the all-servers approach. In many situations the client has to maintain the communication with one server only. This requirement generally occurs when a client not only download readable data, but also transmits data to server in an interactive way, such as in business transactions, shopping carts and search engine requests. In these application scenarios, the client must be connected with only one server. Another great advantage in binding a client to the same server for consecutive transactions (during the same session) is related to a better exploitation of the cache memory and to improve server performances [15]. In the literature the comparison of different strategies in the Replication Model is made taking into account mainly the URT (or similar statistics). Moreover, the evaluation regards few clients that apply the same strategy. Hereafter, we compare the *QoS based* and all-RWS used techniques also in term of load balancing and overheads. In the following we neglect the amount of bandwidth requested from the clients to send their requests, but we consider mainly the bandwidth involved by the servers' responses. Both methods, in the initial phase, produce a similar amount of requested bandwidth in addition. This is equal to $M \cdot DummyRequest$, where M is the number of RWSs and *DummyRequest* is the dummy response size. In the *QoS based* approach the overhead ends when the data download starts, instead when all-RWS are used (see [19] strategy) an additional overhead mainly occurs during the last part of download. To better understand how this overhead occurs let us focus on the last block to retrieve. First of all we consider as a start-point for our consideration the following *Lemma*. **Lemma 1.** Let N be the number of RWSs and *DimBlock* defines the block size: when a strategy presented in ([19]) with fixed block size is adopted, the average number of requests in addition to all servers generated by each client is $(N-1)$ and consequently, the amount of wasted bandwidth is $(N-1) \cdot DimBlock$.

Proof. Let us define *RequestCounter* as the counter of the number of block requests to send to the RWSs. When the *RequestCounter* assumes the value 1, it means that only one block lacks for the completion of the download. When *RequestCounter* is set to 1, the first useful response, i.e. related to the necessary block that arrives, determines the end of the download. At this time instant all the RWSs, except the one returning the last block are active and hence they will return $(N-1)$ useless blocks. During the amount of time that the *RequestCounter* is equal to 1, all requests that occur are additional respect to the request that makes the transition to 0 of *RequestCounter* take place. The number of these additional requests is less or equal to $(N-1)$. In term of wasted bandwidth in the network and in transmission through the network the overhead is proportional to the block size, that is $(N-1) \cdot DimBlock$.

$$N_{req} = \frac{<Data>}{N\alpha} + \frac{N-1}{N} . \tag{1}$$

$$B_{req} = \frac{<Data>}{N} + \frac{(N-1)\alpha}{N} . \tag{2}$$

This simple estimation gives also an idea in term of time wasted to compute useless operations at the client and server side. If we consider persistent connections this time means of maintaining the resources for all download operation, otherwise the resource occupation is intermittent. In the case of pipelining use, the possibility to have wasted resources is greater because we decide a priori the requested blocks. If we consider the simple case in which the RWSs and network areas are balanced in term of available resources the total amount of requests made to each RWS is shown in Equation (1), where *<Data>* is the average Web page size that is around 32 KB [16] and α belongs to the set [2 KB, 4 KB, 8 KB]. *<Data>/α* represents the number of block of the same size in which the data to download are divided. From Equation (1) is clear that the requests' number is proportional to the number of blocks in which the data is divided. Moreover by decreasing the block size we have an increase of the N_{req}. The total amount of requested bandwidth (B_{req}) on each RWS from each client is expressed in Equation (2). In Equations (1) and (2) the second term represents the introduced overhead. As expected the wasted network bandwidth is proportional to the block size. Multiplying Equation (2) for N we obtain the total bandwidth requested from a client. In Fig. 3 are shown the percentage of additional requested bandwidth[a], i.e. wasted bandwidth, introduced into the system for N in the set [2,4,6,8] and *DimBlock* belonging to [2 KB, 4 KB, 8 KB]. They show that by increasing the block size or/and the number of RWSs the requested bandwidth increases.

4 Performance Comparison

In this section, via simulation, we quantitatively contrast the performance of client-side strategies. There are in the literature several studies of client-based strategies based on measurements on real test-beds ([3], [11], [12], [14], [19], [20], [21], [22]). Apparently, measurement studies have the advantage to take into consideration all the aspects of the problem (real network conditions, real servers' behavior, exact characterization of the Internet protocols, etc.). However, in a real testbed several important study parameters cannot be controlled (e.g., the load on the replicated servers, the network load conditions, etc.). In addition, and even worse, in the real testbeds it is almost impossible to have a large number of clients distributed into the Internet that access the RWSs by applying the same client-side strategy. Indeed, currently available experiments in the literature have been obtained with few clients (e.g., 4-5 clients). Therefore, these studies do not highlight the possible negative impact on the performance that may occur when several clients apply a parallel strategy (e.g., load fluctuations on the RWSs, RWSs overloading, etc.). On the other hand, with our simulative approach, even though we provide an approximate model of the environment (yet representative of the system bottlenecks), we are able to study the performance of the client-side strategies when a large clients' population adopts the same criterion to download data. The client-side strategies analyzed in the following have been selected by applying the qualitative criteria: simplicity, load balancing and overheads. Specifically, we contrasted the QoS-based strategy, presented in [8] and the Parallel strategies defined as follows. The class of Parallel strategy is derived from [19], however, in our study we analyze the performance of the parallel strategies to download Web Pages instead of documents of several hundreds of KBs. In the parallel-strategy approach a client browser that wishes to retrieve a Web page: *i)* contacts the DNS to resolve the URL; when receives the RWSs' IP addresses, *ii)* sends a HEAD request to all the RWSs to know the amount of data to download; *iii)* when the HEAD response returns to the client, the total amount of data to retrieve is divided in fixed-size blocks and a block of data is

---

[a] The percentage is calculated as the additional bandwidth respect to that requested from a client that uses a single server approach.

requested to each RWS, *iv)* until the download is completed, when a RWS returns the requested block (to the browser), the browser issues the request for a new block to that RWS. Therefore, the most responsive server automatically satisfies more requests. In our simulative study, we decided to use the following block size: 2 KBs, 4 KBs, 8 KBs. We selected these values to make the block size close to a Web-object size[a]. By adopting several block sizes we will assess the impact of the block size on the URT. Hereafter, the Parallel strategies with a 2, 4 or 8 KBs block size are named 2K-block, 4K-block and 8K-block, respectively. Furthermore, we name the QoS-based strategy as "single-block strategy" or "single-block" in the figures.

4.1 System Model

In this section, we describe the system model used in the experiments. Fig. 2 presents the reference scenario of our simulations. The simulation scenario is an extension of the realistic scenario adopted in [8]. Specifically, we extended that model to emphasize the Internet bottlenecks described in Section 2. In our simulative scenario there are four AS located in four geographical areas (e.g. USA, Europe, Asia and Australia). Hereafter the term Area and AS are used interchangeably. Each AS contains a RWS (or more generally a cluster of RWSs) and a pool of clients. These clients request data via their own browsers from (potentially) all the RWSs (i.e., not only those of their AS) according to a common client-side policy. To define our scenario we needed to specify the modeling of the main system components: i) the servers' behavior (i.e. RWSs), ii) the Internet infrastructure, and iii) the clients' behavior. Particular attention was devoted to represent the bottlenecks in the Internet infrastructure because we are particularly interested to evaluate the impact of the different client-side policies on the network congestion and to discover the effects that the network has on the URT.

i) The Server Modeling

We adopted the same server model used in [8]. We assume that each server can serve up to 200 requests per second (*rps*), i.e. the *capacity* of each server is 200 rps. The service time to process the *extra-data* requests (e.g., the dummy request of the QoS-based strategy) is one order of magnitude less respect to *content-data* requests (e.g., GET requests) processing. The amount of time to process a *content-data* request is assumed to be independent from the *content-data* size (i.e., amount of requested data). This assumption is based on the observation that most of the server operations have the same complexity if a file or a fragment of the file itself is requested. For example, the cache system mainly uses the file as its operating unit (a fragment is in the cache only if the overall file containing it is in the cache). Furthermore, to manage the request of a fragment that is not already in the cache the overall file containing that fragment must be retrieved from the secondary storage[b].

---

[a] We think that it is useful, if possible, to download a single object rather than fragments. When we download a fragment, the browser cannot generally render the object to show it to the user.

[b] In addition, simple considerations induce us to think that the greater block size the more likely the amount of data requested is in cache than in memory or in the worst case into the disk (whose retrying is the most expensive). In fact, by increasing the block size it increases the

ii) The Internet Modeling

To model the Internet we take into consideration the bottlenecks of the Internet infrastructure (see Section 2) as explained below. Our model is shown in Fig. 2.

First mile. Each RWS is located on a LAN that is connected to Internet via a router (*access router*). The *access router* has a finite buffer and a tail drop discard policy. This connection to Internet has (in our simulation) a 4-Mbps capacity and represents the *first mile effect*.

Backbone capacity. For each AS we introduced in our model an *area router*.(i.e. the most congested router of the AS). With the *area router* we represent a backbone router capacity. The router is represented by a FIFO queue and a finite buffer. This router is crossed by i) the client requests to the RWSs and the relative response to them, ii) all other packets generated by the rest of Internet users and servers. The latter packets represent the congestion level of the router. For this reason the Data coming from the RWS and client requests to the RWS that cross *area router* are served in a time negligible respect to the flowing of all other Internet data that goes through it. This means that the client requests provide negligible contribution to the congestion of the *area router* while the congestion influences the client URT. In our experiments its interface is set to 10 Mbps. In other words the available bandwidth among areas is set to 10 Mbps.

Peering points. To represent the peering points problem the connection between each couple of different area's routers is modeled by using a FIFO queue and a fixed inter-area delay. The service rate of the FIFO queues represents the available bandwidth. Inter-area delays are used to model the communication latency among different geographical areas. Their value is in the discrete set [50,500] milliseconds in average. The values 50 and 500 ms are used to model wide area distribution cross-countries via fiber or satellite connections, respectively ([18]).

Last mile. The last mile problem, related to the client connection to the Internet, is modeled by a FIFO queue to represent an access line of 56 Kbps or 10 Mbps. 56 Kbps represents a connection to the Internet via modem, while 10 Mbps represents a high-speed connection of a user on a LAN.

Accordingly to our model, the URT is the sum of the queueing delays in the queues (routers, servers), inter-area delays and service time delays. In other words, the URT involves the amount of time to satisfy a request when it starts from the client until the last content-data packet has crossed the Internet bottlenecks and arrived to the client. In the considered Internet scenario, the four geographical areas experience daily different loads in different periods of time (e.g. early morning, rush hour, late afternoon, night). We used different network and query load values to represent a particular period of the day. These values are reported in Table 1[a]. They show that only the router and server(s) in Area 1 are heavily loaded, i.e., they have a utilization

---

probability that an object is requested only to one RSW and hence the corresponding file is stored only in its cache. On the other hand, if small fragments are requested the file containing an object will be stored in several RSWs' caches hence decreasing the efficiency of the cache system.

[a] Network load represents the utilization of the *area router*. The query load value defines the utilization of the RWS's capacity.

(0.98) close to their saturation point. We model the packet fragmentation in the Internet by dividing data in 1Kbyte block size when data is delivered between client and servers.

Table 1. Load configuration for the examined realistic scenario.

Server	Area 1	Area 2	Area 3	Area 4
Network	0.98	0.80	0.50	0.10
query rate	0.98	0.80	0.50	0.10

iii) The Client Modeling

To model the amount of data requested by a client, in our simulation model, we have used a lognormal distribution (with $\sigma=2.16$ and $C=8.27$ [16]) to characterize the amount of data requested during a Web-Access[a] operation. The time intervals between consecutive Web-Access operations are independent and exponentially distributed [8]. We focused our attention to reduce the URT observed to satisfy these operations because this reduction means a reduction of all "session response time" ([5]). The client request has a dimension of 200 bytes. In addition, in the initial probing of the QoS-based strategy (i.e. a HEAD request), the dummy request corresponds to the retrieval of a 1000-byte page. The client, before deploying a particular strategy to download data, needs to have the IP addresses of the all RWS. We don't consider in the simulation the delays introduced by contacting the DNS (for IP address resolution of the RWS) as its impact is an invariant quantity for all techniques that we analyzed. In the steady state there are on average 60 clients adopting the same client-side strategy in each AS.

The results presented below have been obtained with the RESQ simulation tool using the independent replication method with a 90% confidence level. The width of the confidence intervals in these results is between 2% and 3%. We estimate both the average and the tail of the aggregated URT distribution for the 1st and the 4th AS (most and least congested, respectively). In the single-block strategy the URT includes the delay to select a replica with satisfactory URT. For each strategy, we have run a set of simulative experiments. In the simulations of the different strategies the system is under the same incoming requests condition (i.e., for a given scenario, the clients' requests per second is the same in the analysis of all client-side strategies). It is worth noting that the system offered load depends on the client-side strategy and the block size. Hereafter, we will use as a reference point the offered load related to the 4K-block strategy assuming a symmetric load case[b].

---

[a] We consider as a Web-Access operation the volume of data a user requests from the network before stopping and performing some user level action. This means that we model also the requests of more pages launched from the same browser by opening different windows ([Mol00]). We don't consider more requests interleaved by think times.

[b] In the symmetric case the inter-area congestion level (i.e. router utilization) and the query-generation rate are the same for each area, i.e. the service rates of all servers are equal.

4.2 Block-Size and Parallel Strategies Performance

In this subsection we focus on the Parallel strategies and we evaluate the block-size effect on the URT. In Fig. 4 and Fig. 5 we contrast the 2K-block, 4K-block and 8K-block strategies when the inter-area delay is set to 50 ms, and the last mile connection is 10 Mbps, i.e. a fast Internet connection. Specifically, the Fig. 5 plots the tail of the URT distribution shown in the Fig. 4. For each Parallel strategy we report the results of the most and least congested area, i.e., Area 4 and 1, respectively (see Table1 for the load distribution in the different areas). Results reported in Table 2 show that by increasing the block size the URT decreases both in the minimum and maximum values[a]. This is easily explained since the number of requests for each server decreases by increasing the block size (see Section 3). When the 2K-block strategy is used the server processing capacity is faster (with respect to 4K-block and 8K-block) becoming a system bottleneck. The greater the block size is, the less is the number of requests generated from each client. Therefore the 2K-block strategy shows the highest server utilization (see Table 3). By increasing the query rate the RWSs in the 2K-block strategy became totally congested (let us remember that in our model the service time to serve a request is independent from the block size). From the obtained results, it is worth noting that the Parallel strategies guarantee a load balancing among RWSs when the inter-area delay is set to 50 ms. On the other hand, load balancing is not achieved when the inter-area delay is set to 500 ms (see Table 3). In this case the time to retrieve a block from the client's own area is much smaller than from the other areas. Thus most of the blocks are obtained from a single area, i.e., the client area where the requests are generated. For example, the percentage of request generated from Area 1 and served from the same area in the 4K-block strategy is 61% and 93% with 50 and 500 ms, respectively. Hence, we can understand why the minimum URT (it corresponds to the 4th area, i.e. the least congested area) with 500 ms, and the 2K-block strategy is less than the correspondent value measured for 50 ms. Similar considerations explain the URT values estimated in the 500 ms case, e.g. the increase of the gap between the minimum and maximum URT values shown in Table 2. Differences between the 50 and 500 ms inter-area delay cases are visible also in the Fig. 6. In this figure we report the tail of the URT distribution in the case of 500 ms. To summarize, from the results presented so far, the 8K-block strategy seems to be the best approach. With this strategy when the network congestion is relatively low we reach a load balancing among the RWSs. However, from the overhead standpoint this approach has side effects in term of the wasted bandwidth. As expected (see equation 3 in Section 4), it has the greater overhead respect to the other strategies. For example by analyzing the *access router* interface for the Area 1 when the inter-area delay is 500ms, we measure an utilization of about 54% with 8K-block while it reduces to 48% and 29% in the 4K-block and 2K-block, respectively. This means that if the *access router* bandwidth is 2 Mbps instead of 4 Mbps the router in Area 1 saturates by applying the 8K-block strategy or in other words 8K-block strategy provides an inefficient utilization of a critical resource. This result is intuitive if we think for example to the ideal case of RWSs with exactly the same performance. In

---

[a] The values reported in Table 2 are obtained as follows. We compute the Average User Response Time per Area (seconds) for each Inter-area delay value (50, 500 ms). Among the four values obtained we select the maximum and minimum value.

this case the last block related to the same client request is downloaded from all RWSs. The larger is the block the greater is the amount of wasted resources in term of bandwidth and resources utilization (see Section 3).

Table 2. Average User Response Time per Area (seconds) with 10 Mbps in the first mile servers' connection.

10 Mbps in the last mile	Inter-area delay			
	50 ms		500 ms	
	Min	Max	Min	Max
2k-block	1.69	1.76	0.36	2.07
4k-block	0.17	0.25	0.18	0.53
8k-block	0.11	0.15	0.12	0.22
single-block	0.39	0.45	0.40	1.24

Table 3. Load distribution with 10 Mbps in the first mile servers' connection.

10 Mbps in the last mile	Inter-area delay							
	50 ms				500 ms			
	A1	A2	A3	A4	A1	A2	A3	A4
2k-block	0.99	0.99	0.99	0.99	0.99	0.99	0.99	0.52
4k-block	0.72	0.70	0.65	0.49	0.88	0.73	0.61	0.34
8k-block	0.49	0.47	0.44	0.35	0.57	0.48	0.42	0.28
single-block	0.08	0.08	0.07	0.07	0.09	0.08	0.07	0.05

4.3 Parallel Strategy vs Single-Block Strategy

In this subsection we contrast the Parallel strategies with the single block strategy. The results of the experiments are obtained under the conditions described in the previous subsection. In particular two types of experiments have been performed: medium and high inter-area delay (i.e. 50 and 500 ms). The average URT values are reported in Table 2 because they are part of the same set of experiments. Fig. 7 and Fig. 8 show the tail of the URT distribution of 8K-block, 4K-block and single-block strategy with medium and high inter-area delay (i.e. 50 and 500 ms). To increase the figures readability, we omit the 2K-block results as the performance of this strategy (as already shown in the previous section) are quite far (worse) from the other strategies (single-block, 4K-block and 8K-block). From Table 2 we can note that in the single-block strategy the average URT has values between the 2K-block and 4K-block case. From Table 3 we observe that the utilization of the RWS in Area 1 when a single-block strategy is adopted is (in comparison with the Parallel approaches) extremely low. This result is justified if we remember that the 4K-block strategy was used as a reference for the load parameter setting (e.g. query rate) and the number of requests per server with the single-block strategy is minimized. Therefore, all the results related to the single-block strategy are obtained with lightly loaded RWSs. However, the values in Table 2 show that the URT is greater in the single-block than in 4K-block or 8K-block case. In this situation the presence of the Internet bottlenecks is more emphasized. Analogue considerations to that explained in the previous

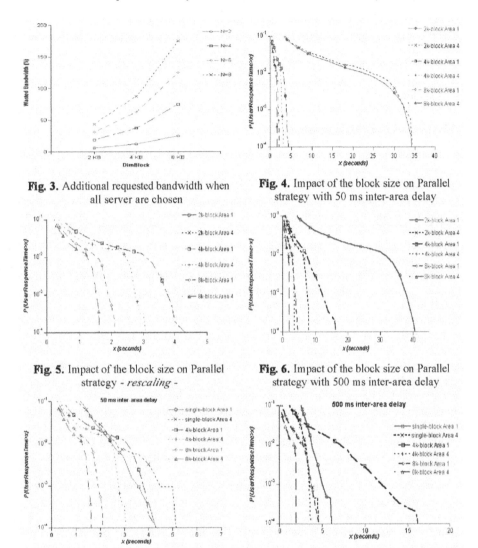

Fig. 3. Additional requested bandwidth when all server are chosen

Fig. 4. Impact of the block size on Parallel strategy with 50 ms inter-area delay

Fig. 5. Impact of the block size on Parallel strategy - *rescaling* -

Fig. 6. Impact of the block size on Parallel strategy with 500 ms inter-area delay

Fig. 7. Parallel *vs* single-block strategy with 50 ms inter-area delay

Fig. 8. Parallel *vs* single-block strategy with 500 ms inter-area delay

subsection can be made in term of load balancing if we consider the results showed in Table 3. For example, the percentage of the request generated and satisfied by Area 1 when single-block strategy is used is 49% and 78% with 50 and 500 ms respectively. Instead, with the 4K-block strategy, the percentage is 61% and 93% with 50 and 500 ms, respectively. From the overhead standpoint the single-block strategy has the great advantage that it doesn't introduce additional load in the server and in the network when a RWS is selected in the initial probing. However in the single-block strategy the initial probing is extremely critical because it binds the client to the selected RWS for all download duration. An incorrect assessment of the URT that a RWS can provide may lead to a strong QoS degradation. To verify the effectiveness of the initial probing we have estimated the probability to make a wrong choice. To this end, we estimated the probability that the selected server has less resources than those estimated in the initial probing. The results indicate that the probability to commit an error is low and confirms that during a session with only one server, performance varies smoothly [17].

4.4 Impact of Last Mile Bottleneck

Let us consider the case in which we introduce the bottleneck in the last mile connection, that is we consider a typical user connected via a 56 Kbps modem to the Internet. In Table 4 is presented (for each strategy) the Average URT with 50 and 500 ms inter-area delay. In Table 5 are shown the values of the load distribution in the RWSs with 50 and 500 ms inter-area delay. With reference to the results presented in Table 2, in Table 4 we note a large increase in the average URT, due to the introduction of the modem bottleneck. However, from the showed results (see Table 4) it is evident that there is not a winner strategy among analyzed strategies in term of URT. In addition, the impact of the inter-area delay is not so meaningful as in the case of direct connection (10 Mbps) to the Internet. In Fig. 9 are reported, as an example, the tail of the URT distribution in the case of single-block and 4K-block strategy. These curves are almost identical. The tail of the URT distribution is the same independently from i) the strategy, ii) the Area and iii) the inter-area delay level considered. The introduction of the last mile bottleneck tends to level the URT values. Moreover, the results presented in Table 5 show an almost perfect load balancing on each RWS. From a load balancing standpoint there is not impact if the congestion level is varied. The last mile problem introduces an increment of URT due to the limited interconnection bandwidth but presents advantages for the global system in term of load balancing and server utilization. Simulation results highlights that, if we exclude the delay introduced by the limited bandwidth (that involve an URT increase for the limited bandwidth), the last mile problem is in reality not a big problem. In other words, if we remove this last mile problem we don't obtain relevant advantage but make the other bottlenecks problems became more apparent [1]. However, we point out that even if the analyzed techniques show similar results in term of URT, it doesn't imply that all techniques give same results. In particular we expect that the Parallel and single-block strategy (i.e. dynamic techniques) provides better performance respect to static techniques (e.g. Mirror-based or DNS-based techniques[a]). However this issue needs further investigations. From the overhead standpoint the considerations already presented in the previous subsections on the number of requests per RWS and wasted bandwidth still apply. However, from results presented in this subsection, the Parallel strategy overhead seems not producing any effect on the last mile bottleneck. This can be explained because our performance index is the URT of clients that perform a single Web-Access operation at a time. The URT of a single Web-Access operation is almost unaffected by the overhead produced in term of wasted bandwidth generated during the request itself. In fact the

---

[a] In the Mirror-based technique the RWS closer to the client is chosen. In the DNS-based technique the RWS is selected in a RoundRobin way among the available RWSs.

computation of the URT ends when the last blocks returns. Consequently, the rest of the useless data to download located at the tail of the client's pipe doesn't appear in the URT. We can expect that their impact it is not negligible if the client performs other operations in parallel or performs other Web-Access operation as it happens during a client's session.

Table 4. Average User Response Time per Area (seconds) with 56 Kbps in the last mile servers' connection.

56 Kbps in the last mile	Inter-area delay			
	50 ms		500 ms	
	Min	Max	Min	Max
2k-block	4.30	4.36	4.19	4.50
4k-block	4.16	4.40	4.23	4.42
8k-block	4.39	4.51	4.34	4.53
single-block	4.23	4.45	4.48	4.58

Table 5. Load distribution with 56 Kbps in the last mile servers' connection.

56 Kbps in the last mile	Inter-area delay							
	50 ms				500 ms			
	A1	A2	A3	A4	A1	A2	A3	A4
2k-block	0.54	0.55	0.55	0.54	0.53	0.54	0.54	0.40
4k-block	0.32	0.33	0.33	0.32	0.31	0.32	0.32	0.28
8k-block	0.21	0.22	0.22	0.22	0.20	0.21	0.21	0.20
single-block	0.04	0.04	0.04	0.04	0.04	0.04	0.04	0.02

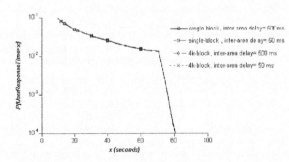

Fig. 9. Impact of the first mile congestion on the User RT

References

1. www.fp.akamai.com/resources/pdf/Internet_Bottlenecks.pdf
2. J. W. Byers, M. Luby, M. Mitzenmancher, *Accessing Multiple Mirror Sites in Parallel: Using Tornado Codes to Speed Up Downloads*. Proceedings of IEEE INFOCOM'99, New York, March 1999
3. R. L. Carter, M. E. Crovella, *Dynamic Server Selection using Bandwidth Probing in Wide-Area Network*.

68   Marko Conti, Enrico Gregory, and Willy Lapenna

4. R. L. Carter, M. E. Crovella, *Server Selection using Dynamic Path Characterization in Wide-Area Networks*, In Proceedings of IEEE Infocom'97, April 97, Kobe, Japan
5. L. Cherkasova ; M. DeSouza and S. Ponnekanti, *Performance Analysis of Content-Aware Load Balancing Strategy FLEX: Two Case Studies*, Thirty-Fourth Hawaii International Conference on System Sciences, HICSS-34 2001:Maui, Hawaii, January 3rd –6th, 2001
6. L. Cherkasova, P. Phaal, *Peak Load Management for Commercial Web Servers Using Adaptive Session-Based Admission Control*, Thirty-Fourth Hawaii International Conference on System Sciences, HICSS-34 2001:Maui, Hawaii, January 3rd –6th, 2001
7. M. Conti, E. Gregori, F. Panzieri, *Load Distribution among Replicated Web Servers: A QoS-based Approach*, Proc. Second ACM Workshop on Internet Server Performance (WISP'99), Atlanta, Georgia, May 1, 1999
8. M. Conti, E. Gregori, F. Panzieri, *QoS-based Architecture for Geographically Replicated Web Servers*, Cluster Computing Journal, 4, 2001, pp. 105-116
9. M. Conti, E. Gregori, W. Lapenna, *Replicated Web Services: Comparison of Client-based and Server-based solutions*, in Proceedings of XV Convegno Annuale CMG-Italia, Rome, 4-6 june 2001, Italy
10. M.Conti, E. Gregori, W. Lapenna, *Quality of Service in Internet Web Services: Issues and Solutions*, in Proceedings of 8th HP-OVUA Plenary Workshop, june 24-27, Berlin 2001, Germany
11. S. D. Dykes, K. A. Robbins, C. L. Jeffery, *An Empirical Evaluation of Client-side Server Selection Algorithms*, IEEE INFOCOM, VOL. 3, March, 2000, pp. 1361-1370
12. V. Ghini, F. Panzieri, M. Roccetti, *Client-centered Load Distribution: A Mechanism for Constructing Responsive Web Services*, 34th Hawaii International Conference on System Sciences (HICSS-34), Maui (Hawaii), 3-6 January 2001
13. wwwfp.akamai.com/resources/pdf/Network_Providers_Business_Case.pdf
14. J. Kangasharju, J. W. Ross, J. W. Roberts, *Performance Evaluation of Redirection Schemes in Content Distribution Networks*, In Proceedings of 5th International Web Caching and Content Delivery Workshop, Lisbon, Portugal, 22-24 May 2000
15. http://www.alteonwebsystems.com/collateral/vma_white_paper.pdf
16. M. Molina, P. Castelli, G. Foddis, *Web Traffic Modeling Exploiting TCP Connections' Temporal Clustering through HTML-REDUCE*, IEEE Network, May/June 2000, pp. 46-55
17. A. Myers, P. Dinda, H. Zhang, *Performance Characteristics of Mirror Servers on the Internet*, IEEE Infocom 1999, NY, March 1999
18. L. L. Peterson, B. S. Davie, *Computer Networks: A System Approach*, Morgan Kaufmann, San Francisco, CA, 1996
19. P. Rodriguez, A. Kirpal, E.W. Biersack, *Parallel-Access for Mirror Sites in the Internet*, Proceedings of IEEE/Infocom 2000, Tel-Aviv, Israel, March 2000
20. M. Sayal, Y. Breitbart, P. Scheuermann, R. Vingralek, *Selection Algorithms for Replicated Web Servers*, Workshop on Internet Server Performance, SIGMETRICS, Madison, USA, June 1998
21. M. Sayal, Y. Breitbart, P. Scheuermann, R. Vingralek, *Web++: A System For Fast and Reliable Web Service*, Proceedings of 1999 USENIX Annual Technical Conference, June 6-11, 1999, Monterey Conference Center, Monterey, CA, USA
22. E. W. Zegura, M. H. Ammar, Z. Fei, S. Bhattacharjee, *Application-Layer Anycasting: A Server Selection Architecture and Use in a Replicated Web Service*, IEEE/ACM Transactions on Networking, Vol. 8, NO. 4, August 2000

Internet Cache Location
and Design of Content Delivery Networks

Adam Wierzbicki

Institute of Telecommunications, Warsaw University of Technology,
ul. Orzycka 8 m.37,
02-695 Warsaw, Poland

Abstract. The paper studies the problem of where to locate caches
in a network of a general topology with many servers. The problem is
formulated using mixed integer programming (MILP). The goal is to
develop new models for cache location that overcome the limitations of
the basic model. A secondary goal is to evaluate the practical complexity
of using MILP for cache location and to improve existing heuristics using
the new model formulations.

The basic CLP model is studied as a multi-criteria problem to address
the possibility that some servers or clients may be discriminated. The
basic model is modified to allow searching for efficient solutions according
to user preferences, for example for fair solutions. Using multi-criteria
methods, the CLP can be extended to determine the optimal number of
caches or to minimize average delay and bandwidth consumption. The
paper studies modifications of the CLP that account for the effect of
client assignment and cache size on cache hit rate.

Medium-sized topologies of the order of 100 nodes can be solved optimally using modern MILP solvers. The model modifications can be used
to improve heuristics for larger networks.

1 Introduction

Caching and replication are methods used to improve network and system performance of the HTTP and FTP protocols. Caching works by saving network
bandwidth, reducing delays to clients, and reducing origin server load. Companies offer services to content providers who can deliver their content through the
caches owned by the company. These caches form an overlay network called a
Content Delivery Network (CDN). Significant research has gone into optimizing
cache performance, and recently the subject of designing CDNs by choosing appropriate locations for caches or replicas of the origin server in the network has
received attention of researchers. In [15], Krishnan et al. formulated the Cache
Location Problem (CLP) and extensively studied heuristics and special-case optimal solutions of that problem. The authors showed that cache location had
a significant impact on overall performance, and that commonly used rules-of-
thumb for cache location were not always appropriate.

Krishnan et al. and other work that studied the CLP, such as [16], [5], focused
on the single-server version of the problem. Several heuristics for that problem
were studied. However, the subject of the fully general CLP with many servers
on a general topology was left as an open question.

The area of facility location contains much work on problems that resemble the CLP – for example, hub models [4]. Many useful approaches for formulating and solving location models can be found in [1]. Location models were also used in other areas, such as hierarchical reliable multicasting [6]. Other areas, such as the design of overlay networks for application-level multicast, can benefit from location models [2].

The aim of this paper is not to study the computational complexity of the problem (which has been the main subject of previous work) but to improve models used for cache location. Too simple models that cannot be adapted to user preferences or ignore phenomena that can significantly influence efficiency will not give good solutions. Improved model formulations that are too computationally complex to be solved optimally for large problems can be used to improve existing heuristics.

In this paper, the CLP is formulated as a Mixed Integer Linear Problem (MILP). This allows to study the fully general CLP with many servers. It is shown that the general CLP can benefit from a multi-criteria reformulation, which has not been attempted before. For multiple servers, the average delays of a server are non-compensating: a decrease of delay of one server at the cost of increasing the delay of another server does not always improve the solution, even if the average delay of all servers is decreased. It is found that using the basic CLP model, less popular servers can be discriminated. The reformulated CLP gives solutions that are more fair with respect to individual servers or clients. The paper studies several model extensions that find the optimal number of caches, minimize average delay and bandwidth consumption, and account for effect of client assignment on hit rate.

A secondary goal of the paper is to evaluate the practical complexity of using MILP programming for cache location on topologies that closely resemble realistic internetworks. The paper describes an attempt to modify the greedy heuristic described in [15] to use an objective function derived from multi-criteria methods.

The rest of the paper is organized as follows. In Section 2, the MILP formulation of the CLP is given. Section 3 explains the need for a multi-criteria reformulation of the basic CLP model. Model modifications introduce additional criteria of average client delay. Two multi-criteria methods are compared that allow the user to find solutions that fit his preferences. Section 4 presents model extensions: methods for fair cache location, finding the optimal number of caches, minimizing bandwidth consumption, and variable hit rate. Section 5 discusses the practical complexity of MILP models for cache location and the extension of the greedy heuristic to use multi-criteria methods. Section 6 concludes.

2   The Cache Location Problem as a MILP Problem

In this section, the CLP is formulated as a Mixed Integer Linear Problem (MILP). The model described in this sections shall be referred to as the basic CLP model. It can be shown that the basic model is equivalent to the model in [15].

2.1 Input Data

The input data of the cache location problem problem consists of a network topology and user demands. The topology is a general graph, $G = < V, E >$, where V is the set of vertices and E is the set of edges. Edges $e \in E$ are *directed*, that is, they are ordered pairs of vertices. The graph G is assumed to be arc connected, which is reasonable on the Internet. Since G is arc connected, there exists a shortest path between any two nodes $u, v \in V$. The delay of this path will be denoted by $\delta(u, v)$. This delay can be specified for all pairs of nodes, based on end-to-end measurements. This is reasonable if this delay is determined by the available throughput of the TCP protocol, which is an end-to-end property. Note that delays need not be additive.

V_S is the subset of nodes in the graph that are servers. Every node $v \in V$ can have a demand from any server $s \in V_S$ (possibly zero). This demand shall be denoted by z_v^s. For each demand, the user can specify the cache hit rate of that demand, h_c^s, which is the fraction of data that can be served from the cache's local memory. This hit rate could depend on the type of data that is requested from the server by the client. For the sake of simplicity, but without loss of generality, the hit rates of all demands will be considered as equal and denoted by h. If the use wishes to find locations for replicas of the origin server, the problem can be modeled by setting the hit rate to $h = 1$. Further on, the influence of client assignment on the hit rate will be discussed (see Section 4.3.)

Another subset of nodes that has a special significance is the set V_R of possible locations for caches in the network. This is a useful user input; if the user wishes to consider all nodes, he can choose $V_R = V$. Nodes in the set V_R shall be denoted by w. The final user input is the number of caches that the user wants to locate, denoted by m. This quantity can be introduced into the model as a decision variable using multi-criteria methods.

The input data of the CLP model can be gathered from an analysis of logs from chosen Web servers, for example the main users of a CDN. These logs can be used to map a relevant portion of the network topology. Next, a measurement of end-to-end network characteristics such as available TCP throughput needs to be carried out for all pairs of nodes.

2.2 Decision Variables

There are two types of decision variables. The first, called the *location variables*, are necessary to constrain the number of caches to m. For every $w \in V_R$,

$$L_w = \begin{cases} 1 \text{ iff a cache is located at } w \\ 0 \text{ otherwise} \end{cases}$$

The second type are the *assignment variables*. The number of the assignment variables is equal to the number of nonzero demands times $|V_R| + 1$. For every z_c^s, $w \in V_R \cup \{s\}$,

$$P_{cw}^s = \begin{cases} 1 \text{ iff demand } z_c^s \text{ is served by } w \\ 0 \text{ otherwise} \end{cases}$$

2.3 The CLP Objective Function

The objective function of the basic model can be formulated as the sum, for all servers, of the average delay of a server. This function will be referred to as the *simple sum* and denoted by $Q^S = \Sigma_{s \in V_S} \Sigma_{c \in V} \, z^s_c \, \Sigma_{w \in V_R \cup \{s\}} \, P^s_{cw} \, (\delta(w, c) + (1 - h)\delta(s, w))$.

Note that $Q^S = \Sigma_{s \in V_S} Q^1_s$, where Q^1_s is the average delay of serving the data from the server s to all its clients. Also, $Q^S = \Sigma_{c \in V} Q^2_c$, where Q^2_c represents the average delay of a single client c.

2.4 Model Constraints

The first constraint specifies the number of caches: $\sum_{w \in V_R} L_w = m$. Models can be solved for various values of the parameter m – but such an approach is computationally intensive, and does not give the user the answer to the question: how many caches should be located? The first constraint can be modified if the user wants to find the optimal number of caches: $\sum_{w \in V_R} L_w = Q^m$, where Q^m will be one of the criteria of the model. For this criterion, the smallest and largest value are easily determined.

The second constraint specifies that the assignment of clients to caches and the origin server is a function: a client can be assigned to only one cache or the origin server, as follows: $\forall_{s \in V_S} \forall_{c \in V \setminus \{s\}} \; \sum_{w \in V_R \cup \{s\}} P^s_{cw} = 1$.

The third constraint ties the two groups of variables. It states that if a client is assigned to a node $w \in V_R$, then a cache must be located there: $\forall_{s \in V_S} \forall_{c \in V \setminus \{s\}} \forall_{w \in V_R \setminus \{s\}} \; P^s_{cw} \leq L_w$.

In [15], a constrained version was formulated that forced caches to be located at the shortest paths from the client to the server for some demand. This model, called the TERC (Transparent En-Route Caches) was shown to be as computationally difficult as the basic CLP model. To formulate the TERC model as a MILP it suffices to add constraints that forbid the assignment of demands to caches that are not on the shortest path from the client to the server. The ability to adapt the model to TERC caches is important because this form of caching is frequently used as an efficient form of cache discovery by clients. For the more general client assignments, tools such as Proxy Auto-Discovery (PAC) can be utilized.

Using the above formulation, multi-server cache location problems with general topologies can be solved using standard mixed integer linear programming solvers. However, the formulation presented in this section is not the best for the case of multiple servers. Specifically, using the above formulation can result in the discrimination of less popular servers. In the next section, the problem is explained and the model is reformulated using multi-criteria optimization methods. This will allow to extend the basic model in various directions, such as finding the optimal number of caches or minimizing consumed bandwidth while providing fair delays to the clients.

3 Multi-criteria Methods for Cache Location

For multiple servers, the objective function of the basic model is a sum of average delays of each server. If the user wishes to create a CDN that charges a fixed

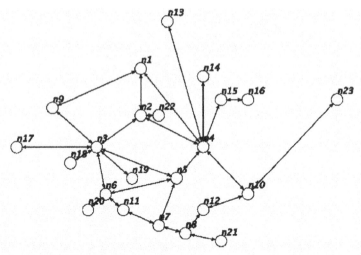

Fig. 1. A medium-sized topology for cache location.

fee from each server for content distribution, he should attempt to treat each server fairly. Caches can also be installed by a popular content provider, who charges a fixed fee from all his users. In this case, there is only one server, but the average delays of all clients should be fair. Using multi-criteria methods described in this chapter, a content provider can design a caching system that provides information with fair delays to the user while at the same time minimizing the consumed bandwidth.

It was shown above that the objective function of the basic model can be viewed as a sum of average client delays. Whether or not the criteria for client delay should influence the solution more than server criteria, depends on the preferences of the designers of the caching system. If the caches form a CDN that is employed to disseminate content from servers (and that is financed by the content providers) then the client criteria do not have to be included. On the other hand, if the cache administrators wish to design a public caching infrastructure, the reverse is true: client criteria should influence the solution most.

The basic CLP model is inadequate for these purposes. The average delays of various servers or clients are non-compensating: a decrease of delay of one server at the cost of increasing the delay of another server does not always improve the solution, even if the average delay of all servers is decreased. Using the basic CLP model, less popular servers can be discriminated, since the average delays of a server are not scaled by the range from their largest and smallest value. These values can be obtained by optimizing all the individual criteria separately, and choosing the largest value from the values of a criterion when any other criterion is optimized. For a criterion Q_v (either the average delay of a server, or a client), the largest and smallest value will be denoted by q_v^{hi} and q_v^{lo}, respectively. An objective function that scales the criteria and uses weights to express user preferences is the *weighted sum*: $Q^W = \sum_v \frac{\alpha_v}{q_v^{hi} - q_v^{lo}} Q_v$.

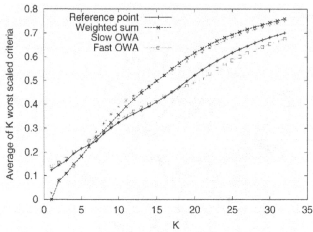

Fig. 2. Comparison of reference point and weighted sum, m=5, h=0.5.

However, an objective function that uses a sum of criteria can only choose solutions from the convex hull of all efficient (Pareto-optimal) solutions [7]. This means that it may not find a solution that is closest to user preferences, although such a solution exists and is efficient. To avoid such problems, the objective function of the basic model is reformulated using an approach called the reference point method. The objective function (which will be maximized) is formulated as follows: $Q^R = \min_v \sigma_v(Q_v, q_v^R) + \epsilon \sum_v \sigma_v(Q_v, q_v^R)$, where $\sigma_v(Q_v, q_v^R) = \frac{q_v^R - Q_v}{q_v^R - q_v^{lo}}$. Note that since the individual criteria are minimized, the objective function incorporates them with negative coefficients (since Q^R is maximized). The parameters (q_v^R) form the coordinates of the so-called *reference point*, which can be thought of as specifying the direction in which the Pareto border is approached. ϵ is a small positive number (usually, 1%). The objective function Q^R contains a minimum. It can be formulated as a linear function, by introducing additional variables (one for each criterion).

If the user chooses a weighted sum, he would use equal weights for all criteria to obtain a fair solution. If he chooses the reference point method, he would use a neutral reference point given by the formula: $q_i^R = q_i^{hi} - 0.5(q_i^{hi} - q_i^{lo})$, that is, halfway between the largest and smallest value. For the remaining part of the paper, we shall assume that the user wishes to obtain a fair solution with respect to all criteria   both client and server criteria and, if the user searches for the optimal number of caches, the criterion Q^m. For a neutral reference point, the effect would be an appropriate scaling of the client and server criteria in the objective function.

It can be shown that the objective function specified by the reference point method always gives a Pareto-optimal solution (the same is true for the weighted sum) and that by varying the coordinates of the reference point, any Pareto-optimal solution can be found (provided that the tradeoffs between Pareto points are bounded by $M = 1 + \frac{1}{\epsilon}$) [7]. Therefore, the reference point method should be more suitable for cache location than a weighted sum. Further on, this hypothesis

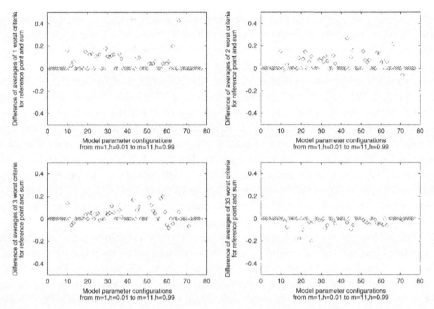

Fig. 3. Difference of averages of 1,2,3 and 33 worst criteria for weighted sum and reference point methods.

will be investigated further: the reference point method and the weighted sum will be compared on an example topology.

3.1   Comparison of the Reference Point and Weighted Sum Methods

In this section, multi-criteria methods for cache location shall be evaluated on a medium-sized topology. The topology is patterned after the Polish national academic network. The edge costs of the topology were chosen randomly. There were 11 servers in this topology. Caches can be located at 12 potential nodes. Any node in the topology could be a client, and demands were chosen randomly in such a way that the total sum of the demands was constant. The hit rate was chosen from values: $h \in \{0.01, 0.21, 0.41, 0.5, 0.61, 0.81, 0.99\}$ and the number of caches: $m \in \{1, 2, \ldots, 11\}$. Together, there are 77 different model configurations. Each model has 11 server criteria and 22 client criteria.

It remains to define a measure of fairness for the comparison of the reference point and weighted sum methods. A measure of fairness that is commonly used in economics is the Lorenz curve. In this section, a closely related measure will be used for the comparison. The individual (client or server) criteria Q_i are scaled by the function: $\frac{q_i^{hi} - Q_i}{q_i^{hi} - q_i^{lo}}$, obtaining numbers from 0 to 1. The scaled individual criteria are ordered from worst (smallest) to best. Next, the averages of k worst criteria are calculated for increasing k – they shall be denoted by M_k. These averages can be plotted against k. If the resulting curve is close to a straight horizontal line, the distribution is fair, since each of the criteria is equal to the average. Two such curves for $m = 5$, $h = 0.5$ are shown on Figure 2: one for the solution obtains by the reference point method, and the other – for the weighted sum. The curve of the reference point method is closer to a horizontal line than the curve of the weighted sum. (The two curves labeled "Fast OWA" and "Slow OWA" will be described further on in section 4.1).

To evaluate the two methods further, the differences of the averages M_k for $k \in \{1, 2, 3, 32\}$ are shown on Figure 3 for all 77 models. Each point on the Figure is the result of subtracting the average of k worst criteria of a solution found by the weighted sum from a similar average of criteria from a solution found be the reference point method. Most points form a line at zero, showing identical performance of the two methods. For $k = 1, 2, 3$ most points that are not at zero lie above zero, indicating a better performance of the reference point method. With increasing k, the reference point method performs increasingly worse than the weighted sum – which is consistent with common sense, since for $k = 33$ the average is optimized by a simple sum.

The results of the comparison indicate that the reference point method is more fair than the weighted sum. There is no difference between the two methods for $m = 1$ and $m = 11$, since there are much fewer efficient solutions in these cases. The difference is largest for medium values of m, when there are many efficient solutions, which indicates that for larger topologies the reference point method would perform even better.

4 Model Extensions

The multi-criteria analysis of the basic model lead to a reformulation that introduced criteria for average client delay and changed the objective function. The goal was to allow the user to express his preferences in a precise way. The search for fair and efficient solutions was considered as an example of user preferences.

In this section, new model extensions will be considered that take into account new user preferences or make the model more realistic. First, the subject of searching for fair solutions shall be explored further. Next, the model will be extended to optimize bandwidth consumption along with delay. Finally, the effect of client assignment on the cache hit rate will be examined.

4.1 Fair and Efficient Cache Location

In the previous section, it was shown that the reference point method performs better than a weighted sum in searching for fair and efficient solutions. Still, the reference point method does not attempt explicitly to choose fair solutions: it merely is able to choose among all efficient solutions, while the weighted sum does not consider some efficient solutions. To search explicitly for fair solutions, one must use other methods, which require a further extension of the model.

User preferences that require fairness (also called equity) and efficiency can be defined mathematically [14]. Intuitively, these preferences require an even distribution of outcomes, and do not change if the outcomes are permutated (in other words, the order of the outcomes is not relevant for fairness). Solution concepts that try to satisfy such preferences are usually based on the minimization of some measure of inequality. In the previous section, the averages M_k were used as such a measure. It can be shown that fair and efficient solutions can be found using these averages. It is important that these solutions are also efficient (Pareto-optimal) – the same is not true for all inequality measures, and it is easy to imagine fair solutions that are not efficient (equally bad for all). For location models, the center model (minimizing the maximum of the criteria) is frequently used in problems that require fairness. However, it can be shown that this model does not choose efficient solutions [13] – this occurs when the center model minimizes the distance to a single isolated node, leaving the other nodes unoptimized.

In this subsection, the model for cache location shall be extended to include an inequality measure similar to the averages introduced in the previous section. This measure can be expressed using a linear model with additional variables. For a proof of this fact the reader is referred to [11].

Let m be the number of criteria in the model, and let all criteria Q_i be scaled by the function: $\sigma_i(Q_i) = \frac{q_i^{hi} - Q_i}{q_i^{hi} - q_i^{lo}}$, $i \in \{1, \ldots, m\}$. (The original criteria Q_i are to be minimized, and the scaled criteria – maximized.) The average of k worst (smallest) criteria will be denoted by M_k. The following linear program minimizes M_k:

$$M_k = max\{t_k - \frac{1}{k}\sum_{i=1}^{m} d_{ik} \ : \ d_{ik} \geq t_k - \sigma_i, \ d_{ik} \geq 0 \ \text{for} \ i = 1, \ldots, m\}$$

Note that the method outlined in this section is parametrized by k: the user can specify how many of the worst-off criteria he wishes to optimize. Thus, he can control the tradeoff between fairness and efficiency.

An even better, although most complex method is to use to Ordered Weighted Averaging (OWA). The OWA objective function is defined as a linear combination of the sorted criteria, from worst to best. If the weights of this combination decrease monotonically, it can be shown that such a model chooses equitably efficient solutions [12]. The OWA model is hard to express using MILP models, since a large number of constraints is required. However, the OWA objective function with monotonic weights can be expressed using the averages M_k. This leads to an LP formulation for such a model, with the weights w_k, $k = 1, \ldots, m$:

$$max\{\sum_{k=1}^{m} k w_k t_k - \sum_{k=1}^{m}\sum_{i=1}^{m} w_k d_{ik} \ : \ d_{ik} \geq t_k - \sigma_i, \ d_{ik} \geq 0 \ \text{for} \ i = 1, \ldots, m\}$$

The weights w_k have to be positive. If the weights are chosen in such a way that they decrease quickly for increasing k, the model will optimize the worst criterion, then the next worst, and so on. If the weights decrease more slowly, the model will perform more similarly to a sum. In the evaluation of these models for cache location, the weights were chosen from a geometric sequence: $w_1 = 1 - q$, and $w_n = w_1 q^{n-1}$, $n \geq 2$, where $0 < q < 1$.

On Figure 2, the results of applying the above model with $q = 0.6$ is labeled as "Fast OWA", while the solution found by the model with $q = 0.95$ is labeled as "Slow OWA". The first solution improves fairness of the solution found by the reference point method (it is more close to a horizontal line). The second solution is close to the solution found by the weighted sum, but is more favorable to medium criteria at the cost of the best criteria. On Figure 4, "Fast OWA" and the reference point method are compared together against the weighted sum, by

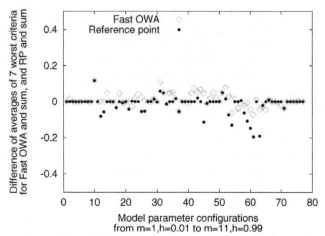

Fig. 4. Comparison of Fast OWA, reference point and weighted sum by averages of 7 worst criteria.

averages of 7 worst criteria. As before, the figure plots the difference between averages for solutions obtained by the reference point method with a neutral reference point and by the weighted sum (smaller black circles). Additionally, the figure shows similar differences for the "Fast OWA" model and the weighted sum (larger empty diamonds). It can be seen that for an average of 7 worst criteria, the "Fast OWA" model performs not worse than the weighted sum for a majority of model configurations. This is not true for the reference point approach. For $k > 7$, the "Fast OWA" model performs slightly worse than the weighted sum for those model configurations that do not have identical solutions for the two methods.

4.2 Bandwidth Consumption

In the basic model, the costs of transferring the data were end-to-end delays for each pair of nodes. To consider bandwidth consumption along with delay, the input data must include bandwidth costs of each edge, b_e. These bandwidth costs are additive, in other words, the cost of a path $delta_b(u, v)$ is the sum of the costs of all edges on that path. The bandwidth costs of all edges can all be equal to 1 to simplify the model. It is also possible that a provider wishes to consider only the costs of links that connect his network to exchange points (and which he has to pay for to his ISP). In such a case, all the bandwidth costs of the provider's own links can be zero.

To extend the model to optimize bandwidth consumption, note that the cost of serving a demand z_c^s from a cache w in terms of bandwidth is similar to the average delay: $z_c^s(\delta_b(w, c) + (1 - h)\delta_b(s, w))$. Still, this cost need not to be introduced into the model like the average delay of a client or a server. The difference lies in the fact that use of bandwidth is compensating, that is, it does not matter which client or server used the bandwidth. Therefore a function like the simple sum is entirely appropriate as a criterion of used bandwidth. The situation would change if the user wished to take into account the bandwidth consumption of certain critical links – perhaps in order to avoid overloading them, which is difficult to express in linear models. Then there should be separate criteria for the bandwidth use or the load of each critical link.

4.3   Variable Hit Rate

All the models described so far depended on the assumption that the hit rate is a fixed value, given as input data to the model. (The hit rates could vary for different demands, but they were still fixed during optimization). This is an assumption that makes the model linear. However, it may be too simplistic.

Several studies have investigated the influence of cache size on the hit rate. Nowadays in practice caches can be large enough to store several days of traffic, and the hit rate depends critically on coherence protocols. Still, if the user wishes to create a fast CDN based on main memory caches, the influence of cache size on hit rate may be of significance. If that is the case, the model can be modified in the following manner. Instead of locating whole caches, the model would locate units of memory of a fixed size. The location variables could still be binary, but there would be more of them: for every location $w \in V_R$, there would have to be variables for all possible amounts of memory units in that location. However, the main change is in the objective function.

To incorporate an influence of cache size on the hit rate in the model, the objective function would need to contain products of the location and assignment variables, since the hit rate is a function of the location variables that specify how much memory is at the given location. (The exact form of the dependence of the hit rate on cache size can be obtained from one of several studies, such as [8].) Thus, the model cannot be linear, but may still be studied by nonlinear methods or be the basis of useful heuristics.

However, the influence of cache size on the hit rate is not the only phenomenon that is ignored by the basic model. The number of clients that are assigned to a given cache also has an impact on the cache hit rate [8, 10]. The reason is that clients usually have their own caches, and therefore the request stream from one client has little reference locality. The reference locality and the hit rate of a cache increase rapidly as more clients are added, and above a certain number of clients, the hit rate stabilizes at an almost constant value.

The influence of the number of clients on a cache can be incorporated in the basic model in the following way. For every server $s \in V_S$ and every cache $w \in V_R$, let $C_w^s = \sum_{c \in V} P_{cw}^s$ be the number of clients of that cache that request data from s. The hit rates h_c^s of all demands from the server s would depend on C_w^s. The form of that relationship should be obtained from relevant studies, but it can be approximated by a piecewise linear function. Therefore, the model can be quadratic. Heuristics can incorporate the relationship directly by modifying their objective function.

5   Complexity of MILP Programming for Cache Location

All experiments described in this paper used the commercial MILP solver cplex, versions 7.1 and 6.6, on a SUN SPARC Ultra-4 with processor speed of 250MHz (not dedicated to the MILP computations). The Georgia Tech Internetwork

Topology Models [9] (GT-ITM) was used to generate the network topologies used in the evaluation of the practical complexity of using MILP for cache location. The topologies were generated from the "transit-stub" models to obtain graphs that more closely resemble the Internet than pure random construction. GT-ITM generates a transit-stub graph in stages, first a number of random backbones (transit domains), then the random structure of each backbone, then random "stub" graphs are attached to each node in the backbones. For the structure of both transit domains and stubs , the "locality" model was used.

The CLP is by its nature an off-line problem. The use of multi-criteria methods requires several iterations in the search for solutions that best fit user preferences, but still the task of locating caches and designing a CDN can be supported by MILP tools if the running time is not too long. For networks up to a 100 all models were solvable in reasonable time (not exceeding one hour). Note, however, that the complexity of these models depends on the number of non-zero demands and the size of the set of potential cache locations, V_R. Model complexity does not depend directly on the size of a topology.

Additionally, the integer assignment variables for one demand are related by the second constraint of the CLP, which allows only one of them to be positive. This greatly reduces the complexity of branch-and-bound procedures. Taking this into consideration, the complexity of using MILP for cache location depends mainly on the number of demands. This number cannot be too large if the problem is to be solved using MILP. In the experiments the number of demands was set at 500. Since this is a factor that cannot be easily decreased, it remains to consider if the size of the set V_R can be reduced. The problem is, that if an optimal solution is to be found, the set V_R must be equal to the entire set of nodes in the topology. If it were possible to find ways to reduce the set V_R, it would be possible to solve location problems even for very large topologies.

The present-day topology of the Internet is several orders of magnitude larger than a hundred nodes. Therefore, cache locations in a large public network can only be found using heuristics. On the other hand, network administrators that are designing a CDN will be creating a high-bandwidth network under a the control of a single administration (for purposes of control over network reliability and Quality of Service). This implies that the number of potential cache locations will not be very large. A study of the Internet core (using the Skitter tool) was conducted by CAIDA in October, 2000 [3]. The study selected $626,773$ IP addresses as belonging to the Internet core. These addresses were part of $7,563$ autonomous systems. This leads to the conclusion that on the average, the portion of the autonomous system that was part of the Internet core consisted of 82 IP addresses. While these numbers cannot be generalized to the case of large Internet Service Providers, they can be thought of as representative of a case when a CDN is constructed that wishes to reach a large part of the global Internet. If potential cache locations are constrained to a network under a single administration, their number can be of the order of a hundred nodes.

The greedy heuristic proposed in [15] is a good candidate for finding approximate solutions for larger topologies . However, it should be modified to use an objective function similar to the reference point objective function, so that the user can specify his preferences with respect to the individual criteria (client or server delays, bandwidth consumption, number of caches). To do so, the utopia and nadir points need to be found before the heuristic is executed. This involves optimization of only single criteria, which can be performed quickly even for large topologies. In this way, the heuristic can be adapted to use multiple criteria, which increases the likelihood of finding good potential cache locations. It was found that the value of $\epsilon = 1\%$ that was used in the reference point objective function does not lead to good performance of the heuristic. A value of $\epsilon = 33\%$ was best for the considered examples. This implies that the greedy heuristic will perform like the weighted sum and will have similar drawbacks when compared to the exact solutions of the reference point method. The comparison of the reference point method and the weighted sum should be a good indication of the performance of the greedy heuristic in searching for solutions that match user preferences.

Instead of using a heuristic to find an approximate solution directly, one can use it as an automatic method of choosing potential cache locations in a very large topology. If the user wishes to locate $m < 100$ caches, the heuristic could be used to select 100 nodes from the topology to form the set V_R. Next, a MILP model could be used to optimally locate m caches in the set V_R. This procedure cannot be guaranteed to find optimal locations, but it should be a reasonable approach to finding approximate solutions in large topologies.

The described procedure was evaluated on 20 topologies of sizes of 100 nodes and 500 demands, generated by GT-ITM. First, the greedy heuristic was used to find a set V_R^H of potential cache locations such that $|V_R^H| = 50$. Next, the optimal solution was found for $V_R = V$ for $m \in \{5, 10, 20\}$. In all cases, the optimal solution was a subset of the set V_R^H. Concluding, it seems likely that for topologies of up to 200 nodes the optimal solution could be found using the procedure described in this section. For larger topologies, the procedure should also perform well, although perhaps not optimally. Still, the procedure is limited by the number of caches that the user wants to locate. If $m > 50$, the set V_R should probably be larger than 100 nodes, which may lead to high running times of the MILP solver.

6   Conclusion

Cache location models can be adapted to a variety of circumstances using MILP programming. The choice of the most appropriate model depends on the problem, but MILP programming is very flexible and allows the user to adapt the model and to specify his preferences. Multi-criteria methods are an essential tool for the formulation of cache location models for multiple servers. Using multi-criteria methods, a content provider can design a CDN that provides information with fair delays to the user while at the same time minimizing the consumed bandwidth. Heuristic approaches are not likely to perform as well as advanced multi-criteria MILP models in finding solutions that best match user preferences.

Medium-sized topologies can be solved optimally using modern MILP solvers. For larger topologies, it is necessary to search for approximate solutions using heuristics. The proposed models can be used to improve heuristics for cache location. These heuristics can be extended to use multi-criteria methods that allow to express user preferences. If the number of caches that the user wants to locate is not too large, a solution can be found using heuristics to reduce the set of potential cache locations.

References

1. M. S. Daskin. *Network and Discrete Location.* John Wiley, 1995.
2. J. Jannotti et. al. Overcast: Reliable multicasting with an overlay network. *Proceedings OSDI'01*, 2000.
3. Kimberly Claffy et al. Visualizing internet topology at a macroscopic scale. World Wide Web page, http://www.caida.org/analysis/topology/as_core_network, CAIDA, 2002.
4. J. Klincewicz. Solving a freight transport problem using facility location techniques. *Operations Research*, January-February 1990.
5. G. Voelker L. Qiu, V. Padmanabhan. On the placement of web server replicas. *Proceedings of IEEE Infocom*, 2001.
6. A. Markopoulou. Hierarchical reliable mutlicast: performance analysis and placement of proxies. *Proceedings of NGC 2000*, 2000.
7. A. P. Wierzbicki, M. Makowski, J. Wessels, editor. *Model-Based Decision Support Methodology with Environmental Applications.* Kluwer Academic Publishers, 2000.
8. B. Duska, D. Marwood, M. Feeley. Measured access characteristics of worl-wide-web client proxy caches. *Proceedings of the USENIX Symposium on Internet Technologies and Systems*, 1997.
9. E. Zegura, K. Calvert, S. Bhattacharjee. How to model an internetwork. In *Proc. IEEE Infocom*, pages 40–52, 1996.
10. Michal Kurcewicz, Adam Wierzbicki, Wojtek Sylwestrzak. Filtering algorithms for proxy caches. *Computer Networks and ISDN Systems*, 1998.
11. W. Ogryczak, M. Zawadzki. Conditional center: A parametric solution concept for location problems. Technical report, Institute of Control and Computation Engineering, Warsaw University of Technology, 2000.
12. W. Ogryczak, T. Sliwinski. On solving linear programs with the ordered weighted averaging objective. Technical report, Institute of Control and Computation Engineering, Warsaw University of Technology, 2001.
13. W. Ogryczak. On the lexicographic minimax approach to location problems. *European Journal of Operational Research*, 1996.
14. W. Ogryczak. Inequality measures and equitable approaches to location problems. *European Journal of Operational Research*, 1999.
15. Y. Shavitt P. Krishnan, D. Raz. The cache location problem. *IEEE/ACM Transactions on Networking*, October 2000.
16. D. Estrin P. Radoslavov, R. Govindan. Topology-informed internet replica placement. *Proc. of the Sixth International Workshop on Web Caching and Content Distribution*, 2000.

A Server Placement Algorithm Conscious of Communication Delays and Relocation Costs

Junho Shim[1]   Taehee Lee[2]   Sang-goo Lee[2]

[1]Department of Computer Science
Sookmyung Women's University
Seoul 140-742, Korea
jshim@sookmyung.ac.kr

[2]School of Computer Science & Engineering
Seoul National University
Seoul 151-742, Korea
{ thlee, sglee }@europa.snu.ac.kr

Abstract. The server placement algorithm is to locate the given number of cache servers at "proper" coordinates in the network. A typical objective to determine good locations may be simply to find the set of client clusters in which the Euclidean center of each cluster is the location of the cache server. We claim, however, that the objective should also consider 1) the network communication delays and 2) the cost of relocating cache servers, if any. We exploit both hierarchical and partitioning approaches, and present our server placement algorithm. We evaluated the performance of the algorithm, and its result is promising.

1 Introduction

In distributed systems, mobile networks and Web, servers and clients are distributed over the system and clients may need data from servers to continue their process. The idea of placing cache server (or simply server here below) is to have the benefit of reducing the communication delays for the data to be transferred from server to client. In addition, caching may also help balance the system load by replicating multiple copies of a data on different locations throughout the network, and also help the system to be fault tolerant in that copies of a data are available even if certain servers are down or unreachable. [6,11]

There may be numerous objectives such as balancing server loads and reducing network latency regarding where to place the servers over the network. We claim, however, that servers should be deployed at the locations where the total communication delays between clients and servers can be minimized. Practically in a network system like Web and mobile environments, however, figuring out the communication delay of a data or the amount of data is not feasible due to the nature of network in which the environment such as bandwidth, network load, routing topology, and client population continuously changes.[10,12] Therefore without

E. Gregori et al. (Eds.): Networking 2002 Workshops, LNCS 2376, pp. 83–89, 2002.

knowing the topology of the network, we simplify the problem by the supposition that cities in the network area represent the clients and the population of a city represents the amount of data communication the client makes. Then the total communication delay between servers and clients may be reduced to the Euclidean distance between them multiplied by the population of the client city.

1.1 Problem Statement

Let us say that in a network we have n number of clients $c_i \in C = \{c_1, c_2, ..., c_n\}$, and k number of servers s_j, $1 \le j \le k$. Let us assume that S_j is the set of c_i such that c_i download the data from the server s_j, and $\bigcup_{j=1}^{k} S_j = C$, $S_l \cap S_m = \Phi$, if $l \ne m$. In other words, any client $c_i \in C$ should download data from at least one and only one server. Let $S = \{S_1, S_2, ..., S_k\}$. Then the given C and k, the objective of server placement algorithm is to find k number of servers such that the total communication delays defined as below can be minimized,

$$D(C, S, k) = \sum_{j=1}^{k} \sum_{c_i \in S_j} \left(|c_i - s_j|^2 \cdot p_i \right) \qquad (1)$$

where p_i is population of client city c_i, and $|c_i - s_j|^2$ is the Euclidean distance between the server s_j and the client c_i.

If we consider the situation where we place additional servers to existing server locations, no matter which data placement algorithm we use, the cost of placing δ new servers is inevitable since the enterprise needs to install them at first. The cost of relocating existing servers, however, may vary depending on the algorithm: from relocating all k servers to not relocating any server at all, in which the former demands high relocation cost as the later requires no cost of relocation.

Let k' out of k be the number of servers to be kept at current locations when we add δ new servers to the network. Let $s_1, s_2, ..., s_{k'}$ be the servers to be kept at current locations, $s_{k'+1}, ..., s_k$ be the servers of which locations could be changed, and $s_{k+1}, ..., s_{\delta + k}$ be the new servers. Then the objective Equation (1) can be rewritten as following:

$$D_{reorg}(C, S, k, k', \delta) =$$
$$\sum_{j=1}^{k'} \sum_{c_i \in S_j} \left(|c_i - s_j|^2 \cdot p_i \right) + \sum_{j=k'+1}^{k} \sum_{c_i \in S_j} \left(|c_i - s_j|^2 \cdot p_i \right) + \sum_{j=k+1}^{\delta + k} \sum_{c_i \in S_j} \left(|c_i - s_j|^2 \cdot p_i \right) \qquad (2)$$

Note that $D_{reorg}(C, S, k, k', \delta)$ is the extension of $D(C, S, k)$ in that if in $D_{reorg}(C, S, k, k', \delta)$ both k' and δ are zero, two objective functions (1) and (2) generate the same result. Then a good server placement algorithm conscious of relocation cost should be able to construct the set $S = \{S_1, ..., S_{k'}, S_{k'+1}, ..., S_k, S_{k+1}, ..., S_{\delta + k}\}$ such that its $D_{reorg}(C, S, k, k', \delta)$ objective function is minimal.

In this paper, we present a new server placement algorithm SEPA (Server Placement Algorithm) of which highlighted features are as following.

1. Delay conscious algorithm: SEPA aims at finding k server locations to minimize the communication delays shown in Equation (1).
2. Relocation-cost conscious algorithm: When we add δ new servers, if k' out of k server locations can not be changed, then SEPA aims at finding $k+\delta$ server locations to minimize the communication delays shown in Equation (2).

SEPA is based on the partitioning clustering approach, and its methodology we adopted here is one based on the experimentation.[10] We show in this paper that how we adapt CLARANS to become SEPA, and the experiments to illustrate the performance of SEPA.

1.2 Related Work

Works on optimizing client response time in the Web with a pre-determined set of cache servers should be distinguished to our work. [11,13] For example, [13] analyzes several well-known algorithms that find out a "closest" cache server from a client when a set of server locations is already determined. [11] suggests a delay-conscious cache replacement algorithm within a server in order to minimize the client response time. Recently, several works were done regarding the replica placement problem. [4, 9] They assumed the network topology as a graph and used several heuristics on K-center [4] optimization problem. [4] shows that increasing the number of replicas is effective in reducing client download time for a small range of values, which is consistent with our result. [9] proposed that the greedy algorithm is the best among several previous heuristics, but it's not applicable if the network topology and candidate locations of replicas are not known.

2 Algorithm Development

Since we don't take the network topology into consideration, we considered the clustering approach as the candidate solution to our problem defined in Equation (1) because of the similarity of its objective function with ours.[3] Clustering techniques in the literature can be at large categorized into *partitioning* methods and *hierarchical* methods.[3] Among the *partitioning* methods, CLARANS[8] has been experimentally shown to be more effective in large datasets than other algorithms such as PAM and CLARA. [3,8] Another category is *hierarchical* methods, which create a hierarchical decomposition of the given set of data objects. An agglomerative method for hierarchical method starts with each object forming a separate group, and successively merges each cluster until the number of clusters becomes k. We thought, at first, hierarchical clustering approach such as [2,14] would be desirable one for relocation cost conscious algorithm, in that it keeps at least $k-\delta$ servers in place whenever it adds δ new servers to the network with k existing servers. Surprisingly we found through extensive experiments that partitioning approach like CLARANS does not underperform hierarchical clustering approach even for the problem in Equation (2), while partitioning approach consistently performs better than hierarchical clustering approach for the problem in Equation (1). [10]

2.1 SEPA (Server Placement Algorithm)

We develop our algorithm SEPA (Server Placement Algorithm) based on our modification of CLARANS.[8] CLARANS outputs $S = \{S_1, S_2, ..., S_k\}$ which minimizes Equation (2). From the output, we can obtain the server location

$$x = \sum_{c_i \in S_j} x_i \cdot p_i \Big/ \sum_{c_i \in S_j} p_i, \quad y = \sum_{c_i \in S_j} y_i \cdot p_i \Big/ \sum_{c_i \in S_j} p_i \tag{3}$$

of each cluster S_i, by the parallel axis theorem in physics. What we should more to minimize the Equation (2) are as following:

① Input: In addition to the inputs of CLARANS, SEPA needs the number of servers to be kept at current locations, the number of new servers, and the output of CLARANS.

② Output: SEPA returns the k sever locations to minimize the Equation (2).

SEPA algorithm

Input : the number of clusters k and the object set C with n objects c_i, *max_neighbor*, and *num_local*, the set $S = \{S_1, S_2, ..., S_k\}$ from the output of the CLARANS, k': the number of servers to be kept at current locations, and δ : the number of new servers to the network

Output : A set of $k+\delta$ clusters $S = \{S_1, S_2, ..., S_{k+\delta}\}$ that minimizes Equation (2), and their server locations $s_1, s_2, ..., s_{k+\delta}$

Method :

(1)
① If k' and δ are 0, then SEPA works like CLARANS. Exit.
② Otherwise Set *local* = 1.

(2) repeat
① Set *num_no_change* to 0.
② Find k objects each of which is nearest to centers of $S_1, S_2, ..., S_k$ by Equation (3), and set them to initial medoids m_j, $1 \leq i \leq k$. Randomly select δ more medoid objects and set them $m_{k+1}, m_{k+2}, ..., m_{k+\delta}$.
③ repeat
  A. Assign each remaining object to the cluster with the nearest medoid. Assign c_i to the cluster S_i with the minimal $(p_m + p_i) \cdot |m_i - c_i|$. Find $k+\delta$ objects each of which is nearest to center by Equation (3), and set them to s_j, $1 \leq i \leq k+\delta$. Compute the total cost D by Equation (2).
  B. Randomly select a non medoid object, c_{random}.
  C. If swaping c_{random} with a medoid m_i, $k'+1 \leq i \leq k$ results in more than $(k-k')$ changes of medoids, do not swap. Repeat B.
  D. Compute the total cost, D_{new}, of swapping m_i with c_{random} with a medoid m_i, $k'+1 \leq i \leq k$ by Equation (2)
  E. If $D_{new} < D$ then swap m_i with c_{random}, to form the new set of k medoids.
  F. Otherwise, increase *num_no_change* by 1.
④ Until *num_no_change* $\leq$ *max_neighbor* do ③.
⑤ Set S_OPT_{local} to the current set $S=\{S_1, S_2, ..., S_{k+\delta}\}$, increase *local* by 1.
⑥ Until *local* $\leq$ *num local* repeat (2) to find out next local optimal set.
(3) Find a S from $S\_OPT_1, S\_OPT_2, ..., S\_OPT_{num\_local}$, which results in the minimal cost. And also calculate k number of server locations
(4) Find centers for each cluster by Equation (3).

Fig. 1. Our server placement algorithm: SEPA

③ Method: Selection and swapping, if necessary, of non-medoid may be performed on upto *(k-k')* number of servers rather than one. Note that the cost of current cluster is obtained by Equation (1) as the one of new cluster is obtained by Equation (2).

The time complexity of SEPA is $O(num\_local*max\_neighbor*n*k'+n)$, and again becomes $O(n^2*k'*(n-k))$ if we use the same *num_local and max_neighbor* to the settings in [8]. It takes linear space to hold input data and the set of clusters. And the space complexity of SEPA is $O(n)$.

3 Experimental Result and Conclusion

We evaluated the performance of SEPA on a USA County Statistical Data obtained at U.S. Census Bureau. [12] The data contains the stats of 3141 number of US counties. Among numerous statistical items on the county, what we are interested in are the population and the location in its latitude, and longitude of each county. In our case, each county represents a client c_i, the latitude and longitude of a county represents the geographical coordinates x_i, y_i of a client, and the population of a county represents p_i, the amount of data communication of a client. We extensively compared the performance of SEPA to various approaches. [10] Among them, we in this paper show the performance comparison between SEPA and a well-known hierarchical clustering algorithm CURE.[2]

We performed experiments with seven different k from 5 to 45: $k=5, 7, 10, 15, 20, 25, 30, 45$. In each experiment, *0%, 10%, 20%, 30%, 50%, 80%* of k are set to the number of servers which can be relocated in order to see the effect of k' on the performance. Note that in Fig. 1, k' is the number of servers in place. Therefore, for example, with the setting of 50% for $k=10$, k' becomes 5.

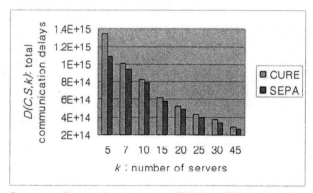

Fig. 2. Performance Comparison between CURE and SEPA in $D(C,S,k)$

Fig. 2 shows the performance of SEPA compared to CURE with no regard of relocation cost, i.e., k' and δ are 0. The x-axis is for k numbers and the y-axis is for $D(C,S,k)$ of SEPA and CURE. As Figure indicates, SEPA provides consistently better performance than CURE for all k numbers. SEPA gives on average 9.0% improvement over CURE, maximal improvement over CURE is 19.0% for $k = 5$.

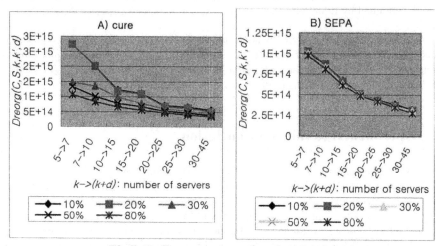

Fig.3. Performance comparison in $D(C,S,k,k',d)$

Fig. 3 shows the performance comparison in $D_{reorg}(C,S,k,k',\delta)$. $k{\to}k{+}d$ in x-axis represents that $d(\delta)$ new servers are added to the network with existing k servers. The results are obtained for different settings of percents: 10%-80% numbers of k can be relocated. Fig. 3-(A) shows the performance of CURE and Fig. 3-(B) shows the one of SEPA. For all cases, SEPA gives better performance than CURE. The figure shows that as the number of servers to be relocated is increasing, the value of $D_{reorg}(C,S,k,k',\delta)$ is decreasing for all cases in both algorithms. The result makes sense since both algorithms can find better solutions as they can relocate more number of servers.

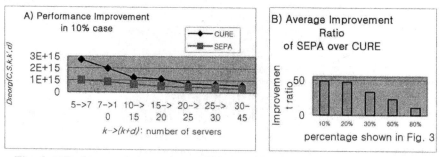

Fig. 4. A) Performance improvement of SEPA over CURE for 10% case shown in Fig. 3
B) Average performance improvement of SEPA over CURE for all cases shown in Fig. 3

Fig. 4-(A) shows in detail the performance comparison of two algorithms at a 10% case of Fig. 3. As the figure says, SEPA provides the maximal improvement ratio 53% over CURE at 5$\to$7, and the improvement becomes smaller at higher number of $k{\to}k{+}d$. And Fig. 4-(B) shows the average performance improvement ratio of SEPA over CURE for all different percent cases shown in Fig. 3. As the figure says, we can conclude that SEPA provides on average 10%-50% improved performance over CURE.

In this paper, we present our server placement algorithm SEPA. SEPA is an experimental driven algorithm.[10] In addition to CLARANS and CURE which are illustrated in this paper, we also surveyed other clustering approaches including Simulated Annealing [3], Genetic Algorithm [1], AutoClass [7], CLARA [3,8] and Universal Gravitation [14]. Based on CLARANS which suits our objective most among them, we developed SEPA.

The benefits of caching on the network may include to decrease the communication delays between the servers and the clients, to balance the network traffic load, and to help the network to be fault tolerant. A good server placement algorithm would help the first. As a future work, we plan to integrate our algorithm SEPA with some algorithms in those areas. Our model assumes that the average communication delay of a data may be reduced to the Euclidean distance, and the amount of data to the population of the client. We plan to investigate different network communication models to estimate the communication delays and data traffic, and to apply them in our algorithm.

References

1. D.E. Goldberg, Genetic Algorithms in Search, Optimization and Machine Learning, Addison-Wesley, 1991.
2. S. Guha, R. Rastogi, and K. Shim, "CURE: An Efficient Clustering Algorithm for Large databases," Information Systems, Vol. 26, No. 1, Pergamon, 2001.
3. J. Han, and M. Kamber, Data Mining : Concepts and Techniques, Morgan Kaufmann, 2001.
4. S. Jamin, C. Jin, A.R. Kurc, D. Raz, and Y. Shavitt, "Constrained Mirror Placement on the Internet," IEEE INFOCOMM, 2001
5. K. Leung, J. Shim, D. Tcherevik, and A. Vinberg, "A Scalable Yet Transparent Infrastructure for Distributed Applications," Proc. of the 8th International Conference on Parallel and Distributed Systems, IEEE Computer Society, 2001.
6. P. Krishnan, D. Raz, and Y. Shavitt, "The Cache Location Problem," IEEE/ACM Transactions on Networking, Vol. 8, No. 5, ACM, 2000.
7. NASA, The AutoClass Project, http://ic.arc.nasa.gov/ic/projects/bayes-group/autoclass/.
8. R.T. Ng, and J. Han, "Efficient and Effective Clustering Methods for Spatial Data Mining," Proc. of the 20th Very Large Data Bases Conference, Morgan Kaufmann, 1994.
9. L. Qiu, V.N. Padmanabhan, and G.M. Voelker, "On the Placement of Web Server Replicas," IEEE INFOCOMM, 2001
10. J. Shim, and T. Lee, "Survey on Clustering Algorithms for Optimal Server Placement," Technical Report, Sookmyung Women's University, 2001.
11. J. Shim, P. Scheuermann, and R. Vingralek, "Proxy Cache Algorithms: Design, Implementation, and Performance," IEEE Transactions on Knowledge and Data Engineering, Vol. 11, No. 4, IEEE Computer Society, 1999.
12. U.S. Census Bureau, United States County Statistics, http://www.census.gov/.
13. R. Vingralek, Y. Breitbart, M. Sayal, and P. Scheuermann, "A Transparent Replication of HTTP Service," Proc. of the 15th International Conference on Data Engineering, IEEE Computer Society, 1999.
14. W. E. Wright, "Gravitational Clustering," Pattern Recognition, Vol. 9, Pergamon Press, 1977.

The Yoix[1] Scripting Language
as a Tool for Building Web-Based Systems

Richard L. Drechsler and John M. Mocenigo

AT&T Labs - Research, Shannon Laboratory, 180 Park Avenue
Florham Park, NJ 07932-0971, USA
{drexler,john}@research.att.com

Abstract. The Yoix scripting language is ideal for building web applications. Implemented using Java[2] technology, the Yoix interpreter runs wherever Java runs. The Yoix language includes many features and constructs from both the Java and C languages. Because it uses Java technology, it is cross-platform, GUI-capable and both network and thread friendly, yet requires less coding than using Java directly. The interpreter can use URLs to access Yoix scripts via a web server. CGI interactions are equally simple. Though socket level communication methods are also available, robust and scaleable web applications can be constructed using straightforward, familiar client interactions with a web server. Such a model is being successfully used by AT&T for one of its fraud management systems, which is utilized 24/7 by hundreds of users at diverse locations. This paper briefly describes the Yoix language and focuses on its use as a tool for building web-based systems.

Keywords: scripting language, Java, application development, web applications

1. Introduction

A fully realized web application, namely one that provides remote users a reliable, easily distributed and easily maintained interface to an organization's information technology resources, is a wonderful thing. Unfortunately, when that web application requires more than basic HTML and JavaScript, it becomes a much more elusive goal. Differences in browsers and operating systems can complicate application development or exclude users that do not conform to the environment required by the application.

Java technology, with its credo: *Write Once, Run Anywhere*, appears to offer the best hope for a solution to this predicament However, applets are victims of the Browser Wars and often disappoint when pushed beyond simple, short-lived tasks. Java applications, on the other hand, can give satisfaction, but need a good deal of careful, sometimes tedious, development and testing to deliver on the *Run Anywhere* part of the bargain.

---

[1] Yoix is a trademark of AT&T Corp.
[2] Java is a trademark of Sun Microsystems.

E. Gregori et al. (Eds.): Networking 2002 Workshops, LNCS 2376, pp. 90–103, 2002.

1.1 Background

In the Spring of 1998, we were directly confronted by these issues when we found ourselves compelled to deliver a reliable web application in support of a critical business function by the end of that year. Moreover, we knew that, for the first year after delivery, just the two of us would be responsible for maintaining and updating the GUI to hundreds of users on different platforms around the United States.

Fairly quickly, for the reasons alluded to above, we decided we needed a Java application, but the thought of maintaining and updating Java jar files distributed on file servers and PCs across the nation *on our own* was daunting. Fortunately, one of us had built a special-purpose Java application that could be configured by interpreting tables loaded at runtime. Thus, we realized that by making the installed Java application an interpreter that could be configured over the network at runtime, we could have the reliable, maintainable web application we sought.

After delivering the application, every customer request for modification or fix to a GUI bug showed us how valuable even a rudimentary interpreter could be. All we had to do was change or add files on a web server and the end-user application was updated. However, we understood that for development organizations to profit from our experience, the interpreter would need a language. So, in the Autumn of 1999, we began work on what became the Yoix scripting language and interpreter, which we released publicly in the Autumn of 2000.[3]

Since that time, we have built several web applications using Yoix technology, including a re-implementation of the original application that had been using the Yoix prototype. In all cases, the results have been positive. Because the Java Virtual Machine and the Yoix interpreter perform so well, users, even on 333 MHz Pentium II processors, do not realize that their application is running on an interpreter that is written in Java. Moreover, our experiences with these applications have led us to improve and expand the Yoix interpreter and language both in general and as regards web applications in particular. Furthermore, we have confronted and overcome as best as possible many subtle barriers to the *Run Anywhere* promise so that developers can have confidence that the application they build using Yoix technology will be as close to *Write Once, Run Anywhere* as possible.

1.2 Why a New Java Scripting Language?

In the list of programming languages for the Java virtual machine assembled by Robert Tolksdorf, there are over twenty entries in the section for scripting languages.[4] It is not unreasonable to ask, therefore, why we chose to develop a new Java scripting language.

As our target applications include those requiring a high degree of reliability, we can immediately pare from the list the experimental, first-draft and research-sandbox languages. Several other of the languages are inappropriate because they are designed

---

[3] Yoix technology is available from AT&T Labs at http://www.research.att.com/sw/tools/yoix/ at no cost under a form of open source licensing.

[4] Tolksdorf's list can be found at http://flp.cs.tu-berlin.de/~tolk/vmlanguages.html.

for specific tasks that differ from the tasks we require. The remaining possibilities, which include some widely respected languages, share a feature that we view as a failing: seamless integration with the Java platform. We do not want to call Java methods directly via reflection or through bytecode. We want an intermediate layer that we can use to provide robustness, bug workarounds, a degree of uniformity and a way to smooth over those little incongruities that cause the *Write Once, Run Anywhere* promise to fall short. Although we knew when we started that we were taking the road less traveled and more arduous, we believe that road has led us to a stronger application development tool.

For example, we want screen resolution consistently standardized to 72 points per inch across platforms. Not only do we feel that script writers should not have to deal with making the appropriate conversions, but on certain platforms, the OS does not even accurately provide the information needed to make those conversions. As other examples, we find it annoying that Java's GridLayout ignores the supplied columns value unless the rows value is zero, or that suddenly with JDK1.3 the value returned by `System.getProperty("user.timezone")` is the empty string. More serious obstacles present themselves when trying to interrupt a thread blocked during I/O[5] or when trying to treat I/O using the *RandomAccessFile* class like I/O from other Java classes. For these reasons and many more, we feel a great deal of value is added by actively intervening between the script writer and the Java virtual machine.

Once convinced of the need for a new language for building reliable, cross-platform applications, we wanted to spare users the pain of learning a new language as much as possible. Thus, we borrowed grammar, syntax, pointer arithmetic and even many standard library functions from the C language. In addition, we modeled most of the data types and a few of the grammar components from the Java language.

Finally, some readers may be surprised that we included pointers as part of the language. When implemented in a safe manner, however, pointers can provide a convenient shorthand for specifying common activities. Moreover, pointers allowed us to realize these shorthand constructs through the use of familiar (i.e., C style) syntax and grammar elements.

1.3 Overview of This Paper

Through this paper we hope to persuade the reader that the Yoix scripting language and interpreter can both simplify and assure the development of reliable, cross-platform applications. Specifically, in this paper, we want to focus on using Yoix technology for building the client side of scaleable web applications. Consequently, after a brief introduction to the Yoix language in Section 2, we present, in more depth, two illustrative examples that highlight language features particularly suited to web applications (Section 3). Section 4 then discusses Yoix performance. Section 5 lists the software components typically needed by a Yoix web application and Section 6 touches on our near-term plans for enhancements. Finally, Section 7 summarizes the key points of this paper and provides an opportunity for concluding remarks.

---

[5] For those with access to the *Java Developer Connection*[SM], a description of this situation can be found at http://developer.java.sun.com/developer/bugParade/bugs/4154947.html.

2. A Brief Introduction to the Yoix Language and Interpreter

The Yoix language was designed to be learned easily by programmers familiar with C and Java. Grammar constructs such as declarations, conditionals and loops will be recognizable instantly. There are also *try/catch* statements for Java programmers and pointers (without access violations) for C programmers. In addition, work-alike versions of many C library functions, such as *fprintf, fscanf, regcmp, regex* and *strtok*, and Java methods, such as *endsWith, startsWith* and *toLowerCase*, are also available.

Yoix modules are much like Java packages. Modules contain built-ins (i.e., pre-defined functions), pre-defined variables or both. Since the Yoix interpreter reads and executes one statement at a time, much like the Unix shell, a module is not loaded until the first time a line that references a component in that module is executed. Certain fundamental modules, however, are always loaded at start-up. An *import* statement can be used explicitly to load a module. For example, one can say:

```
yoix.stdio.printf("Hello, World.\n");
```

or:

```
import yoix.stdio.*;
printf("Hello, World.\n");
```

The contents of a module can be viewed by conversion to a *String* in any of several ways. For example, a simple way to view the contents of yoix.stdio is:

```
stdout.nextline = toString(yoix.stdio);
```

Although the Yoix language is not object oriented, it does have objects. Currently, there are over 90 data types. These types range from fundamental, such as *Array, Dictionary, int* and *String*, to simple, such as *Color, Dimension* and *Point*, to complex, such as *File, SecurityManager, TextArea* and *Tree*. Most data types have fields that describe the characteristics of a type instance. For example, an instance of a *Color* is declared fully as follows:

```
Color turquoise = {
  double red   =  64. / 255.;
  double green = 224. / 255.;
  double blue  = 208. / 255.;
};
```

Often fields can be modified in an existing instance to change its characteristics. For example, a visible AWT *Frame* referenced by the variable *myframe* can be made invisible succinctly and efficiently as follows:

```
myframe.visible = FALSE;
```

Some data types even have executable methods associated with them. For example, a key/value pair can be added to a *Hashtable* referenced by the variable *myhash* as follows:

```
myhash.put("turquoise", turquoise);
```

Many of the complex data types behave like the *Dictionary* type by accepting arbitrary fields when they are declared so that additional, application-specific information can be carried along with the type instance and modified as needed.

Data types and built-ins are available for regular expressions and text substitution. Standard regular expression patterns, shell-like (i.e., glob) patterns and fixed text (i.e., fgrep) patterns are supported. Text substitution built-ins are provided and low-level access to pattern matching information is available. Regular expressions can also be used in *case* expressions as part of *switch* statements.

Essentially all of Java's AWT capabilities are available, including all five of the AWT layout managers. Unlike the Java AWT, however, coordinates are expressed in terms of 72 points per inch so that GUI constructions are more likely to appear the same across platforms.[6] Yoix syntax for event handling is notably simple. One need only define the appropriate event handler function (e.g., *actionPerformed*) within the context of the component where the event is to be handled. For example, a quit button becomes simply:

```
Button quit = {
  String text = "Quit";
  actionPerformed(ActionEvent ev) {
    exit(0);
  }
};
```

XML parsing is another Yoix capability. When XML documents are parsed, their structure and content are stored in an instance of the *Tree* data type, which permits easy traversal of the document structure and selective extraction of its content.

Input/Output capabilities are particularly flexible and easy to use. *File, URL* (including CGI) and *String* streams are all treated the same way. Additional functionality such as checksum, ZIP or GZIP filtering is obtained trivially. Programmers comfortable with C *stdio* library functions will find many old friends available. The following simple script to extract just the HTML directives from the AT&T home page illustrates some of these points.

```
import yoix.stdio.*;
Stream  att = yoix.io.open("http://www.att.com/", "r");
String  text;
if(att != NULL) {
  do {
    if((cnt = fscanf(att, " <%[^>]>", &text)) > 0)
      printf("<%s>\n", text);
    else cnt = fscanf(att, " %*s"); // discard
  } while(cnt >= 0);
} else fprintf(stderr, "ERROR: open failed.\n");
```

One could replace the URL in the open request above with a local file path and expect the same behavior.

---

[6] Microsoft OSs need a one-time test provided during the Yoix installation process to establish the actual screen resolution, which is then mapped into the 72 points per inch standard.

Extending the language by adding user-defined built-ins is straightforward. Static Java methods written in conformance with some simple guidelines and compiled into an accessible class file can be made available to a Yoix script by appropriate use of the import statement just as with standard Yoix built-ins.

Since the Yoix interpreter is implemented entirely in Java, any task a Yoix script is capable of performing could also be accomplished using Java directly. However, a Yoix script will most likely require less code than the corresponding Java program. The next example illustrates this point. The script below will read a list of file names or URLs from the invocation argument list, retrieve and compress the content of each and place it in a zip archive that was created in the current directory with a unique name automatically generated by the tempnam built-in.

```
import yoix.io.*;
import yoix.stdio.*;
ZipEntry ze;
Dictionary init = { int filters = ZIPPED; };
if(output = fopen(tempnam(".","y",".zip"),"w",init)) {
  setZipLevel(output, BEST_COMPRESSION);
  for(i=1;i<argc;i++) {
    if(input = open(argv[i],"r")) {
      buf = readStream(input);
      close(input);
      ze.name = argv[i];
      output.nextentry = ze;
      output.nextbuf = buf;
    } else fprintf(stderr,"could not open %s\n",argv[i]);
  }
  close(output);
  fprintf(stdout,"Zip file is: %s\n",output.fullname);
} else fprintf(stderr,"could not open zip file\n");
```

The corresponding Java program is left as an exercise for the reader, but even a few moments of reflection regarding the Java code needed for the opening of a buffered stream for reading either a file or a URL should be sufficient to make the point.

This section provided a brief introduction to the Yoix language as a general-purpose scripting tool. It should not be considered as a substitute, however, for a thorough investigation of the documentation available at the Yoix website, http://www.research.att.com/sw/tools/yoix/.

3. Building a Web Application Using Yoix Technology

We will show now how Yoix technology can be applied to the specific problem of building a web application. Although thorough, step-by-step instructions are beyond the scope of this paper and some subtleties are omitted, we hope to present enough detail as part of two substantive examples in this section to make a persuasive case for the efficacy of the technology.

3.1 Threaded, Interruptible Communications

Perhaps the most important component of a web application is client/server communications. From the end-user's perspective, this component should be innocuous, informative and interruptible. Active communications should not prevent an end-user from interacting with the GUI (innocuous), yet the status and progress of a communication should be available (informative) and any unnecessary or undesirable communication should be stoppable (interruptible).

To avoid interfering with GUI interactions, our first Yoix implementation example will have a thread for handling communication requests. For efficiency, we will make it persistent, meaning that the internal Java thread will wait rather than die when it completes its task, thereby saving the need to create a new Java thread for each task. To fully avoid interfering with the GUI, the thread's priority needs to be less than the priority of the Java event thread.

```
Thread RqstThread = {
  int   priority = 1 + MIN_PRIORITY; // reasonable
  int   persistent = TRUE; // optional, but efficient
};
```

Next, we need a way to queue requests onto this thread. The following function makes use of the Thread object's *queue* built-in to do the job:

```
QueueRequest(URL cgi, String arg, ...) {
  RqstThread.queue(PostRequest, unroll(&cgi));
}
```

The ellipses in the function argument list indicate that a variable number of arguments beyond the two specified may be supplied. The Yoix *unroll* built-in provides an easy way to pass the argument list to other functions.

The heart of this approach is the *PostRequest* function. Before presenting it, we need to state some assumptions about our model. Firstly, a request and response communication can be specified by these arguments: a URL for the CGI script handling the request,[7] zero or more string arguments associated with the request, a NULL string, which acts as a separator, and zero or more string pointers for storing the response.[8] Secondly, a session cookie is needed by the CGI script to validate the request as coming from a legitimate source. Lastly, a header prefacing the response consists of lines of the form *name=value*, contains at least status information and is terminated by a blank line, which acts to separate the header from the response data. The text for *PostRequest* is below. Its readability suffers somewhat from its compact rendering, but we hope the description following it will clarify matters. The details regarding the evocatively named functions, *ShowStatus* and *ShowAlert*, and variable, *SessionCookie*, as well as several module imports are omitted for brevity.

---

[7] In practice, we prefer using a single CGI script for all requests to facilitate a disciplined approach to activity logging and other administrative activities.

[8] A better approach, though one that is beyond the purposes of this paper, is to provide object pointers that are programmatically loaded from the string responses based on their type.

```
PostRequest(URL cgi, String arg, …) {
 String      buf[4096, …]; // a growable string buffer
 String      name, value;
 Array       args, data;
 Dictionary  header[2, …] = { // a growable dictionary
  String status  = "missing";
  String separator = NULL;
 };
 ShowStatus("Contacting " + cgi.host);
 if((s = open(cgi.name, "r+")) != NULL) {
  ShowStatus("Sending data to " + cgi.host);
  s.nextline = SessionCookie;
  for(args=&arg; args@sizeof>0 && *args!=NULL; args++)
   s.nextline = urlEncode(*args, TRUE);
  ShowStatus("Reading data from " + cgi.host);
  while(fscanf(s,"%[a-z]=%[^\r\n]%*c",&name,&value)==2)
   header[name] = urlDecode(value, TRUE);
  s.nextline; // skip blank line ending header
  if(strcasecmp(header.status, "OK") == 0) {
   total = 0;
   while((count = read(s, buf, buf@sizeof)) >= 0) {
    total += count;
    buf += count;
    buf[total<32768?total:32768] = '\0'; // grows buf
    ShowStatus("Reading data from " + cgi.host +
               "(" + toString(total) + " chars)");
   }
   ShowStatus("Transfer complete from " + cgi.host);
   buf -= total; // reposition pointer to beginning
   args++;         // get rid of NULL, if present
   data = strsplit(buf,header.separator,-args@sizeof);
   while(args@sizeof > 0)
    **args++ = *data++;
  } else ShowAlert(cgi.name+" status: "+header.status);
 } else ShowAlert("Cannot contact " + cgi.name);
}
```

The script starts by opening a read/write stream to a CGI script on the server and sending the session cookie to validate the communication. The script then writes the supplied arguments to the server up to the NULL separator. Here, one argument per line is ensured by using the Yoix built-in, *urlEncode*, to encode the arguments in IETF RFC 2396 format, which can be easily decoded by *perl*, for example, on the server side. Next, the script uses *fscanf* to read and parse the response header, placing each decoded value into the dictionary, *header*. After skipping the empty line marking the end of the response header, the script checks the header status and reads the CGI output in chunks, which allows feedback on the progress of large transfers to be reported. The chunks, initially of size 4,096, are doubled, as needed, up to a size of 32,768. This progressive read operation employs several Yoix capabilities:

growable buffers, pointer arithmetic, the *sizeof* attribute, which gives the size of an object from its current offset,[9] and initialization policies that easily allow the new portions of the growing buffer to be zeroed out. If a separator string was supplied in the header, the *strsplit* built-in uses it to split the buffer into an array of strings. The array will be no larger than the number of pointer arguments supplied to *PostRequest*. If too few string elements are in the response, the array will be NULL filled. If too many elements are in the response, the extras (and their separators) will be put into the last array slot. Finally, using a *while* loop and pointer arithmetic, the strings in the array are assigned to the (dereferenced) string pointers in the argument list.

The interrupt function is short and simple:

```
Interrupt() {
 RqstThread.alive = FALSE;
 ShowStatus("Interrupted");
}
```

These four Yoix code samples form the basis of reliable, threaded and interruptible communications between a Yoix web application and a CGI script on a web server.

3.2 Screen Management

Screen management, the downloading and caching of screens or windows that display the GUI, is the other major component of a web application. Simply downloading, as needed, Yoix scripts that define and display screens has several drawbacks: uncontrolled access, difficulty caching and difficulty using variations of the same basic screen. Control over access is achieved by serving the screens through a CGI script. The other drawbacks are overcome by downloading not a script defining the screen, but a script that defines a function whose return value is the screen, namely a screen builder. The advantages to this approach are several. Firstly, the return value is easily cached. Secondly, the function only needs to be downloaded and parsed once, no matter how many screens are to be built. Lastly, variations on a screen can easily be built by passing parameters to the function. For example, message text for an alert screen might be one of the parameters. Of course, it is possible to vary a built screen by calling a function within the screen to adjust certain parameters before making it visible. Both approaches are valuable and both have their place.

Note that the screen builder approach involves two types of cacheable objects: screen builder functions and instances of built screens. Normally when we think of caching in this context, we have in mind screen instance caching since one would expect to cache a screen builder one time for the life of the application invocation. However, during development or when updating an application, it can be useful to clear and reload the cache of screen builders. For example, the server might trigger cache clearing by including an appropriate indicator in its response header.

Our second Yoix implementation example starts with a builder directory that also serves as a screen builder cache. It is declared as a growable dictionary and, initially, should contain only non-standard directory entries, if any. Ours will start empty:

---

[9] Whereas the *length* attribute gives the size of an object always from the zero offset.

```
Dictionary BuilderDirectory[0,…];
```

We use a function for retrieving existing entries or creating standard directory entries:

```
LookupBuilder(String name) {
  if(!defined(name, BuilderDirectory)) {
   BuilderDirectory[name] = new Dictionary {
    URL      cgi = cgiURL("getlayout.pl");
    Function Builder = NULL;
    int      cachebuilder = TRUE;
   };
  }
  return(BuilderDirectory[name]);
}
```

The special Yoix built-in, *defined*, checks whether the supplied name refers to an element in *BuilderDirectory*. Let us assume that the function *cgiURL*, which generates an appropriate URL object, is defined elsewhere in the application.

Now we can define a function that returns a builder:

```
LoadBuilder(String name) {
  Dictionary buildinfo = LookupBuilder(name);
  Function   builder = buildinfo.Builder;
  if(builder == NULL) { // get it from the CGI script
   String script;
   PostRequest(buildinfo.cgi, name, NULL, &script);
   if(script != NULL) {
    builder = execute(script, name, global);
    if(buildinfo.cachebuilder)
     buildinfo.Builder = builder;  // may be NULL
   }
  }
  return(builder);
}
```

This function requires some discussion. Firstly, we make use of *PostRequest* defined in the previous section, but we do not queue it onto *RqstThread* because this request is to display a GUI component and we would not want to delay that by possibly queuing it behind a data retrieval request. Secondly, we note that we are referencing elements in *buildinfo* that may not exist if the application writer has explicitly added an entry into *BuilderDirectory* in a sloppy manner. Efficient validation schemes to prevent such errors are easy to concoct, but these, again, are beyond the scope of this paper. Finally and most importantly, we are using the special Yoix built-in, *execute*. This built-in executes the Yoix statements in *script* in a new global context with the additional arguments supplied to it available in that context as argv[0], argv[1] and so on. By convention, we pass the screen name as argv[0]. The next argument, however, is more interesting. Since *execute* always starts a new global context, we pass the current global context as an argument to *execute* so that it is available to the statements in *script*. Note that Yoix contexts are *Dictionary* objects. The return value of *execute* is determined by an executed Yoix *return* statement in *script*. The builder script outlined below will help to clarify these points:

```
import yoix.awt.*;
Dictionary Appl = argv[1]; // supplied global context
Builder(String name, Array args) {
 Frame screen = {
  int cachescreen = TRUE;
  // other variable declarations, as needed,
  // including the layout manager
  Array layout = {
   // screen layout components
  };
  HideScreen() {
   Appl.HideScreen(this); // access global function
  }
  LoadArgs(Array args) {
   for(; args@sizeof > 1; args += 2)
    this[args[0]] = args[1];
  }
  // other functions used by the screen
 };
 screen.LoadArgs(args);
 return(screen);
}
return(Builder); // return the Builder function
```

As the Yoix documentation for **functions** at the Yoix website indicates, the global context of the script will be available to the builder function whenever it is executed. Thus, the application's global context passed in as argv[1] and assigned to the dictionary *Appl* will be available to the builder function simply by referencing *Appl*. Notice that an indicator for screen caching, *cachescreen*, is included among the screen variables. Also, there is a function, *LoadArgs*, for setting screen variables from arguments passed to the builder function with the assumption that the variables' names and values alternate in the argument list.

We are almost ready to describe our screen loader, but it is going to need a cache lookup function, which we define here:

```
GetCachedScreen(String name) {
 Object screen; // could be Frame, Dialog, etc.
 if(defined(name, ScreenCache)
  if((screen = ScreenCache[name]) != NULL)
   if(screen.dispose)
    screen = NULL;
 return(screen);
}
```

GetCachedScreen checks if the supplied name indicates a defined, occupied entry in *ScreenCache*, which is just a growable dictionary. If it does, then we need to check if the screen has been disposed, since a disposed screen cannot be reused and should be treated as an uncached screen.

Now we are ready for the screen loader function:

```
LoadScreen(String screenname, String buildername, ...) {
  Object    screen;
  Function builder;
  if((screen = GetCachedScreen(screenname)) == NULL) {
   if((builder = LoadBuilder(buildername)) != NULL) {
    screen = builder(screenname, &buildername + 1);
    if(defined("cachescreen",screen))
     if(screen.cachescreen)
      ScreenCache[screenname] = screen;
   }
  }
  return(screen);
}
```

Note that we need the second argument of *builder* to be a single *Array* argument rather than an array of single arguments. Consequently, instead of using the *unroll* function as we had earlier, we use an offset into the *Array* of *LoadScreen* arguments directly.

In this section, we have summarized how Yoix technology can be used to succinctly build the screen management portion of a web application. The implementation described takes advantage of Yoix capabilities to expand the concept of downloading screens over the web to downloading screen building functions, which in turn offers greater flexibility and more features to the application.

3.3 Other Components

Naturally, there are many other components involved in a web application. Administrative features such as activity logging and broadcast messaging are just two among many examples of needed capabilities. However, while we cannot address all the issues in this paper, we hope that we have given sufficient indication of the value Yoix technology brings to the task of building a web application.

4. Yoix Performance

When Java technology was first introduced, one of the major obstacles to its widespread acceptance was its performance characteristics. Compared to the many C and C++ applications then prevalent, it was deemed too slow. Over the years, however, improvements to the Java virtual machine, substantial increases in the speed of processors and the application of Just-In-Time compiling techniques have made Java performance much less of an issue in a great many instances. Nonetheless, the thought of using the Yoix language to write an application that runs on an interpreter that is itself a Java application may well give one pause. After all, the time it takes a

Yoix application to perform a task is bounded by the time it takes a Java application to perform that same task.

We address the performance issue by presenting some timing studies comparing a Yoix program to a Java program performing the same task. The studies were done on a Compaq Deskpro Workstation with an Intel Pentium 4 1.3GHz processor under the RedHat 7.2 Linux operating system using version 1.3.1 of the Java virtual machine distributed by Sun Microsystems. The mean, median, low and high values for 100 consecutive trials were recorded. Each trial involved one Yoix and one Java program invocation. For the *start-up* trial, timing was obtained using the *real* (i.e., clock) value of the shell `time` command. For the other trials, timings were obtained by differencing `System.currentTimeMillis()` calls bracketing the trial code.

At start-up, a `Toolkit.getDefaultToolkit()` call is made by the Yoix interpreter to get screen size and font information. However, a corresponding call is not made by the Java virtual machine until specific display activity requires it. These behaviors affect the timings in the *start-up* and the *display* trials. Consequently, additional trials were run in which an explicit call was included in the Java programs to force *Toolkit* loading. In the *start-up* trials, including the call slowed Java, while in the *display* trials, Java performance improved since the effect of the implicit *Toolkit* call was removed from the timed portion of the program.

Table 1. Performance Comparison between Java and Yoix Test Programs for 100 Trial Runs

Trial	Tool	Mean	Median	Low	High
Start-up and simply exit	Java	0.255s	0.250s	0.250s	0.400s
	Yoix	1.228s	1.230s	1.220s	1.340s
Start-up and exit (load default Toolkit explicitly)	Java	0.658s	0.660s	0.640s	0.680s
	Yoix	1.233s	1.220s	1.210s	1.410s
Read text of *Don Quixote* into a String (2.37Mb)	Java	0.247s	0.245s	0.215s	0.281s
	Yoix	0.718s	0.717s	0.712s	0.745s
Create and display a frame with 100 buttons	Java	0.733s	0.736s	0.657s	0.776s
	Yoix	0.716s	0.728s	0.549s	0.757s
Display a frame with 100 buttons (preload Toolkit)	Java	0.332s	0.336s	0.262s	0.403s
	Yoix	0.706s	0.719s	0.546s	0.756s

As expected, the trial results show that Yoix performance lags Java performance (Table 1). Nonetheless, the results are reasonably close. The GUI results, in particular, indicate that Yoix technology is capable of performing client-side application tasks with alacrity.

5. Client and Server Requirements

Building a quality web application using Yoix technology can be achieved, in most cases, by downloading all the necessary components from reliable sources at no cost.

On the client side, two software tools are needed: the Java Runtime Environment, available from Sun Microsystems at http://java.sun.com and, of course, Yoix, available from AT&T Labs at http://www.research.att.com/sw/tools/yoix/.

On the server side the possible choices depend more on the particular application, but, generally, at least two software tools are needed: a web server and a CGI scripting language. The most popular choices for these are the Apache web server, available at http://www.apache.org, and the perl scripting language, available at http://www.cpan.org.

6. Future Enhancements in the Near Term

The version of the Yoix interpreter described in this paper works with versions of the Java Development Kit (JDK) or Java Runtime Environment (JRE) from release 1.1.8 through the current release, 1.4.0. However, we have not yet had an opportunity to incorporate into the Yoix interpreter any of the Swing or Java2D capabilities. We have kept those capabilities in mind throughout the development of the Yoix language and interpreter and have made certain design decisions to allow natural evolution to Swing and Java2D. We expect this evolution to happen shortly.

Another enhancement associated with the addition of Java2D will be graph drawing. Although it was not mentioned earlier in this paper, capabilities for building and manipulating graphs of nodes and edges are already a part of Yoix technology. However, we have held off from adding a means of displaying such graphs out of a preference for the graphical model provided by Java2D.

7. Concluding Remarks

We have introduced Yoix technology: a general-purpose scripting language and associated interpreter. In particular, we have tried to show through a few practical examples that Yoix technology is a valuable tool for building web applications. In addition to its ability to succinctly implement substantive tasks, certain of its features are well suited to the sorts of tasks required by web applications. We also indicated, through mention of our experiences in constructing critical applications used within AT&T, that a properly constructed Yoix web application performs reliably, at scale, and is easy to both maintain and update.

We mentioned that the Yoix interpreter is implemented completely using standard Java technology and runs wherever Java runs. Moreover, we discussed how the Yoix interpreter is designed to allow a Yoix application to come as close as possible to achieving the Java promise of *Write Once, Run Anywhere*.

We also pointed out that Yoix technology is freely available under a form of open source licensing from our web site at: http://www.research.att.com/sw/tools/yoix/.

Finally, we hope that this tool will prove useful to the software development community. We know firsthand that it can allow a small team to quickly build, trivially distribute and easily maintain a reliable, corporate-wide web application. We encourage readers to try Yoix technology for themselves.

XGuide - A Practical Guide to XML-Based Web Engineering

Clemens Kerer, Engin Kirda and Christopher Krügel

Technical University of Vienna, Distributed Systems Group
Argentinierstr. 8/184-1, A-1040 Vienna, Austria
Phone: +43 1 58801 18418, Fax: +43 1 58801 18491
{C.Kerer, E.Kirda, C.Kruegel}@infosys.tuwien.ac.at

Abstract. *Various approaches have been proposed in the field of Web engineering that attempt to exploit the advantages of XML/XSL technologies. Although a strict separation of presentation and content achieved through XML/XSL has many advantages, a considerable effort is involved in using these technologies to develop Web sites. The lack of experience in XML/XSL can be a major cause for the extra effort. In several XML/XSL-based Web projects, we felt the need for a methodology that systematically guides the developer in the field through the development process while taking into account the limitations and strengths of XML. In this paper, we present XGuide, a practical guide for XML-based Web Engineering that focuses on parallel development. XGuide is a methodology for XML/XSL-based Web development that is tool-independent and hence, can be used with a broad range of development tools. We are currently using the XGuide approach in several Web projects.*

Keywords: XML, Web Engineering, Methodology, Web Service Life Cycle, Parallel development

1 Introduction

For more than seven years the World-Wide Web has been growing rapidly. Organizations were quick to realize the Web's huge potential and it became a powerful and important means to stay in contact with customers, provide online services, express opinions and make money from e-commerce applications. As the functionality of Web sites increased, many new features were implemented that made Web applications more dynamic, interactive and complex. Thus, as the offered information grew and the management complexity of Web sites increased, maintenance often became difficult, too.

Many Web applications and services are developed in an ad-hoc manner today and the main reason is the lack of *practical*-oriented, easy-to-use methodologies, approaches and guidelines. Some authors have referred to the current situation on the Web as the *Web crisis* (e.g., [1]) and have likened it to the *software crisis* (e.g., [2]) in the 1960s when much of the produced software was not reliable and failed to reach basic levels of quality and user satisfaction.

E. Gregori et al. (Eds.): Networking 2002 Workshops, LNCS 2376, pp. 104–117, 2002.

In order to eliminate HTML's shortcomings and to define flexible, extensible standards that address current Web requirements, the World Wide Web Consortium (W3C) defined the eXtensible Markup Language (XML) and the eXtensible Stylesheet Language (XSL). XML is ubiquitous today and is widely used in areas such as data representation and data exchange, repositories and in domain-specific languages (e.g., SVG, MusicML, MathML or VoiceXML).

Although the majority of existing Web sites are not XML-based, there is general consensus that XML will be the Web language of choice in the future. The somewhat slow adoption of XML on the Web is probably because of the complexity of XML and its related technologies (e.g., XSL transformations, XSL formatting objects, XML schema, etc.) in comparison to HTML. Furthermore, tool support for XML-based Web development is still in its infancy compared to the large number of available HTML-based development tools.

Although a strict separation of presentation and content achieved through XML/ XSL has many advantages, a considerable effort is involved in using these technologies to develop Web sites. The lack of experience in XML/XSL can be a major cause for the extra effort. In several XML/XSL-based Web projects, we felt the need for a methodology that systematically guides the developer in the field through the development process and supports parallel development to decrease development time.

In this paper we present XGuide, a practical guide for XML-based Web Engineering. XGuide is a methodology for XML/XSL-based Web development that is tool-independent and that can be used with a broad range of development tools. We are currently using the XGuide approach in several Web projects.

The remainder of this paper is structured as follows: in Section 2 we briefly discuss our previous experiences engineering XML-based Web sites. Section 3 presents the XGuide methodology with the eight important steps we identified for XML-based Web engineering. Section 4 briefly evaluates the XGuide approach. Section 5 presents related Web engineering approaches and Section 6 concludes the paper and lays out future work.

2   Our Previous XML-Based Web Engineering Experiences

Our group started working in the area of Web engineering in 1995 when we first implemented the Web presence of the Vienna International Festival (VIF) [3]. The VIF is an annual cultural festival in Vienna that attracts a national and international audience from Europe, Japan and the US.

Since 1995, we have been trying to improve the development processes and the deployed tools to effectively meet the customer requirements and to be able to finish the development work in the short time frame of 5-6 weeks. This is especially important since both the appearance and the functionality of the VIF site evolves every year and we often cannot reuse functionality and components from previous years.

Based on our previous experiences [4] and with the aim of improving our old tools, we built a new tool called MyXML [5, 6]. MyXML fully relies on XML and related technologies to support the development and maintenance of flexible, extensible Web applications. Some of the key requirements for this tool were:

- the strict separation of the content, the layout and the application logic (similar to the Model-View-Controller Pattern [7]),
- a reuse oriented resource management,
- the easy creation of static and dynamic pages,
- built-in support for common concepts on the Web such as database access or CGI parameters
- independence from a particular implementation model or programming language.

We deployed MyXML for the VIF Web presence in the 2001 season and, at the same time, started deploying it in the implementation of the Web site of the Austrian Academy of Science (AAS) [8]. This project had completely different characteristics (many more pages, longer project duration, emphasis on maintenance and evolution, etc.) and helped us to evaluate the versatility of the tool.

Although the deployment of MyXML and XML/XSL technology helped us in general, we also observed several problems when doing XML-based Web site development. We reported our positive and negative XML-based Web engineering experiences in [9].

We observed that the majority of the problems stems from the lack of experience in how to do XML-based Web development. Many developers did not know what challenges (as opposed to HTML-based development) were to be expected. Separating the presentation from the content, for example, was not always easy for the developers to understand and many questions came up that were not always easy to answer: Should a Document Type Definition (DTD) be used? What should be put in the DTD? How do you provide multi-language support using XSL? What should the graphical designers deliver? What is expected from the content managers?

After experiencing similar problems and questions in both the VIF and the AAS project, we realized that a set of guidelines for doing XML-based Web engineering are needed. Such guidelines should not exclusively cover the development process but include the analysis and design phases. Tasks for different roles (such as developers, graphical designers and content mangers) need to be taken into account and support is needed to enable parallel development to decrease development time.

In the next section we present XGuide, a methodology for XML-based Web engineering that covers the basic decisions and requirements that need to be considered in an XML-based Web project.

3   The XGuide Methodology

Web development involves many different tasks and requires different skills to solve them [10, 11]. We define four roles to represent the different kinds of activities involved in the process: the project manager, the content manager, the graphical designer and the programmer.

Clearly, a single person can play several of the above roles in small projects whereas in large ones, a single role can be represented by many people. In the following, we only distinguish between roles, abstracting from who or how many people a role represents.

3.1   Define the Goal and the Characteristics of the XML-Web Site

Before starting the design or implementation, it is important to make sure that all involved roles understand what the key aspects of the Web site are. With the characteristics of a Web site, we refer to functionality-oriented aspects such as the support for multiple languages and the ability to seamlessly switch between them. Another requirement might be that different output devices and/or formats must be supported (e.g., HTML browsers, simple HTML for hand-held devices, WML for mobile phones and PDF for a paper version).

In the following enumeration, we present the aspects we found to be important in our XML projects:

The Lifetime of the Web site is critical to determine how much effort should go into the various tasks. In the case of the VIF, for example, the lifetime of the Web site usually is half a year, in the case of the AAS it is several years.

Multi-lingual support per se is relatively easy to accomplish; this task becomes trickier if the user should be able to switch from a page in one language to the same page in the other language - especially if the pages are created dynamically (e.g., search results, shopping carts, etc.). The complexity further increases if more than two languages have to be supported.

Multi-device support affects the content manager, the graphical designer and the programmer. The content manager has to decide *what* content should be presented on different devices, the graphical designer has to plan the corresponding rendering of the content and the programmer has to take the different output formats and device capabilities into account.

Integration of legacy data/applications mainly concerns the programmer and content manager. The migration of the data or application might be an option if it is exclusively used for Web purposes; this might save time and money in the long run.

Browser-less access to the Web site is increasingly becoming important with the wide-spread use of Web services (i.e., XML-based machine-to-machine communication). Support for browser-less access can also be seen as another output device which must be supported.

External data sources such as remote databases or third-party Web services add additional complexity in terms of performance and/or maintenance. Especially if the data sources do not provide XML data, conversion might be costly.

Evolution of the Web site is another important factor. If new or extended functional requirements are likely to be added frequently, the development process needs to put even more emphasis on flexible and easy-to-change data structures and application logic. If high availability is required, appropriate update mechanisms have to be in place to support the evolution of the site with a minimum interference.

3.2   Decide on the Technology and Infrastructure

Based on the preliminary understanding of the Web site's functionality developed in step 1, the next question that needs to be answered is whether the use of XML technology for the realization of the project makes sense.

According to our experience, this step is sometimes skipped because people implicitly assume that a new technology such as XML is better suited for a task than an existing one. This is not necessarily the case. On the one hand, all parties involved in XML-based Web engineering have to be (or become) knowledgeable in XML and its related technologies; in the latter case this can take considerable educational effort. On the other hand, not all kinds of Web projects are suitable for an XML implementation – especially if the project deals with a small Web site, a Web site with a short time-to-live, or a creative Web site with many different pages that lack any commonalities. Thus, commitment to XML technology might sometimes be counterproductive.

3.3   Develop a Means of Communication

One of the key problems in the Web projects we implemented was the lack of communication among the different roles. For example, content managers did not communicate their requirements or intentions to the graphical designers. Likewise, the graphical designers did not make explicit their constraints. As a result, the content managers did not know what kind of content the graphical designers expected and vice versa. Eventually, either one or both of these roles had to adapt their work to conform to the other's requirements.

We use a simple graphical notation to represent pages, graphics and content and relations between them (rectangles and arrows or anything else the participants feel comfortable with). Figure 1 shows an example diagram illustrating the structure of a class of pages that contain navigational elements, a header and a footer and a content area. The content area contains a list consisting of images and corresponding descriptive texts. On this foundation, it is much easier for the roles to communicate on the same level. To record the outcome of the discussion and make it more explicit and binding, annotations can be added to the diagrams. The annotation number 3 in the diagram (usually a post-it in practice), for example, could be a constraint such as: "Every item in the list consists of an optional image and a text. There must be at least one item in the list and at most five". Similar constraints can also hold for the other annotations on the diagram.

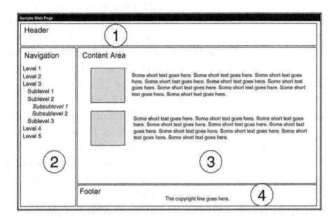

Fig. 1. Example of a graphical notation used in discussions showing the structure of a class of pages

3.4 Use a DTD as Contract

In the VIF project, the only way to meet the deadline was to extensively develop in parallel. Thus, our desire was to enable the content managers, layout designers and programmers to work in parallel and independently of each other.

```
<!--
  <in>
    <param name="studentname" type="String" />
    <param name="grades" type="String[]" />
  </in>
-->
<!ELEMENT webpage (text*, grades, text*)>
<!ELEMENT text (#PCDATA | studentname)*>
<!ELEMENT grades (grade+)>
<!ELEMENT grade (#PCDATA)>
<!ELEMENT studentname (#PCDATA)>
```

Fig. 2. The DTD contract for a page in the Web site

Our approach to achieve this is to define a *contract* that specifies the high-level constraints and interfaces and is binding for all roles. We use a document type definition (DTD) for this purpose. In terms of content, the DTD specifies the structure and the type of the content to be expected; for the graphical designer, this structure is the only important information needed to create corresponding stylesheets to render the content; finally, the programmer must be able to derive from such a contract how the interfaces to the layout/content templates described in Section 2 look like. Figure 2 depicts a contract for a page in the Web site that lists the grades of a student. In addition to the structure and content model of the elements, the interface to the layout/content is specified in the contract. In the example, the student's name (a string) and a list of grades (a string array) are used as input parameters. Similarly, output parameters can be specified to describe the results a Web form may return. Once this contract is fixed, all roles can work independently, i.e., the application logic can be developed without the actual content and layout at hand, the content can be created without any knowledge of the layout and the layout can be designed based on the content's structure as opposed to the content itself.

Since tool support for WYSIWYG creation of XSL stylesheets is only rudimentary compared to HTML tools, in practice an additional step is required to transform HTML layout templates into XSL/CSS stylesheets - again strictly conforming to the content's structure as defined in the contract (i.e., DTD). We obtained good results using this technique. For instance, the application logic of the VIF 2001 Web site could be finished *before* the first layout drafts or content information was available.

3.5   Develop in Parallel

Based on the contract defined in the previous step, the content managers, layout designers and programmers can start to do their job independently of each other. In this section, we briefly discuss each role's task and the main XML-related issues they need to consider.

The Content Management Content management is about storing and maintaining content. In the context of XML-based Web development, this means that the content has to be stored permanently and can be delivered in XML according to the structure defined in the contract (i.e., DTD). A content manager has several options for storing content: in XML files in the file system, in a relational database, in an XML repository or any combination of these. Furthermore, existing content sometimes has to be integrated, too. In any case, a way to generate the XML representation of the content from the actual repository has to be provided. If the content is natively stored in XML format, this is relatively easy. If a relational database or any other non-XML repository is in use, appropriate transformation mechanisms have to be installed.

In the VIF project, we provided prefabricated word processor templates for content managers that were then automatically processed to gather the content.

In the AAS project, we developed WebCUS [12], a Web-based content management tool for relational databases, and used MyXML's ability to query relational databases and present the result as XML. This approach facilitated the reuse of existing relational databases know-how in the AAS, supported a flexible way to edit content via the Web, and provided transparent creation of XML documents using MyXML.

The Layout Definition The aim of layout definition is to provide a set of layout templates that can be applied to the XML content. As mentioned before, direct generation of XSL stylesheets is currently difficult due to missing satisfactory tool support. As a result, graphic companies frequently deliver HTML templates as design mockups that have to be manually transcoded into stylesheets. This process is guided by the structure of the content as defined in the contract. Depending on the graphical appearance of the site, commonalities of these stylesheets can be further extracted, thus facilitating reuse of layout fragments. Using stylesheets has the advantages of separating the layout from the content, supporting reuse of layout definitions and ensuring layout consistency across all pages using the same stylesheet. Despite these desirable properties, the use of stylesheets also bears some restrictions in that exceptions for single pages (e.g., to change the background color for a single page, to add an image only on one page, etc.) are difficult to implement.

The Application Logic The focus of this task is on the functionality (usually) taking place on the server. The programmer is not interested in how the pages look or what other content is available on the site. His only interest is how dynamic content can be given out in the appropriate layout. In other words, he needs access to the 'executable form' of the layout and the static content. Furthermore, dynamically generated content must be integrated at runtime. One way of achieving this is by using generated user interface classes as in MyXML (e.g., [6]). Another possibility is to merge the static with the dynamically generated content first and apply the stylesheet at runtime (e.g., [13–15]).

3.6   Navigational Structures

Navigation bars and hierarchical menus can be found on almost all Web sites today. Especially in large Web projects, the consistent implementation and maintenance of navigational structures for static and dynamic pages can be a difficult and tedious task.

A good solution for this problem is to separate the navigational information from the content. Instead of integrating slightly different navigational constructs in all pages, the whole navigational information is specified only once and stored externally. From this single source of information all navigational structures are generated depending on the actual target page (contextual links).

As we reported in [9], we usually use a separate XML structure to hold the navigational information including the hierarchy or list of all hyperlinks, their representation as text or images and the destination URLs.

3.7 Integration

When the parallel tasks are concluded, they can be integrated to form the final Web site. In the first step, the content documents are processed with stylesheets containing the layout information. In the next step, the navigational information is added. This leaves us with the task to integrate the application logic by calling the appropriate layout classes as discussed in Section 3.5. The above steps are what worked best in our projects, but alternative integration paths can easily be imagined: if CSS stylesheets are used, the browser performs the first step; if the navigational structures need further decoration with layout information, the content should first be merged with the navigational information before applying the style, and so on.

Although the final integration can only take place when all other tasks are concluded, we found the early integration of subsets as soon as they are finished useful. This gives a first indication of whether the specified contracts hold and supports early detection of necessary changes, thus, reducing the overall cost of such changes. Furthermore, it helps the content manager to review parts of the content in the final layout as well as the layout designer to test the layout with real content.

3.8 Implementation, Evolution and Maintenance

Just as in software engineering, in Web projects the requirements keep changing and evolving all the time. To maximize the benefit of parallel development as discussed above, it is crucial to distinguish between implementation and evolution and not to continuously extend the functionality and/or requirements for the Web project. Instead, only when the integration of a given set of features is finished, another round of parallel development dealing with extensions should be started.

The distinction between the evolution and the maintenance of a Web site is often difficult to make; e.g., is the adaptation of a stylesheet part of the site's evolution or maintenance? We usually define activities as maintenance if they affect only a single role but have no consequences for other roles or the contract (e.g., changing the value of a content item or formatting properties of a stylesheet). Due to the independence of the roles with respect to the contract, these activities can be performed easily. If a change of the contract is necessary to implement a new requirement, we talk about evolution of the site that automatically involves all roles and usually requires major updates. While maintenance activities can be performed continuously, evolution cycles are scheduled less frequently and result in a new release or version of the whole site.

4   A Web Site Example

In this section, we discuss a Web site that we implemented according to the steps we define in this paper and illustrate the presented ideas. The Web site offers information about an introductory course on XML and related technologies (see [16]) and is the primary source of information for students. The functional requirements for the site were quickly defined: a news section should inform about recent updates and accompany more general information about the lecture such as the dates or the grading scheme. Furthermore, the description of the lab examples is offered, a download section provides the lecture slides and required tools for the lab, a grading service reports the points a student earned so far, and a feedback form allows students to contact the lecturer.

The characteristics of this Web site, as discussed in Section 3.1, are presented in the following list:

- the site's lifetime is several years (as long as the course is offered),
- the content is only available in English,
- different output formats shall be supported (i.e., a full-fledged HTML version for Web browsers, a light-weight HTML version for hand-held devices and a printable version in PDF),
- no legacy applications have to be integrated,
- no browser-less access is envisioned,
- only a (relational) database with student information serves as additional source of information, and
- the evolution of the site happens only for the next semester's lecture, i.e., in 6 months steps.

The target environment for our Web site consisted of a Redhat Linux system with Apache as a Web server and Jakarta Tomcat as servlet container. For XML processing, we used Xerces and Xalan in combination with our MyXML development tool.

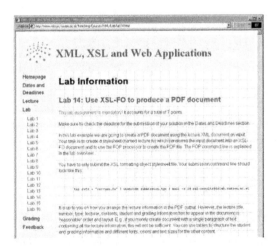

Fig. 3. A full-fledged Web page for viewing in an HTML browser.

In the VIF and AAS projects, we had several different kinds of pages and thus needed several DTDs to describe them. In the course Web site, we planned to have only a single type of page with a header, footer, navigation and content area as shown in Figure 3. A flexible set of content definitions and structures helped to map the content requirements of different pages to the same contract.

We started and finished the application logic before any content or layout was defined. In a second step, we defined the layout based on some test content; the content was added only as the last step. The development of the layout, content and the application logic was thus independent of each other.

The navigation of the site is managed by a hierarchical menu that provides access to the main sections of the Web site and shows shortcuts to the subsections of the currently selected section. As proposed in this paper, we defined the whole navigational structure external to the content and layout and automatically added the appropriate representation to all pages.

The integration of the content with the layout and the application logic worked smoothly. Some changes were made to the layout definition after the actual content had been added; this was mainly done for stylistic reasons and to better render the content on different browsers. Furthermore, the generation of different versions of the site for the different output formats also worked without major problems. A slight adaptation of the content structure was necessary to incorporate information that was only to be present in the printable PDF version of the site. Figure 4 shows the same sample lab exercise depicted in Figure 3 in the alternative output formats of light-weight HTML and PDF.

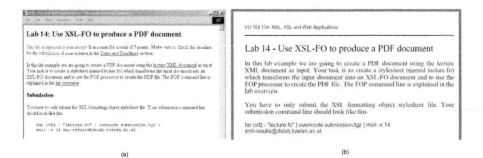

Fig. 4. Additional output formats (a) light-weight HTML for hand-held devices and (b) printable PDF for the same content.

5   Related Work

The Relational Management Methodology (RMM) and the Object Oriented Hypermedia Design Methodology (OOHDM) are two well-known Web site development methodologies. RMM [17] is based on the Entity Relationship (ER) model [18] and focuses on database-backed Web development. A severe restriction of the original RMM is that the mapping of contents from several entities onto a single Web page was not possible. The extended RMM [19] explicitly introduces the separation of content, layout and application logic (storage level, presentation level and logical level) and focuses on the logical level of a Web application to provide formalized mappings of the content through the logical level onto the presentation level. OOHDM [20] is an object-oriented hypermedia design methodology based on the HDM data model [21] that focuses on the database application domain. In OOHDM, separate phases for the conceptual design, the navigational design and the user interface design are introduced. The conceptual design models the application domain using the notation of Rumbaugh; the navigational design distinguishes nodes, links between nodes and access structures that are the equivalent to our navigational structures.

A graphical design technique, W3DT, is introduced in [22] and extended into eW3DT in [23]. eW3DT represents pages and classes of pages in a hierarchical diagram and has an explicit notion to model database interactions. This methodology is solely targeted at HTML generation, though.

In [24], the authors discuss the analysis and design of Web-based information systems. A *sequential* methodology based on ER analysis, scenario analysis, architecture design, attribute definition and construction is proposed. The architecture is represented in an extended version of RMM's diagram notation. Attributes can be viewed as meta data for later maintenance use. The different stages in the life cycle of a Web application are presented and traditional methodologies such as RMM are used in the design phase.

Another Web application design methodology for mainly data-centric Web sites is WebML[25]. WebML defines a structural model for the content, a hypertext model for content composition and navigation, a presentation model and a personalization model. The proposed design process covers similar aspects as our methodology, but does not support parallel development and does not have much support for logic development.

The Extensible Web Modeling Framework (XWMF) [26] is an RDF [27] based approach towards Web engineering. It focuses on the specification of a reusable hierarchy of fragments that eventually form a Web page. These specifications are extensible and can be enriched with other meta data. Although the implementation of such a model can be generated automatically, no strict separation of layout, content and logic is possible.

6 Conclusion and Future Work

We are currently deploying XGuide for the design, development and maintenance of this year's VIF Web presence. Currently, we are using MyXML for the logic, but also plan to test XGuide with other development tools such as Cocoon [14].

We are also extending the contract model to better describe the properties of a Web page and add extensibility with respect to new aspects such as security or workflow. Furthermore, we extend our ideas to support components (e.g., content components, layout components, logic components, etc.) and their reuse in the Web development process.

Easy support for different output devices is another area of our active research. The goal is to define an architecture to support arbitrary output formats with minimal changes to existing components. We are working on a runtime environment where support for new devices is transparent to the programmer and the content manager. Only the person responsible for the layout needs to take the capabilities of the output devices into account.

We presented a Web engineering methodology that focuses on XML-based Web development. We exploit the strengths of XML and its related technologies to achieve flexibility and design for change by strictly separating the content, the layout and the application logic information. Furthermore, parallel development supports a reduced time-to-market – a critical factor in most Web projects.

Many Web applications and services are developed in an ad-hoc manner today and the main reason is the lack of *practical*-oriented, easy-to-use methodologies, approaches and guidelines. Unlike many other development methodologies, XGuide is based on standards such as XML and XSL, thus enabling a rich set of tools to be used. In this context, XGuide attempts to combine the abstract concepts of a Web engineering methodology with the actual technology used for the implementation.

Acknowledgments

The authors would like to thank the Vienna International Festival and the Austrian Academy of Science for their financial support and cooperation.

References

1. Ginige, A., Murugesan, S.: Web Engineering: An Introduction. IEEE Multimedia, Special Issue on Web Engineering **8** (March 2001) pp. 14–18.
2. Sheppard, D.: An Introduction to Formal Specification with Z and VDM. The McGraw-Hill International Series in Software Engineering (1995)
3. Vienna International Festival: VIF homepage, http://www.festwochen.at/ (2001)
4. Kirda, E., Jazayeri, M., Kerer, C., Schranz, M.: Experiences in Engineering Flexible Web Services. IEEE Multimedia **8** (January - March 2001) pp. 58–65.
5. Kirda, E., Kerer, C.: MyXML: An XML based template engine for the generation of flexible Web content. In: Proceedings of Webnet 2000 Conference, San Antonio, Texas. (Nov 2000)
6. Kerer, C., Kirda, E.: Logic, Layout, and Content Separation in Web Engineering. In: Proceedings of the 9th World Wide Web Conference, 3rd Web Engineering Workshop, Amsterdam, The Netherlands. (May 2000)
7. Gamma, E., Helm, R., Johnson, R., Vlissides, J.: Design Patterns: Elements of Reusable Object-Oriented Software. Addison-Wesley, Reading Mass. and London (1995)
8. Austrian Academy of Science: AAS homepage, http://www.oeaw.ac.at/ (2001)

9. Kerer, C., Kirda, E., Jazayeri, M., Kurmanowytsch, R.: Building XML/XSL-Powered Web Sites: An Experience Report. In: Proceedings of the 25th International Computer Software and Applications Conference (COMPSAC), Chicago, IL, USA, IEEE Computer Society Press (October 2001)

10. Rosenfeld, L., Morville, P.: Information Architecture for the World Wide Web. O'Reilly & Associates (Feb. 1998)

11. Streitz, N.A.: Designing Hypermedia: A Collaborative Activity. Communications of the ACM **38** (August 1995)

12. Kerer, C., Kirda, E., Kurmanowytsch, R.: WebCUS: A generic Web-based Database Management Tool powered by XML. IEEE Internet Computing (to appear) (2002)

13. Barta, R., Schranz, M.W.: JESSICA – An Object-Oriented Hypermedia Publishing Processor. Computer Networks and ISDN Systems **30** (Apr. 1998) p. 281.

14. Mazzocchi, S.: The Cocoon Project Home Page, http://xml.apache.org/cocoon/ (1999-2001)

15. Webmacro: Webmacro Home Page, http://www.webmacro.org (2001)

16. Kerer, C.: XML, XSL and Web Applications Homepage, http://www.infosys.tuwien.ac.at/xml/ (2001)

17. Isakowitz, T., Stohr, E.A., Balasubramanian, P.: RMM : A Methodology for Structured Hypermedia Design. Communications of the ACM **38** (August 1995) pp. 34–44.

18. Teorey, T., Yang, D., Fry, J.: A logical Design Methodology for Relational Databases Using the Extended Entity-relationship Model. ACM Computing Surveys **18** (1986) pp. 197–222.

19. Isakowitz, T., Kamis, A., Koufaris, M.: The Extended RMM Methodology for Web Publishing, Working Paper IS98 -18, Center for Research on Information Systems (1998)

20. Schwabe, D., Rossi, G.: The Object-Oriented Hypermedia Design Model. Communications of the ACM **38** (August 1995) pp. 45–46.

21. Garzotto, F., Paolini, P., Schwabe, D.: HDM - A Model-based Approach to Hypermedia Application Design. ACM Transactions on Information Systems **11** (1993) pp. 1–26.

22. Bichler, M., Nusser, S.: Modular Design of Complex Web-Applications with W3DT. In: Proceedings of the 5th Workshops on Enabling Technologies: Infrastructure for Collaborative Enterprises (WETICE '96), IEEE Comput. Soc. Press., Los Alamitos, CA, USA (1996) pp. 328–333.

23. Scharl, A.: Reference Modeling of Commercial Web Information Systems Using the Extended World Wide Web Design Technique (eW3DT). In: Proceedings of the 31st Hawaii International Conference on System Sciences (HICSS-31), Hawaii, USA, IEEE Computer Society Press (1998)

24. Takahashi, K., Liang, E.: Analysis and Design of web-based Information Systems. In: Proceedings of the 6th International World Wide Web Conference, Santa Clara, CA, USA. (1997)

25. Ceri, S., Fraternali, P., Bongio, A.: Web Modeling Language (WebML): a modeling language for designing Web sites. In: Proceedings of the 9th World Wide Web Conference, Amsterdam, Netherlands. Volume 33 of Computer Networks., Elsevier Science B.V (2000) pp. 137–157.

26. Klapsing, R., Neumann, G.: Applying the Resource Description Framwork to Web Engineering (2000)

27. Lassila, O., Swick, R.R.: Resource Description Framework (RDF) Model and Syntax Specification. Technical report, World Wide Web Consortium (1999)

Process-Based Optimisation of Data Exchange for B2B Interaction

Christian Zirpins[1], Kevin Schütt[1], and Giacomo Piccinelli[2]

[1] Dept. of Computer Science (VSYS)
University of Hamburg
Hamburg, Germany
zirpins@informatik.uni-hamburg.de
[2] Hewlett-Packard Laboratories
Stoke Gifford Park
Bristol BS34 8QZ, UK
giacomo_piccinelli@hp.com

Abstract. The automation of business-to-business (B2B) interaction depends on considerable amounts of data being exchanged between companies. Moving from paper-based to EDI-like communication (Electronic Data Interchange) can be complex and expensive for a company. In many cases, the solution adopted is to use the electronic version of documents. Business documents are stored into files encoded in the native format of the applications from which they derive, and attached to electronic messages. In some parts of typical business transactions (e.g. negotiation) documents are often exchanged several times with only slight changes of content.The same files can be transferred a number of times between the participants, with minor structural modifications. In this paper, we propose a methodology for optimising the amount of data exchanged between business partners. The methodology focuses on automatic reconstruction of the process logic behind business interactions. Based on process information, document modifications are automatically detected and transmitted. The optimisation procedure is transparent to existing applications. A prototype is presented that explicitly targets RosettaNetcompliant systems.

1. Introduction

Efficiency is essential in business-to-business (B2B) interaction. Just-in-time models reduce costs and improve business agility. Very little room is left for delays. If a transaction with an end customer is delayed, the risk is to lose one sale. If a transaction with a business partner is delayed, the risk is to lose all the sales that depended on such transaction. Automatic processing and exchange of information become crucial [1, 3, 14].

Exchanging data in electronic format is a first step towards automation, but the format of the data can make the difference [6]. In order for data to drive business processes, it must be possible to convert them into automatically tractable information. For example, receiving an order form as a word-processor file in attachment to an electronic message can be preferable to receiving the printed form as a fax. Still, a human being probably needs to read the form and enter the appropriate

E. Gregori et al. (Eds.): Networking 2002 Workshops, LNCS 2376, pp. 118–126, 2002.

data in an order-management system. Solutions based on the EDI model (Electronic Data Interchange) effectively support end-to-end automation. The main issue with traditional EDI is that it requires complex and expensive changes to the IT and often even business structures of a company. Only big companies make use of EDI, and on a limited scale. Hybrid solutions are emerging (e.g. RosettaNet), based on the Internet and XML [2, 7, 13]. Still, data exchange is among the issues that most companies have to face; small and medium enterprises in particular.

Data format and data flow represent specific characteristics in the B2B world. Concerning the format in which information is encoded, information systems are partially victims of their success [1, 3]. The user-friendliness of most software packages allows users to concentrate on the informational content of artefacts like spreadsheets, documents, or pictures. Users are not immediately concerned by parameters like the size of a file. Concerns arise instead from the waiting time for the data transfer. Concerning the flows of business information, redundancy is a reality justified by business-level concerns. In the B2B space, the economic value of even individual transactions encourages extensive information exchanges. For example, a few words can change in one of the two hundred pages of a product specification. Almost certainly, the entire document needs to be exchanged multiple times between multiple parties, together with specific notification forms until mutual agreement.

The work presented in this paper is based on two observations. The first observation is that B2B interaction processes involve big volumes of data; and redundancy is a business requirement. Network bandwidth is a bottleneck for many companies. The second observation is that business interaction tends to follow regular patterns. Independently from the use of technology such as workflow management systems [9], the activity of business resources is strictly aligned with the operational logic of specific business processes. From the first observation, we derive the objective of our work. Taking into consideration requirements and peculiarities of B2B interaction, our goal is to optimise data exchange across organisational boundaries. From the second observation, we derive a specific line of investigation on how to address the problem. In this paper, we propose a methodology for automatic detection and management of redundancy in process-driven data exchange. The methodology involves the process logic behind B2B interaction, but the assumption is that information on process logic may not be explicitly available. The requirement for the solution is to be transparent with respect to the existing components of the business information system.

In section 2, we describe and motivate the need for a technique for the automatic inference of process logic from a flow of business messages. In section 3, we propose a methodology for the optimisation of data exchange based on process logic. In section 4, we describe a prototype infrastructure deriving from the methodology proposed. The prototype has been initially applied in the specific context of RosettaNet-compliant interaction. Future developments of the work and final considerations conclude the paper. A2B-ml

2. Dynamic Discovery of Interaction Logic

Business interaction represents the external manifestation of internal business processes [11]. On the one hand, interaction logic is regulated by specific business rules. The body of rules governing the information exchange shapes the interaction in accordance with specific patterns. On the other hand, different parts of a company use different processes. Different rules are applied in different contexts. For example, the notification process used by the finance department can be quite different from the one used by the sales department. Formal specifications and enforcement mechanisms can be quite different, if at all available.

In an ideal-case scenario, all the business processes of a company are captured in formal specifications, and enforced by some form of workflow management system. Initiatives such as the ISO 9000 certification programme are an attempt to move businesses in such direction. In practice, cost-effectiveness evaluations often discourage companies from formalisation and automation. Workflow management technology can be quite expensive, and the cost of the technology is just a fraction of the costs of process (re)engineering. Individual applications automate specific aspects of different business processes, and ad-hoc solutions are usually put in place to achieve coordination. The actual logic behind business interaction emerges from diversified reality of applications and procedures. Direct communication is one of the few points of convergence for interaction logic.

In practical terms, different data-mining techniques and information models can be applied to the communication channels of a company in order to derive information on interaction patterns [4, 8]. For the purpose of our work, we identified two major requirements. The first requirement is that the information model has to focus on individual business transactions. Given the messages related to a transaction, the model should represent the type of causal and temporal relations used in static business-process definitions. The second requirement is that the interaction process associated to a specific transaction has to be derived at the same time as the transaction unfolds. At a given time t, the model must provide a precise description of the history of the transaction up until t. The model can also provide indications of possible developments of the transaction. Considering the example in (Figure 1), at the end of time T2 the model must provide a representation of the first four interactions. An interaction node X2Y-m indicates that X has sent the message m to Y. The model can indicate that at a future time C might send a reply to A for m3, possibly indicating a degree of confidence. History is essential. Prediction is desirable.

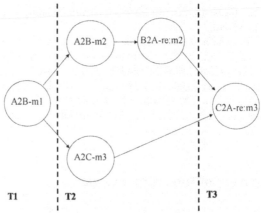

Fig. 1. Interaction process at time T3

The information model we propose revolves around three capabilities: aggregation, structuring, and prediction. The techniques adopted for the enforcement of the model exploit the peculiarities of B2B interaction. The structure of a typical business message is presented in (Figure 2) [13].

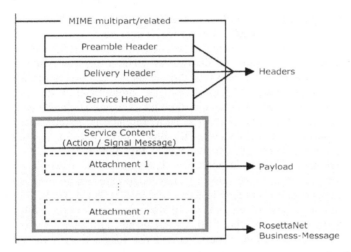

Fig. 2. An example of business message extracted from the RosettaNet Implementation Framework specification

2.1. Aggregation of the Data

Given the overall flow of business messages, the first level of aggregation is based on the set of business partners involved. One-to-one is the most common form of business interaction, but multiparty is also quite important. Information on the business partners involved in a message can be extracted from the headers of a message. The second level of aggregation is based on the business transaction to which the message is related. Different parts of a company can use different processes and systems. However, the concept of transaction as unifying element for business activities is well established at business level. Some form of identification for business transactions is always present in business communication [7, 13]. In order to route efficiently the message to the appropriate business entity, information are usually present also on the type of both the message and the transaction. For example, the message confirming the payment of an invoice contains indications on order number, invoice number, and the indication that the message relates to the financial aspect of a transaction.

From a technical perspective, the data needed for the level of aggregation we require are accessible from the headers and the content descriptor of messages. Such data are exposed in a structured format, and can be accessed quite efficiently. Other parts of the message can be subject to some form of application-level encryption. Headers and service description are usually sent in clear, or subject to transport-level encryption (e.g. SSL).

2.2. Process-Oriented Structuring of Data

As the messages pertaining to a specific transaction accumulate, the information model requires a specific structure to be imposed on the data. Causal and temporal dependencies are the key elements of the structure required. The goal is to reconstruct on -the-fly an a-posteriori description of the interaction process between the parties. New messages monotonically extend the process structure.

Temporal dependencies have been modelled using the basic concept of time intervals (Figure 1). Information on the time at which a message is sent or received can be derived from transport metadata. All the messages observed in a given time interval are consider part of parallel threads, unless causal dependencies are identified. Messages observed in distinct time intervals are assumed sequential. The sequential relation is transitive, and it can be represented in an intentional form. All the parties require a consistent view of the observation time for a message, hence standard solutions are p ut in place to avoid ambiguity on border cases.

The management of causal dependences is based on the message type and on specific knowledge on message flows. A knowledge base contains the general rules describing the dependencies at type level. In addition , instancespecific information is used. For example, a general rule can state that a payment message is followed by an acknowledgment of a given type. Still, there can be multiple payments within the scope of a specific transaction. Type-specific and instance-specific rules are used at the same time. From a technical perspective, the level of information exposed by the message structure allows a rich set of rules to be inserted in the knowledge base. In practice, message flows reflect the structural and efficiency-driven simplicity of business processes. For example, RosettaNet PIPs (Partner Interaction Processes) [13] provide correlation information for atomic interaction in cooperative processes.

2.3. Flow Prediction

Predictions on the future directions of a message flow provide useful information for optimisations. As it will become apparent in the following sections, cache management is particularly relevant to our work. The type of information we use derives in part from the same knowledge base used fo r causal correlation and in part from statistical information. Both types of information are represented in the form of process patterns. From an operational perspective, we apply pattern -matching techniques to process branches. The order of application go es from the most recent leaves towards the root. Matches from the static knowledge base have precedence over statistical information.

The objective of the prediction technique is to indicate likely developments for an interaction process. Multiple possibilities can be explored at the same time. The information on the actual development observed for the process contributes to the continuous refinement of the statistical component of the knowledge base used for the predictions.

3. Optimisation Technique

As a reference scenario, we can consider the interaction process behind a direct sale. The data concerning an order can be initially generated in the sales department of a company A. Among others, the same data can then be used by the finance department for the payment procedures. Similar distinctions can be made for the customer company B. Different applications can be involved at different stages of the process.

In practice, internal coordination at application level can be complex and expensive [3]. Implicit coordination is maintained at the level of internal business processes, and it becomes explicit at communication level. The interaction process between companies is independent from specific applications on any side. New applications can be added to the IT systems of a company. Existing applications can be consolidated into or replaced by a single application. The enforcement mechanisms for the interaction logic can also change within the company. Manual procedures can be embedded into specific applications, or enforced by workflow management technology. A formal specification of the interaction process is not always available.

The objective of the optimisation technique is to avoid sending information that is already available on the receiver side. The idea is for all the parties involved in an interaction process to maintain knowledge of the information already sent to and received from a business partner. New information can then be exchanged in the form of variations of the existing data. The optimisation works at channel level, and it is transparent to existing applications.

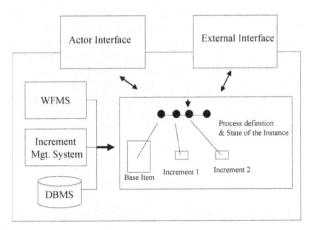

Fig. 3. Functional architecture for an interaction filter

Main aspects of the optimisation technique are data correlation and data transformation. For the correlation of the different data items in a message flow, we focused on the on-the-fly reconstruction of the interaction process between the parties. The technique adopted is the one described in the previous section. The historic part of an interaction process gives specific information on the data exchanged between the parties up to the current time. Such information can be immediately used in two ways. Knowing that a given version of a document was exchanged in the past (sent or received), sending the new version of the document can be reduced to sending the changes with respect to the older version. On the receiving end, it is possible to identify the old version of the document and recreate the new version by applying the changes. For example, company A may want to place an order for a product based on the specification document previously received from company B. From a business perspective company A may need to enclose a copy of the entire product specification with indications of the customisation required (e.g. colour or type of material). From a technical perspective, the new specification can be reconstructed by B based on the few changes made to the original document.

Concerning data transformation, different options are available for managing the incremental changes applied to documents [5, 12]. Format-aware algorithms can be devised for specific data formats and document structures. The approach we chose is to be both format and content independent. Given two related documents X an X∗, we apply standard comparison techniques to their binary representation. As a result, we obtain a compact representation of the transformation to apply to X in order to become an exact copy of X∗. The size of the description for the transformation is quite important. A complete discussion on the efficiency achievable in different circumstances can be found in the literature [12]. However, the main priority is not to lose any information. In the worst case, the strategy adopted is to consider X∗ itself as the most compact representation of its differences with respect to X. Hence, any problem in terms of data correlation can only result in efficiency loss. The correct information is always made available at application level.

From an engineering perspective, the optimisation technique requires the cooperation of all the parties involved in an interaction process [10]. The functional model in (Figure 3) describes the general architecture for the interaction filter that each party has to use. The outbound message flow is diverted towards the actor interface, from which the inbound messages are also received. Within the filter, messages are aggregated, data are stored, and data transformations are computed. The external interface of the filter enforces the actual inbound and outbound communication with business partners. New incoming data are stored, and transformations applied to existing data before sending them to the applications through the actor interface. New outgoing messages and transformations are sent to the specific recipient.

4. Prototype

The current version of the prototype focuses on the RosettaNet standard for business messaging. The metadata used for message aggregation are taken from the message-independent data model described in the RNIF 2.0 (RosettaNet Implementation Framework) [13]. The information for process reconstruction is taken from the specification of a number of PIPs. In accordance with the current state of RosettaNet specifications, the type of interaction modelled is one-to-one. In the case of multiparty interaction, extensions are required only to the content of the knowledge base of process reconstruction.

Each party is equipped with an interaction filter (Figure 3) that implements the techniques descried in the previous sections. The MIME-encoded stream of RosettaNet messages is captured at HTTP-server level. Filters are transparent to back-end applications. Messages are then processed within the filter in order to extract the process logic for the transaction. Possibly optimisations are computed for the data in the specific message, and the result is then transmitted to the business partner. A similar procedure is applied on the receiving end of the message. The implementation of the filters is substantially based on Java technology. In particular, most of the components have been developed as EJBs (Enterprise Java Beans) and are deployed on a J2EE-compliant application server. The main exception is the component in charge of the differential compression of data files, which is based on a C library. A web-based interface allows basic monitoring and management of the filter.

5. Future Work

Validation of the work against live business networks is the main objective in the immediate future. Simulations based on two business partners and artificially generated message flows show promising results, but a more comprehensive evaluation is required. Initial experiments have been conducted using copies of real RosettaNet messages taken from HP's procurement system. We are currently planning to deploy the system alongside the main RosettaNet backbone connecting a limited number of business partners. The focus is on the dynamics of real message flows.

In order to validate the methodology in a more general context, we also plan to extend the knowledge base and the message processing capabilities of the prototype to handle flows that are not in RosettaNet format.

6. Conclusions

The shift of business interaction towards electronic messaging is a source of technical challenges as well as business opportunities. As traditional business interaction processes are moved on-line, very little reengineering is applied to the process logic in order to incorporate the peculiarities of the new channel. On the contrary, electronic exchange of data seems to encourage redundancy at both content and structural level. The technique proposed in this paper aims at automatic reduction of redundancy in B2B message exchanges.

Exploiting metadata associated to business messages, the interaction process used for a specific transaction is automatically derived. Process information is then used in order to prevent at channel level duplicate data to be transmitted. The activity required for the optimisation is transparent to business applications.

References

1. AA.VV. "The third imperative of e-business. The role of collaboration networks in e-business" *CAP Ventures*, 2000.
2. Aankolekar A. and others "DAML-S: semantic markup for web services" Proc. Int. *Semantic Web Working Symposium* (SWWS), Stanford University, California, 2001.

3. Anderson L. "Emerging network technologies. Digital document workflow" *CAP Ventures*, 2000.
4. Agrawal R., Gunopulos D., and Leymann F. "Mining Process Models from Workflow Logs" Proc. 6th Int. Conference on Extending Database Technology (LNCS 1377), Valencia, Spain, 1998.
5. Black A.P. and Burris C.H. "A compact representation for file versions: A preliminary report." In *Proc. of the 5th International Conference on Data Engineering*, 1989, pp.321–329.
6. Bartelt A. and Lamersdorf W. "A multi-criteria taxonomy of business models in electronic commerce" Proc. *IFIP/ACM International Conference on Distributed Systems Platforms* (Middleware'01), LNCS 2232, Springer-Verlag, 2001, pp. 193-205.
7. ebXML, http://www.ebxml.org
8. Heinl P., Horn S., Jablonski S., Neeb J, Stein K., and Teschke M. "A comprehensive approach to flexibility in workflow management systems." In G. Georgakopoulos, W. Prinz, and A.L. Wolf, editors, Proc. *Work Activities Coordination and Collaboration* (WACC'99), San Francisco, California, 1999, pp.79-88.
9. Holligsworth D. "The workflow reference model" *Workflow Management Coalition* (WfMC), TC00-1003, 1994.
10. Neueschwander M. "Commercial peer-to-peer: alternative architectures for e-business networks" *The Burton Group*, 2001.
11. Piccinelli G. "Exposing Models of Behaviour of E-Service Components" Proc. *6th London Communication Symposium*, London, UK, 2001.
12. Reichenberger C. "Delta storage for arbitrary non-text files" In *Proc. of the 3rd International Workshop on Software Configuration Management*, Trondheim, Norway, 1991, pp.144–152.
13. RosettaNet, http://www.rosettanet.org
14. Seaborne A., Stammers E., Casati F., Piccinelli G., and Shan M. "A framework for business composition" In Proc. *W3C Workshop on Web Services*, San Jose, CA, USA, 2001.

Client–Side Profile Storage

Stéphanie Riché[1], Gavin Brebner[1], and Mickey Gittler[2]

[1] HP Laboratories Grenoble, 5 avenue Raymond Chanas, 38053 Grenoble Cedex 9, France.
[2] HP Laboratories Bristol, Filton Road, Stoke Gifford, Bristol BS34 8QZ, U.K.
{stephanie_riche, gavin_brebner, mickey_gittler}@hp.com

Abstract. As Internet users, we provide personal information to a growing number of service providers with little or no control over its usage, and no means to properly track subsequent access of this information. Some companies have recently made announcements proposing to handle our personal information centrally, offering the possibility of a unified repository, but raising additional trust and privacy concerns. We have chosen to investigate an alternative to this trend by storing personal information on client devices, increasing the possibility of putting the user in control of his or her personal information. A user can have multiple heterogeneous devices, so this generates a need for the distribution of profile data. We report on work that addresses this distribution issue using a coherency protocol well adapted to handle data migration, and are extending this protocol to incorporate trust-related features.

1   Introduction

In today's approach to personalization, the technology is created and applied by those with a strong vested interest in tailoring commercial offerings to end users. Typically, personalization solutions are sold to e-commerce sites wishing to present the user with the combination of goods that will generate the most profit for the provider. Although personalization may, in some cases, be aligned with the user's best interests, this is not the priority of the e-commerce provider. Personal details of end users are a valuable commercial resource, and are often bought and sold without the users knowledge or consent[1].

We believe that an alternative exists, where the primary objective is to supply a better customer experience at the interface to the virtual world that includes, but is not restricted to, the Internet and web services. Given this, we work to the following:

1. A vision where devices, in contact with an end user, have permanent access to information and knowledge on the user and the surrounding environment. This information is used to personalize interaction with the user, making interaction with the virtual world simpler, and more intuitive.

2. A view of privacy as a key enabler of this vision. The user has to trust the device / system to store personal data with respect for privacy and to restrict access to sensitive data by non-trusted 3rd parties.

In our work, we anticipate client-side profiles being used by existing "legacy" client-side applications via "bridges" between the profile and the existing preference data

E. Gregori et al. (Eds.): Networking 2002 Workshops, LNCS 2376, pp. 127–133, 2002.

store, and also by "enhanced" applications, e.g. for instant messaging, that will directly exploit the available middleware.

2   A User-Centered Architecture

A rich database of user preferences and context, a profile, is a key enabler for the personalization of local and remote services. However, many existing personalized solutions lack reliable and rich profiling data. Personal data can be used to customize remote web services, local services, applications, and man-machine interfaces [2]. We are motivated by the needs of devices working in ad hoc networks where reliable, high bandwidth, low latency access to remote servers may not always be possible[3]. We consider that in such scenarios, there is a clear advantage in storing data locally, as depicted in Figure 1, permitting personalized actions even if the device is not connected to a network. In addition, we are of the opinion that client-side storage of personal data offers the possibility of better privacy, increasing still further our motivation for working in this area.

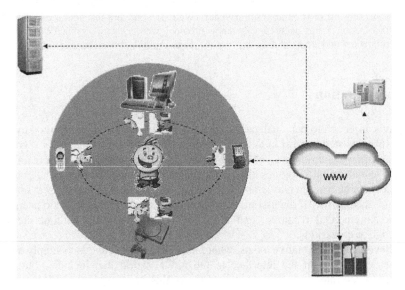

Figure 1: User Centered architecture. User devices form a cluster. Each device can store part of the profile represented by the jigsaw pieces. For instance, the mobile phone and the game console both have a copy of the same jigsaw piece. External systems can access profile information, but each exchange of data is potentially under user control.

We have identified three profile usage models by service providers that restrict personal information exposure. The first alternative is client side personalization as illustrated by our previous work on VAL[4], where the matching of services with user preferences is made on the user device, data is stored client side, and remote services receive only that client data that is necessary for a particular request. Client-side service execution[5] [6], the second alternative, consists of the importation of the service to the local device for client-side execution in a protected environment. Limited communication with other remote services or service components remains possible if appropriate. The third alternative is to provide a mechanism that can tell a remote service to use the local device as a source of user preference data, as opposed to the default centralized information store. The user's client device is therefore intimately involved in the personalization process, and be equipped with simple monitors and filters, e.g. that warn the user that personal data is being accessed.

We see the exchange of profile information with an external entity as being a process of negotiation, where the requester credentials have to match what the user is willing to disclose. P3P[7] is one well-known way to express privacy preferences, and control of the access to personal information can be achieved via mechanisms such as those described in IDSec[8].

3   System Overview

The design decisions made for our initial experiment reflect our main requirements:

- A unique profile per user, that keeps up to date with user-made changes on any machine identified as belonging to that user. Initial work makes the simplifying assumption of one user, multiple machines, with each machine being owned by only one person.
- Protection for user privacy.
- A system that does not preclude extension to the case where devices are intermittently connected, however the current implementation does not yet support connection failures.

3.1   Synchronization or Shared Storage?

Personal information management system approaches typically make use of a synchronization paradigm, like TrueSync[9]. This approach has the advantage of simplifying the management of communication; communication takes place relatively rarely and is explicitly triggered by a user event (e.g. putting a PDA in its cradle), and a failure of communication is not a major problem for the system (data is left unsynchronized).

However, the synchronized approach has a number of significant drawbacks:

- *Conflict resolution.* In a general purpose profile (as opposed to a limited data type system such as a contact database or calendar) conflict resolution has to be addressed. Reconciliation functions require an understanding of the data being synchronized; thus the profile store, and not just the applications, must be capable of understanding data types. In today's world, in the absence of reliable reconciliation models, the user is typically forced to intervene. We would prefer a solution where the profile store does not have to consider the semantics of the data, and where user intervention is rare.

- *Weak coupling of devices.* Synchronization is a weak coupling between copies of data. Data update occurs at specific synchronization time. We want a solution that offers better visibility of the current state of data copies.

For these reasons, we have chosen to start our investigations using an approach based on a shared storage paradigm. Our idea is to use the shared storage approach as much as we can, eventually combining this with synchronization approaches as a backup mechanism.

3.2   System Design

This section describes a current implementation of the initial version of a research vehicle. It is not the final solution proposed for this problem; we describe it merely to show the current status of the project. The distributed profile forms an object space, where a profile element is an object. The object space is distributed among hosts, i.e. user devices. Several copies of the same object can exist but only one copy is writable: the master copy. Object copies are scattered on different memory hosts. Before writing to an object, a host has to gain master rights. On each host, a middleware component handles requests coming from other hosts via the network to support the coherence protocol, manage the local cache, and handle requests coming from local applications.

The coherence protocol we have initially chosen is a write-invalidate protocol with conditional object-copy caching: before being authorized to cache a readable or a write-able object-copy a decision algorithm that takes into account the requester host capabilities and data sensitivity is performed. The current master of an object runs a policy engine to check if the requester host is allowed to cache the object; if caching is not authorized, the current master may return a readable value but with no cache rights.

There are several reasons to limit the presence of some objects on certain hosts. First, hosts are heterogeneous devices, so some of them have limited power or storage resources, a policy rule will determine whether an object should be cached. In some cases, it may be inappropriate or even infeasible to cache an object-copy and so object access would have to be achieved remotely, if at all. Secondly, devices are not equally trusted, for example, a mobile device is more prone to be stolen than a PC at workplace, or a PDA may not support the same security capabilities as a laptop equipped with a smart card reader peripheral. Hence, as a function of the level of data confidentiality, objects may or may not be stored on certain devices. This can be expressed by a policy rule as shown in Figure 2: "if data is confidential and security capabilities is medium or less grant no cache right". Finally, impeding the migration of an exclusive object-copy on a sporadically connected device is a way to provide higher data availability. In our current trial implementation, when the master of an exclusive object copy is disconnected from the system, there is no way of getting a guaranteed up-to-date object-copy.

Different decisions can be taken following the defined policy, the object sensitivity attributes, and device capabilities:

- Allow caching of object-copy and migration of the master authority (exclusive or shared master).
- Allow caching and migration of the shared-master authority only. The migration of the exclusive master authority is forbidden.
- Allow only caching of a shared object-copy, i.e. no migration of the master authority,
- No caching allowed for this object on this device. Access to a copy of this object will have to occur remotely each time the given host wishes to read or write the given object based on access authorization in effect.

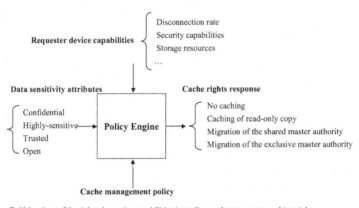

Figure 2: Access policy

We have implemented the system described here by extending Java RMI [10] client server model to a peer-to-peer model. When a device needs to get some object value it invokes a method on the local representative for that object –the object proxy- that may answer immediately, or collaborate with other representatives for the given object to get an accurate value. Our first implementation of a profile storage system reflects our main objectives as explained in previous sections, but we have designed a flexible (object oriented) architecture to get a modular structure. This permits us to replace components of the system (e.g. the coherence protocol) without major architectural changes. Indeed, a possible direction in the future is to associate specific coherence protocols to specific types of profile data and usage model. However, we currently work on migratory objects, and this implementation only supports the protocol described above. Access to a profile node by a client application is location transparent. The client application accesses profile node values by invoking a

JNDI[11] interface. This first design and implementation provides no provisions for disconnection. We intend to make experiments and get knowledge on profile data locality and access patterns. We expect to use this information to form hypotheses on how to address the problem of disconnection.

4   Experiments and Demos

In parallel to the development of our research vehicle, we are developing a test framework. This framework allows us to experiment with access patterns on the distributed system, and capture relevant information to characterize the research vehicle behavior. An access pattern description associates access sequences and machines on which are run the sequences. A test central module triggers access sequence execution on each machine. Experimentation results will be analyzed to determine the effect of altering cache migration policy, pro-active caching, or the usage of different coherence algorithms on performance, distribution of data and accuracy of accessed data (in the case of weakly coherent protocol use). In parallel, research will continue on the generation of realistic access patterns from existing preference usage, and extrapolation based on our vision.

In order to be able to demonstrate client side profiling technology, we have implemented some simple demo applications designed to allow us to use a distributed profile in what we hope are reasonably realistic scenarios. One of these basic applications is a profile manager that allows a user to observe and manage the profile. The user can browse the profile structure, add and remove profile nodes, and control the sensitivity of profile information by modifying a sensitivity level attribute combined with each profile node. By having a profile store able to store and spread information relative to user habits, user devices can offer personalized interfaces, ideally simplifying the access to information or services.

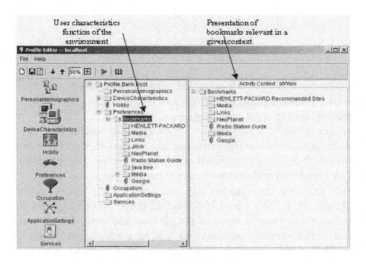

Figure 3: Profile manager

5   Conclusion

Consumer acceptance of personalized e-commerce and user interfaces depends on the availability of reliable, secure, and especially trusted profile information. We believe that a user's feeling of trust is related to a sense of ownership and control of profile data, and that a client-side approach is more appropriate for this.

We have made the choice to start with a strictly coherent model for distribution across multiple-clients, and have taken an approach to trust that restricts the permitted location of data items based on data sensitivity, device capabilities, and a user-specified trust policy. This allows us to deal with the heterogeneity of device capabilities. The implementation of this model uses a coherence protocol based on a write invalidate protocol with dynamic and conditional caching rights.

A research vehicle has been implemented in Java using RMI object level services such as persistence and communication management. Further research entails running experiments on this system to collect information on system behavior when accessed following identified patterns. We foresee that this will permit us to define mechanisms that may enable profile access in an intermittently connected infrastructure.

References

[1]   K.SCRIBBEN - Privacy@net An international comparative study of consumer privacy on the Internet- Consumers International. January 2001. ISBN 19023 91 31 68.

[2]   J. NEILSON - *Noncommand User Interfaces*- Communications of the ACM 36, 4 (April 1993), 83-99

[3]   G. BREBNER, Y.DURAND, S.PERRET. - *Position Paper - A Middleware Architecture for Personalized Communities of Devices*- The Fourth International Conference on Distributed Communities on the Web 3-5 April 2002, Sydney, Australia.

[4]   G. BREBNER - *Matching user needs to product offerings in a friendly way* - In Proceedings of the COST 254 workshop on Intelligent Terminals, Bordeaux, March 23-24, 2000. pp 75-78.

[5]   E. RAFFAELE, G. BREBNER - *Consumable Services* - HP Labs Technical Report HPL 2000-161 December 2000.

[6]   BELARC INC. http://www.belarc.com/

[7]   WORLD WIDE WEB CONSORTIUM – *Platform for Privacy Preferences Specification 1.0* - http://www.w3.org/TR/P3P/

[8]   INTERNET ENGINEERING TASK FORCE – *IDsec: Virtual Identity on the Internet*- http://www.ietf.org/internet-drafts/draft-zandbelt-idsec-00.txtSTARFISH

[9]   SOFTWARE, INC *TrueSync* - Http://www.starfish.com/solutions/solutions.html

[10]   SUN MICROSYSTEMS, INC – *Java Remote Method Invocation Specification*- Revision1.7, Java2SDK, Standard Edition, v1.3.0, December 1999.

[11]   SUN MICROSYSTEMS, INC- *Java Naming and Directory Services*- http://java.sun.com/products/jndi/

Boosting the Performance of Three-Tier Web Servers Deploying SMP Architecture

Pierfrancesco Foglia[1], Roberto Giorgi[2], and Cosimo Antonio Prete[1]

[1] Dipartimento di Ingegneria dell'Informazione, Universita' di Pisa , Via Diotisalvi 2,
56126 Pisa, Italy
{foglia,prete}@iet.unipi.it
[2] Dipartimento di Ingegneria dell'Informazione, Universita' di Siena, Via Roma 56,
53100 Siena, Italy
giorgi@unisi.it

Abstract. The focus of this paper is on analyzing the effectiveness of SMP (Symmetric Multi-Processor) architecture for implementing Three-Tier Web-Servers. In particular, we considered a workload based on the TPC-W benchmark to evaluate the system.
As the major bottleneck of this system is accessing memory through the shared bus, we analyzed what are the benefits of adopting several solutions aimed at boosting the global performance of the Web Server. Our aim is also to quantify the scalability of such a system and suggest solutions to achieve the desired processing power. The analysis starts from a reference case, and explores different architectural choices as for cache, scheduling algorithm, and coherence protocol in order to increase the number of processors possibly connected through the shared bus.
Our results show that such an SMP based server could be scaled (up to 20 processor) quite above the limits expected for this kind of architecture, if particular attention is used in solving problems related to process migration and coherence overhead.

Keywords: Multiprocessor, Shared-Memory, Coherence Protocol, Performance Evaluation, Process Migration.

1 Introduction

Web-Servers are often used as three-tier systems for E-Commerce applications [10], [21]. On tier one, the user machine runs a client program, typically a web-browser and/or Java applets; the client sends its requests to the server and receives the results to be shown to the user. Tier two includes a web-server that satisfies application specific requests, takes care of the task management and delivers standard services such as transaction management and activity log. Tier three contains data and their managers, typically DBMS systems, to furnish credit-card information, catalog information, shipping information, and user information. Tier two and three elements can be merged onto a single platform, or they can be distributed on several computers (clustered solution [26]). The single-computer solution has the advantage of a lower cost and a simplified management. The distributed solution has flexibility, scalability,

E. Gregori et al. (Eds.): Networking 2002 Workshops, LNCS 2376, pp. 134–146, 2002.

and fault-tolerance. In both cases, the systems can be based on multiprocessor architecture [29].

We considered servers based on shared-bus shared-memory multiprocessor systems. In this case, design issues are scalability and speedup, which may be limited by memory latency and bus traffic. Using cache memories can reduce both. Unfortunately, multiple cache memories introduce the coherence problem [22], [32]. The coherence protocol may have a great influence on the performance. Indeed, to guarantee cache coherence, the protocol needs a certain number of bus transactions (known as *coherence overhead*) that add up to the basic bus traffic of cache-based uni-processors. Thus, a design issue is also the minimization of the coherence overhead. A commonly adopted solution to coherence problem is the use of MESI protocol [31]. This protocol might not be performance effective for shared-bus architecture, and in particular when process migration is allowed to maintain the load balancing among processors. The scheduling algorithm plays an essential role in such systems in order to obtain load balancing. The consequent process migration generates *passive sharing*: private data blocks of a process can become resident in multiple caches. Coherence has to be enforced even on those data, but generates useless coherence overhead, which in turn may limit system performance [13], [23].

In our evaluation, the workloads have been setup as specified in the TPC-W benchmark [35]. TPC-W simulates the activities of a business-oriented transactional web server. Our aim is to quantify the scalability of such a system and suggest solutions to achieve the desired processing power. We considered the major bottlenecks of the memory system of this architecture. The results we obtained show that, by reducing the coherence overhead and the effects of process migration on the memory sub-system –acting on the affinity scheduler and the coherence protocol, - we could scale this kind of architecture up to 20 processors.

2 Related Work

Several important categories of general purpose and commercial applications, like web-server and database applications, motivated a realistic evaluation framework for shared memory multiprocessing research [29]. Several studies started to consider benchmarks like TPC-series (including DSS, OLTP, WEB-server benchmarks) representative of commercial workloads to evaluate the performance of multiprocessor servers [4], [5], [6], [19], [36].

Cain et al. [5] implemented TPC-W as a collection of Java servlets and present an architectural study detailing the memory system and branch predictor behavior of this workload. They used a 6-processor IBM RS/6000 S80 SMP machine, running AIX 4.33 operating system. They also evaluated the effectiveness of a coarse-grained multithreaded processor, simulated using SimOS, at increasing system throughput. However, their evaluation uses only no more than 6 processors. They found that the false sharing is almost absent in the user part as we also verified.

Other evaluations considered TPC-based benchmarks [4], [6], [19], [36] for database workloads. Most of the conclusions found in these evaluations present analogies with our evaluation. In particular, large caches, more associativity, and larger blocks help in the case of large working set. The major drawback of large caches is the increase coherence overhead. In our case, instead of considering single query execution, we run multiple concurrent query streams. We consider also configurations with more processors and with different solutions for the cache parameters, coherence protocol, and scheduling policies (in particular cache affinity).

3 Web-Server Setup and Workload Definition

The typical software architecture of Web-Servers for e-commerce applications is based on a three-tiered model: tier one is constituted by the e-commerce clients (typically a Web Browser), which access the server by the Internet; tier two is constituted by the Web Server, a transaction management process and the application processes (which also provide accounting and auditing); tier three is constituted by data and their managers [10].

The activity of e-commerce systems typically involves data scan (to access product list, product features, credit card information, shipping information), update (to update customer status and activity status) and transactions (for instance to buy products, make payments). These activities involve the interaction between tiers according to the following model: the user (i.e. the client, tier one) sends its requests by means of a Web-Browser. A process (a daemon, which constitutes part of the tier two) waits for the user request, and sends the request to a child application process. Then, the daemon waits for new requests, while the child process handles the incoming request. This activity may require accessing html pages and/or invocating service processes at tier three.

As for workloads, we implemented a software architecture based on the following freeware components. The system front-end (part of the tier two) includes an Apache Server [24] (which is currently the most popular HTTP server [9]) Client requests that involve database activities are forwarded, via CGI interface, to the Data-Base Management System (DBMS) PostgreSQL [38]. PostgreSQL is constituted by a front-end (also part of the tier two), which intercepts requests and by a backend (part of the tier three), which executes the queries.

We configured the Apache server, so that it spawns a minimum of 8 idle processes, a maximum of 40 idle processes. The number of requests that a child can process before dying is limited to 100. PostgreSQL utilizes shared memory to cache frequently accessed data, indices, and locking structures [36].

We considered general cases of workloads not depending on the specific system. To this end, we setup the experiments as described in the TPC-W benchmark [35], which specifies how to simulate the activities of a business-oriented transactional web server and exercises the breadth of system components. The application portrayed by the benchmark is a retail store with customer browse-and-order scenario.

In a typical situation, application and management processes can require the support of different system commands and ordinary applications. To this end, Unix utilities (`ls`, `awk`, `cp`, `gzip`, and `rm`) have been considered in our workload setup. These utilities [14] are important because: i) they increase the effects of process migration as discussed in detail in the Section 5; ii) they may interfere with the shared data and code footprint of the other applications.

4 Methodology and Hardware System Configuration

The methodology used in our performance evaluation is based both on trace-driven simulation [30], [37] and on the simulation of the three kernel activities that most affect performance: *system calls*, *process scheduling*, and *virtual-to-physical memory address translation*. We used the Trace Factory environment [12]. The approach used in this environment is to produce a process trace (a sequence of user memory references, system-call positions and synchronization events in case of multi-process programs) for each process belonging to the workload by means of a modified version of Tangolite [15]. By using this tool, we have also traced the system calls of a Linux kernel 2.2.13 [20].

Process scheduling is modeled by dynamically assigning a ready process to a processor. The process scheduling is driven by time-slice for uniprocess applications, whilst it is driven by time-slice and synchronization events for multi-process applications. Virtual-to-physical memory address translation is modeled by mapping sequential virtual pages into non-sequential physical pages.

By using this methodology, the TPC-W benchmark specification, and the freeware components, we generated our target workload. We traced the execution of the workload programs handling of 100 web interactions in a specific time interval corresponding to 130 millions of references.

Table 1. Statistics of source traces for some UNIX utilities, in case of 32-byte block size

Application	Distinct blocks	Code (%)	Data (%)	Data Write (%)
AWK	9876	76.23	23.77	8.83
CP	5432	77.21	22.79	8.88
GZIP	7123	82.32	17.68	2.77
RM	2655	86.18	13.82	2.11
LS -AR	5860	80.23	19.77	5.79

Table 2. Statistics of multi-process application source, in case of 32-byte block size

Number of processes	Distinct Blocks	Code (%)	Data (%)		Shared blocks	Shared data (%)	
			Access	Write		Access	Write
8 (PostgreSQL)	24141	71.94	28.06	9.89	5838	2.70	0.79
13 (Apache)	34311	73.84	26.16	6.99	1105	1.84	0.60

The target workload is constituted of 13 processes spawned by the Apache daemon, 8 by PostgreSQL, and 5 Unix utilities. Table 1 (for the uniprocess applications) and Table 2 (for the multi-process ones) contain some statistics of the traces used to generate the workloads for a 32-byte block size. Table 3 summarizes the statistics of the resulting workloads.

Table 3. Statistics of target workload, in case of 32-byte block size

Number of processes	Distinct blocks	Code (%)	Data (%)		Shared blocks	Shared data (%)	
			Access	Write		Accesses	Write
26	112183	75.49	17.12	7.39	6101	1.68	0.54

The simulator of Trace Factory characterizes a shared-bus multiprocessor in terms of CPU, cache, and bus parameters. The CPU parameters are the number of clock cycles for a read/write CPU operation. The simulated processors are MIPS-R10000 ones; paging relays on 4-Kbyte page size. The cache parameters are cache size, block size, and associativity. The caches are non-blocking ones using a LRU (Least Recently Used) block replacement policy. We assumed a constant cache access time by the processor for all configurations.

Each processor uses a write buffer thus implementing a relaxed model of memory consistency, in particular the processor consistency model [1], [17]. Finally, the bus parameters are the number of CPU clock cycles for each kind of transaction: write, invalidation, update-block, memory-to-cache read-block, cache-to-cache read-block, memory-to-cache read-and-invalidate-block, and cache-to-cache read-and-invalidate-block. The bus supports transaction splitting.

We considered in our analysis three coherence protocols: MESI [31], AMSD [8], [28] and PSCR [13], which we describe here briefly. Although MESI is considered the industry standard, we added for comparison other two coherence protocols that perform better than MESI, in order to widen our view of possible solutions that could be combined to enhance the performance of a TPC-W workload.

Besides classical MESI protocol states, our implementation of MESI [25] uses the following bus transactions: *read-block* (to fetch a block), *read-and-invalidate-block* (to fetch a block and invalidate any copies in other caches), *invalidate* (to invalidate any copies in other caches), and *update-block* (to write back dirty copies when they need to be destroyed for replacement). The invalidation transaction used to obtain coherency has, as a drawback, the need to reload a certain copy, if a remote processor uses again that copy, thus generating a miss (*Invalidation Miss*). Therefore, MESI coherence overhead (that is the transactions needed to enforce coherence) is due both to *Invalidate Transactions* and *Invalidation Misses*. SMP architectures based on MESI have been extensively analyzed in the case of scientific, engineering, DBMS and web workloads.

AMSD is designed for Migratory Sharing, which is a kind of true sharing that is characterized by the exclusive use of data by a certain processor for a long time interval. The protocol identifies migratory-shared data dynamically, in order to reduce the cost of moving them. Although designed for migratory sharing, AMSD may have some beneficial effects also on passive sharing. AMSD coherence overhead is due to invalidate transactions and invalidation misses.

PSCR (Passive Shared Copy Removal) adopts a selective invalidation scheme for the private data, and uses the *write-update* scheme for the shared data. A cached copy belonging to a process private area is invalidated locally as soon as another processor fetches the same. This technique eliminates passive sharing overhead. Invalidate transactions are eliminated and coherence overhead is due to write transactions.

The most significant metric for our evaluation of the machine is the GSP (Global System Power) [3], [12], which includes the combined effects of processor architecture and memory hierarchy. We recall the definition GSP:

$$GSP = \Sigma U_{cpu}$$

where

$$U_{cpu} = (T_{cpu} - T_{delay})/T_{cpu}$$

T_{cpu} is the time needed to execute the workload, and T_{delay} is the total CPU delay time due to memory operation.

We used the miss rate to identify the main sources of memory overhead. The simulator classifies also the coherence overhead by analyzing the access patterns to shared data (true [33], false [33], e passive sharing [2], [23]). In particular, it classifies coherence transactions (write or invalidate) and misses due to a previous invalidate transaction (invalidation misses). The type of access pattern to the cache block determines the type of the coherence transaction or invalidation-miss. The classification [11] is based on an existing algorithm [18], extended to the case of passive sharing, finite size caches, and process migration.

Table 4. Timing parameters for the multiprocessor simulator (in clock cycles)

Class	Parameter	Timing			
		32 bytes	64 bytes	128 bytes	256 bytes
CPU	Read/Write operation	2	2	2	2
Bus	Invalidate transaction	5	5	5	5
	Write transaction	5	5	5	5
	Memory-to-cache read-block transaction	68	72	80	96
	Memory-to-cache read-and-invalidate-block transaction	68	72	80	96
	Cache-to-cache read-block transaction	12	16	24	40
	Cache-to-cache read-and-invalidate-block transaction	12	16	24	40
	Update-block transaction	8	12	20	36

5   Simulation Results

Our aim in this section is to show our quantitative data on solutions that could enhance the performance of a shared-bus multiprocessor utilized to as a three-tier web-server. For this reason, we first considered a reference case study and we varied the parameters that influence mostly the performance. Thus, we show data from our simulations showing how much system power we can get (in terms of GSP), and which are the hardware/software choices that we could adopt in order to build a more powerful machines.

Let us consider the Web-Server workload running on a single multiprocessor as reference case study. We considered a 128-bit shared bus. For the scheduling policy two solutions have been analyzed: random and cache-affinity [34]; scheduler time-slice is equivalent to about 200,000 references. The bus timings relative to these case studies are reported in Table 4.

The GSP graph (Figure 1) shows, as expected, that we can obtain a more powerful machine by increasing the cache size and associativity. The larger are the caches, the more scalable is the machine.

In the following we shall use this definition of scalability: we say that a multiprocessor system is scalable up to N processor, if N is the number of processors that causes the GSP to drop by more than 0.5 when the when switching between a N-to (N+1)-processor machine (this definition is equivalent to the definition of 'critical point' in [13]) By using this definition, the machine we are considering is scalable up to 4 processors in the case of 128-Kbyte direct access cache, and up to 9 processors in the case of 2-Mbyte 4-way caches. The higher scalability is essentially due to lower bus utilization when adopting larger caches (Figure 1). As the cache size and associativity increase, the reduction of bus traffic is due to the lower miss.

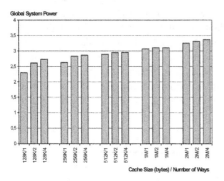

Fig. 1. Global System Power (GSP) versus cache size (128 Kbytes, 256 Kbytes, 512 Kbytes, 1 Mbytes, 2 Mbytes) and number of ways (1, 2, 4), for a 4-processor system, random scheduling policy, and 32-byte block size. The sum of processor utilizations (GSP) switches from 2.2 to 3.4 as the cache size and associativity increases

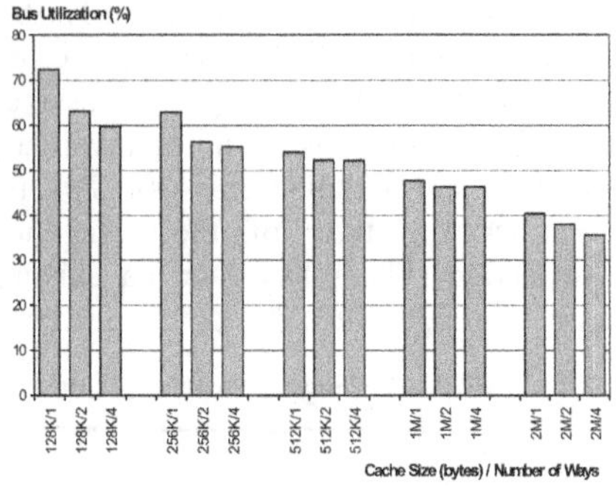

Fig. 2. Bus Utilization (in percentage) versus cache size (128 Kbytes, 256 Kbytes, 512 Kbytes, 1 Mbytes, 2 Mbytes) and number of ways (1, 2, 4), for a 4-processor system, random scheduling policy, and 32-byte block size. The less the bus utilization, the more system power can be gained by adding new processors to the system

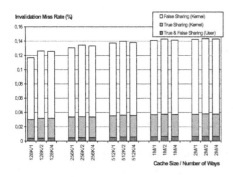

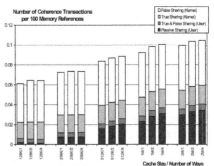

Fig. 3. Breakdown of invalidation miss rate versus cache size (128 Kbytes, 256 Kbytes, 512 Kbytes, 1 Mbytes, 2 Mbytes) and number of ways (1, 2, 4), for a 4-processor system, random scheduling policy, and 32-byte block size. Invalidation misses are basically due to the kernel, and false sharing is the main source of those misses. They slightly increase with cache size

Fig. 4. Number of coherence transactions (*invalidate transactions*) versus cache size (same conditions as previous figure). Passive sharing overhead increases with cache and associativity, becoming significant in case of cache sizes larger than 256 Kbytes. Passive sharing increases due to a larger average lifetime for a cached copy when the cache size is increased

Coherence overhead increases with the cache size and associativity (Figures 3 and 4), and it weighs, in percentage, more and more on the performance. Indeed, the coherence overhead, in terms of bus utilization, changes from about 5%, in the case of 128-Kbyte direct access cache, up to 20% in the case of 2-Mbyte 4-way set associative cache. In this case, most of the coherence overhead (Figure 3) is due to false sharing generated in the kernel. True sharing is present in the kernel, whilst it is limited in the application user area. Passive sharing increases as the cache capacity is increased (Figure 4), since average lifetime of cached copies increases as well. This also shows that even a low sharing may have an important impact on the global performance: this will be more clear as the number of processors is scaled up, as we shall discus in the following paragraph. The importance of coherence traffic on performance as the cache size increases has been also highlighted in previous studies [7], [19].

As a second step, we compared the 4- and the 8-processor case. We discuss briefly the results: we found that the 8-processor configuration is near the scalability limit of the machine. In fact, the bus utilization in the 8-processor case is very high (more than 90%). Despite the fact that the GSP increases, due to higher number of processors, each processor has a lower utilization. This is essentially due to the increased bus latency.

By acting only on cache size and associativity, however, we cannot significantly increase the scalability of the machine. Thus we considered other optimizations. In particular, we can increase the performance of the 8-processor system by intervening: i) on the classical misses (sum of cold, conflict and capacity misses), ii) on the kernel false sharing, iii) by limiting the effects of process migration.

We can intervene on the point i) and ii) by modifying the block size. As for the effects on performance caused by the process migration, we can modify both the scheduling policy and the coherence protocol.

As the block size increases, we observed lower bus utilization in all the cache configurations, and a higher GSP. This is due to the decrease of miss rate, in particular due to the reduction of "classical" misses. Anyway, increasing block size become soon not so effective for block sizes above 128 bytes. In fact we should consider both higher transaction cost and coherence overhead. As we increase the block size from 32 bytes to 256 bytes, in case of 2-way caches and 2-Mbyte cache sizes, GSP increases from 5.6 to 7, and bus utilization decreases from 71% to 43%. This allows us to increase architecture scalability up to 18 processors, corresponding to a 14.5 GSP value.

This technique has the disadvantage of a higher cost to transfer the block on the bus. Another drawback is false sharing overhead, which varies with the block size. Moreover, intervening on the block size connects system performance to the program locality more tightly. Considering that program locality may vary, it is not convenient to use too much larger block sizes. Therefore, we considered in the following the results related to a system having a 128-byte block size.

As a further step, we analyzed the system when the kernel adopts a scheduling policy based on cache affinity [27]. Cache affinity produces 'other miss' (i.e. classical misses) rate reduction (Figure 6), and in particular the reduction of context-switch miss portion. Also, the coherence transactions are lower (Figure 7), due to the reduction of number of passive sharing related transactions. As for invalidation misses (not reported in figure), there is no substantial difference compared to the base scheduling policy case.

In the case of 2-Mbyte, 2-way set associative cache, we observed a miss rate reduction, which causes a GSP increase from 6.9 to 7.4 (Figure 5) and a bus utilization change from 47% to 32%. This situation would allow us to extend the number of system processors up to 14, with a related increase of GSP equal to 11.3. Cache affinity reduces context switch misses, while still tolerating process migration for load balance.

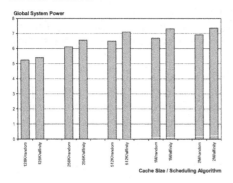

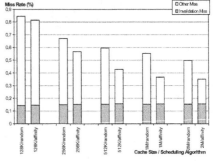

Fig. 5. Global System Power versus cache size (128 Kbytes, 256 Kbytes, 512 Kbytes, 1 Mbytes, 2 Mbytes) and scheduling policy (random, affinity), in case of 8 processors, 128-byte block size, and two-way set associative cache

Fig. 6. Breakdown of miss rate versus cache size (128 Kbytes, 256 Kbytes, 512 Kbytes, 1 Mbytes, 2 Mbytes) and scheduling policy (random, affinity), in case of 8 processors, 128-byte block size, and two-way set associative cache. Miss reduction due to cache affinity technique is evident

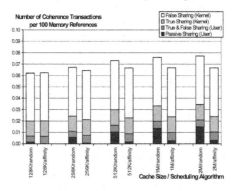

Fig. 7. Number of coherence transactions *(invalidate transactions)* versus cache size (128 Kbytes, 256 Kbytes, 512 Kbytes, 1 Mbytes, 2 Mbytes) and scheduling policy (random, affinity), in case of 8 processors, 128-byte block size, and two-way set associative cache. Cache affinity scheduling reduces only passive sharing component, while the other components remain constant

Based on our experiments, the best way to further increase the system scalability is to reduce the coherence overhead by adopting a special coherence protocol, as we show below.

We considered two additional coherence protocols that reduce or eliminate passive sharing. The first is based on Write-Update technique and the second on a Write-Invalidate technique. They are respectively, PSCR [13] and AMSD (Adaptive Migratory Sharing Detection) [8], [28]. We described briefly these protocols in Section 2.

As shown (Figure 8), as the number of processors increases, the performance difference among protocols becomes more evident. In particular, the choice of MESI protocol appears the most penalizing. This is due to the non-selective invalidation technique of MESI.

AMSD has beneficial effects on passive sharing although it does not eliminate it completely. The benefits on passive sharing are due mainly to a decrease of coherence transactions (Figure 11). The reduction of coherence transaction number is due to the behavior of AMSD on shared copies. When AMSD detects a block that has to be treated exclusively for a long time interval, it invalidates the copy locally during the handling of a remote miss, thus avoiding a necessary consequent bus transaction.

PSCR is based on the update of effectively shared copies, thus minimizing invalidation misses. By using the write-update technique, the number of coherence transactions results higher compared to other protocols (Figure 11). On the other side, the reduction of total number of misses produces a more consistent bus utilization decrease than with the other protocols. Moreover, the cost of the coherence overhead is somewhat limited by the lower cost of the coherence maintaining write transactions (Table 4). Finally, the write transaction cost is independent from the block size. More generally, in non-technical workloads has been noticed that there is a scarce reuse of data and there are large working sets [16]. This will give further advantage to such solutions that are based on write-update techniques, like PSCR.

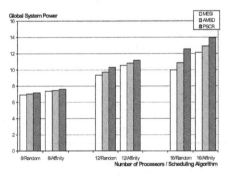 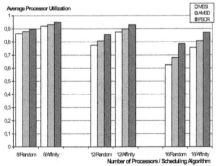

Fig. 8. Global System Power versus number of processors (8, 12, 16) and scheduling algorithm (random, affinity). Cache is a 2-way set associative with 128-byte block size, and 2-Mbyte size

Fig. 9. Average Processor Utilization versus number of processors (8, 12, 16) and scheduling algorithm (random, affinity). Cache is a 2-way set associative with 128-byte block size, and 2-Mbyte size

Let us now analyze the scalability offered by the various protocols. As observed previously, the system is in saturation when the GSP does not increase of a minimal quantity as the number of processors is increased. In our experiments we calculated that this minimal quantity is equal to a GSP of 0.5 for each added processor. As a rule of thumb, this corresponds to a GSP increase of 2 when switching among different configurations in Figure 8. Thus, as shown in Figure 8, we can state that MESI (in case of random scheduling policy) is already near the saturation threshold for a 12-processor configuration. AMSD performs slightly better since the saturation is reached for some number of processors between 12 and 16, for both scheduling policies. In the shown configurations, PSCR is never in saturation. This justifies its adoption when higher performance (GSP) is needed.

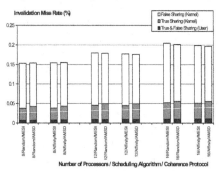 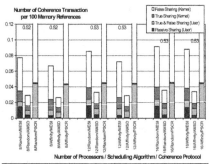

Fig. 10. Invalidation Miss Rate versus number of processor (8, 12, 16) and scheduling algorithm (random, affinity). The cache has a 128-byte block size, 2-Mbyte size, and it is 2-way set associative

Fig. 11. Miss Rate versus number of processor (8, 12, 16) and scheduling algorithm (random, affinity). The cache has 128-byte block size, 2Mbyte size, and it is 2-way set associative

When the performance is pushed to the limits (and consequently the system works near saturation) the designer should take advantage of more optimization techniques like smart coherence protocols. The combination of all analyzed techniques (adequate block size, cache affinity, and PSCR) allows us to push system scalability up to 20 processors with a corresponding GSP of about 16.

In Table 5, we report a summary of the configuration that we tested, and how effective the solutions were, in increasing the scalability of a machine.

Table 5. Scalability that can be reached on our shared-bus multiprocessor

SYSTEM PARAMETER	NUMBER OF PROCESSORS	4	8	8	8	16
	CACHE CAPACITY (BYTES)	2M	2M	2M	2M	2M
	CACHE BLOCK SIZE (BYTES)	32	32	256	128	128
	SCHEDULING POLICY	RANDOM	RANDOM	RANDOM	AFFINITY	AFFINITY
	COHERENCE PROTOCOL	MESI	MESI	MESI	MESI	PSCR
PERFORMANCE	GSP	3.3	5.6	7	7.4	14
	BUS UTILIZATION	38%	71%	43%	32%	55%
SCALABILITY	MAX NUMBER OF PROCESSORS	9	9	18	14	20
	CORRESPONDING (ESTIMATED) GSP	~6	~6	~14	~11	~16

6 Conclusions

In this paper we analyzed a three-tier Web-Server used for e-commerce applications (TPC-W benchmark), based on a shared-bus multiprocessors SMP architecture. We analyzed what are the benefits of adopting several solutions aimed at reducing the major bottlenecks in this kind of architecture. In particular, we have analyzed in detail the memory subsystem, whose performance depends heavily on the miss rate and traffic on the shared-bus. We tried to quantify the scalability of such a system and suggested solutions to achieve the desired processing power.

As the number of processors increases, the goal of reducing coherence overhead and bus traffic becomes essential, in order to achieve good performance. When designing Web-Servers for e-commerce applications as well as other processing power demanding applications, the first goal is the reduction of classical misses. This can be achieved by using techniques that enhance the locality of the program, and other traditional solutions. Then, kernel designers should take into account false sharing. False sharing misses have to be reduced by using kernel data restructuring techniques. This could be easily achieved, since the kernel is a well-know part of the system at design time.

The use of cache affinity scheduling produces also good results for reducing classical misses and passive sharing overhead, even if its applicability is somewhat limited by the load conditions (and in particular, by the difference between number of processors and number of processes). As for architectural aspects, in the case of bus-based multiprocessors, MESI protocol is sufficient for configurations having a not so high number of processors (8 in our experiments). If a higher computing power is needed, the increase of number of processors really produces benefits, if other miss reduction techniques are considered. Coherence protocols like PSCR and AMSD, produce performance benefits. In particular PSCR eliminates coherence overhead due to passive sharing, without generating useless invalidation misses, and thus achieve better results. The adoption of PSCR allows us to extend the multiprocessor scalability at least up to 20 processors when we choose also cache affinity scheduling for the experiments that we carried out.

References

1. S.V. Adve and K. Gharachorloo: Shared Memory Consistency Models: A Tutorial. IEEE Computer, pp. 66-76, December 1996.
2. A. Agarwal and A. Gupta: Memory Reference Characteristics of Multiprocessor Applications under Mach. Proc. ACM Sigmetrics, Santa Fe, NM, pp. 215-225, May 1988.
3. J.K. Archibald and J. L. Baer: Cache Coherence Protocols: Evaluation Using a Multiprocessor Simulation Model. ACM Transactions On Computer Systems, vol. 4, pp. 273-298, April 1986.
4. L.A. Barroso, K. Gharachorloo, and E. Bugnion: Memory System Characterization of Commercial Workloads. Proc. 25th Int. Sympo. on Computer Architecture, Barcelona, Spain, pp. 3-14, June 1998.
5. T. Cain, R. Rajwar, M. Marden, and M. Lipasti: An Architectural Characterization of Java TPC-W. 7th International Symposium of High-Performance Computer Architecture, pp. 229-240, January 2001.
6. Q. Cao, J. Torrellas, et al.: Detailed characterization of a quad Pentium Pro server running TPC-D. International Conference on Computer Design, pp.108-115, October 1999.
7. J. Chapin, et al.: Memory System Performance of UNIX on CC-NUMA Multiprocessors. ACM Sigmetrics Conf. on Measurement and Modeling of Computer Systems, pp. 1-13, May 1995.

8. A. L. Cox and R.J. Fowler: Adaptive Cache Coherency for Detecting Migratory Shared Data. Proc. of 20th International Symposium on Computer Architecture, San Diego, CA, pp. 98-108, May 1993.
9. J. Edwards: The changing Face of Freeware. IEEE Computer, vol. 31, no. 10, pp. 11-13, October 1998.
10. J. Edwards: 3-Tier Client/Server At Work. Wiley Computer Publishing, New York, NY, 1999.
11. P. Foglia: An Algorithm for the Classification of Coherence Related Overhead in Shared-Bus Shared-Memory Multiprocessors. IEEE TCCA Newsletter, pp. 53-58, January 2001.
12. R. Giorgi, C.A. Prete et al.: Trace Factory: a Workload Generation Environment for Trace-Driven Simulation of Shared-Bus Multiprocessor. IEEE Concurrency, vol. 5, no. 4, pp. 54-68, October 1997.
13. R. Giorgi and C.A. Prete: PSCR: A Coherence Protocol for Eliminating Passive Sharing in Shared-Bus Shared-Memory Multiprocessors. IEEE Transactions on Parallel and Distributed Systems, pp. 742-763, vol. 10, no. 7, July 1999.
14. GNU Free Software Foundation. http://www.gnu.org/software/
15. S.R. Goldschmidt and J.L. Hennessy: The Accuracy of Trace-Driven Simulations of Multiprocessors. Sigmetrics Conf. on Measurement and Modeling of Computer Systems, CA, pp. 146-157, May 1993.
16. A. M. Griffazzi Maynard et al.: Contrasting characteristics and cache performance of technical and multi-user commercial workloads. Proc. of the 6th International Conference on Architectural Support for Programming Languages and Operating Systems, pp. 158-170, October 1994.
17. J. Hennessy and D.A. Patterson: Computer Architecture: a Quantitative Approach, 2nd edition. Morgan Kaufmann Publishers, San Francisco, CA, 1996.
18. R.L. Hyde and B.D. Fleisch: An Analysis of Degenerate Sharing and False Coherence. Journal of Parallel and Distributed Computing, vol. 34, no. 2, pp. 183-195, May 1996.
19. K. Keeton, D. Patterson et al.: Performance characterization of a quad Pentium Pro SMP using OLTP workloads. Proc. of the 25th International Symposium on Computer Architecture, pp. 15-26, June 1998.
20. Linux on SGI/MIPS, http://oss.sgi.com/mips/
21. V. Milutinovic: Infrastructure for Electronic Business on the Internet. Kluwer Publishers, 2001.
22. C.A. Prete: RST Cache Memory Design for a Tightly Coupled Multiprocessor System. *IEEE Micro*, vol. 11, no. 2, pp. 16-19, 40-52, April 1991.
23. C.A. Prete, G. Prina, R. Giorgi, and L. Ricciardi,: Some Considerations About Passive Sharing in Shared-Memory Multiprocessors. IEEE TCCA Newsletter, pp. 34-40, March 1997.
24. D. Robinson: APACHE – An HTTP Server. Reference Manual, 1995, http://www.apache.org
25. T. Shanley and Mindshare Inc.; Pentium Pro and Pentium II System Architecture, 2nd edition. Addison Wesley, Reading, MA, 1999.
26. R. Short, R. Gamache, et al.: Windows NT Clusters for Availability and Scalability. In Proceedings of the 42nd IEEE International Computer Conference, pp. 8-13, San Jose, CA February 1997.
27. M.S. Squillante and D.E. Lazowska: Using Processor-Cache Affinity Information in Shared-Memory Multiprocessor Scheduling. IEEE Transactions on Parallel and Distributed Systems, vol. 4, no. 2, pp. 131-143, February 1993.
28. P. Stenström, M. Brorsson, and L. Sandberg: An Adaptive Cache Coherence Protocol Optimized for Migratory Sharing. 20th Int. Symposium on Computer Architecture, San Diego, CA, May 1993.
29. P. Stenström, E. Hagersten, D.J. Li, M. Martonosi, and M. Venugopal. Trends in Shared Memory Multiprocessing. IEEE Computer, vol. 30, no. 12 pp. 44-50, December 1997.
30. C.B. Stunkel, B. Janssens, and W.K. Fuchs: Address Tracing for Parallel Machines. IEEE Computer, vol. 24, no. 1, pp. 31-45, January 1991.
31. P. Sweazey and A.J. Smith: A Class of Compatible Cache Consistency Protocols and Their Support by the IEEE Futurebus. Proc. of the 13th Intnl. Symph, on Computer Architecture, pp. 414-423, June 1986.
32. M. Tomasevic and V. Milutinovic: The Cache Coherence Problem in Shared-Memory Multiprocessors – Hardware Solutions. IEEE Computer Society Press, Los Alamitos, CA, April 1993.
33. J. Torrellas, M.S. Lam, and J.L. Hennessy: False Sharing and Spatial Locality in Multiprocessor Caches. IEEE Transactions on Computer, vol. 43, no. 6, pp. 651-663, June 1994.
34. J. Torrellas et al.: Evaluating the Performance of Cache-Affinity Scheduling in Shared-Memory Multiprocessors. Journal of Parallel and Distributed Computing, vol. 24, no. 2, pp. 139-151, Feb. 1995.
35. TPC BENCHMARK W (Web Commerce) Specification, version 1.0.1. Transaction Processing Performance Council, February 2000.
36. P. Trancoso, et. al.: Memory Performance of DSS Commercial Workloads in Shared-Memory Multiprocessors. 3rd Int. Symp. on High Perf. Computer Architecture, pp. 250-260, February 1997.
37. R.A. Uhlig and T.N. Mudge: Trace-Driven memory simulation: a survey. ACM Computing Surveys, pp. 128-170, June 1997.
38. A. Yu and J. Chen: The POSTGRES95 User Manual. Computer Science Div., Dept. of EECS, University of California at Berkeley, July 1995.

Overload Behaviour and Protection of Event-Driven Web Servers

Thiemo Voigt*

SICS, Tel. +46 86331598, Fax +46 87517230, Box 1263, SE-16429 Kista, Sweden
thiemo@sics.se

Abstract. Web servers need to be protected from overload, since server overload can lead to low server throughput and high response times experienced by clients. Most architectures for overload protection have been developed for the Apache web server. Event-driven web servers handle many more simultaneous connections than the Apache server. Thus, they exhibit a different behaviour during server overload. In this paper, we study the behaviour of event-driven servers during overload. We show that an overload protection architecture that we developed earlier successfully protects event-driven web servers from overload.

Keywords: web server, event-driven, overload protection, admission control

1 Introduction

In this paper, we study the overload behaviour of event-driven web servers and compare it to the well-known overload behaviour of the Apache web server. Due to the fact that event-driven web servers handle many more connections simultaneously than Apache does, the behaviour during overload differs between the two architectures. Many event-driven servers accept established connections in a greedy manner even during high demand. This means that the number of requests waiting in the listen queue is low. Many traditional overload protection and service differentiation schemes for web servers trigger rejection of requests when queue lengths exceed certain threshold. Thus, schemes such as WebQoS [4] and Web2K [5] work well with Apache-style web servers, but it is unclear if they work with event-driven web servers.

We have previously presented an architecture that protects web servers from overload [16]. The architecture is kernel-based and can thus be used in combination with any user space web server. This architecture supervises critical web server resources by monitoring the resource utilization and adapting the acceptance rate for requests that are the main consumers of each critical resource. In addition, the architecture uses an early discard mechanism called TCP SYN policing that protects the server from overload during very high demand. The adaptation of the acceptance rate for this mechanism is based on the length of

* This work is partially funded by the national Swedish Real-Time Systems research initiative ARTES (www.artes.uu.se).

E. Gregori et al. (Eds.): Networking 2002 Workshops, LNCS 2376, pp. 147–157, 2002.

the listen queue. This means, that using event-driven web servers, this mechanism might not work as expected. Nevertheless, our results demonstrate that our admission control architecture is efficient even with event-driven web servers. During high load, decreasing the acceptance rate of resource-intensive requests reduces the task of the web server to serving mostly static, small requests, which is the strength of event-driven web servers. Thus, in our workload scenarios, the fact that TCP SYN policing is not put into play when the listen queue starts growing does not hinder effective overload protection. For Apache-style web servers, on the other hand, the deployment of TCP SYN policing is crucial during high load.

The contribution of this paper is demonstrating the behaviour of event-driven web servers during overload compared to Apache-style web servers and showing that an architecture presented earlier [16] efficiently protects event-driven web servers from overload.

Our paper is outlined as follows. In the next section we present related work. Section 3 describes the different types of web servers and our overload protection architecture. Section 4 presents a set of carefully chosen experiments. Section 5 summarizes our results.

2   Related Work

Several schemes for overload protection and service differentiation of web servers trigger rejection of requests when queue lengths exceed certain thresholds. Web2k a QoS-aware middlelayer, uses the occupancies of queues as a guide for enforcing admission control [5]. In a similar way, WebQoS starts rejecting requests when the number of queued requests reaches a programmable trigger point [4]. These schemes will not work with event-driven web servers since event-driven web servers accept requests from the listen queue in a greedy manner.

Other researchers handle a peculiar bottleneck that is caused by the interaction between the Apache web server and persistent connections used by HTTP 1.1 [9, 14]. After each request on a persistent connection, the server keeps the connection open for another period of time (usually 15 seconds) to await further requests on the same TCP connection. Thus, all server processes can be idle waiting for new requests on persistent connections while incoming requests must wait in the listen queue. This peculiar bottleneck is not important for event-driven servers which handle much more concurrent connections.

Paj et al. point out several features of event-driven servers that are important for the understanding of our work [13]:

- Event-driven servers provide much better performance for static workloads, in particular small, static files, than the Apache web server.
- Since event-driven web servers make use of a single process and a single thread of control, the overheads of context switching and thread synchronization of other web server models are avoided.
- In a wide-area network, servers handle a significantly larger number of concurrent requests than a server tested under LAN conditions.

The last point has also been confirmed by studies of other researchers, for example by Nahum et al. [11].

3 Background

In this section we briefly present the multi-process and event-driven web server architectures as well as an architecture for overload protection for web servers we have developed earlier [16].

3.1 Multi-process and Event-Driven Architectures

In a multi-process architecture, one process is assigned to handle each client request. Each process performs all the steps from accepting the connection, reading and handling the request until the client has received the requested object. The popular Apache web sever is an example of that architecture. In Apache, the default maximum number of processes is 150 which limits the number of connections this web server can handle concurrently.

Event-driven architectures have one main process that performs concurrent processing of multiple requests. Typically, the web server uses an operation like select() to select one of the requests that is currently not blocked and performs the next required processing step for this connections. This way, event-driven servers can handle many requests concurrently. Example web servers are the commercial Zeus web server [17], Boa web server [8], mathopd [6] and thttpd [1].

3.2 Overload Protection Architecture

In previous work, we have presented an architecture that avoids server overload by preventing overutilization of critical server resources using adaptive inbound controls [16]. For each supervised resource, we adapt the acceptance rates for requests that are the main consumers of one critical resource. In our architecture, we adapt the acceptance rate for large static files based on the queue length to the network interface and the acceptance rate of CGI-scripts based on the current CPU utilization. We call this approach resource-based admission control (Figure 1).

When the request rate reaches above a certain level, resource-based admission control alone cannot prevent server overload. When such situations arise, we use *TCP SYN policing* [15]. This mechanism is efficient in terms of resource consumption of rejected requests because it provides "early discard" dropping of TCP SYNs that exceed the acceptance rate. The admission of connection requests is based on network-level attributes such as IP addresses and a token bucket policer. When designing the architecture we used Apache as our user-space web server. TCP SYN policing should come into play when resource-based admission control alone is not sufficient to prevent overload. When such situations arise, the length of the listen queue starts growing. Therefore, the

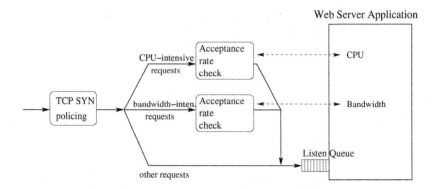

Fig. 1. Resource-based Admission Control

adaptation of the acceptance rate for TCP SYNs is based on the length of the listen queue.

The architecture is implemented as a loadable kernel module in the Linux OS. We have earlier shown that overload protection mechanisms implemented in the kernel are much more efficient and scalable than the same algorithms implemented in user space [15]. Another advantage of our architecture is that it can be used in combination with any user space web server.

4   Experiments

Our testbed consists of a server and a traffic generator connected via a 100 Mbit/sec Ethernet switch. The server machine is a 600 MHz Athlon with 128 MBytes of memory running Linux 2.4. The traffic generator runs on a 450 MHz Athlon. Note that this setup does not allow us to assess the effect of network latency on the response times. We use the following web servers in our experiments: An unmodified Apache web server, v.1.3.9., with the default configuration, i.e. a maximum of 150 worker processes. We use three event-driven web servers: Zeus, thttpd and mathopd. For mathopd we set the number of maximum connections to 512 (Mathopd 512) or the default number of 24 connections (Mathopd 24). All web servers were used with their default configuration and we assume that their performance could be enhanced with performance tuning.

For load generation we use the sclient traffic generator [2]. Sclient is able to generate client request rates that exceed the capacity of the web server. This is done by aborting requests that do not establish a connection to the server in a specified amount of time. This timeout is set to 50 milliseconds in our experiments. The exact timeout value does not impact the results, as long as it is chosen low enough to avoid that TCP SYNs dropped by the server are retransmitted. However, the larger the value, the higher the risk that the request generator runs out of socket buffers. Sclient does not take into account aborted requests when calculating the average response time.

For the first experiments we just request a single file, as sclient in its unmodified version does. For experiments with a complex workload, we have modified sclient to request files according to a workload that is derived from the surge traffic generator [3]:

1. The size of the files stored on the server follows a heavy tailed distribution.
2. The request size distribution is heavy tailed.
3. The distribution of popularity of files follows Zipf's Law [3]. Zipf's Law states that if the files are ordered from most popular to least popular, then the number of references to a file tends to be inversely proportional to its rank.

We made 20% of the requests for small files dynamic. The dynamic files used in our experiments are minor modifications of standard Webstone [12] CGI files and return a file containing randomly generated characters of the specified size. In the Internet the fraction of dynamic requests varies from site to site. Some sites experience more than 25% dynamic requests [7, 10].

4.1   Overload Behaviour

In this section we present some experiments that compare the overload behaviour of event-driven servers to Apache. In the experiments, the server does not deploy our overload protection scheme.

Requests for large static files. In the first experiment, the sclient traffic generator requests a file of size 140 KBytes with varying request rates. We choose this large file size in order to make the bandwidth on the outgoing interface a bottleneck. The results are shown in Figure 2. For request rates up to 80 reqs/sec, all web servers achieve maximum throughput, i.e. the server throughput is as high as the request rate, and response times are low. However, at a request rate of slightly above 80 reqs/sec the response time increases quickly for all web servers. Packets drops on the network interface are responsible for the low throughput and in particular the higher average response times. Packet drops do not only lead to retransmissions but also cause TCP to back off and reduce its transmission rate.

At high request rates, response times are high with all servers, except Mathopd 24. Using Apache the average response time is slightly higher compared to the other servers due to the additional time that requests to the Apache server spend in the listen queue. Connections to the event-driven web servers only have to wait for a very short time in the listen queue, i.e. the listen queue does not build up and mostly has a length of zero. Hence, in this workload scenario, the listen queue length does not indicate the overload situation and the long response times.

At a request rate of about 100 reqs/sec, Mathopd 512 handles about 500 connections concurrently while thttpd handles more than 800 connections. The

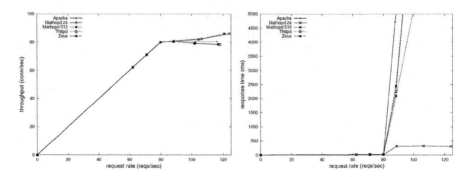

Fig. 2. Throughput and response time for large file

numbers are that large since event-driven web servers greedily accept new connections despite that the connections that are already accepted do not make fast progress due to the packet drops on the network interface. Mathopd 24 avoids packet drops on the interface since it only handles 24 connections concurrently and resets excessive connections.

Complex workload. In this experiment we use the complex surge workload described earlier. Figure 3 shows that Apache and the event-driven web servers behave similarly. At a request rate of about 400 reqs/sec, the web servers become overloaded. This overload is caused by the CPU-intensive CGI requests. Using Apache and Zeus, the listen queue builds up which leads to additional latency as depicted in Figure 3.

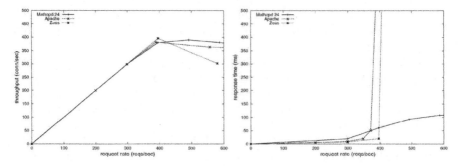

Fig. 3. Throughput and response time for surge workload (20% dynamic)

As in the previous experiment, Mathopd 24 manages to keep response times low during high demand. Mathopd 512 caused very high response times even with low request rates and is excluded from this figure[1].

The example of Mathopd 24 shows that restricting the number of concurrent connections is a simple solution to protect web servers from overload. However, there is a risk that such a system is underutilized, in particular when faced with low bandwidth connections with large round-trip times. Furthermore, due to the varying demand and resource consumption of requests, the "optimal" number of maximum connections is inherently non-steady.

4.2 Overload Protection

In this section, we study if our overload protection architecture is able to efficiently protects event-driven web servers from overload. In all experiments presented in this section, the server deploys our overload protection architecture.

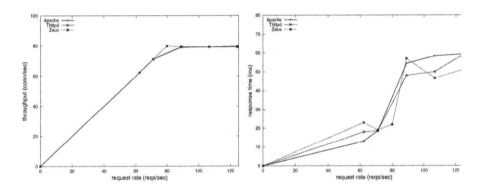

Fig. 4. Throughput and response time for large file with overload protection

Requests for large static files. Figure 4 demonstrates that our overload protection architecture can prevent the dramatic increase of the response times when the large file is requested at high rates. The response times shrink from more than five seconds (see Figure 2) to below 70 ms at request rates between 80 and 125 reqs/sec. Our experiments have not shown any packet drops on the network interface. When the queue to the network interface grows, the overload protection architecture reduces the acceptance rate for large static requests. This avoids packet drops and at the same time keeps the number of concurrent connections low. For example, using thttpd the number of concurrent connections rarely exceeds 10 at a request rate of about 100 reqs/sec while it was above 800 in the experiment without overload protection.

---

[1] For thttpd we cannot report any results because we did not get the CGI scripts to work.

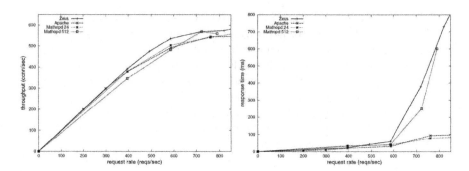

Fig. 5. Throughput and response time for surge workload supervising CPU and listen queue

Complex Workload: Supervising CPU and listen queue. In this experiment shown in Figure 5 we control the acceptance rate for CGI-scripts and deploy TCP SYN policing. The figure shows that our overload protection architecture increases the throughput and keeps the response times much lower than without any controls (see Figure 3).

Figure 5 shows that at request rates above 700 reqs/sec the average response time for Mathopd 512 and Zeus increases. The log revealed that large number packet drops on the network interface caused these larger response times. While using Apache, TCP SYN policing is activated at requests rates above 700 reqs/sec, SYN policing is not activated with any of the event-driven servers.

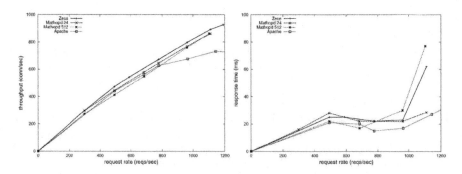

Fig. 6. Throughput and response time for surge workload with all controls active

Complex Workload: All controls active. In this experiment, we also control the acceptance rate for large files. Figure 6 demonstrates that this leads to lower response times and much higher throughput. For example, at a request rate of

825 reqs/sec, the response time experienced by Zeus is reduced from 730 ms (see Figure 5) to 23 ms when we also supervise the bandwidth on the network interface. It is obvious that the response time decreases and the throughput increases when the admission control mechanisms reject requests for large static files, since handling requests for large files is more demanding than handling requests for smaller files. However, in this scenario the main improvement is achieved by avoiding packet drops on the network interface.

Table 1. The impact of packet drops on the response time

server	min. acceptance rate large reqs.	resp. time (ms)	packet drops
Apache	5	29	110
Apache	20	67	6000
Zeus	5	57	6500
Zeus	20	680	126000

Table 1 compares the number of packet drops experienced by the Apache and Zeus web servers for 60000 requests at a request rate of about 1120 reqs/sec for two different scenarios. In the first scenario, we set the minimum acceptance rate for large requests to 20 and in the second scenario we set this minimum rate to five, i.e. no matter how much packet drops we experience, the acceptance rate for large requests is not set lower than 20 in the first scenario and five in the second scenario. The table illustrates that Zeus experiences much more packet drops than Apache and therefore the response time is higher. Event-driven web servers use only one process and a single thread of control and thus, there is no need for expensive context switching between processes. Therefore, event-driven servers can process requests faster and cause more packet drops.

TCP SYN policing. In the experiments above where our overload protection scheme was deployed, none of the event-driven web servers ever made use of TCP SYN policing. Even during very high demand, resource-based admission control has been sufficient to protect the event-driven web server from overload. Since event-driven web servers are able to handle requests for the non-policed requests, in our experiments mainly static files smaller than 50 KBytes, efficiently, the deployment of SYN policing is not as vital for overload protection of these servers as it is for Apache-style web servers. In Apache-style web servers the overhead of handling these requests is much higher [13], causing almost constantly 100% CPU utilization. The same is true for Mathopd 512 while it is not the case for the efficient Zeus web server. When repeating the experiment in the previous section (Figure 6) without deploying SYN policing, the Apache server becomes overloaded at high request rates.

The experiment with the surge workload and no overload protection in Section 4.1 demonstrates that in some overload scenarios, event-driven web servers do not accept requests as fast as they arrive and the listen queue starts growing. We have also seen that when the Zeus web server gets exposed to a sudden high demand (about 1800 reqs/sec), the listen queue grows and thus TCP SYN policing becomes active. In this situation, TCP SYN policing was active until resource-based admission control became effective, i.e. the acceptance rates for resource-intensive requests had been sufficiently reduced. Thus, there are workload scenarios where event-driven web servers benefit from TCP SYN policing.

5   Summary

We studied the behaviour of event-driven web servers and compared it to Apache's behaviour during overload. We demonstrated overload scenarios that caused long response times while at the same time the length of the listen queue did not increase using event-driven servers. Using the Apache server, the listen queue filled up to its maximum size in the same scenario. Overload protection schemes that use the listen queue length as their single overload indicator will not be effective with event-driven web servers in such scenarios. Since the listen queue does not increase, they are not able to discover the overload situation and to take corresponding action.

We have also shown that our admission control architecture successfully protects event-driven web servers from server overload. However, while TCP SYN policing is vital for the Apache server at high request rates, event-driven servers rarely made use of TCP SYN policing in our workload scenarios. Since the single process architecture of event-driven web servers avoids expensive context switches and enables them to process static requests fast, in these scenarios the major bottleneck for event-driven servers was the capacity of the network interface.

6   Acknowledgements

We want to thank the developers of the different web servers for extremely low response times on several questions on their web servers. We also want to thank Zeus Technology Ltd for granting us an extended evaluation license for their web server.

References

1. ACME Laboratories: thttpd, http://www.acme.com/software/thttpd
2. Banga G., Druschel P.: Measuring the Capacity of a Web Server. Usenix Symposium on Internet Technologies and Systems (1997)
3. Barford P., Crovella M.: Generating Representative Web Workloads for Network and Server Performance Evaluation. Proc. of SIGMETRICS (1998)
4. Bhatti N., Friedrich R.: Web Server Support for Tiered Services. IEEE Network (1999) 36–43

5. Bhoj P., Ramanathan S., Singhal S.: Web2K: Bringing QoS to Web Servers. Tech Report: HPL-2000-61 (2000)
6. Boland M.: Mathopd, http://mathop.diva.nl
7. Challenger J., Dantzig P., Iyengar A.: A Scalable and Highly Available System for Serving Dynamic Data at Frequently Accessed Web Sites. Proc. of ACM/IEEE SC 98 (1998)
8. Doolittle L., Nelson J.: Boa Webserver, http://www.boa.org
9. Lu C., Abdelzaher T., Stankovic J., Son S.: A Feedback Control Approach for Guaranteeing Relative Delays in Web Servers. Real-Time Technology and Application Symposium (2001)
10. Manley S., Seltzer M.: Web Facts and Fantasy. Usenix Symposium on Internet Technologies and Systems (1997)
11. Nahum E., Rosu M., Seshan S., Almeida J.: The Effects of Wide-Area Conditions on WWW Server Performance. Proc. of ACM Sigmetrics Conference on Measuring and Modeling of Computer Systems (2001)
12. Mindcraft: Webstone, http://www.mindcraft.com
13. Paj V., Druschel P., and Zwaenepoel W.: Flash: An Efficient and Portable Web Server. Proc. of Usenix Annual Technical Conference, June 1999.
14. Pradhan P., Tewari R., Sahu S., Chandra C., Shenoy P.: An Observation-based Approach Towards Self-managing Web Servers. Int. Workshop on Quality of Service (2002)
15. Voigt T., Tewari R., Freimuth D., Mehra A.: Kernel Mechanisms for Service Differentiation in Overloaded Web Servers. Usenix Annual Technical Conference (2001)
16. Voigt T., Gunningberg P.: Handling Multiple Bottlenecks in Web Servers Using Adaptive Inbound Controls. Int. Workshop on Protocols for High-Speed Networks (2002)
17. Zeus Web Server, http://www.zeus.co.uk

Scalable Benchmarking and Performance Monitoring: A Coordination and Mobility Perspective

Kyungkoo Jun[1], Dan C. Marinescu[2], Yongchang Ji[2], and Gabriela M. Marinescu[2]

[1] Samsung Electronics Co., LTD.
Suwon, Kyungki-Do, Korea.
[2] School of Electrical and Computer Engineering
University of Central Florida
Orlando, Florida, 32816, USA
{dcm, yji, magda}@cs.ucf.edu

Abstract. *In this paper we introduce the concept of an ad hoc cluster as a scalable solution to benchmarking and performance monitoring. We discuss coordination and mobility and present results of a case study.*
Keywords: *Web, benchmarking, performance monitoring, software agent, coordination, mobility*

1 Introduction

Benchmarking and performance evaluation are an integral component of the development cycle of any technology, they provide the necessary feedback for further improvement. Therefore, it is important that the Web benchmarking and performance monitoring techniques keep up with the developments in Web server architecture.

The scalability of Web server architecture has been investigated for some time and the studies have produced important results; today's clusters of Web servers are capable of sustaining very high request rates of millions of requests per second or even more. Moreover, content-delivery services such as those provided by Akamai help reduce the response time by caching objects at Internet sites located close to clients and eliminate hot-spot contention at the sole server site.

This paper addresses questions related to scalable benchmarking techniques capable to place a realistic load on clusters of Web servers as well as performance monitoring techniques to determine the variability of the response time when content-delivery services are present. Though we restrict our discussion to Web server benchmarking and performance monitoring, the basic architecture we propose could be extended to other Internet services.

A survey of mobile agent applications to network management [7] presents agent–based approaches to network management, fault management, configuration management, and performance management. Applications of agent–based monitoring in telecommunication are reported in [3, 6].

E. Gregori et al. (Eds.): Networking 2002 Workshops, LNCS 2376, pp. 158–164, 2002.

2   Ad Hoc Benchmarking and Performance Monitoring Cluster Architecture

Throughout this paper the term *benchmark server* refers to a system hosting benchmarking softw are including statistical analysis tools; a*performance monitoring server* is a system hosting performance monitoring and analysis tools. A benchmark server mimics the behavior of a number of Web server clients and, in addition, has the means to analyze the results of measurements. A benchmark server should be capable to: (i) create the workload data files; (ii) generate the HTTP requests; (iii) receive the responses; and (iv) process the results.

Placing a realistic load on a powerful cluster of Web servers is impractical with a single-system benchmark server; the resources av ailable to a single-system, namely the CPU cycles and primary and secondary storage restrict the maximum request rate and limit our abilit y to analyze the results. T o o vercome these limitations we mirror the solution supporting the scalability of Web servers and instead of a single-system use a *cluster of benchmark or performance monitoring servers*.

Yet, the results produced by a benchmark or by a performance monitoring cluster could be seriously affected by the placement of the cluster. If a conten t-deliv ery serv er is present in the vicinity of the cluster, then the results will reflect the efficiency of the caching algorithms at that particular server as well as the local netw ork load, but will not be able to predict the response time experienced by clien ts located elsewhere in the Internet. Moreover, the connection of the cluster to the Internet must be capable of providing the communication bandwidth required by the aggregate HTTP request and response rate.

Thus, it seems more reasonable to consider a distributed approach to benchmarking and performance monitoring. Instead of a cluster with co-located components we could imagine an *ad hoc cluster* where the individual servers in the cluster are mobile and can be placed at strategic points throughout the Internet. This approach requires the ability to coordinate the activities of multiple servers. In this vision mobile agents are dispatched at selected locations throughout the In ternet and at each site an agent assembles dynamically the software and the corresponding data needed for benchmarking or performance monitoring; then the agent controls all phases of the benchmarking or performance monitoring process.

Throughout this paper whenever we talk about a *software agent* or an *agent* w e mean an activ e mobile object with some degree of intelligence. *Active* means that at least one thread of control is running. *Mobile* means that the code, the data, and the state can be moved from one physical location to another. *Strong mobility* means that the request to migrate can be answered immediately while *we ak mobility* restricts the moments in time when the migration could take place. *Intelligence* refers to the ability to infer new facts given a set of rules and a set of facts, as well as planning, and learning capabilities.

Coordination implies the abilit y to reac h some consensus about the global state of the system and to control the flow of activities in the system. Barrier sync hronization is an example of coordination when all activities must reach a w ell-defined poirt before any one of them could proceed. Coordination could be supported by a shared data server, for example, a tuple space server.

We propose to use existing benchmarking and performance monitoring tools rather than dev elopnew tools written in some net w ork-oriemed programming language supporting mobility such as Java. Thus, we avoid a prolonged development phase and the potential inefficiencies of Java-based programs. To gain the additional functionality we extend existing tools with software agents rather than design agents to replace the tools.

This approach raises a number of delicate questions. A first question is how to ac hieve an aggregate distribution with desired characteristics when the servers of a benchmark cluster are co-located or are distributed across the netw ork and we have to combine the request streams from multiple servers. Another question is how to guarantee the statistical characteristics of the benchmarking stream at the Web server site, knowing that the *round trip time (RTT)* to/from different different hosts to a single host connected to the Internet could be different. The failure of any component of the ad hoc benchmark cluster must be promptly detected and a decision to stop the measurements or, alternatively, a fast recovery procedure must be initiated; thus, we need efficient fault detection and, possibly, fault recovery algorithms.

Sev eraltypes of experiments could be conducted with an ad hoc cluster. Some experiments could be designed to optimize the placement of the conten t-delivery servers; other experiments could be designed to study the efficiency of the caching algorithms used by a conten t-deliv ery server. Of course, in many cases we are primarily interested in the response time as seen by clients throughout the Internet, regardless of the source of the response. In such cases, rather than compute an average response time with a very large variance we propose to provide an Internet map revealing the average response time experienced by clients at different locations.

This paper focuses upon the architecture of an hoc cluster and addresses only a subset of the questions posed above.

3   A Case Study

The experimental set-up for our ad hoc benchmark cluster consists of a mobile agent platform and a Web workload generator.

The Bond mobile agent framework [4] supports agent control, synchronization, and fault–detection and agent recovery. Two types of agents participate in our monitoring system: *coordinator* and *field* agents. The coordinator agent assigns each step to a field agent. The field agents perform tasks such as software installation, workload generation, and carry out measurements. Each field agent performs simple tasks. For example, we have tw o separate agerts, one to install a tool and the other to monitor the execution of the tool. This decision leads to simpler and more effective design and agent implementation.

Surge [2] is a tool made of three components: the *workload data generator*, the *client request generator*, and the *server file generator*. These components separate workload generation from the actual benchmarking. The tool needs as input several empirical statistics: the file size distribution, the request size distribution, the relative file popularity, the embedded file references, the temporal locality of reference, and the user think time.

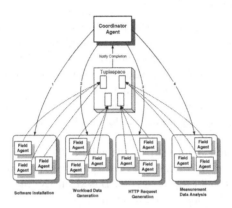

Fig. 1. Agent–based Web benchmarking system: a coordinator agent manages each step of the process and controls a set of field agents. A tuple space is used for barrier-synchronization.

The process described in Figure 1 consists of four steps: softw are installation, workload dataset generation, request generation, and analysis. Before the next step of this process is initiated, all field agents go through a barrier synchronization.

The coordination agent carries out the steps sequentially , a step is started only after the previous one was completed. The barrier synchronization at the end of each step is implemented using the tuple space extension to Bond [5]. Before the coordinator agent initiates a step, it creates a barrier in the tuple space then starts up the group of field agents and assigns to them the tasks required for that step. After finishing a task a field agent deposits a token in the tuple space. The control agent is notified when the specified n umber of token was collected.

The failure of an agent during benchmarking may lead to incomplete workload generation or to loss of measurement data. The agents constantly monitor each other using the distributed adaptive fault detection algorithm described in [5]. A t each step the field agents and the coordinator form a ring monitoring topology. A t the beginning of each step the monitoring topology is initialized with a new set of field agents. The coordinator agent is the initial contact point providing the current list of fault–free agents and it is responsible for fault recovery in the case of failure detection.

3.1   Implementation

The blueprint of the coordinator specifies the states and the transitions for the finite state machine of the agent, are described elsewhere [5]. The states of the coordinator can be classified into four groups, each corresponding to one of the four steps of the benchmark. The workflow for each step consists of four sequential sub-steps: build a list of agents to be deployed, create a barrier in the tuple space, deploy the agents in the list, and start the agents. The states are interconnected by transitions to create the workflow required for each step.

The coordinator is given a list of field agents for each step. The blueprints, model data, and dispatching addresses are provided. At the deployment time, the control agent provides the field agents with the information for barrier-synchronization: the address of the tuple space and the name of the barrier. Agent failures during tuple space access do not affect the synchronization because the barrier access operation is atomic.

The fault detection algorithm described in [5] requires that participating agents to have unique identifiers. The coordinator assigns non–negative unique integer aliases to the field agent agents. Based on the integer aliases, the ring monitoring topology is constructed at each step.

During the software installation step a field agent downloads the C version of the Surge tools from a Web server and then compiles them using the C compiler and libraries available on the target system. At the time of this writing only Linux–based systems are supported because the thread libraries required by Surge are not available on other systems.

During the workload dataset generation step, a field agent invokes a sequence of command–line programs with parameters specifying the number of files, maximum number of file reference, as required by Surge [2].

Linux processes invoked by a field agent handle the actual HTTP requests and data processing during the last two steps. The field agent checks the correct completion of the Linux processes by comparing the output strings with the expected ones. To process the measurements we use Perl–written scripts.

3.2   Measurements

We measured the workload generated by the ad hoc cluster as well as the overhead caused by operation of the agents.

Experimental Setup. We use the Apache 1.3.12 as a Web server. The Web server runs on a Linux system with a 300 MHz Intel Pentium II processor, 128 MBytes of main memory, and 100 Mbps network connection. IPtraf [1] is used to measure the network traffic.

We configure the benchmark servers, the Surge processes controlled by the agents, to use HTTP 1.0 instead of 1.1. The benchmark servers run on Linux systems, each system has a 400 MHz Intel Pentium II processor, 128 MBytes of main memory, and are connected to the Web server by a 100-Mbps network.

Surge uses multiple processes to avoid the typical system limitations placed upon the number of open sockets per process. Each process spawns multiple threads and each thread corresponds to one user. Such a unit is called *User Equivalent (UE)*.

Comparison of the workloads generated by benchmark servers. We performed three experiments. Each experiment involves different number of servers and UEs; one server and 20 UEs for the first; one server and 120 UEs for the second; and three servers and 120 UEs (40 UE on each) for the third.

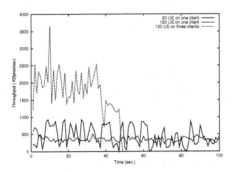

Fig. 2. Web server throughput (in KBytes) for the three server configuration.

Figure 2 shows the Web server throughput for the three server cluster. As expected, the server responses show patterns similar to those of the requests.

The results confirm the limitations of a single-server approach. The experiments show that a multi server cluster is capable to generate an workload that cannot be achieved by a single server.

Now let us turn our attention to the qualitative aspects of the benchmark. If the temporal characteristics of the workload pattern generated by multiple servers differs from the one generated by a single server the benchmarking results are questionable.

The aim of the second experiment is to show that the load generated by the three server cluster is equivalent to the one produced by the single server of the first experiment. We used a facility of Surge to split a workload dataset; we divided the dataset of the first experiment into three sub-sets and assigned one sub-set to each server.

Figure 3 shows the data rates of the cumulative traffic between the benchmark servers and the Web server. Two time-series graphs are similar, but a more elaborate analysis to determine the degree of similarity of the throughput is necessary.

4   Conclusions

In this paper we introduce the concept of an ad hoc cluster, a collection of systems distributed throughout the Internet and capable to support scalable benchmarking and/or performance monitoring.

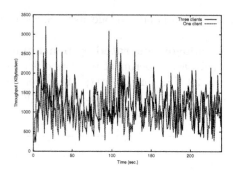

Fig. 3. Time series describing the traffic intensity between the Web server and the benchmarking cluster. The traffic intensity for the single and for the three server cluster exhibit similar patterns.

An important lesson is that Web benchmarking results depend upon both benchmark and Web servers. We have to be extremely careful when comparing Web server performance using benchmarking results. The same benchmark of the same Web sever could produce significantly different results depending upon the ability of the ad hoc benchmark cluster to generate the prescribed workload.

5   Acknowledgements

The research reported in this paper was partially supported by National Science Foundation grants MCB9527131, DBI0296107, ACI0296035, and EIA0296179.

References

1. IP Network Monitoring Software. URL http://cebu.mozcom.com/riker/iptraf/.
2. P. Barford and M. Crovella. Generating Representative Web Workloads for Network and Server Performance Evaluation. *Proc. SIGMETRICS 98*, June 1998.
3. A. Bieszczad, B. Pagurek, and T. White. Mobile Agents for Network Management. *IEEE Communications Survey*, Fourth Quarter 1998.
4. L. Bölöni, K. Jun, K. Palacz, R. Sion, and D. C. Marinescu. The Bond Agent System and Applications. In *Proc. 2nd Int. Symp. on Agent Systems and Applications (ASA/MA 2000)*, pages 99–112. Springer-Verlag, Heidelberg, 2000.
5. K. Jun. *Monitoring and Control of Networked Systems with Mobile Agents: Algorithms and Applications.* PhD thesis, Purdue University, May 2001.
6. J. Nic klish, J. Quittek, A. Kind, and S. Arao. INCA: An Agent-based Network Control Architecture. In *Proceedings of the 2nd International Workshop on Intelligent Agents for Telecommunication Applications*, 1998.
7. Y. Wijata, D. Niehaus, and V. Frost. A Scalable Agent-Based Network Measurement Infrastructure. *IEEE Communications*, September 2000.

Towards Specification-Based Web Testing

Jessica Chen and Steve Chovanec

School of Computer Science, University of Windsor
Windsor, Ont. Canada N9B 3P4
xjchen@cs.uwindsor.ca

Abstract. As testing has always been our primary device to gain the
confidence in the correctness, robustness, and reliability of a system, a
typical issue in web engineering is how to automate effective testing on
web applications. Many factors have contributed to the new dimensions
of the complexity in the automated testing in this regard. Here we present
our work in progress towards the specification-based testing of the presentation logic in web applications. This work is realized by extending
an existing testing technique for window-based applications.

Keywords: Web applications, Finite state machines, Specification-based testing, Capture/Replay, Java AWT and Swing.

1 Introduction

With the advances of software development and the wide use of web programming technologies, web applications are gaining increasing popularity. The development of web applications has raised a lot of new issues from the perspective
of software engineering. To address these issues and search for suitable solutions
to the emerging problems in engineering web applications is undoubtedly an important task we are facing. Typically, as testing has always been our primary
device to gain the confidence in the correctness, robustness, and reliability of a
system, a prominent issue in web engineering is how to automatically and effectively perform testing on the developed and/or developing web applications.
Many factors have contributed to the complexity in web testing. These factors
include, for example,

- the distributed nature of the architecture of the Application Under Test
  (AUT),
- the adopted network infrastructure,
- the complex Graphical User's Interface (GUI) given in various presentation
  languages.

In this paper, we present our technique focused on testing the *presentation
logic* in web applications. It is realized by extending our previous work on testing
window-based applications, and it enjoys the following three main features: (i) a
specification-based testing technique; (ii) a *visual* environment for manipulating

E. Gregori et al. (Eds.): Networking 2002 Workshops, LNCS 2376, pp. 165–171, 2002.

test specifications; (iii) a *generic* and *scalable* tool with respect to the various types of presentation languages that can be adopted in the AUTs.

As we know, a precise description of the functionality of an application is essential not only for the implementation, but also for testing and maintenance purposes. In regard of software development methodologies, the assumption of the availability of such a description has long been the starting point of many specification-based testing techniques. In particular, for text-based applications, much work on specification-based testing techniques has been based on given specifications of the systems functionality in terms of Finite State Machines (FSM) (See e.g. [8, 15, 11, 6, 13]). Here we follow our previous work (see [5]) to assume the availability of FSM-based specifications. A presentation logic usually takes the form of graphical user's interactions. Thus, in our context, we assume that the specifications are provided in terms of the input and output of the system, which are actually the graphical user interactions. More precisely, the transitions on the FSMs represent the system moves according to the graphical user interactions denoted on the labels of the transitions. Adopting FSMs to describe graphical user interactions actually offers us the opportunity to combine our technique with other FSM-based testing techniques, which can be used on testing the business logic of web applications.

To automatically test the presentation logic in a web application obviously requires the proper acquisition, simulation and presentation of the user's graphical input and output. Unlike in text-based applications, input and output in GUI-based applications may have a lot of different context, such as mouse clicks on different GUI-components. These contexts are usually related to the GUI-components, which can have fairly complicated structures and relationships. This makes the descriptions of the systems functionality much more difficult. Moreover, to automate specification-based testing, we need to have the specification internally represented in a certain format so that it can be directly used in automated testing. In doing so, it is important that the components denoted in the specification be identified with the same ones in the AUT. In [5], we have presented our solution to these problems: We have developed a *visual specification editor* to be associated into the test development environment for testers to manipulate specifications. The internal representation of a specification, which contains the contexts of GUI input and output, is generated interactively through this visual specification editor. Such an editor runs the AUT under its own control, so that test users can edit test specifications within the true GUI environment of the AUT without knowing the details of the internal representation. Furthermore, the recorded input and output contain the same references as those in the AUT, so that the test cases generated from the edited specification can be used directly by test oracles to perform automated testing. By extending this work, we naturally inherited the above two characteristics that are common to testing ordinary applications with graphical interface and to testing web applications.

Finally, the presentation logic to be tested can be given in various languages. Window-based applications are the typical stand-alone applications with their own window containers. Applet is a new emerging type of web applications that can be dynamically loaded to and actually run on different client machines across the network. It realizes its graphical interactions with the end-users through the web browsers on the client sides. The widely used HyperText Markup Language (HTML) also provides some basic functionalities for graphical user's interactions. It is our goal to make our testing environment generic in terms of handling the presentation logic given in different languages, and also scalable to those presentation languages to appear in future.

In the following, we give a brief introduction to our previous work, and then present our work towards testing the presentation logic of web applications.

2   Automated Testing for Window-Based Applications

To automate specification-based testing, first of all we need to have the specification internally represented in computer so that it can be further used for the testing procedure. Such an internal representation of a specification (called *internal test specification* below) can be obtained by manual editing, via a text-based tool, or via a visual tool. For example, RationalRose [12] supports the visual editing of FSMs. One of the main features in our testing architecture is that such internal test specification is obtained via a special visual editing tool that *uses AUT as an input*. In other words, the editor runs the AUT under its own control and allows test users to interact with the AUT in order to describe the given specification.

The visual specification editor provides an integration of two environments to testers: one is the *AUT environment*, i.e. the GUI environment of the AUT obtained by running the AUT, and the other is the *FSM editing environment*, i.e. the GUI for editing the test specification. To designate input and output, testers can click on a GUI-component in the *AUT environment* to indicate the target component, and then go to the *FSM editing environment* to describe the event on this target component (input) or the change of values in this target component (output). For example, to express input *click close button in the information dialog box*, the tester can simply move the cursor to the proper dialog box of the AUT to make a click on the *close* button, and choose the mouse-clicked event from the given list of possible events associated with this dialog box object given in the *FSM editing environment*. Then the event is recorded.

Since the input and output are obtained while running the AUT, the editor is capable of obtaining related object references in the AUT. For example, when the editor receives event *click close button in the information dialog box*, the object reference of *close button* is obtained from this same object in the AUT. As the recorded input and output contain the same references of the context of the input/output event as those in the AUT, the test cases generated from the edited specification can be used directly by test oracles to perform automated testing.

A running prototype of such a technique is implemented in Java 1.2 with Swing and Abstract Window's Toolkit (AWT), for Java applications.

3   Towards Testing Web Applications

The target AUT of our previous work is window-based stand-alone applications. We are currently working on the same testing environment and architecture for applets. An on-line registration program developed with applets is a typical example of the AUTs in this setting.

Compared with window-based stand-alone applications, applets do not have the top-level window containers: An applet is normally displayed in the web browser of the client. As a consequence, to run an applet under the control of our visual specification editor, we need to simulate the browser environment. To avoid implementing a complex browser, we have identified a subset of the functionalities of the web browser to be implemented. This subset of functionalities includes for example, (i) to call all the necessary methods to start the applet (e.g. *init()*, *paint()*, *start()*); (ii) to load an applet from remote site; (iii) to make a request to the server in the same format of those sent by a normal web browser.

As we mentioned at the beginning, there are many languages that allow us to express the presentation logic in web applications. Furthermore, along with the advances of web technologies, we should be prepared for the new languages and formats to appear. In this regard, we have modified the previous design of the visual specification editor into a generic and scalable one with respect to the presentation languages in AUT.

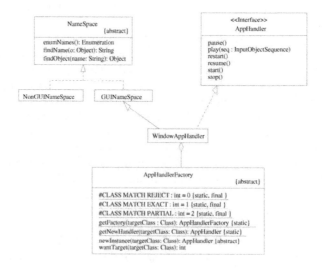

Fig. 1. Visual specification editor class diagram for handling window-based applications

Figure 1 shows the modified class diagram for handling the window-based applications. Class *NameSpace* defines the hierarchy of the reference names of the

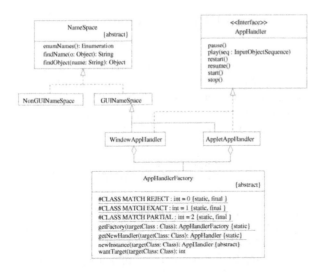

Fig. 2. Visual specification editor class diagram for handling window-based applications and applets

objects of the AUT. The objects in AUT are classified into two parts: those GUI-components and those related to the business logic of the AUT. Correspondantly, we have *GUINameSpace* and *NonGUINameSpace* as subclasses of *NameSpace*. The *GUINameSpace* is an essential component to handling the AUT.

Interface *AppHandler* defines the functionalities such as loading the application, replaying inputs, etc. For each type of AUT, we need to provide an *AppHandler* class that implements this interface and defines the set of GUI-component objects within the AUT. The reference names of these objects are maintained in *GUINameSpace*. In the design of Figure 1, we handle only one type of AUTs, i.e. the window-based applications. The functionalities for the related handling is defined in *WindowAppHandler*.

When the testing tool is started, there is an *AppHandlerFactory* object automatically created for each type of applications. Such a factory object is responsible for creating the instance of the proper *AppHandler* whenever necessary, that is, when we have the corresponding type of application for test. Through the use of the *AppHandlerFactory*, the editor is able to *recognize* the type of the given AUT, and calls for the proper *AppHandler* object to handle it.

With this setting, for each new type of applications, we can develop the related *AppHandler* class and easily plug it into the existing system. Figure 2 shows the class diagram where new handling for applets is plugged into the previous structure (Figure 1).

4   Related Work and Future Work

We have proposed a framework for specification-based testing for the presentation logic in web applications, by extending previous work for window-based ones. The development of the visual specification editor for web applications is under progress. We are currently considering AUTs that are applets. Our prototype itself is being developed under Java 1.2 with Swing and Abstract Window's Toolkit (AWT).

Although web testing technique has not been well discussed and developed, people have studied various aspects of the visual environment and graphical user's interactions.

Rather than a general specification-based testing framework as proposed in this paper, special testing techniques on particular GUI paradigms such as spreadsheet have been investigated (See e.g. [2, 10]). In [9], we can find a related work on testing/replaying Swing-based Java applications. However, the work described there only considered the handling of input from testers, and it was not oriented by studying a *systematic* way to conduct tests.

Many of current testing tools for GUI-based applications are based on the Capture/Replay technique (see for examples [1, 12, 14]). This technique suffers the following two major drawbacks:

- It is not specification-based. In general, there is no specification showing *what should be considered the correct behavior of the system*. As a consequence, test cases are picked up in an *ad hoc* manner.
- It is difficult to edit test scripts. If the specification of the systems behavior changes, the test scripts recorded during the first run of the system may need to undergo related modifications. In order to have these changes take effect, testers have to manually edit test scripts according to a specific script language.

The limitation of using FSMs is its non-scalability when the number of potential execution paths dramatically increases due to the large number of possible input events in each state. For future work, we are interested in looking for a suitable way to handle the large number of possible execution paths in our context. As we have mentioned in [5], although we have used FSMs in our experiment, our testing framework itself is not restricted to FSMs. A related work in this regard is given in [7] where the authors have discussed solutions on how to automatically generate user events in an unpredictable but controlled manner to produce test scripts.

To investigate the testing techniques on presentation logic and business logic individually follows the software engineering discipline: *separation of concern*. The study on testing business logic for distributed systems with middleware is also under progress [3, 4], and it is within our plan to integrate the tools from these two parts in future.

5   Acknowledgements

This work is supported in part by the Natural Sciences and Engineering Research Council of Canada under grant number RGPIN 209774.

References

1. AutoController. See http://www.autotester.com.
2. M. Burnett, A. Sheretov, and G. Rothermel. Scaling up a "what you see is what you test" methodology to spreadsheet grids. In *IEEE Symposium on Visual Languages*, 1999.
3. X. Cai and J. Chen. Control of nondeterminism in testing distributed multi-threaded programs. In *Proceedings of the First Asia-Pacific Conference on Quality Software (APAQS 2000)*, pages 29–38. IEEE Computer Society Press, 2000.
4. J. Chen. On using static analysis in distributed system testing. In *Proceedings of the 2nd International Workshop on Engineering Distributed Objects (EDO'2000), LNCS 1999*, pages 145–162, 2000.
5. J. Chen and S. Subramanian. A GUI environment to manipulate FSMs for testing GUI-based applications in Java. In *Proc. of the 34th IEEE Hawaii International Conference on System Sciences (HICSS-34)*. IEEE Computer Society, 2001.
6. T. Chow. Testing software design modeled by finite state machines. *IEEE Transactions on Software Engineering*, 4(3):178–187, 1978.
7. D. Kasik and H. George. Toward automatic generation of novice user test scripts. In *ACM Conference Proc. on Human Factors in Computing Systems*, pages 244–251, Vancouver, Canada, April 1996.
8. D. Lee and M. Yannakakis. Testing finite state machines: State identification and verification. *IEEE Transactions on Computers*, 43:306–320, 1994.
9. J. Newmarch. Testing Java swing-based applications. In *The 31st Internaltion Conference on Technology on Object-Oriented Language and Systems*, Nanjing, China, September 1999.
10. G. Rothermel, L. Li, C. DuPuis, and M. Burnett. "what you see is what you test: A methodology for testing form-based visual programs. In *Proc. of International Conference on Software Engineering*, pages 198–207, 1998.
11. K. Sabnani and A. Dahbura. A protocol test generation procedure. *Computer Networks and ISDN Systems*, 15(4):285–297, 1988.
12. R. V. Test. See http://www.rational.com/products/visual_test/index.jtmpl.
13. H. Ural, X. Wu, and F. Zhang. On minimizing the lengths of checking sequences. *IEEE Transactions on Computers*, 46(1), January 1997.
14. XRunner. See http://www.merc-int.com/products/xrunner6.
15. M. Yannakakis and D. Lee. Testing finite state machines: Fault detection. *Journal of Computer and System Sciences*, 50:209–227, 1995.

Routing in Mobile Ad-hoc and Peer-to-Peer Networks
A Comparison

Rüdiger Schollmeier[1], Ingo Gruber[1], and Michael Finkenzeller[2]

[1] Lehrstuhl für Kommunikationsnetze, Technische Universität München,
Arcisstr. 21, 80333 München, Germany
{Schollmeier, Gruber}@lkn.ei.tum.de
[2] Siemens Corporate Technology, Siemens AG
Otto-Hahn-Ring 6, 81730 München, Germany
Michael.Finkenzeller@mchp.siemens.de

Abstract. The goal of this paper is to make the similarities and differences of Peer-to-Peer (P2P) and Mobile Ad Hoc (MANET) networks clear. Thus we want to show the synergetic potential hidden in these two decentralized and self organizing networks. As well as both networks are established on a different physical layer, both networks hold similarities concerning their routing and network management principles. The reason therefore is, that both of them have to solve a similar goal, namely to provide networking functionalities in a completely unmanaged and decentralized environment. One of the most interesting tasks in these networks is thus how queries are guided through the network. Therefore we concentrate in this work on the different routing algorithms employed in Peer-to-Peer and mobile ad hoc networks. Finally, the similarities of both networks can be used, to bring up the synergetic effects of looking at both networks at the same time.

1 Introduction

Since the first appearance of wireless ad hoc networks as the DARPA packet radio networks in the 1970s [8, 10], they became an interesting research object in the computer industry. During the last couple of years tremendous improvements are made in the research of ad hoc networks. The wireless LAN standard 802.11 [18] is used as a wireless connection of portable computers with the local network. However it still does not supply completely self configuring ad hoc networking. With the development of Bluetooth [3] a first product, designated only for ad hoc networking, is available. Due to its possibility to create and organize a network without any central management, ad hoc networking is characterized as the art of networking without a network [5].

On the other hand, a similar concept without infrastructure can be observed in the Peer-to-Peer networking area. Peer-to-peer networks are first discussed in the mid 1990s, and became famous in the late 1990s as file sharing platforms. For P2P the IP-layer provides the basic communication medium and enables IP capable terminals to reach anyone attached to the IP-network. However the IP-layer does not tell a terminal how and where to find content or other participants. These peer-to-peer

E. Gregori et al. (Eds.): Networking 2002 Workshops, LNCS 2376, pp. 172–186, 2002.

networks, like e.g. Freenet [9] or Gnutella [6] are completely self organizing networks.

Similarities between both networks arise, as the basic problem, how to enable terminal to terminal communication in an unmanaged environment, is the same. However, beside the similarities there are also great differences, due to the different utilized network layers and different motivations for creating an ad hoc or P2P network.

As the routing is one of the most important modules within an unmanaged network, the routing algorithms of these two kinds of networks, will be compared in this work. As a result we want to point out similarities and differences between the Peer-to-Peer and the wireless ad hoc networking world. Thus it could be possible to make use of the synergetic effects even with completely different physical layers but the same goal, to provide networking functionalities without a given network.

The paper is structured as follows: a brief overview of the main attributes of wireless ad hoc networks is given in Section 2. In Section 3 we present the characteristics of peer-to-peer networks, followed by an overview about some important ad hoc routing algorithms in Section 4. Section 5 then enfolds the routing algorithms in peer-to-peer networks, and their differences and similarities to ad hoc networks are discussed in Section 6. Finally Section 7 concludes this work and gives an outlook to further possible developments and research topics in this area.

2 Ad Hoc Networks

Ad hoc networks are self configuring wireless networks. An ad hoc terminal is by definition a source of information, a drain for information and a router for information flows from other users. A wireless ad hoc network allows unrestricted mobility of the enlisted terminals, as long as at least one terminal is within transmission range. Direct neighbors can be used as relay stations to connect to nodes beyond a terminals own coverage (see **Figure 1**). The transmission range of a wireless ad hoc node is restricted by its power consumption due to the limited battery power of a wireless node. Therefore the node transmission range is typically small compared to the span of the network. All nodes within a wireless ad hoc network use the same frequency band as a shared medium for receiving and transmitting data. Unpredictable errors can occur on the transmission channel, and therefore a reliable data transmission is mandatory to reliably send out packets from source to destination.

An ad hoc network is mostly user driven, not data driven. The purpose of an ad hoc network is establish connections to other users, instead of redundantly distribute data over the network. This means, that a route is setup from a source to a specified destination, which are defined by their unique addresses, for the reason of enabling a communication between both users.

The advantage of this kind of network is, that it does not require any kind of infrastructure, like a base station in cellular networks. Therefore ad hoc networks are best suited for an environment, unable to provide any infrastructure, e.g. in hostile environment or for disaster recovery.

However the lack of infrastructure also has great disadvantages. One disadvantage is the insecure communication path, over several intermediate nodes. Nodes within transmission range of forwarding nodes can overhear the communication between source and destination. Therefore an encrypted end-to-end connection is important for a private communication, and is easy to put into practice with the existing tools known from the Internet. In contrast to that, authentication of communication partners might be impossible to guarantee, because public key infrastructures (PKI) as in the internet are not feasible in wireless ad hoc networks.

Ad hoc networks according to the definition outlined above, thus suffer from the lack of an infrastructure and from terminal mobility, therefore links between neighboring nodes are dynamic. While two nodes are diverging, the link between these two nodes will break, when the distance between both is large then their radio range. If this happens, both routing tables must be updated and used for new connection requests. As terminals are not only sources and destinations, but also relays for others, they must notify all other nodes relying on this link about the break.

As described, breakups of connections between adjacent nodes leads to frequent topology updates and must be announced to all other nodes relying on this link. While terminal mobility is low and the number of nodes is small, updates are send seldom. However, if the terminal mobility or the number of nodes increase, topology updates are getting more frequently, and signaling messages are utilizing more link bandwidth. Therefore ad hoc networks do not scale well for large numbers of terminals, especially with high mobility patterns. To limit this behavior it is important to employ optimized routing algorithms using the scarce available bandwidth optimal.

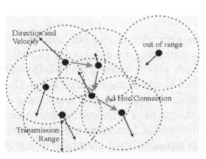

Fig. 1 A simple ad hoc network: nodes have different directions and velocities and a multi-hop ad hoc connection is established (grey pointers)

Fig. 2 Schematic network topology of a Peer-to-Peer network

3 Peer-to-Peer Networks

Since a few years Peer-to-Peer (P2P) networks came into discussion, which provide the capability to establish virtual overlay networks. So called "pure" P2P networks which are completely self organizing and therefore do not need central instances to manage the network. In this work, our understanding is according to the understanding of Peer-to-Peer networks, as described in [17]. The main characteristic of Peer-to-Peer networks is from our point of view, that the terminals of these networks communicate in a bidirectional and symmetric way with each other. Therefore a virtual overlay network is established above the IP-Layer (see **Figure 2**). Such a network consists in most cases only of the nodes and the TCP/IP connections between the different nodes. The term node in this context represents the fact, that each participant in a Peer-to-Peer network acts as a server and as a client, as understood in the common sense, at the same time. Therefore the artificial word node has been created, which is constituted of the first syllable of the term server and the second syllable of the term client.

The nodes itself are mostly computers with standard computing capacities, nearly infinite power supply (as they are connected to the electricity network) and at least with a network connection of about 56 kbit/s. Thus the terminals in Peer-to-Peer networks are more powerful than the terminals normally used in a wireless environment.

The virtual network, based on the nodes and the TCP/IP connections between them, is used to satisfy the different demands of the users operating in this network, may it be the search for an mp3 compressed audio file, or for another participant to whom a Voice over IP connection should be established. The data which is exchanged between the peers directly, may range from file data, over Internet Relay chat data up to real time voice communication and interaction data streams.

Basically there are no hierarchies given by the IP-Layer or the peers themselves. However this does not exclude the possibility to establish a routing architecture for the Peer-to-Peer network, which brings in central entities and thus adds hierarchies to the network. These central entities may be used as central look up tables to route queries, or as a kind of dynamic proxy server for low-bandwidth clients (see Section 0). Depending on the way, central entities are added to the routing architecture, we distinguish between several routing approaches, e.g. flat, hybrid and hierarchical, as described in Section 0.

However, employing central entities may on the one hand be of advantage because of management and scalability issues. On the other hand central entities also impose new problems like a single point of failure. Thus depending on the kind of application the Peer-to-Peer network is employed for, it must be carefully decided, what kind of routing architecture is used.

In contrast to wireless Ad hoc networking, Peer-to-Peer networking is already widely accepted e.g. in Napster [12] or Gnutella [6]. The cause therefore can be found in the easy availability and accessibility of the IP-Layer, which makes the development of Peer-to-Peer networking terminals much easier, than in the wireless world, with its additional physical constraints.

4   Routing in ad Hoc Networks

Several different routing algorithms for ad hoc networks, with their special advantages and disadvantages have been proposed until now. They can be divided in two main branches, the proactive or table drive routing algorithms and the reactive or on demand routing algorithms. A node running a proactive routing algorithm has the full network view at every time, like a regular router in the Internet. All topology updates are broadcasted immediately or with a small time shift to all other nodes in the network. Therefore the route establishment can take place very fast. The disadvantage of proactive routing algorithms is the number of required topology updates within a time period. In case the number of nodes belonging to a network rises over a certain threshold, this kind of routing algorithm is not feasible anymore.

In contrast to that, nodes using a reactive routing algorithm do not send any kind of topology updates to its neighbors. Only in case they want to set up a route to another node, they flood a route request through the network, and get a response from the destination or an intermediate node, which knows the route to the destination by a formerly made route request.

4.1 Destination Sequenced Distance Vector Routing (DSDV)

The Destination Sequenced Distance Vector Routing protocol [13] is the best known protocol for a proactive routing scheme. It is based on the classical Distributed Bellman Ford (DBF) routing mechanism [2]. The basic algorithm is optimized to guarantee the avoidance of loops in the routing tables. Like every other table driven routing algorithm it maintains several routing tables which provide information about every possible destination within the network. The tables contain the minimum number of hops and the next hop in direction of a specific destination. Further on, they also include sequence numbers for every destination. The sequence numbers guarantee that the node can distinguish between stale and new routes. Therefore it can update its routing tables with more actual information (higher sequence numbers), and thereby avoid route loops. Route updates can be sent as two types. Either a full route update, where all information of all tables of the node are exchanged, or an incremental update to save link bandwidth. The incremental updates only contain information about changes since the last full update.

Broadcasted route updates contain the address of the destination, the number of necessary hops to reach the destination, the sequence number of the route information regarding the destination, and a new sequence number unique to the broadcast. Receivers of this route updates can thus update their own routing tables, and if necessary broadcast their own routing tables. While every node maintains all necessary information of the full network, a route setup can be processed very fast with the locally stored information. Unlike the reactive routing algorithms, no more flooding of a route request through the network is required to discover a route from the source to a destination.

4.2 Ad Hoc On-demand Distance Vector Routing (AODV)

Ad hoc On-Demand Distance Vector Routing [14] is one of the major ad hoc on demand routing algorithm.

AODV uses route request (RREQ) and route reply (RREP) messages. The route request packet is used, if a source wants to send a message to a destination. If its routing cache does not contain a route to the destination, it broadcasts a RREQ to its neighbors. The RREQ contains the source address, the destination address and a unique sequence number. Every node receiving a RREQ saves the node address, from which it first received the RREQ, before it forwards the message to its neighbors. In case a node receives copies of the same RREQ, the copies are discarded. The RREQ is forwarded through the network until the RREQ reaches a node with a valid route to the destination, or the destination itself. The intermediate node or the destination creates a RREP message, and sends it to the node from which it first received the RREQ. The RREP is forwarded by the nodes on the reverse path the RREQ traveled. Every node saves the node's address from which it received the RREP. When the RREP reaches the source, the path is established, and the source can send data packets to the destination, without knowing the exact path to the destination. Information about this RREQ in nodes, which are not part of the established route, times out and will be deleted, because no RREP is received. This mechanism reduces packet overhead, because the complete path needs not to be coded within every packet. On the other hand extra memory in every node is needed to save the next hop information of all connections using this node.

When an intermediate node notices a movement of a downstream node, it generates a RREP packet with an infinite next hop metric. The RREP travels upstream to the source, informing all intermediate nodes, about the impossibility of reaching the moved node. All nodes can therefore delete existing routes, and set up new RREQ messages for their destination.

4.3 Zone Routing Protocol (ZRP)

The Zone Routing Protocol [7] is often called a hybrid ad hoc routing protocol as it combines proactive and reactive elements. The ZRP maintains routing information for a local zone, and establishes routes on demand for destinations beyond this local neighborhood. It limits the scope of the local zone by defining a maximum hop number for the local zone (e.g. 3 hops). Using ZRP with a maximum hop count of zero for the local neighborhood creates a reactive routing algorithm, and using it with maximum hop count $\to \infty$ creates a pure proactive routing algorithm. A route to a destination within the local zone can be established from the proactively cached tables of the source node. The routing algorithm used in the local zone can be based on every table-driven routing algorithm, but it has to be extended in that way, that packets contain the "time to life" (TTL) information, which describes the maximum hop count of the local zone. For routes beyond the local zone, route discovery happens reactively. The source node sends a route requests to its border nodes, containing its own address, the destination address and a unique sequence number. Border nodes are nodes which are exactly the maximum number of hops to the defined local zone away from the source. The border nodes check their local zone for the destination. If the requested node is not a member of this local zone, the node adds its own address to the route request packet and forwards the packet to its border nodes. If the destination is a member of the local zone of the node, it sends a route reply on the reverse path back to the source. The source node uses the path saved in the route reply packet to send data packets to the destination. To reduce the signaling messages during a route discovery copy-detection mechanisms are used to detect unnecessary forwarding of route request packets. The main advantage of the ZRP is a reduced number of required RREQ messages and further on the possibility to establish new routes without the necessity to completely flood of the network. The main disadvantage is the increased complexity of the routing algorithm, especially the copy-deletion algorithms are difficult to implement. This also imposes additional requirements to the already limited processing power of mobile nodes.

5   Routing in Peer-to-Peer Networks

5.1 The Gnutella Protocol v0.4

The most prominent example for flat routing architectures in the area of Peer-to-Peer networks is the network established by the Gnutella protocol [6]. The Gnutella network is made up of nodes distributed throughout the world, which are interconnected by TCP/IP connections. Within this virtual overlay network the nodes provide the content and perform routing tasks, to make networking possible.

Every node is connected dynamically to an average of 7 nodes [16], depending on the bandwidth of the node's network connection. The messages, routed via these connections can be divided into two categories. One type are the query messages, and the second type are the respond messages. The query messages are used to explore the structure of a terminals neighborhood and to search for user demanded content.

The Gnutella network employs a routing concept, known as "viral propagation" for the query messages. This means that a node searching for content or exploring the network, sends out a query message, i.e. a QUERY() or a PING() message, to all the neighboring nodes it is currently directly connected to via TCP/IP connections in the virtual overlay network.

The second type of messages, which are used in the Gnutella network, are the respond messages, which are used to answer received query messages. These respond message are of no interest to the rest of the network, and they therefore have to be routed only to the querying node. To avoid flooding, respond messages are routed back to the querying terminal on the same way backwards, the original query message traveled to the receiving node.

Beside the – application routed - signaling messages, i.e. the respond and query messages, the content a node is querying for must also be distributed through the virtual overlay network. However, to minimize the load on the existing overlay network and especially of its nodes/routers, the demanded data is transmitted "out-band". "Out-band in this context means, that with the address provided in the QUERY_HIT message, a direct - only IP routed - connection between the querying and the responding node is established. This connection is used to transmit the content directly between both peers.

The major problem of the Gnutella protocol v0.4 is that parts of the virtual overlay network are flooded to a certain extent with ping and query messages, which causes a high signaling load. To reduce this load, a time-to-live value (TTL) is attached to each query message in the Gnutella protocol v0.4. Thus a certain transmission range for these messages is defined, which prevents the network from being flooded by query messages.

5.2 Table Driven Query Routing

Chord [21] follows a different approach to locate content in a P2P network. Instead of flooding the whole network in search of a certain file one could think of storing information about the location of all content in form of tables. An entry to this table basically consists of key/value pairs like file-name/destination-node. The table itself is stored in a distributed manner. A hashing algorithm applied to the key results in the destination address of the node that stores and maintains this key/value pair. The lookup of key/value pairs e.g. to resolve a search query for key=file-name is done by hashing the requested key and resolving the node address for the value lookup. In fact those node addresses are also hashed and incrementally arranged in form of a circle that spans the whole range of possible hash values. Hashed node addresses are also called *identifiers*.

Consistent hashing [22] guarantees a balanced distribution and computation of table entries but also implies that every node has to know about at least one successor node to forward lookup requests. The actual lookup is fast. By comparing the included identifier with it's own hashed address a node determines if the lookup has to be resolved by itself or by one of its successors.

To speed up the forwarding of lookup requests Chord maintains more than one successor node entry in form of finger tables where the distance between successor address entries grows to the power of 2.

Chord also adapts to the dynamic nature of P2P networks. by failure-handling and replication mechanisms.

Distributed hash tables offer a fast and reliable way to route queries at the cost of an increased need for processing power and memory. Additional examples for table driven P2P routing algorithms are Pastry [23], CAN [24] or Query Routing [15].

5.3 Dynamic Hierarchical Routing

Due to the eventual scalability problems of flat routing architectures as described in chapter 0 and 0, another P2P routing architecture has recently appeared, which tries to combine the advantages of centralized and decentralized routing. Within this approach, which is the basis for the FastTrack [4] architecture, nodes are elected at logon to become so called SuperNodes, if they offer sufficient bandwidth and processing power. Further on they additionally receive a list of already active SuperNodes, to which they connect. These SuperNodes thus establish a network, with high bandwidth connections to each other and high computing power at each SuperNode.

If a node without sufficient capabilities logs on to this network, it is bound to one of the existing Supernodes in it's neighborhood. Thus clusters are established, which consist of several "normal" nodes, and one SuperNode. After having connected to a SuperNode, the node uploads information about hosted data on to its SuperNode, and thus becomes "visible" to the overlay network.

As a normal node directs queries only to the SuperNode of its cluster. Upon receiving a query, the SuperNode first searches its own database, whether the demanded data is available in its own cluster. In this is the case, the IP-addresses of the nodes hosting the demanded data is sent back to the querying node. Otherwise, the

SuperNode broadcasts this query in the upper layer, the SuperNode layer. Every SuperNode, which receives this query, searches its database and in case of success sends back the according IP-address of the node of its cluster, to the querying SuperNode. This SuperNode then forwards this response to the querying node.

6   Similarities and Differences between Mobile ad Hoc Networks and Peer-to-Peer Networks

6.1 Differences between Mobile ad hoc Networks and Peer-to-Peer Networks

The most important difference between a mobile ad hoc network (MANET) and a peer-to-peer network (P2P) is the motivation to create such a network. A MANET is created to connect terminals with other terminals for communication purposes. We refer to this as user driven.

The reason to use a P2P network is different. Due to the large capacity of a P2P network, the primary goal of most P2P users is to search for data in the network and do not necessarily want to communicate with other users. However using Peer-to-Peer for distributed collaboration on the same document via a groupware tool, is gaining more and more attention

In P2P networks, the exchange of data is done with a direct link from one computer to the other. The intermediate computers used to setup a connection between these two computers are neither required nor wanted as relay stations for the transmission of the requested data.

An ad hoc network works different. In a MANET, the route discovery as well as the established connection must use the intermediate nodes. Therefore, data connections are indirect, whereas a P2P data connection – from the "Overlay" network view - is a direct link. **Figure 4** is a schematic picture, which shows the difference between P2P and ad hoc networks in maintaining an established connection. It should be outlined, that the direct link of a P2P connection is much easier to maintain than an indirect link over multiple hops of an ad hoc network. Due to the mobility of intermediate nodes the number of route reestablishments increases.

Another difference in the network is the structure of a network in P2P and MANET. A virtually overlay network is created to connect computers in a P2P network. Thus the P2P network is separated from the physical network. Computers directly connected in the P2P overlay network may be separated by thousands of kilometers in the real world. In contrast to that, the physical position of an ad hoc network member can roughly be estimated, because the members are densely distributed in an area. Beside this, the physical network structure of an ad hoc network can usually be mapped directly to the logical structure of such a network. Exceptions are subsequently added virtual hierarchies to the logical network structure of the MANET. While a P2P network can possibly span the world, the position of a single computer is fixed. In contrast the position of a complete MANET is approximately known, the position of a single moving node within the MANET cannot be forecasted.

There are also some differences in the usage of routing algorithms between P2P networks and MANET. Several publications [19, 20] show, that a proactive ad hoc routing scheme only works in small MANETs, with a number of nodes less then 100. With larger numbers of nodes, update messages must be sent too frequently, so the network is mainly concerned with signaling instead of data traffic. Beside the scaling problem, proactive routing algorithms are feasible in ad hoc networks, whereas they do not work at all in a P2P network. The reason therefore is, that the load, generated by the usage of a Bellman-Ford [2] routing algorithm, is too high for large P2P networks. Using a proactive routing algorithm in a P2P network, would mean, to transmit lists of addresses and/or containing subjects of all peers to all other peers, which would certainly fail.

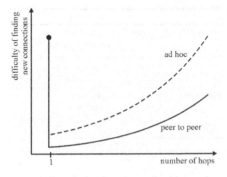 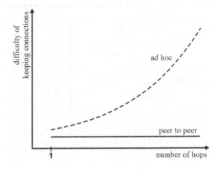

Fig. 3 Schematic comparison of MANET and P2P networks: Difficulty of establishing new connections over multiple nodes

Fig. 4 Schematic comparison of MANET and P2P networks: Difficulty of keeping an established connections alive

As mentioned, the P2P routing algorithms is only executed during a search-query, therefore it can be stated as a reactive routing algorithm. Despite the usage of similar reactive routing algorithms in both networks, the execution differs in both networks. In an ad hoc network the search ends, i.e. the request is not forwarded anymore, when the destination is found, or an intermediate node knows a fresh route to the destination. In contrast to that, the query request does not stop in a P2P network, although that node hosts the searched file. The query request is still forwarded by the node and only stops when the TTL field is equal to zero.

points out another difference between the P2P routing architecture and a reactive MANET algorithm. The main difficulty for setting up a new connection in P2P networks is to gather information for the first hop, because there is no possibility in the P2P-overlay network to receive information about the structure of the underlying IP network. Whereas in a MANET network, the adjacent nodes within transmission range are the possible nodes for the first hop, which can easily be found.

The reliability of the physical channels of the underling network infrastructure differs in P2P and ad hoc networks. Whereas wired links show very high reliability, wireless links always suffer from unpredictable changes, causing numerous bit errors. Therefore, the bit error rate of a wireless link is magnitudes greater then the bit error rate of a wired link. Thus, as shown in **Figure 3**, the creation of a new route over multiple hops is easier in a P2P network. The behavior of executing a broadcast is also different at both networks. A P2P network is a single cast network. It can only generate a virtual broadcast, consisting of numerous of single cast messages. In contrast to that, an ad hoc network always performs a physical broadcast. Every neighbor within transmission range receives a message broadcasted by a node. On the other hand, a logical single cast message is a physical broadcast, and the receiver must be determined with help of a logical address within the message.

Table 1 Differences between Peer-to-Peer and Mobile Ad hoc Networks

Difference	Peer-to-Peer	MANET
Reason for network creation	virtual infrastructure, independent from physical one	create an initial/physical infrastructure for connectivity
Connection between two nodes	wired and direct connection (at P2P layer)	wireless and indirect connection over several intermediate nodes
Reliability of connections	high, due to the wired links	Low, due to the wireless links
Structure	virtual overlay separated from physical structure	logical and physical structure corresponds
Physical diameter of network	can span the world	members are densely distributed
Routing	stops when TTL field is 0	stops when destination is found
Proactive routing	not possible	Limited by network size
Reactive routing	possible	Possible
Reliable routing	not required, not implemented	Exist
Broadcast	virtual broadcast, realized with multiple unicasts	physical broadcast performed
Mobility of nodes	fixed	Mobile
Available resources	practical unlimited	Limited
Usage of a PKI	possible	not feasible

The fixed position of a P2P node or the mobile position of an ad hoc node also impact the available resources. Resources in this context are transmission bandwidth, battery power, memory and processing power. While a P2P terminal has nearly unlimited resources, they are certainly limited in an ad hoc node.

As a summary of this chapter, it can be stated that wireless ad hoc networks and wired peer-to-peer networks have differences, summed up in **Table 1**. However beside all differences there are also a lot of similarities, as shown in the next section.

6.2 Similarities between Mobile ad Hoc Networks and Peer-to-Peer Networks

The basis of both networks, i.e. Peer-to-Peer and wireless ad hoc networks, is the concept of self organization. In most cases, except the hybrid Peer-to-Peer approach (see [17]), no central entities, which manage and coordinate the network, are given nor is such a network in any form preconfigured. The network is established, as soon as the single participants decide to create a network, by establishing connections to each other. Thus although the nodes stay the same, the network alters permanently, because the nodes most probably change their connections to each other.

The frequently changing topology is another parallel of Peer-to-Peer and wireless ad hoc networks and results from the permanent change of connections. In the wireless area, this is caused by the terminal mobility of the nodes. Thus previously established connections to other nodes may break down, as the node might leave the transmission range of previously neighboring nodes. As a result new connections have to be established to other nodes which can be reached now.

In Peer-to-Peer networks, the geographical mobility is not an issue, but the frequent on and of switching of the nodes itself. The average session duration is only 2 hours per day, which results in an average availability of 0.083 [16]. Further on the dynamic assignment of IP-addresses by DHCP servers and network address translators causes further problems, as a certain member cannot be located at a stable IP-address. This could be compared to the geographical mobility of wireless nodes. As a result, a statement concerning the current network situation can hardly be given, as it is nearly impossible to gather in a short time all the information about the whole network, due to the dynamic network topology.

However, the availability of the terminals is important, as the initial connection request to a demanded objected, may it be a file or a user, and additionally in case of success the possible reply message must be forwarded via multiple hosts. A direct connection cannot be established, as it is not known, where a certain object can be found in the network.

A further critical issue which arises from the self organization, is that flooding is necessary to a certain extent in both networks. As both networks are based on a continuously changing topology, the network must be periodically probed, whether certain links and nodes are still available. This is only possible via broadcasting or flooding messages, as a central management entity is not available. Thus the question of up to what number of participants the network is able to scale, is of high interest in the wireless as well as in the Peer-to-Peer area.

A further problem occurring in both networks is, how a new participant can log on to an existing Peer-to-Peer or mobile ad hoc network. As a central managing entity is in general not given, it is necessary, that any new node has to find active members of the network. By connecting to the active nodes, the new node becomes also an active member of the network. To find active members of the network, a kind of portal is used, which works more or less like a beacon to announce to not yet connected participants, at which addresses active members can be found. Thus any new node must know at least the address of the portal, to be able to log onto the ad hoc network. In Peer-to-Peer networks this portal is located under fixed and preconfigured IP-addresses. A new node first contacts the portal, from which it receives a certain number of IP-addresses of active nodes, to which the new node is now able to connect and thus to become an active member of the Peer-to-Peer network.

In the wireless area a similar procedure is necessary. However in this case not a specific IP-address of a portal must be known, but a specific frequency range, within which the signaling channel of the wireless ad hoc network is located. On this signaling channel, the new terminal has to announce its presence, and thus is able to become an active member of the network. However, a restriction, which does not occur in Peer-to-Peer networks is, that at least one active member of the ad hoc network must be located within the transmission range of the new terminal. Otherwise no logon is possible.

Due to the basic principle of self organization and independence of each participant, it is not easy in wireless ad hoc and Peer-to-Peer networks to offer network management functionalities, like authorization, authentication and accounting, or even Quality of Service features. Especially the two topics authorization and authentication lead to the basic question of trust in an untrustworthy environment, as a central authority unit is missing. How can e.g. a participant be sure, whether it's communication partner, is the one which originally answered a request?

Concerning secure transmission, no lower layer security approaches, as e.g. IPSEC [1], can be used. The reason is the necessity, that user and signaling data has to be routed at least partly via other participants of the network. Thus an end-to-end security can not be granted by IPSEC tunnels, but only by encryption techniques implemented on higher layers, e.g. by the use of PGP.

As mentioned above, Quality of Service is also an issue which is not easy to solve in any ad hoc network. Guarantees of connection parameters can hardly be given, as the connections are established and managed by independent peers. Thus delay and bandwidth critical applications, like e.g. video communication can hardly be provided in wireless ad hoc or Peer-to-Peer networks, independent from their additional physical constraints.

Table 2 Similarities between Peer-to-Peer and Mobile Ad Hoc Networks

Similarity	Peer-to-Peer	MANET
Basic routing principle	Virtual broadcast, flooding	Physical broadcast, flooding
Network topology	Flat and frequently changing topology,	Flat and frequently changing network topology
Reliability of nodes	low	Low
Connection establishment	Hop by hop, via TCP links, unlimited range	Hop by hop via radio links, limited by the transmission range
Network log on	Via a portal ("beacon server").	Via a portal (broadcast radio channel).
Scalability	Limited by signaling traffic s($\rightarrow$ approx. 50.000-60.000 currently)	Limited by consuming signaling traffic ($\rightarrow$ approx. 100 users)
Network management	QoS and AAA are difficult (no central management)	QoS and AAA are difficult to realize (no central management)
Security	No lower layer security (e.g. IPSEC) useable. (separation from. phys. layer)	No lower layer security concepts for MANET implemented until now.

Although some difficulties arise from the lack of a central authority in Peer-to-Peer and wireless ad hoc networks, such a form of networking also offers the advantage that no additional hardware is necessary for the establishment and basic management of the network. Communication and data exchange is made possible in a fast changing environment, where possibly fixed or static network elements could mean too much overhead. Further on, there is no single point of failure in Peer-to-Peer and ad hoc networks, which makes these networks as whole comparable robust and reliable. An overview of further similarities is given in **Table 2**.

Conclusion

The former sections only can give an overview on ad hoc and Peer-to-Peer networking but should be sufficient to understand the basic principles of the two worlds. As mentioned before the motivation of routing in both networks is different the approaches however show similarities. This stems from the fact that both networks – ad hoc and application layer networks – have to deal with same problems, namely *self-organization, scalability* and *robustness*. Moreover there exist a lot of more or less unsolved questions in both disciplines e.g. bootstrapping in a total distributed manner, dynamic address assignment or consistent naming of nodes and resources.

We want to conclude with four examples to show how to make use of the comparisons and tables in section 6.

The first two examples should clarify how to interpret the similarities of section 6.2. Table 2 offers a – yet incomplete – means to quickly identify areas where solutions might be exchanged between Peer-to-Peer and ad hoc networks. Evaluation of ideas inspired by our comparison are subject of further investigations.

Example 1: Looking at the former mentioned self-organization with respect to table-driven approaches of distributed information management it might be interesting to investigate in more detail a proactive ad hoc routing algorithm like DSDV and a table-driven Peer-to-Peer lookup service like Chord. Though a Chord like ring organization of routing information in a network with basic connectivity depending on indirect links is questionable, a star like organization into hashing zones could be appealing. Not only would hashing reduce storage needs for routing info but also open new possibilities of hierarchical organization from center to edge.

Example 2: Scalability is not only an issue in ad hoc networks but also in Peer-to-Peer networks. Although the information to deal with differs in magnitudes between ad hoc nodes and Peer-to-Peer resources, there are interesting solutions in both areas. Whereas a cluster based organization of nodes like the FastTrack framework enables fast and effective resources lookup, zone based ad hoc routing differentiates between two zones and therefore also introduces sort of a hierarchy. Investigating a zone based routing concept in Peer-to-Peer networks might be an idea. This would allow an efficient handling of local resource information, combined with the robustness of a flat, Gnutella like network at the edge. Who belongs to a local zone and what node is part of a outer zone can depend on response times, contribution of resources or availability of a peer.

The comparison of differences in Section 6.1 allows an identification of topics where both networks could complete and extend each other. Also it should allow to identify issues where a direct exchange of concepts is difficult and requires adaptations.

Example 3: Gnutella like Peer-to-Peer networks, which use virtual broadcasts to explore their neighborhood, could benefit from the already existing physical broadcast in a wireless LAN. Interlayer communication between application, routing and MAC layer has to be defined and evaluated to get the best out of both worlds.

Example 4: The virtual structure of Peer-to-Peer networks offers the possibility to integrate different ad hoc radio technologies into one unique overlay network. But again context awareness and communication between Peer-to-Peer and ad hoc routing layer is needed to adapt e.g. query and hello messages to the limited resources of low rate radio links.

We think there is a lot of hidden treasure in both areas. Ad hoc can learn from Peer-to-Peer and vice versa. The complementary effects of both worlds should not be underestimated and are subject to our further investigations.

References

1. R. Atkinson, S. Kent. "Security Architecture for the Internet Protocol". RFC2401. November 1998
2. O. Bertsekas, R. Gallager, Data Networks, 2nd Edition, Prentice Hall Inc., 1992
3. The Bluetooth Specification, see http://www.bluetooth.com/dev/specifications.asp
4. http://www.fasttrack.nu/index_int.html. January 2002
5. M. Frodigh, P. Johansson, P. Larsson, "Wireless ad hoc networking: The art of networking without a network" Ericsson Review, No. 4, pp. 248-263, 2000.
6. The Gnutella Protocol Specification v0.4. http://dss.clip2.com/GnutellaProtocol04.pdf. August 2000.
7. Z. Haas, M. Pearlman, "The Performance of Query Control Schemes for the Zone Routing Protocol", IEEE/ACM Transactions on Networking, Vol. 9, No. 4,August 2001
8. J. Jubin, J. Tornow. „The DARPA Packet Radio Network Protocols", in Proceedings of the IEEE volume 75, 1, pages 21-32, Jan 1987
9. A. Langley. "Freenet". ". Appeared in "Peer-to-Peer Harnessing the Power of Disruptive Computing". Editor: A. Oram. Publisher: O'Reilly & Associates, Incorporated. March 2001
10. B. Leiner, D. Nielson, "Issues in Packet Radio Network Design, Proceedings of the IEEE Special issue on "Packet Radio Networks", 75, 1:6-20, 1987
11. Limewire. "Current Network Size". http://www.limewire.com/historical_size.html. January 2002
12. The Napster Protocol. http://opennap.sourceforge.net/napster.txt. September 2001
13. C. Perkins, "Highly Dynamic Destination Sequence Distance Vector Routing (DSDV) for Mobile Computers", ACM SIGCOMM'94, 1994
14. C. Perkins, E. Royer, "Ad hoc On demand Distance Vector Routing", Proceeding of 2nd IEEE Workshop on Mobile Computing Systems and Applications, February 1999
15. Christpher Rohrs. "Query Routing for the Gnutella Network". http://www.limewire.com/developer/query_ routing/keyword%20routing.htm. December 2001.
16. S. Saroiu, P. K. Gummadi, S. D. Gribble. "A Measurement Study of Peer-to-Peer File Sharing Systems" Technical Report # UW-CSE-01-06-02. July 2001
17. R. Schollmeier. "A definition of Peer-to-Peer Networking towards a Delimitation against Classical Client-Server Concepts". Proceedings of WATM-Eunice 2001. pp. 131-138. 2001.
18. The IEEE 802.11 Standards, see   http://grouper.ieee.org/groups/802/11/
19. P.Johansson et al. "Scenario Based Performance Analysis of Routing Protocols for Mobile Ad-hoc Networks", Mobicom '99, 1999 Seatle, USA
20. J. Broch et al., "A Performance Comaprison of Multi-Hop Wireless Ad hoc Network Routing Protocols", MobiCom '98, 1998, Dallas, USA
21. I. Stoica et al "Chord. A scalable peer-to-peer lookup service for Internet applications. Technical Report TR-819, MIT, March 2001

22. D: Karger et al "Consistent hashing and random trees: Distriubuted caching protocols for relieving hot spots on the World Wide Web", Proceedings of the 29th Annual ACM Symposium on Theory of Computing (El Paso, TX, May 1997), pp. 654-663
23. P. Druschel, "Past: Persistent and anonymous storage in a peer-to-peer networking environment. In Proceedings of the 8th IEEE Workshop on Hot Topics in Operating Systems (HotOS 2001) (Elmau/Oberbayern, Germany, May 2001), pp. 65-70
24. S. Ratnasamy "A scalable content-addressable network" in Proc. ACM SIGCOMM (San Diego, CA, August 2001)

Multi-layer Clusters in Ad-hoc Networks
– An Approach to Service Discovery

Michael Klein and Birgitta König-Ries

Institute for Program Structures and Data Organization
Universität Karlsruhe
D-76128 Karlsruhe, Germany
{kleinm,koenig}@ipd.uni-karlsruhe.de
http://www.ipd.uni-karlsruhe.de/DIANE

Abstract. One of the core functionalities needed in ad-hoc peer-to-peer networks is service discovery. However, none of the existing solutions for service discovery work well in these dynamic, decentralized environments. Therefore, in this paper, we propose a new approach to service discovery which is based on the dynamic organization of the services into multi-layer clusters. These clusters are formed based on both physical and semantic proximity.

1 Introduction

Anna is a graduate student majoring in computer science. Currently, she prepares for the finals in her information systems class. She has downloaded some of the official course material onto her laptop computer. She also stores the solutions to some exercises and her personal summary of the first few chapters there. Of course, Anna is not the only student about to take the exam, others are in the same situation. They, too, will have stored some information on their computers - information that might be a good complement to the one Anna already possesses. Thus, the idea to connect the computers of these students to a peer-to-peer network and to allow the exchange of information stored on these devices is pretty natural. However, a classical peer-to-peer network (if such a thing exists) is not sufficient for our needs. Like Anna, some of the students will own laptop computers or other mobile devices and will want to have access to the network from wherever they are at a certain point of time regardless of the existence of an underlying network infrastructure. Therefore, in the DIANE project [1], we attempt to use wireless ad-hoc networks to offer the functionality described.

Assuming we have succeeded in technically connecting the computers to such a network, what is needed next is a possibility for the students (or their computers) to find information (or more generally services) in the network. Due to the distributed and dynamic nature of ad-hoc networks, a centralized approach which is based on a service directory is not feasible. Because of the characteristics of wireless networks, a Gnutella-like gossiping approach involving a large

E. Gregori et al. (Eds.): Networking 2002 Workshops, LNCS 2376, pp. 187–201, 2002.

message overhead is not feasible, either. Therefore, we present a new approach to discovering services in wireless ad-hoc peer-to-peer networks.

The basic idea of our approach is to take advantage of the fact that nodes in an ad-hoc network are naturally grouped along two dimensions: The first of these dimensions is the physical proximity of nodes; the second is their semantic proximity. Two nodes are considered to be physically close, if they are within radio range of each other. Two nodes are considered to be semantically close, if the services they offer are similar. For our work we assume that a common ontology exists within the network that is used to describe the services offered by a node. The structure of this ontology is very simple: Terms are related via *isSubTopicOf* links only. Thus, if two nodes offer services described by the same term or by terms that are close in the ontology, they are considered to be semantically close.

Based on these dimensions we now define multi-layered clusters on the nodes which will be used for service discovery. Let us first have a look at how these clusters are defined. Afterwards, we are going to explain how the clusters can be used to find specific services. The bottom layer of our cluster hierarchy, the leaf level, is formed by grouping nodes that offer services that are described by the same leaf term of the ontology and that form a connected sub net. On the next layer several of these leaf-level clusters are combined to form larger clusters offering services that belong to the same term on the next level of the ontology and so on.

This cluster hierarchy can be used for service discovery as follows: When a node looks for a certain service, it first checks, whether that service is available in its own leaf-level cluster. If this is not the case, the query is moved to higher-level clusters until one that might contain an appropriate service is reached. In this cluster, the query is moved back down through the hierarchy to the appropriate leaf-level cluster. In the following sections, we will describe the details of this process.

The remainder of this paper is organized as follows: In Section 2 we review related work. Then, Section 3 describes multi-layer clusters in more detail. Section 4 explains how this concept is used for service discovery. The paper concludes with a discussion of the advantages of our approach and an outlook to future work (Section 5).

2   Related Work

This section contains a short introduction to ad-hoc networks in general and an overview of approaches to service discovery taken by different research communities.

An ad-hoc network, as the name suggests, is a spontaneous community of mobile devices communicating via wireless links without the support of an underlying infrastructure [3]. In the simplest case, all the devices are within radio-range of each other, thus forming a single-hop ad-hoc network. More interesting are multi-hop ad-hoc networks, where devices may need the help of intermediate nodes to communicate with one another. In this case, the intermediate nodes take over the functionality classically provided by routers. In an ad-hoc network, nodes interact as equals, thus, they can be regarded as a special kind of peer-to-peer network. However, in contrast to peer-to-peer networks in wired environments, a number of additional problems need to be solved in ad-hoc networks. The most obvious of these problems is the need to offer a possibility to route messages in ad-hoc networks. The topology of an ad-hoc network may change frequently. The nodes that take part in an ad-hoc network typically have a limited power supply only, thus restricting the amount of messages they can process and in particular send. These characteristics make the development of appropriate routing protocols a challenging task. Thus, in the past, most of the research effort has been concentrated on this topic. Much of this work has been done in the context of the IETF MANET working group [4].

While routing protocols determine a way from a given node A to a given node B, service discovery protocols try to find a node B that is able to fulfill a certain task that node A is looking for. Traditionally this problem is solved by maintaining a directory server that contains the necessary information to identify node B. A typical representative of this class of solutions is Jini [5], a Java based network technology that aims at facilitating integrated usage of services in dynamic networks. The core component of a Jini system is a service directory, the Lookup Server. Devices that offer services register with this directory. Devices looking for services query the directory and obtain an appropriate service stub from the directory. Other approaches like UPnP [6], the Corba Naming and Trading Services [7], the Bluetooth Service Discovery Protocol [8], operate similarly. The same is true for Napster [9] and related systems.

For ad-hoc networks, approaches that rely on a directory server do not apply for two reasons: First, nodes can join and leave the network at any time, thus the set of services offered in the network changes frequently, making it difficult to maintain an up-to-date directory. More severely, in an ad-hoc network, there is no guarantee, that a certain node will be available at any given time. Thus, in a true ad-hoc network, none of the participating nodes could serve as a directory server.

Similar problems have resulted in peer-to-peer systems trying to avoid the need for a centralized service directory altogether. Gnutella [10], for instance, relies on a gossiping approach that propagates searches throughout the network. Its main drawback is that they necessarily involve a large message overhead. This may be acceptable in wired networks; however, it is a major disadvantage in wireless environments with limited bandwidth and limited power resources, where minimizing communication is a major requirement.

A major prerequisite for service discovery is that the devices have agreed on some common scheme to describe services. Jini, for example, uses the Java class hierarchy to achieve this goal. In our work, we assume that services are described by a common ontology [2] that is known to every node.

To summarize, in order to support service discovery in a mobile ad-hoc network, we need an approach with the following characteristics: It allows to find services without relying on a centralized directory server. At the same time, it minimizes message overhead and is able to deal with the high dynamics and ever changing topology of ad-hoc networks. In the next sections, we present such an approach.

3   Ad-hoc Nets as Multi-layer Clusters

In this section, we describe how ad-hoc networks can be conceptually organized into multi-layer clusters. After introducing this structure, we will explain in Section 4 how it can be used to support efficient service discovery.

The main idea of our approach is to naturally combine the conceptual structure given by an ontology with the technical structure of the devices caused by the current state of reachability between the nodes. We present the details of this process in this section starting with explaining and formalizing the two different types of structures that have to be merged: the ontological structure and the technical structure. After that, we combine the two structures to form multi-layer clusters.

3.1   The Ontological Structure

The network consists of devices that offer services. In the context of this paper, we are interested in information services, i.e., services that deliver documents. To describe the content of information that is delivered by information services, we use very simple, single-rooted, hierarchical ontologies consisting only of a set of terms $T = \{t^1, \ldots, t^r\}$ and the relationship type *isSubTopicOf*. Figure 1 shows a sample ontology for the database domain. The top most term (here **database**) is called root term and comprises the whole domain of the ontology. The other terms are subordinated to this root term. We use the notation $t^1.isSubTopicOf = t^2$ to denote the relationship between terms t^1 and t^2.

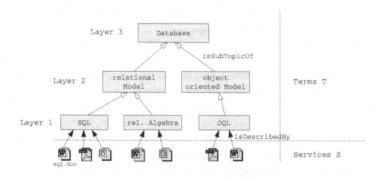

Fig. 1. A database ontology and the documents described by it.

For ease of presentation, we make the following assumptions throughout the remainder of this paper:[1]

- Each service offers exactly one document.
- Each document s can be described by exactly one leaf term t of the ontology: $s.isDescribedBy = t$.

On the ontology and the set of documents described by it, we can define a *parent function* as follows:

Definition 1 (Parent Function).
Let $S = \{s_1, \ldots, s_n\}$ be the set of all services and let $T = \{t^1, \ldots, t^r\}$ be the set of all terms in the ontology with root term t^r. Then, we define the parent *function $p : S \cup T \to T$ as:*

$$p(x) = \begin{cases} t, \ \text{with} \ \ t = x.isDescribedBy & : \ \ x \in S \\ t, \ \text{with} \ \ t = x.isSubTopicOf & : \ \ x \in T \backslash \{t^r\} \\ x & : \ \ x = t^r \end{cases}$$

We will use $p^k(x)$ as a shorthand notation for $\underbrace{p(p(\ldots p(x)\ldots))}_{k-times}$ in the remainder of the paper.

As the ontology should form a tree, we explicitly prohibit cycles:

$$\forall t \in T \ \forall k \geqslant 1 : p^k(t) \neq t \ \lor \ t = t^r.$$

In our example, we have $p(\texttt{sql.doc}) = \texttt{SQL}$ and $p^2(\texttt{OQL}) = \texttt{database} = t^r$.

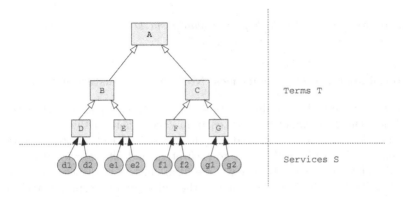

Fig. 2. Generic ontology, which serves as example ontology for the remainder of the paper.

---

[1] Note that the approach will also work if we relax these assumptions. However, the resulting presentation would be a lot less elegant.

The number of layers n in an ontology is the number of nodes on the longest path from a leaf to the root term. Whenever the ontological layer to which a term t belongs is important, we will write t_l with l being the layer, i.e., n minus the distance to the root.

For our example ontology in Figure 1, n is 3, the layer of the term OQL is 1, the layer of the term Database is 3. For the remainder of the paper, we will refer to the generic ontology and services in Figure 2.

3.2   The Physical Structure

Besides the ontological structure, we have to take into account the physical topology of the devices. For our paper, we make the following assumption:

– Each device in our ad-hoc network offers exactly one service $s \in S$. Devices offering no services are useful only for routing purposes and are not further considered in this paper. If a document is offered on more than one device, each of these devices offers its own service instance of the document. Thus, devices are uniquely identified by the service they offer. We will therefore denote devices with the service variables $s_1, s_2, \ldots s_n$.

Devices are connected directly to all the devices within their radio range. Based on these connections, reachability can be defined as follows:

Definition 2 (Device Reachability).
The dynamical relation $\dashrightarrow \subseteq S \times S$ describes the (single-hop) reachability between the devices in the ad-hoc network.

Single-hop reachability $i \dashrightarrow j$ is given iff. device $i \in S$ is currently able to send information to device j via a single-hop connection.

As this reachability is transitive, we have multi-hop reachability $i \overset{*}{\dashrightarrow} j$ iff. $i \dashrightarrow \ldots \dashrightarrow j$.

Furthermore, we have multi-hop reachability via D (written $i \overset{*}{\dashrightarrow}_D j$) iff. $i \dashrightarrow d_1 \dashrightarrow \ldots \dashrightarrow d_m \dashrightarrow j$ and $d_1, \ldots, d_m \in D$.

3.3   Combination of the Structures: Multi-layer Clustering

Up to now, we have looked at the two types of structures separately. However, in a real net, the two cannot be isolated from each other. In this section, we describe how devices can be organized into clusters so that each cluster contains devices that are both physically close to each other and offer services that are semantically close. On the bottom layer, we form clusters of devices that offer services described by the same leaf term of the ontology and form a connected graph of reachability. On the higher layers, we combine these clusters to clusters whose semantic description becomes more general when moving up the ontology tree. On the top layer, this results in one big cluster containing all the services offered within the net. (If the network is partitioned, we will have more than one cluster at this layer, too.)

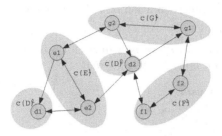

Fig. 3. Clustering on the leaf level. Devices are grouped together if they belong to the same term and reach each other.

In Figure 3, the clustering on Level 1 (i.e., the leaf level) is performed on a net with the help of our generic ontology. As a rule, a set of devices forms a cluster on Level 1 iff. (a) all offered services are described by the same leaf concept and (b) every two devices from this set are mutually reachable via that set of devices. In the example, five rather small clusters have been formed by this definition. Note that this cluster construction rule is non-ambiguous as no parameters like cluster size and shape need to be determined. Only varying radio connections and varying service offerings can change the clustering topology.

On the next layer, we combine clusters that offer services described by the same next layer term in the ontology and form a connected graph of reachability from a cluster point of view (see below). Figure 4 shows how this is done with the clusters of Figure 3. On the left side, the services offered by clusters $c(D)^1$, $c(E)^1$ and $c(D)^2$ have the same parent term B and form a connected reachability graph, so they are grouped to the new cluster $c(B)^1$. On the right side, new cluster $c(C)^1$ is formed. The last clustering step, which is not depicted here, would join those two clusters to one large cluster $c(A)^1$.

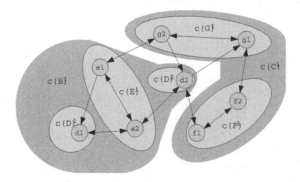

Fig. 4. Cluster are grouped to larger clusters according to higher levels of the ontology and the connectivity between clusters.

Let us now give a formal definition of a cluster on layer l:

Definition 3 (Cluster).
A cluster $c_l(t_l^m)$ on layer l with respect to term t_l^m on ontology layer l is a set of clusters or devices on layer $l-1$, such that

for $l = 1$: $c_1(t_1^m) \subseteq S$ *with*
a) $\forall s_i \in c_1(t_1^m) : p(s_i) = t_1^m$ $\wedge$
b) $\forall s_i, s_j \in c_1(t_1^m) : s_i \dashrightarrow^{*}_{c_1(t_1^m)} s_j$

for $l > 1$: $c_l(t_l^m) \subseteq \{c_{l-1}(t_{l-1}^1)^1, \ldots, c_{l-1}(t_{l-1}^1)^{m_1}, c_{l-1}(t_{l-1}^2)^1 \ldots, c_{l-1}(t_{l-1}^n)^{m_n}\}$ *wit*
a) $\forall c = c_{l-1}(t_{l-1}^i) \in c_l(t_l^m) : p(t_{l-1}^i) = t_l^m$ $\wedge$
b) $\forall c, d \in c_l(t_l^m) : c \dashrightarrow^{*}_{c_l(t_l^m)} d$

Here, t_l^i stands for the i-th term on ontology level l and $c_l(t_l^i)^j$ is the j-th cluster on level l for term t_l^i.

Informally, a cluster on layer l groups together clusters/devices of the next lower layer that belong to the same parent term and are mutually reachable via these clusters/devices. The definition above uses cluster reachability, which we haven't introduced yet. Figure 5 shows intuitively, under which conditions clusters are reachable: Cluster $c(E)^1$ can reach cluster $c(G)^1$ because they can communicate via their directly connected devices **e1** and **g2**. Generally speaking, one cluster c reaches another cluster d if c contains a device/cluster that is directly connected to a device/cluster in d.

Before we formally define cluster reachability, we define a layer of the cluster hierarchy as the set of all clusters on that layer:

Definition 4 (Layer l of the Cluster Hierarchy).
A layer l of the cluster hierarchy is defined as follows:

$$C_l := \{c_l(t_l^1)^1, \ldots, c_l(t_l^1)^{m_1}, c_l(t_l^2)^1, \ldots, c_l(t_l^k)^{m_k}\}$$

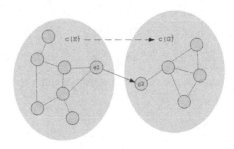

Fig. 5. Intuitive cluster reachability. Cluster $c(E)^1$ reaches cluster $c(G)^1$ because it can send messages over the directly connected devices **e1** and **g2**.

Additionally, we define C as the set of all clusters regardless of their layer:

Definition 5 (Set of all clusters).
The set C of all clusters defined as follows:

$$C := C_1 \cup C_2 \cup \ldots \cup C_n$$

Now, we have all the prerequisites needed to formally define cluster reachability. For that, we extend the $-\!\!-\!\!\rightarrow$ relation from above to clusters:

Definition 6 (Cluster Reachability).
$-\!\!-\!\!\rightarrow \; \subseteq C \times C \; \cup \; S \times S$. *Let c and d be two clusters from C. We have*

$$c -\!\!-\!\!\rightarrow d \quad iff. \quad \exists i \in c \; \exists j \in d : \; i -\!\!-\!\!\rightarrow j$$

In this case, we mark i and j as so called *gateway devices/clusters*, which will help us later to send a message from cluster c to cluster d. In our example in Figure 3, the devices g1 and f2 act as gateway instances for the two clusters $c(G)^1$ and $c(F)^1$.

Now that we have introduced the cluster hierarchy, we can define a parent function on clusters. In analogy to the parent function for terms, this function determines which more general cluster a cluster is part of. Thus, while the parent function for terms operates along the semantic dimension, the parent function for clusters operates along the topological dimension:

Definition 7 (Parent Function of a Cluster).
We define $\bar{p} : S \cup C \to C$, which assigns the parent cluster to services as well as clusters:

$$\bar{p}(x) := c_i(t_i), \quad if \; x \in c_i(t_i)$$

Note, as $\bar{p}$ cannot be derived from other functions like p, it's value has be stored somewhere in the device/cluster $c_i(t_i)$. We do not address this issue in this paper, but give two possible techniques in the last section on future work.

4   Service Discovery via Multi-layer Clusters

In this section, we describe how the multi-layer clusters introduced in the last section can be used for service discovery.

4.1   Layer Architecture

The clustering we described in the previous section leads to the layer architecture depicted in Figure 6. As in every layered architecture, the task of providing complex functionality (here to find a device offering a given information service somewhere in the net) is broken down into several steps each of which increases

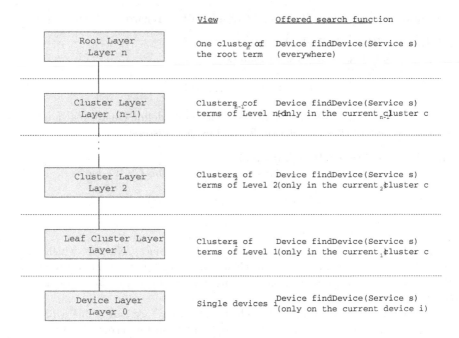

Fig. 6. The layer architecture. The search functionality as well as the cluster sizes increase with every network layer, the number of clusters decreases.

the functionality by using the methods of the underlying layer. Our architecture consists of $n + 1$ layers, one for each of the n ontology layers and one for the lowest device layer. Each layer has a different view on the network and offers two methods: a search and a send method. The first method checks whether the service is available in the current cluster or device; the second one is used to send a message to another cluster or device. Both methods operate within one layer only and are implemented using the respective functions of the layer below.

The bottom-most layer of our architecture is the **device layer** (or Layer 0), where the network is seen as a collection of single devices connected according to the basic reachability relation $-\rightarrow$. Each device i offers one very simple search function that checks whether a given information service request can be met on the own device. If so, it returns i, else it returns NULL:

```
Device findService(Service s)
```

For this very basic layer no ontology is needed - the device answers the request just by checking its own service description. As findService will not always be successful on the current device, the request has to be redirected to other devices. Thus, to send a message (for instance a find request) to a neighboring node with a single hop, we can use the function

```
void sendTo(Device j, Message m)
```

This function results in the message being sent if $i \dashrightarrow j$ and will return an exception else.

Above the device layer, we find the **leaf cluster layer** (or Layer 1). Here, the network is regarded as a collection of clusters consisting of services described by the same leaf terms of the ontology. A cluster $c_1(t_1^j)$ offers the following search function

```
Device findService(Service s)
```

with $p^1(\mathbf{s}) = t_1^j$. It searches for a device in the cluster c that offers service $\mathbf{s}$. As clusters are connected logically via gateway devices, we have the following sending function between two neighboring clusters:

```
void sendTo(Cluster d, Message m)
```

which will result in the message being sent if $c \dashrightarrow d$, and an exception otherwise.

Analogously, we have the functions `Device findService(Service s)` and `void sendTo(Cluster d, Message m)` on all the higher **cluster layers** (Layer 2 to Layer $n-1$). With each layer, the service descriptions we are looking in becomes more general and the physical area we are searching becomes bigger. Finally, the topmost **root layer** (or Layer n) offers the desired function

```
Device findService(Service s)
```

without any constraint to $\mathbf{s}$ because $p^n(\mathbf{s}) = t^r$ for all $\mathbf{s} \in S$.

4.2   Implementation of Layer Functions

After having introduced the declaration of the available functions in each network layer, we want to show how to implement them. We will present a non-centralized implementation, which only considers the locally available information and needs to send method invocation methods to other nodes. The transformation of such an implementation into a network protocol is rather straightforward.

On the device layer, the two functions can be implemented very easily. A device i, on which `Device findService(Service s)` has been called, just compares the service description it stores and returns i if it matches, and `NULL` otherwise. The `void sendTo(Device j, Message m)` is simply delegated to the lower MAC layer if $i \dashrightarrow j$ holds and returns an exception otherwise.

The functions in the Layers 1 to n are a bit more complicated. Generally, if the function `findService` is called in cluster c_l from device i, the `findService` function of all subclusters $c_{l-1}^1, \ldots c_{l-1}^m$ is called. If one or more of these functions deliver a concrete device, one of those is chosen and returned, otherwise `NULL` is returned. It is important that the concrete execution depends primarily on the order in which the subclusters are visited. The pseudocode of the algorithm can be found in Figure 7. It is written for a call in cluster c_l from device i, where c_l is a cluster on Layer $l \geq 1$. First of all, in line (02), the currently visited cluster is marked. We determine the current subcluster c_{l-1}, i.e. the subcluster that contains device i in line (03) and its ontological term t_{l-1} in line (04). If

```
Processing device i on cluster cₗ
(00)      Device findService(Service s)
(01)      {
(02)             mark(cₗ);
(03)             c_{l-1} = p̄^{l-1}(i);
(04)             t_{l-1} = p^{l-1}(i);
(05)             if ((p^{l-1}(s) == t_{l-1}) and (c_{l-1} is unmarked))
(06)             {
(07)                    Device result = (c_{l-1}).findService(s);
(08)                    if (result ≠ NULL) return result;
(09)             }
(10)
(11)             //Send query to the next subcluster
(12)             D := {d_{l-1} ∈ cₗ | c_{l-1} --→ d_{l-1} }
(14)
(15)             if (D is empty) return NULL;
(16)             repeat q times
(17)             {
(18)                    d := pickFrom(D);
(19)                    sendTo(d, "findService(s)");
(20)             }
(21)      }
```

Fig. 7. Pseudocode implementation of findService for a call in cluster c_l from device i. Here, c_l is a cluster on Layer $l \geq 1$.

this term matches the type of the requested service s and if the cluster is still unmarked (line (05)), we start a new search in it in line (07). If a concrete device is found, this is returned to the caller in line (08). Up to now, the search has been strictly local. We have only descended in lower layers of the part of the network the query originated from. Only if this search is not successful, the algorithm will now gradually extend the physical area in which it searches by looking at neighboring clusters. This is done by sending the findService query to the next subcluster of the current cluster c_l. To do that, all possible candidates are determined in line (12). A candidate has to be a cluster or a device that is a descendant of c_l, and can directly be reached by c_{l-1} with one hop. If this set is empty, the search has terminated without success and NULL is returned in line (15). Otherwise, one or more of these clusters/devices are chosen by the loop in line (18), to which the findService query is sent (line (19)).

This algorithms offers some degrees of freedom: First of all, in line (18), the method for fetching an element from the set D is left open. Moreover, the number q of elements is not defined in the condition of the repeat-loop. Depending on the knowledge about the network and the characteristics of the network, one of the following exploration strategies can be chosen:

– **Flooding.** The findService message is sent to *all* members of D, i.e. $q = |D|$. This method is useful if no further information is available. Its performance is poor as many subclusters are reached more than once and possibly an exhaustive search is executed. Nevertheless, if the topology of the subcluster changes very rapidly, flooding may be the only applicable technique.

- **Cycling.** All subclusters are connected to a ring, thus each member knows its ring predecessor and successor. In this case, we choose d as the successor and send the findService message to this cluster only. As in flooding, this can result in an exhaustive search, if, for instance, the suitable cluster is the predecessor of c_{l-1}, but each subcluster is exactly reached once. We can choose this technique, if the dynamics of the subclusters is medium so that a ring structure can be set up. This is not too hard as the structural integrity of a ring can be maintained locally.
- **Direct Routing.** If we have a routing table with an entry for the subcluster d, we send the findService message exactly to the next hop denoted in this entry. To speed up the routing, we could possibly add a flag to the message that prevents descending in intermediate subclusters. This technique can only be used if the subcluster movement is very small so that a routing table can be set up.

The function void sendTo(Cluster d, Message m) is implemented very similar to findService. Because each gateway point stores information about its partner gateway point and the cluster it resides in, sendTo can be seen as a search for an appropriate gateway point. Analogously, the sending process performs in several network layers and the same exploration techniques like flooding, cycling, and direct routing can be used depending on the current knowledge.

5   Conclusions and Further Research

In this paper, we presented a new approach to service discovery in ad-hoc networks based on a multi-layered clustering that results from a natural combination of semantic issues (taken from an ontology) and structural issues (based on radio connectivity). These clusters form the basis for a layered network architecture, in which each layer offers a certain functionality basing on the previous layer. The topmost layer allows a user to search for a device offering a given service.

5.1   Advantages of the Approach

Our layer architecture offers several advantages:

Naturalness. The definition of our multi-layer clustering is very intuitive, natural and easy because only two external parameters are taken into consideration: the semantics within a domain ontology and the structure as a graph of radio connections. No additional parameters like cluster sizes or cluster forms have to be tuned as they evolve automatically.

Decentralization. The approach does not rely on a central device or an infrastructural component as every device is treated in the same way.

Resource-Awareness. Particularly in mobile ad-hoc networks and their limited resources like battery power and bandwidth, it is crucial that services are used in a resource-aware manner. Thus, a client should use a service that matches its query and is physically close to that client in order to avoid expensive package transmission over several intermediate nodes. Our approach achieves this automatically (i.e. without a cost function) by searching local clusters before accessing physically distant regions.

Adaptability. Often, network protocols suffer from the fact that they are specially designed for a certain degree of network stability. In typical ad-hoc networks however, we can spot various regions with highly different dynamics in topology. If we think of a street with two driving lanes leading in opposite directions, for instance, we have a relatively stable network between devices in cars driving in the same direction whereas the network between the two lanes is highly fluctuating. Our clusters are able to adapt to such varying dynamics by choosing an appropriate exploration strategy for each cluster (on each layer) according to the amount of information collected over the time.

Fault Tolerance. In mobile ad-hoc networks, network connections between two devices are not reliable at all: the devices can move out of radio range, they can switch off or fail, and obstacles can disturb the transmission. Many protocols face these problems by setting up a huge list of fault cases in order to handle them. Our approach solves this problem more naturally by moving through the cluster layers and applying exploration techniques dynamically. If, for instance, a connection fails in a cluster on Layer l, the exploration structure in this cluster has to be adapted (for example, routing tables or ring successors will be changed) or changed completely (for example, from cycling to flooding) in more severe cases, i.e., when a gateway node disappears. Nevertheless, the caller on Layer $l+1$ just continues trying to send its message while now using another way of routing. This technique becomes possible because every node only guarantees to send a message or to find a service, but does not state *how* this is done.

5.2   Future Work

The presented approach leaves some important questions for further research. One main question is the management of administrative data like routing tables, information about ring predecessors and successors, information about gateway points, service descriptions, and so on. Within a single instance, these are handled easily by the device itself, but within clusters, we have to decide where to deal with this information. In principle, there are two possibilities: First, electing a cluster head in each cluster and letting this head handle all related tasks. However, this raises the problem, that for clusters on higher levels we approximate a centralized protocol, which is not very robust, if this cluster head fails and not very performant either, as all requests are guided through this head. Another idea could be, to replicate the information on all devices in the cluster so that each device can handle function calls for the cluster on its own. Here, a mechanism needs to be developed that ensures efficient distribution of information even in large clusters. An attractive possibility is a lazy approach, where information is distributed when needed only.

A further point that could be criticized is the assumption from Section 3.1 saying that each device offers exactly one document. This seems to be very unrealistic if we look at laptops with hundreds or even thousands of documents. At the moment, we are dealing with two possible solutions to this: On the one hand, we could consider such a collection of documents as a logical collection of devices forming a complete reachability graph and use our standard clustering rules. On the other hand, we could look at the documents on the device as one virtual document of the lowest common ontological term shared by all documents and cluster it according to that. Advantageously, we can assume that a user in fact has a lot of different documents on its device but shares only a thematically closed subset of them. Also a mixture of both techniques could be possible if the users offers many documents from a few, semantically completely different areas (e.g., peer-to-peer networks and cooking recipes).

Another important issue that we didn't deal with in this paper is the performance of the approach. Currently, we are implementing a simulation using the QualNet tool [11] and are also carrying out a theoretical analysis of the performance.

Finally, the goal of the DIANE project as a whole is to develop a prototype that will support e-learning. Thus, in the not so far future, on our campus, students like Anna will be able to exchange information as described in the introduction.

References

1. DIANE Project. http://www.ipd.uni-karlsruhe.de/DIANE/en.
2. Birgitta König-Ries, Michael Klein. Information Services to Support E-Learning in Ad-hoc Networks. In: Proc. of 1. Intl. Workshop on Wireless Information Systems (WIS 2002), Ciudad Real, Spain, April 2002.
3. Charles Perkins (ed.). Ad Hoc Networking. Addison-Wesley Publishing Company, 2000.
4. IETF Working Group on Mobile Ad Hoc Networks (MANET).
   http://www.manet.org.
5. Jini Network Technology. Sun Microsystems.
   http://www.jini.org
6. Universal Plug-and-Play (UPnP) Forum. Microsoft Corporation.
   http://www.upnp.org
7. Object Management Group. Trading Object Service Specification.
   http://www.omg.org/technology/documents/formal/trading_object_service.htm
8. Bluetooth Specification Part E. Service Discovery Protocol (SDP).
   http://www.bluetooth.com
9. Napster File Sharing. http://www.napster.com, Napster Protocol Specification.
   http://opennap.sourceforge.net/napster.txt
10. Gnutella File Sharing. http://gnutella.wego.com
11. QualNet by Scalable Networks Technologies. http://www.scalable-networks.com

NeuroGrid: Semantically Routing Queries in Peer-to-Peer Networks

Sam Joseph

University of Tokyo, Strategic Software Division,
Tokyo, Japan
sam@mtl.t.u-tokyo.ac.jp, sam@neurogrid.com

Abstract. NeuroGrid is an adaptive decentralized search system. NeuroGrid nodes support distributed search through semantic routing (forwarding of queries based on content), and a learning mechanism that dynamically adjusts meta-data describing the contents of nodes and the files that make up those contents. NeuroGrid is an open-source project, and prototype software has been made available at http://www.neurogrid.net/ NeuroGrid presents users with an alternative to hierarchical, folder-based file organization, and in the process offers an alternative approach to distributed search.

1 Introduction

NeuroGrid is an approach to decentralized search involving adaptation to ongoing network activity, each successive search changing the knowledge that each network node possesses about the contents of other nodes. NeuroGrid aims to use this adaptation to support fast, reliable and efficient decentralized search. NeuroGrid consists of two components that complement one another: a semantic routing technique and a learning algorithm.

The field of P2P has much in common with multi-agent systems since they often require distributed search solutions, and NeuroGrid owes its origins to work in the agent field [9]. However it is in the field of distributed content systems that we find approaches more conceptually similar to NeuroGrid. For example the Whois++ system [5] provides a mechanism for forwarding queries to distributed servers on the basis of the content of those servers. The Harvest system [2] provided a similar service along with caching and replication, as did the Content Routing approach of Sheldon et al. [17], which included query refinement and merging of result sets. However, fundamentally all of these systems rely upon the honesty of the person providing descriptive meta-data or automated parsing of server contents to underpin the validity of the content descriptions they provide. Q-Pilot [13] is a more recent example of this kind of system that routes queries to different search engines based on their specialization.

NeuroGrid's key difference from these systems is that user responses to search results are stored and used to update the meta-data describing the content of remote

E.Gregori et al. (Eds.): Networking 2002 Workshops, LNCS 2376, pp. 202-214, 2002.
© Springer-Verlag Berlin Heidelberg 2002

servers. If a remote server is queried with a word such as "automobile" and returns adverts for weight-loss products, the reliability of this server with respect to this query should be reduced. How does the system know this response was inappropriate? The absence of any positive feedback such as storing links to the discovered data, or explicit negative feedback[1], can be used to reduce the reliability of that server with respect to that query. This crucial "closing of the loop" allows NeuroGrid to try and optimise query results so as to maximize the chance of receiving positive feedback from the user.

Recent Peer-to-Peer (P2P) systems such as Gnutella [8] and Freenet [7] have some points in common with NeuroGrid. Freenet also forwards queries according to beliefs about the contents of other nodes; however, Freenet considers file similarity in terms of closeness in a "key-space" generated by a cryptographic hash. Users must know a file's key in order to retrieve it from the network. Files are inserted into particular locations (as opposed to just shared in the Gnutella network) and combined with aggressive caching activity the arrangement of files ends up reflecting that of the key-space. NeuroGrid does not move files around; rather it gradually learns the existing location of different content. NeuroGrid is different from Gnutella in that it avoids broadcast search, and from Napster [18] in that search is decentralized. A number of other systems have emerged that attempt to deal with the issues of distributed file storage. Chord [19] and CAN [14] provide distributed hashtable functionality, which allow the locations of files to be determined automatically from a single. Tapestry [24] and Pastry [6] are variants of the Plaxton Mesh [20], using prefix/suffix address routing and publishing mechanisms based on this routing to distribute files.

The NeuroGrid approach could be seen as an alternative to these systems if used to track file locations, or it could be seen as a discovery layer that operates on top of one of these systems. In terms of ensuring a file can be retrieved in a limited number of hops for a limited amount of state stored on each node, it follows intuitively that Chord or CAN will outperform NeuroGrid. However, that is to miss the point that NeuroGrid is not intended to provide fast lookup on the basis of a unique key. Given that a robust distributed hashtable was available it would make sense for NeuroGrid to provide a distributed reputation and search mechanism for keys stored in that distributed hashtable. Conceptually one can separate the search process into three parts:

1. identify what you want
2. work out where it is
3. download it

It is possible to imagine a search and retrieval system comprised of three completely separate components, with NeuroGrid supporting just the first part of the process. The assumption in systems like Chord and CAN seems to be that we have

---

[1] It is assumed that the majority of users will not be willing to invest time in terms of ranking the quality of results, and that at best implicit indicators of user satisfaction will be required. However personal experience suggests that a large red button, marked NO! might be used more frequently by users to express displeasure and thus give valuable negative feedback.

already identified the file that we wish to locate. NeuroGrid is there for those situations in which you don't know exactly which file you want. NeuroGrid tries to take advantage of the regularities that exist within file (or file pointer) collections built up by the users in the network.

2 NeuroGrid

Each NeuroGrid node maintains a knowledge base that stores associations between keywords and other NeuroGrid nodes, facilitating search of the network by forwarding queries to a subset of nodes that it believes may possess matches to the search query. NeuroGrid operates under the assumption that files (or file pointers) are referenced by a number of 'keywords'. The knowledge base of keyword-node associations maintained by each node represents local 'belief' concerning the contents of remote nodes. So, for example, given that a node receives an incoming search consisting of keywords A, B, and C, the node will consult its knowledge base and retrieve any remote nodes that are associated with these keywords. The nodes retrieved from the knowledge base are ranked depending on the degree of match to the search query, but the matching algorithm itself and the way the associations get updated over time can be varied.

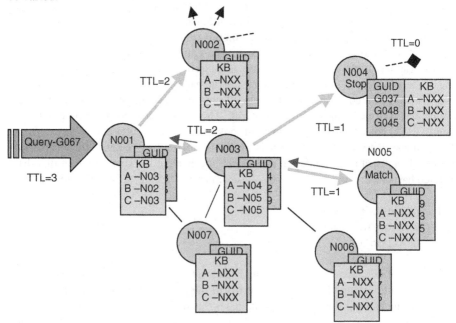

Fig 1. NeuroGrid Knowledge-based Search, in addition to the GUID tables, individual node's knowledge bases (KBs) are shown. Note that the query is not forwarded down all possible connections, but only down to a subset of possible remote nodes (shown by the gold arrows).

For tractability the simulations performed so far use a matching procedure where the possible nodes are ranked according to how many of the search terms they are associated with. For example given a query for keywords A, B and C, a node associated with just keyword C would receive a rank of 1 whereas a node associated with all three terms would receive a rank of 3. The top M matches are then selected and the query is forwarded to these nodes.

Queries in the NeuroGrid network use similar techniques to Gnutella to prevent loops and indefinite propagation: Time To Live (TTL) counters, which limit the range of queries, and Globally Unique Identifiers (GUIDs) which prevent a node forwarding a query twice. However, let us focus on the content based forwarding mechanism or semantic routing. In figure 1 we see that Node N001 will generate a subset of nodes N002 and N003 for a query with terms A, B, and C. Node N003 generates a subset of nodes N004 and N005, and thus the query reaches node N005 where a match is obtained. One possibility is that this node contains the matching file, but another is that it contains a reference to the actual location as specified by, say, a Chord Key or a URL, decoupling the search process from the actual file retrieval.

Note that the number of nodes chosen from the recommended subset is an adjustable NeuroGrid parameter, which gives the equivalent of the Gnutella routing procedure if set equal to the number of connections present at each node. It also offers the interesting possibility of allowing each node to select the degree to forward messages based on its current activity - a throttling mechanism whereby an overactive node can try and reduce the amount of network activity by forwarding to fewer nodes and vice versa. NeuroGrid's search procedure will be effective to the extent that nodes possess knowledge bases that reflect the distribution of documents through the network itself. A simple way to set this up initially is to give all nodes knowledge about the contents of their immediate neighbours.

NeuroGrid nodes also utilize the results of searches in order to update their knowledge bases and add new connections to the nodes that provide results to search queries. The best analogy is to think of the nodes as humans that know something about what their friends know about, and when asked can put you in touch with a friend, who may well be able to put you in touch with a friend who ... and so on.

Just to emphasize the point, the adaptive aspect of NeuroGrid comes into play when a search is successful and the querying node updates its knowledge base to associate the remote node (that supplied the matching file or file-pointer), with the query keywords. The querying node also establishes a direct link[2] to the remote node, adding to the system's existing connections, leading to a gradual increase in connectivity. The important side effect of this is that all of the nodes in the system gradually become a little smarter, developing knowledge bases that reflect the distribution of queries that they receive over time.

---

[2] This is the approach used in the simulations described in the next section where establishing a direct connection occurs no overhead. In the NeuroGrid bookmark implementation this corresponds to knowledge of a remote node's URL. The direct link itself could be avoided in a network supporting point-to-point transmissions that are currently not supported in Gnutella. How to handle this issue in a Gnutella-like network is an open question.

3 Simulation

A preliminary simulation was performed comparing NeuroGrid routing and random routing. Each node in a 1000 node network was randomly assigned 3 documents from a pool of 2000. Each document was randomly assigned 3 keywords from a pool of 1000. Each node was connected to three others that were selected at random. In both simulations nodes received data about the contents of their neighbours. The initial TTL was set to 9 and the forwarding subset M was set to 2. Both simulations were run for 100,000 searches, with each search being started at a randomly selected node. Each search was for a document that shared at least one keyword with the documents in the starting node – the search terms would be the keywords belonging to the target document.

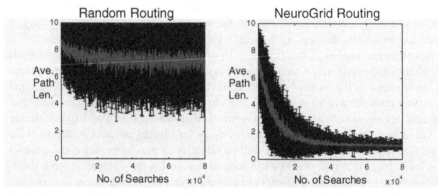

Fig. 2. The first 80000 searches in 1000 node networks, using random routing (left) and NeuroGrid routing (right). Error bars are standard deviation over 50 searches.

The difference between the two simulations was purely in terms of which nodes queries were routed to. In the random routing simulation each node would select two nodes at random to forward the query to. In the NeuroGrid routing simulation a node would examine the query terms of the incoming query and based on the entries in its knowledge base, work out which two nodes would be most likely to contain content with the same keywords. The nodes in both simulations learned from the result of each search. However as is clear from the graphs, the NeuroGrid routing network more quickly establishes the location of documents within the network, and the average path length converges to just above a single hop, whereas the random routing network fails to improve substantially from its starting performance.

Each successful search allows a node to find the location of a document that shares at least one keyword with the documents it holds. This means that over time a node will create connections to other nodes that hold similar content. So after 80,000 searches if a node starts a search for a document that shares a keyword with a document it holds, it will likely find that document in a neighbour (one hop) and if not, then those nodes will be able to quickly recommend nodes that do contain that document.

These initial simulations do not include many features of real world networks. For example they assume a uniform distribution of keywords over documents. It would be more realistic to use a Zipf distribution. Further simulations were performed where the keyword distribution over the various documents follow a Zipf distribution. Immediately the average path length after 80,000 searches increased, and the network showed no signs of converging to a stable state. Surmising that this was due to frequent terms in the Zipf distribution obscuring the effect of the Neuro-Grid routing, information about the distribution was added to the routing algorithm, such that rarely occurring keywords would be weighted more heavily.

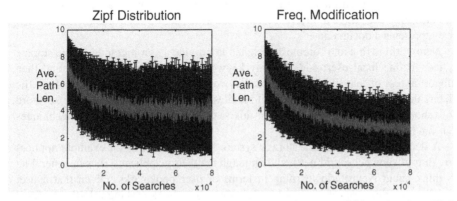

Fig. 3. The first 80000 searches in 1000 node networks, using NeuroGrid routing for a Zipf distribution of keywords over documents in both cases, with the second simulation using keyword frequency information to modify the NeuroGrid routing (right).

Having the routing algorithm focus on rare terms from the Zipf distribution improved performance but there was still no sign of convergence. After 80000 searches each node had on average 120 connections. Further analysis suggests that the Zipf distribution was not affecting routing performance so much as affecting the range of documents that each node was searching for. Under the uniform distribution each node would start searches for content with at most 9 different keywords that on average will be shared by 6 documents and this would mean there are around 54 possible documents that each node might start a search for. Under the Zipf distribution the most popular term might be shared by in excess of 600 documents. This meant that under the Zipf distribution nodes were searching for a much wider variety of content.

It has been suggested that in reality documents will be searched for on the basis of keywords further down the tail of the Zipf distribution that comes closer to a normal distribution. However, in order to move forward it seems we need information about the distribution not just of queries within networked search systems, but also the query distribution for individual users [11][22]. One might hypothesise that in a real system a small number of users would have a large range of interests, whilst most would focus on a smaller area. The effect of this would be to create a small world network [21]. Efforts are currently under way to try and obtain the necessary data to determine the nature of these distributions.

4   NeuroGrid Learning Mechanism

Preliminary "unrealistic" simulations like those presented above suggest that a P2P network using semantic routing and some learning ability can adapt in a fashion similar to Freenet and still provide us with keyword based search, if not anonymity. Of course much is dependent on the learning mechanism employed and the accuracy of the meta-data within the system. Much of the work in the meta-data field seems to go on under the implicit assumption that there is some fundamentally "correct" mark-up of a file, such as the title and keywords provided by the author. NeuroGrid is based on the premise that all meta-data is relative the author of that meta-data; specifically that they may each have a different idea about which set of keywords (or statements) best represents a document.

NeuroGrid is first and foremost designed to provide a non-hierarchical file storage system for the local user; add as many keywords as you like to any file, and then support access of that file through those keywords - no more making shortcuts in file hierarchies. The problem is that if multiple files are associated with the same keyword, how should NeuroGrid rank them? In this section we will look at some techniques that can help solve this problem.

A decentralized bookmark storage system has been built as an example application (http://www.neurogrid.net/), and although the theory applies to files in general let us think about NeuroGrid learning in terms of user bookmarks. Given that a user initially provides a set of keyword associations when bookmarking a URL, the local NeuroGrid node enters these in its index. When subsequent searches take place, NeuroGrid records every time a keyword is used, as well as the URLs (and where they are came from) that are suggested as possibilities. Say I do a search for "rock climbing" on a NeuroGrid node that recommends me a set of URLs. If I click through on a URL that has been recommended directly by the local NeuroGrid node, then we update meta-data about that URL (it has been selected relative to the terms "rock" and " climbing "), but if the URL has been recommended by a remote node, then we can update meta-data not only about the URL, but also the remote NeuroGrid node as well, i.e. that it has been selected relative to the terms "rock" and "climbing". The selection by itself is only a weak indicator, but given subsequent activity, such as bookmarking that URL, we can assume to some degree at least that an implicit "remote node X was able to make a recommendation relating to 'rock' and 'climbing'" judgement has been made.

We can think of each NeuroGrid node as storing two numbers to represent the relationship between any keyword and any URL/Node. In the case of URLs these two numbers represent, firstly the number of times this keyword has been queried and led to a recommendation of the URL, and secondly, the number of times that this URL has been clicked through after a recommendation. One can extend the model further and keep records of further click-throughs (in the case of a node recommending other nodes) or of bookmarking activity or other user feedback schemes.

In the first instance one must address how to transform the ratio of these two numbers into something that can be used to rank the recommendations. Clearly something that has been clicked on very few times, say once in a hundred recommendations, is not a good source of information, or at least it is not very popular; but how does it compare with something that has been clicked through ten times out of a thousand? The ratios are identical. What about when the user is searching on multiple keywords? How do we combine these ratios in such a fashion as to do justice to the actual activity that has produced them?

Let us take the recommendation frequency to be b and the selection frequency to be a. Assuming that there is a certain probability p that if an item is recommended that it will be selected, and assuming that p is fixed but unknown, the ratio a/b can be thought of as an estimate of p. Moreover, it is a "good "estimate in a statistical sense because it is an unbiased estimate, i.e., the expected value of a/b is p. Intuitively, the larger b is, the closer a/b should be to p. However we do not know how likely is that a/b is close to p. For this, we can use the Hoeffding Bound to tell us, given a fixed error epsilon, the probability that a/b is different from p:

$$\Pr[|(a/b)-p|>\text{epsilon}]<=2e^{-2b.\text{epsilon}^2} \qquad (1)$$

Notice that the bound depends only on the number of recommendations that were made (b). Thus, if we consider some different ratios that are superficially identical at 50%, we get adjustments of 0.027 for (1000, 2000), 0.038 for (500, 1000) and 0.054 for (250, 500). Thus, the pessimistic estimates are, with a 95% confidence, 47.3%, 46.2% and 44.6%. The upshot of all this is that if a user is searching for "rock" and this keyword is related to different URLs with different recommendation/selection ratios, we can rank the URLs accordingly. If a URL is associated with multiple keywords then we can take pessimistic estimates of click through probability on each individual keyword before combining them to give an overall rank.

Clearly there are many outstanding issues. A click through on a URL or a node is not necessarily an indicator that the user will be happy with what they find once they receive the data on the other end, but the above approach is easily extended to give estimates based on bookmarking events subsequent to click through, etc. There is also the issue of trying to take into account prior beliefs about associations, and the relative frequencies of the keywords themselves. A Bayesian framework has been suggested and work is underway to combine the Hoeffding and Bayesian approaches into a more general learning framework that will take all these factors into account. Still, much of the NeuroGrid Project's current focus is on trying to create an interface that will support these kinds of learning systems. Without an appropriately designed interface that can accurately discern the meaning of implicit user feedback, the most powerful learning algorithms will be useless.

5   Discussion

Much of the work on NeuroGrid is as yet incomplete and there are very important questions that need to be addressed.

Q1. The analogy with bookmark system is incomplete - how is feedback obtained in the p2p network?
A1. The same feedback model applies to bookmarks as to files downloaded in a p2p network. A user may select a URL from a search result based on a short description or title. They may then choose to bookmark it or not. When a user conducts a search in a p2p network they select a file for download based on a filename, and once they have downloaded it they will delete the item depending on whether it was what they really wanted. Naturally there are more complex situations, such as downloading something that didn't match the original query that nonetheless turns out to be something desirable. These situations will require consideration, but fundamentally it seems possible to implement feedback in both bookmarking systems and file sharing systems.

Q2. Nodes in P2P systems come and go rapidly. What does this imply about how beliefs should be adjusted? Are beliefs wiped out lazily or greedily, or not at all, when a node goes away?
A2. Well, nodes come and go rapidly in **some** P2P systems. Since NeuroGrid nodes rely on there being some degree of regularity for them to learn, any environment in which there is little or no consistency will not support this kind of learning framework. However it is important to consider that a node's ability to supply content is bound up not just with the files it can serve or provide pointers to, but also how frequently it is connected to the network. The statistical learning process presented above will prefer those nodes that are regularly connected to the network. To the extent that a disconnected node provides particularly relevant content it will still be queried. Clearly nodes will be limited in the amount of data they can maintain on other nodes, and a further development of the statistical framework being implemented in the latest NeuroGrid system maintains not just information about the extent to which valid data was returned by a node, but also how long ago that was. An adjustable discounting scheme will be used to follow the stability of different nodes.

Q3. Similarly, content comes and goes rapidly. What does this imply about how quickly the NeuroGrid needs to converge on high quality beliefs? Perhaps NeuroGrid will do OK for popular content, or long-lived content on long-lived nodes, but not for the "harder" but equally important case of short-lived content, or unpopular content on non-long-lived nodes.
A3. In NeuroGrid content that is available for a very short time will not have the chance to affect the reputation of the node in which it is stored – NeuroGrid does not try to address this issue at present, although some sort of automated caching would seem to be in order. However unpopular content will not be a problem. In other systems like Freenet popular content displaces unpopular content, but NeuroGrid knowledge bases give priority to meeting the needs of their local user. Given that at least some NeuroGrid nodes become specialists in a particular type of content, then as soon as one accesses those nodes, the unpopular content can be easily found. The difficulty of finding the right nodes will depend on how broad a range of data can be stored by the largest nodes in the system, and on whether the network connectivity

does form a small world [14]. There are open questions here about how knowledge base storage limits should be enforced (see Q5).

Q4. How much state does each node need to keep? Is it proportional to the number of other nodes in the system? The number of documents in the system? The number of keywords in the system? Is this reasonable to ask?
A4. This is a very reasonable question and it is not yet clear. Realistically it will all depend on the distribution of search queries and content within the system. Efforts are underway to try and get access to the data that would allow these distributions to be understood. The answer to this question is bound up with how limits on state are enforced. The real question is how much state is each node required to keep in order to achieve what? NeuroGrid is not necessarily an attempt to make all content available from every point in the network. Each NeuroGrid node will first and foremost try to serve the needs of their local user(s). The nodes will maintain the data necessary to support local users' navigation of their own data. How much storage space each node devotes to storing additional information will depend on the node's owner. It would seem appropriate to allow old data to expire and maintain state in proportion to the range of keywords that the local user searches for. The state of each node should vary according to local factors, not the number of documents, nodes or keywords in the overall system. This may prevent every document from being locatable from every node in the network, but that is not currently a NeuroGrid goal; being able to find interesting clusters of similar content is.

Q5. What are the trade-offs involved in choosing which nodes to track and which to ignore? What kind of policies will be used to limit the size of the knowledge-bases?
A5. Clearly any node will only be able to devote a certain amount of resources to its knowledge base. Naturally one would try to optimise the use of that resource by tracking the more reliable nodes; reliable that is in terms of being able to respond to queries and being able to supply things the user is interested in. Ideally more storage resources are devoted to things that interest the user, i.e. the keywords being frequently used in queries. The temporal discounting scheme mentioned in A2 could be used to delete old query data, particularly if the users interest in it is transitory.

6 Related Work

There are now a number of systems that try to handle meta-data in peer-to-peer networks. All of these systems, or proposed modifications to existing systems, have come to light in the last year or so, perhaps indicating a desire to move beyond the search capabilities of the first generation of P2P software.

One possible P2P meta-data approach is to try and use Chord to store keyword-document relations [19]. Kronfol [10] suggests that under this scheme popular query terms would drive excessive traffic to certain nodes. As an alternative Kronfol describes and simulates FASD, which adds keyword searching to the Freenet system by inserting meta-data keys that include the TFIDF[3] rankings of keywords in Freenet documents, as well as the Freenet document key. The TFIDF model is also used in the PlanetP architecture of Cuenca-Acuna et al [4], which relies on "gossiping" between nodes in order for information about remote node contents to be updated.

FASD employs a cosine correlation to determine document-query closeness and Freenet routing techniques such that nodes start to take responsibility for similar meta-data keys, distributing meta-data information throughout the network. Babaoglu et al. [1] propose a not dissimilar scheme, although their routing procedure works on hashes of individual keywords to distribute the load, as opposed to TFIDF vectors. Freenet depth first searches can end up exhaustively searching the network and Kronfol proposes iterative deepening as a potential solution; as Yang & Garcia-Molina [23] do for the Gnutella network.

A LimeWire proposal [15] exists to add query routing to the Gnutella network and a subset of this has been implemented as part of the LimeWire ultra-peers framework. The query-routing proposal involves nodes creating indices that summarise their contents and distributing them to other nodes, such that queries can be routed more effectively. Crespo & Garcia-Molina [3] propose a similar approach called "Routing Indices". In addition, there is the Edutella project [12] that describes taxonomy of query types, separating meta-data query languages by the complexity of the queries that can be supported.

While some of the systems mentioned above have some components in common with NeuroGrid, none of them appears to address the issue of how meta-data can be created and maintained to reflect the disparate and sometimes conflicting needs of multiple users.

7 Summary

NeuroGrid nodes adapt the meta-data of their local files to reflect the usage patterns of the local user. As the local user selects, or does not select, recommendations from remote nodes, similar meta-data is built up describing the specialisation of remote nodes from the perspective of the local user. The ultimate objective of the NeuroGrid Project is to use this meta-data to inform semantic routing of queries within a p2p network, while at the same time providing a useful data-management service at the local level.

Acknowledgements

Many thanks to Michael Turner, Roger Dingledine, Brandon Wiley, Justin Chapweske, Kevin Burton, Martin Peck and Raph Levien for helpful discussion and advice.

---

[3] Term Frequency Inverse Document Frequency [16]

References

1. Babaoglu, O., Meling, H. and Montresor, A.: Anthill: a Framework for the Development of Agent-Based Peer-to-Peer Systems. Technical Report UBLCS-2001-09 November (2001).
2. Bowman, C.M., Danzig, P.B., Hardy, D.R., Manber, U., Schwartz, M.F.: The Harvest Information Discovery and Access System. Computer Networks and ISDN Systems 28 (1995) 119-125. http://citeseer.nj.nec.com/bowman95harvest.html
3. Crespo, A. Garcia-Molina, H.: Routing Indices For Peer-to-Peer Systems, to be published in proceedings of ICDCS, (2002).
4. Cuenca-Acuna, F.M., Peery, C., Martin R.P. and Nguyen, T.D.: PlanetP: Using Gossiping to Build Content Addressable Peer-to-Peer Information Sharing Communities. International Workshop on Peer-to-Peer Computing, Pisa (2002).
5. Deutsch, P., Schoultz, R., Faltstrom, P., Weider, C.: Architecture of the WHOIS++ service. RFC 1835, (1995) http://www.ietf.org/rfc/rfc1835.txt
6. Druschel, P., Rowstron, A.: Pastry: Scalable, distributed object location and routing for large-scale peer-to-peer systems. In Proceedings of the 18th IFIP/ACM International Conference on Distributed Systems Platforms (2001).
7. Freenet http://www.freenetproject.org
8. Gnutella http://gnutella.wego.com
9. Joseph, S.R.H., Kawamura, T.: Why Autonomy makes the Agent. In "Agent Engineering" Eds. Liu, J, Zhong, et al. World Scientific Publishing (2001) 7-28.
10. Kronfol, A.Z.: FASD: A fault-tolerant, Adaptive Scalable, Distributed Search Engine. Princeton University Technical Report. (2002). http://www.cs.princeton.edu/~akronfol/fasd/
11. Napster http://www.napster.com
12. Nejdl, W., Wolf, B., Qu, C., Decker, S., Sintek, M., Naeve, A., Nilsson, M., Palmer, M. and Risch, T.: Edutella: A P2P Networking Infrastructure Based on RDF (2001) http://edutella.jxta.org/
13. Plaxton, C.G., Rajaraman, R., Richa, A.W.: Accessing nearby copies of replicated objects in a distributed environment. In Proceedings of ACM SPAA. ACM, June (1997).
14. Ratnasamy, S., Francis, P., Handley, M., Karp, R., Schenker, S.: A scalable content-addressable network. Proc. ACM SIGCOMM (2001). http://www.acm.org/sigcomm/sigcomm2001/p13.html
15. Rohrs, C.: Query Routing for the Gnutella Network (2002). http://www.limewire.com/developer/query_routing/keyword%20routing.htm
16. Salton, G., and Yang, C. On the specification of term values in automatic indexing. Journal of Documentation 29 (1973) 351–372.
17. Sheldon, M.A., Duda, A., Weiss, R., Gifford, D.K.: Discover: A Resource Discovery System based on Content Routing. Proc. 3rd International World Wide Web Conference Elsevier, North Holland Computer Networks and ISDN Systems, (1995). http://www.psrg.lcs.mit.edu/publications/Papers/wwwabs.htm
18. Sripanidkulchai, K.: The popularity of Gnutella queries and its implications on scalability, (2001). http://www-2.cs.cmu.edu/~kunwadee/research/p2p/paper.html
19. Stoica, I., Morris, R., Karger, D., Kaashoek, M.F., Balakrishnan, H.: Chord: A scalable peer-to-peer lookup service for internet applications. Proceedings of the ACM SIGCOMM '01 Conference (2001). http://www.acm.org/sigcomm/sigcomm2001/p12.html

20. Sugiura, A., Etzioni, O.: Query Routing for Web Search Engines: Architecture and Experiments. Proc. 9th International World-Wide Web Conference. Foretec Seminars, Inc., (2000). http://www.cs.washington.edu/homes/etzioni/papers/www9-final.pdf
21. Watts, D., Strogatz, S.: Collective dynamics of `small-world' networks, Nature 393, (1998) 440-442.
22.. Xie, Y., O'Hallaron, D.: Locality in Search Engine Queries and Its Implications for Caching. Infocom (2002). http://www-2.cs.cmu.edu/~ylxie/papers/infocom02.ps
23. Yang, B., Garcia-Molina, H.: Efficient Search in Peer-to-Peer Networks, to be published in ICDCS, (2002).
24. Zhao, B.Y., Kubiatowicz, J.D., Joseph, A.D.: Tapestry: An infrastructure for fault-resilient wide-area location and routing. Technical ReportCSD-01-1141, U.C. Berkeley, (2001).

Storage, Mutability and Naming in *Pasta*

Tim D. Moreton, Ian A. Pratt, and Timothy L. Harris

University of Cambridge Computer Laboratory, Cambridge, UK
{tdm25,iap10,tlh20}@cam.ac.uk

Abstract. We outline the design and operation of *Pasta*, a peer-to-peer storage system that provides traditional file system semantics while offering the wide-spread caching and distribution required for publishing networks. *Pasta* allows users to manipulate shared files and folders with strong consistency semantics and to collaboratively organize them in unmanaged decentralized namespaces. Storage quotas regulate consumption and allow the network to offer permanence of content.

1 Introduction

We are developing *Pasta*, a peer-to-peer system that provides a global mutable data store that acts as a file system, an archive store and a publication tool. In this paper we introduce the system and focus on the techniques that it uses to encourage efficient use of storage space, to support automated replication and caching and to enable flexible and decentralized namespace management.

Pasta is intended for wide-area use over a federated group of well-connected peers in the Internet (perhaps located at ISPs or in medium-size organisations). The peers provide storage space to *Pasta* and, in exchange, receive system-wide quota-credits that they can allocate to users. Although diverse in ownership and physical location, the peers share a trusted third-party that holds a limited storage management rôle in the network. We envisage clients integrating *Pasta* with their local file system to a similar extent as other network file systems – while not designed for workloads with a high turnover of temporary data, we expect files held in *Pasta* to be directly accessible by users.

Pasta builds on the Pastry peer-to-peer routing substrate which it uses to pass messages between peers and to select nodes at which to locate or insert data [9]. Pastry provides fault-tolerance and scalability. In particular, a message can be passed between any two nodes in an n node overlay network in $log(n)$ hops, while maintaining $log(n)$ routing table entries on each node. Further, Pastry preferentially routes messages between nearby nodes in order to minimise the distance travelled in the underlying network.

In Section 2, we briefly assess two other peer-to-peer file system projects. Section 3 outlines the structure of our system. We describe data storage, file mutability and a decentralized naming scheme, and introduce an approach to quota management. Finally, Section 4 discusses the direction of our future work on *Pasta* and its implementation context.

E. Gregori et al. (Eds.): Networking 2002 Workshops, LNCS 2376, pp. 215–219, 2002.

2   Related Work

We outline the two concurrent projects that are most similar to *Pasta*; a brief survey of other large-scale distributed file systems may be found in [3].

As with *Pasta*, PAST [10] is storage system that is built over Pastry. However, unlike *Pasta*, files inserted into PAST are immutable. The system can offer strong data persistence to users by enforcing storage quotas through a scheme of smartcards allocated out-of-band. Storage and retrieval operations are performed at the granularity of whole files rather than through random-access interfaces. No human-readable naming scheme exists by which to reference a stored file: rather, a `fileID` associated with the insertion must be passed by other means.

CFS [3] is implemented over Chord [12], a distributed hash table scheme similar to Pastry. Files are split into fixed-size blocks, which are then distributed to nodes in the network. Storage can be guaranteed for a set time period enabled by per-node storage limits based on IP addresses. Users can store files and arrange them hierarchically in a 'file system', which forms the basis of a per-publisher decentralised namespace. CFS offers coarse-grain file mutability but no means for collaborative update by multiple users.

3   Design

A *Pasta* file system is formed from a network of *storage nodes* that hold data blocks for clients. Each storage node is assigned an asymmetric key pair and, when joining the system, computes its nodeID from the SHA-1 hash of the public key. These IDs are used by Pastry to route messages between nodes.

Files are split into variable-sized immutable *data blocks*. Each data block has an associated blockID, computed as the SHA-1 hash of the block's contents. A block is stored in the network at the node whose nodeID is numerically closest to the blockID. We insert, retrieve or withdraw a block by using Pastry to route an appropriate message with the destination key set to its blockID. Mutable *index blocks* contain file metadata and are the basis of the naming scheme. Each index organises files hierarchically into folders, and describes each file in terms of the ordered list of blocks from which it is composed.

Clients access *Pasta* through their physically-closest storage node. This exposes operations to browse and manipulate the file system hierarchy and to access data via open/close operations and random-access read/write. All these operations are performed at the storage node on which they are invoked, which requests and processes data blocks and index blocks as necessary.

3.1   Data Storage

In this section we describe how *Pasta* clients divide files into blocks in a way that improves storage utilization and cache performance, then how storage nodes replicate and cache these blocks for high availability and low fetch latency.

We adopt the content-based chunking scheme used by the Low Bandwidth File System as a way of splitting files into blocks [5]. This proceeds by calculating a Rabin fingerprint [7] over a sliding window of 48 bytes at each byte offset within the file. Block boundaries are placed whenever the least significant portion of the fingerprint matches a specified break-mark value. Minimum and maximum block sizes avoid pathological cases. Since blocks are stored under their SHA-1 content hash, those that are common to multiple files will be held only once. Our own evaluation, backed by that in [5], shows that content-based chunking can significantly increase sharing of blocks between 'similar' files: unlike fixed-size blocking schemes it is tolerant to insertions and deletions within files.

The primary copy of each block is held on the storage node closest in ID space to the block's SHA-1 content hash. As with PAST and CFS, fault tolerance can be controlled by specifying a replication factor, k, causing copies to be placed on the $k - 1$ nodes adjacent in the ID space to the primary. Techniques similar to those presented for PAST are used to maintain these replicas while the block exists in the network, despite nodes leaving, failing, or joining.

It is highly desirable for blocks to be held on nodes physically close to where they are being requested. This minimises fetch distance for a block and balances the query burden between nodes. Pastry's property of local route convergence [1] means that separate requests for a block from nearby nodes are likely to converge at a node physically near to these while also close in the ID space to the block sought. As such, when a requested block has been obtained, the penultimate node in the lookup path caches a copy before forwarding it toward the client. A frequently requested block will develop cached copies 'drawn out' from its storage nodes along the paths by which requests are being routed.

We anticipate that sharing introduced by content-based chunking will improve the effectiveness of caching: accesses to one file will benefit from previous caching of blocks shared with other files. In particular, when a popular file is modified, cached blocks that are common between the two versions remain valid.

3.2   Mutability and Naming

File system metadata is held in mutable *index blocks*. Each index block has an asymmetric key pair, generated by the user when the block is first inserted; the SHA-1 hash of an index's public key determines its blockID, and any updates to its contents must be signed by the associated private key. As with SFSRO, a voucher is attached to each index block containing the public key and a secure hash of the current contents [4].

Each index block describes a fragment of a user's namespace. Files and mount-points are arranged to form an arbitrary hierarchy of folders, up to the system's maximum block size. This scheme allows file metadata to be modified efficiently by updating a single index block, unlike, for example, CFS where a series of directory and inode blocks must be updated. *Pasta* allows entries in an index block's namespace to be drawn from other index blocks, enabling larger file systems to be constructed either by simply *mounting* subtrees, or by *union mounting* the composite contents of all the index blocks specified.

Files are described as a sorted list of (`file_offset`, blockID, `indirect`) tuples which specify that the bytes of the file at `file_offset` can be read from blockID. Large files may use indirect blocks, each of which can contain further indirection entries, forming a tree. *Pasta* adopts a close-to-open consistency model on the basis of each index block. After inserting any new data blocks, the client attempts to reinsert the updated index block as a commit operation. *Pasta* detects and rejects conflicting updates by including the content hash of the block's previous contents in the update request. The internal tree structure is reminiscent of the Amoeba FUSS File Server which uses similar techniques as the basis of a versioning system and to control concurrent updates [6].

Users may use some out-of-band mechanism to advertise the blockID of the root index block of file systems they wish to publish, allowing other users to 'link' to them, as happens on the Web today. Writing to regions of a namespace stored in another user's index block will cause new entries to be created in a locally-owned index so that the other user's files and folders are overlaid. Similarly, overlays can be used to 'delete' files or folders from the local view of another user's namespace. If two or more users choose to import each other's views then collaborative work spaces may be created.

We envisage that 'authorities' on particular topics will emerge and over time link together to form a structure akin to a Google or Yahoo *directory*, that most users will take as their own root view that they extend and customize as desired.

Pasta adopts the same caching policy for mutable index blocks as for data blocks to distribute file metadata toward clients. To ensure consistency over updates, nodes that cache an index block must subscribe to a multicast tree rooted at the primary store node of the block. Currently, this tree propagates cache invalidation messages – we intend to experiment with incremental updates and differentiating between passively cached copies and indexes in active use. An application-level multicast system similar to Scribe is used [11]. When a node caches a block, it routes a 'subscribe' message with key equal to the blockID, attaching itself in the multicast tree to the node one hop along the original request path. This is the node from which it obtained the block and is therefore already subscribed.

3.3   Quotas and Accounting

Pasta offers persistent storage: any file inserted is maintained until explicitly withdrawn. System-wide per-user quotas are used to regulate consumption. These are enforced by nodes acting as *principal accountants*: when a user inserts a block each node storing a replica informs the user's accountants – a set of nodes generated by iterated hashing of the user's ID. A quorum protocol provides tolerance to Byzantine accountant failures [2].

Storage nodes are responsible for allocating quotas to users: each node provides the system with a fixed unit of storage and may distribute some portion of this as quota credits (the remainder being used for caching). *Storage node accountants* track which users have been credited by which nodes. This structure removes the trusted authority from ordinary operations.

4   Ongoing Work

We are currently incorporating *Pasta* into the Xenoserver [8] project, which is building a *public infrastructure* for wide-area distributed computing. It provides a low-level customizable execution environment over which users can deploy not just their own applications but also their own operating system instances. *Pasta* will fulfil the rôle of a global file system accessible from all Xenoserver nodes. It will be used to hold user-submitted applications for execution on Xenoservers and also to hold the operating system images and standard components necessary for the platform to operate. This context makes *Pasta*'s provision of flexible namespace management with content-based caching particularly attractive.

We intend to evaluate the effectiveness of content-based chunking using file system traces suited to this scenario. We also wish to explore automated methods of structuring files within *Pasta*. For instance, re-organizing index blocks to reflect common access and update patterns, or exploring different chunking policies to reduce false sharing and reflect known file formats.

We are very grateful to Antony Rowstron of Microsoft Research for the public release of the Pastry simulator, and for his support and insightful comments.

References

1. M. Castro, P. Druschel, Y. Hu and A. Rowstron. Exploiting network proximity in peer-to-peer overlay networks. Submitted for publication.
2. M. Castro and B. Liskov. Practical Byzantine Fault Tolerance. In *Proc. OSDI 1999*.
3. F. Dabek, M. F. Kaashoek, D. Karger, R. Morris, and I. Stoica. Wide-area cooperative storage with CFS. In *Proc. ACM SOSP 2001*.
4. K. Fu, M. F. Kaashoek and D. Mazières. Fast and secure distributed read-only file system. In *Proc. OSDI 2000*.
5. A. Muthitacharoen, B. Chen and D. Mazières. A Low-bandwidth Network File System. In *Proc. ACM SOSP 2001*.
6. S. J. Mullender, and A. S. Tanenbaum. A distributed file service based on optimistic concurrency control. In *Proc. ACM SOSP 1985*.
7. M. O. Rabin. Fingerprinting by random polynomials. Technical Report TR-15-81, Center for Research in Computing Technology, Harvard University, 1981.
8. D. Reed, I. Pratt, P. Menage, S. Early and N. Stratford. Xenoservers: accounted execution of untrusted code. In *Proc. HotOS 1999*.
9. A. Rowstron and P. Druschel. Pastry: Scalable, distributed object location and routing for large-scale peer-to-peer systems. In *Proc. IFIP/ACM Middleware 2001*.
10. A. Rowstron and P. Druschel. Storage management and caching in PAST, a large-scale, persistent peer-to-peer storage utility. In *Proc. ACM SOSP 2001*, Oct. 2001.
11. A. Rowstron, A.-M. Kermarrec, P. Druschel and M. Castro. Scribe: The design of a large-scale event notification infrastructure. In *Proc. NGC 2001*.
12. I. Stoica, R. Morris, D. Karger, M. F. Kaashoek, and H. Balakrishnan. Chord: a scalable peer-to-peer lookup service for Internet applications. In *Proc. ACM SIGCOMM'01*.

Text-Based Content Search and Retrieval
in Ad-hoc P2P Communities*

Francisco Matias Cuenca-Acuna and Thu D. Nguyen

Department of Computer Science, Rutgers University
110 Frelinghuysen Rd, Piscataway, NJ 08854
{mcuenca, tdnguyen}@cs.rutgers.edu

Abstract. We consider the problem of content search and retrieval in peer-to-peer (P2P) communities. P2P computing is a potentially powerful model for information sharing between *ad hoc* groups of users because of its low cost of entry and natural model for resource scaling. As P2P communities grow, however, locating information distributed across the large number of peers becomes problematic. We address this problem by adapting a state-of-the-art text-based document ranking algorithm, the vector-space model instantiated with the TFxIDF ranking rule, to the P2P environment. We make three contributions: (a) we show how to approximate TFxIDF using compact summaries of individual peers' inverted indexes rather than the inverted index of the entire communal store; (b) we develop a heuristic for adaptively determining the set of peers that should be contacted for a query; and (c) we show that our algorithm tracks TFxIDF's performance very closely, giving P2P communities a search and retrieval algorithm as good as that possible assuming a centralized server.

1 Introduction

We consider the problem of content search and retrieval in peer-to-peer (P2P) communities. P2P computing is a potentially powerful model for information sharing between *ad hoc* groups of users because of its low cost of entry and explicit model for resource scaling: any two users wishing to interact can form a P2P community. As individuals join the community, they will bring resources with them, allowing the community to grow naturally. Measurements of one such community at Rutgers show over 500 users sharing over 6TB of data. Open communities such as Gnutella [11] have achieved much greater sizes.

A number of open problems must be addressed, however, before the potential of P2P computing can be realized. Content search and retrieval is one such open problem. Currently, existing communities employ either centralized directory servers [16] or various flooding algorithms [11,5,26] for object location when given a name. Neither provides a viable framework for content search and retrieval. On the one hand, a centralized server presents a single point of failure and limits scalability. On the other hand, while flooding techniques can in theory allow for arbitrary content searches [17], in practice, typically only a name search, perhaps together with a limited number of attributes, is performed.

---

* This work was supported in part by NSF grants EIA-0103722 and EIA-9986046.

E. Gregori et al. (Eds.): Networking 2002 Workshops, LNCS 2376, pp. 220–234, 2002.

These techniques currently rely on heavy replication of popular items for successful searches. More recent works studying how to scale P2P communities have put forth more efficient and reliable distributed methods for name-based object location [15,24,21]. The focus, however, has remained on name-based object location because these efforts were intended to support P2P file systems, where there is a natural model for acquiring names.

As the amount of storage per person/device is rapidly growing, however, information management is becoming more difficult under the traditional file system hierarchical name space [10]. The success of Internet search engines is strong evidence that content search and retrieval is an intuitive paradigm that users can leverage to manage and access large volumes of information. While P2P groups will not grow to the size of the web, with the exploding capacity and decreasing cost of storage, even small groups will share a large amount of data. Thus, we are motivated to explore a content search and retrieval engine that provides a similar information access paradigm to Internet search engines. In particular, we present a distributed text-based ranking algorithm for content search and retrieval in the specific context of PlanetP, an infrastructure that we are building to ease the task of developing P2P information-sharing applications.

Currently, PlanetP [6] provides a framework for *ad hoc* sets of users to easily set up P2P information sharing communities without requiring support from any centralized server[1]. The basic idea in PlanetP is for each community member to create an inverted (word-to-document) index of the documents that it wishes to share, summarize this index in a compact form, and diffuse the summary throughout the community. Using these summaries, any member can query against and retrieve matching information from the collective information store of the community. (We provide an overview of PlanetP and discuss the advantages of its underlying approach for P2P information-sharing in Section 2.)

Thus, the problem that we focus on is how to perform text-based content search and retrieval using the index summaries that PlanetP uses. We have adopted a vector space ranking model, using the TFxIDF algorithm suggested by Salton et al. [22], because it is one of the currently most successful text-based ranking algorithm [25]. Under this model, a query is comprised of a set of terms. For each document in the collection, TFxIDF uses the frequency of each query term in that document and the frequency of the term across the collection to compute the likely relevance of the document to the query.

A naive application of TFxIDF would require each peer in a community to have access to the inverted index of the entire communal store. This is costly both in terms of bandwidth and storage. Instead, we show how TFxIDF can be approximated given PlanetP's compact summaries of peers' inverted indexes. (Note that while we present adaptation in the specific context of PlanetP, it should be generally applicable to any framework that maintains some approximate information about the global index at each peer.)

---

[1] We say "currently" because we are actively working to extend PlanetP to be a general framework for building P2P applications, not just information sharing.

We make three contributions:

1. we show how the TFxIDF rule can be adapted to rank the peers in the order of their likelihood to have relevant documents, as well as rank the retrieved documents in the absence of complete global information;
2. we develop a heuristic for adaptively determining the set of peers that should be contacted for a query; and
3. using five benchmark collections from Smart [3] and TREC [13], we show that our algorithm matches TFxIDF's performance, despite the accuracy that it gives up by using only summaries of the individual inverted indexes rather than the inverted index of the entire communal store. Furthermore, our algorithm preserves the main flavor of TFxIDF, returning close to the same sets of documents for particular queries.

PlanetP trades some bandwidth for good search performance. Using our heuristics, PlanetP nearly matches the search performance (we will define performance metrics more precisely later in Section 4) of TFxIDF but, on average, will contact 20–40% more peers than if the entire inverted index was kept at each peer[2].

2   PlanetP: Overview

PlanetP is an infrastructure that we are building to support the indexing, searching and retrieval of information spread across a dynamic community of peers, possibly running on a set of heterogeneous devices [6]. This section briefly discusses relevant features and design/implementation details of PlanetP to provide context for the rest of the paper.

The basic data block in PlanetP is an XML snippet. These snippets contain text, from which we extract terms to be indexed[3], and possibly links (XPointers) to external files. To share an XML document, the user publishes the document to PlanetP, which indexes the document and stores a copy of it in a local data store. To share a non-XML document, the user publishes an XML snippet that contains a pointer to the file and possibly additional description of the file. PlanetP indexes the XML snippet and the external file if it is of a known type (e.g., PDF, Postscript, text, etc.). Also, PlanetP stores the XML snippet in the local data store but not the external file itself.

PlanetP uses a Bloom filter [1] to summarize the index of each peer. Briefly, a Bloom filter is an array of bits used to represent some set A—in this case, A is the set of words in the peer's inverted index. The filter is computed by obtaining n indices for each member of A, typically via n different hashing functions, and setting the bit at each index to 1. Then, given a Bloom filter, we can ask, is some element x a member of A by computing n indices for x and checking whether those bits are 1.

---

[2] 40% only when we average over runs where we assume that users are willing to sort through a very large number of retrieved documents to find what he is looking for. Further, our stopping heuristic currently allows for overly aggressive growth in peers contacted as a function of both community size and of the number of documents to be returned. We are tuning this function to reduce the number of peers contacted without degrading TFxIPF's accuracy.

[3] Currently, we do not make use of the structure provided by XML tags. We plan to extend PlanetP to make use of this structure in the near future.

Once a peer has computed its Bloom filter, it diffuses it throughout the community using a gossiping algorithm [7,6]. (This algorithm is also used to maintain a directory of peers currently on-line.) Each peer can then query for communal content by querying against the Bloom filters that it has collected. For example, a peer m can look for all documents containing the word *car* by testing for *car* in each of the Bloom filters. Suppose that this results in "hits" in the Bloom filters of peers $p1$ and $p2$. m then contacts $p1$ and $p2$ to see whether they indeed have documents containing the word *car*; note that these peers may not have any such documents since a Bloom filter can give *false positives*. On the other hand, this set of peers is guaranteed to be complete—that is, it is guaranteed that no peer other than $p1$ and $p2$ can have a document containing the word car—because Bloom filters can never give *false negatives*.

Our approach of diffusing index-summaries using Bloom filters has a number of advantages, the most significant of which are: (1) The Bloom filter is an efficient summary mechanism, minimizing the required bandwidth and storage at each node. In appendix A, we show that PlanetP only needs approximately 1% of the total data indexed to summarize the community's content. (2) Previous studies of file systems have shown that a majority of files change very slowly [20,8]. If P2P information collections display the same characteristic, then, using Bloom filters, PlanetP will place very little load on the community for searches against this bulk of slowly changing data. (3) Peers can independently trade-off accuracy for storage. For example, a peer a may choose to combine the filters of several peers to save space; the trade-off is that a must now contact this set of peers whenever a query hits on this combined filter. This ability for independently trading accuracy for storage is particularly useful for peers running on memory-constrained devices (e.g., hand-held devices). (4) A peer can know that documents relevant to a query might exist on peers that are currently off-line. Thus, instead of missing these documents as in current systems, the searching peer could arrange to rendezvous with the off-line peers when they reconnect to obtain the needed information.

Using simulation, we have shown that PlanetP can easily scale to community sizes of several thousands. For example, using a gossiping rate of once per second[4], PlanetP can propagate a Bloom filter containing 1000 terms in less than 40 seconds for a community with 1000 peers. This spread of information requires an average of 24KB/s per peer. For communities connected by low bandwidth links, we can reduce the gossiping rate: reducing the gossiping rate to once every 30 seconds would require 9 minutes to diffuse a new Bloom filter, requiring an average of 2KB/s bandwidth.

3   Distributed Content Search and Retrieval in PlanetP

The main problem that we are addressing in this paper is how to search for and retrieve documents relevant to a query posed by some member of a PlanetP community. Given a collection of text documents, the problem of retrieving the subset that is relevant to a particular query has been studied extensively (e.g., [22,19]). Currently, one of the most successful techniques for addressing this problem is the vector space ranking model [22].

---

[4] When there is no new information to gossip, PlanetP dynamically reduces this gossiping rate over time to once-per-minute.

Thus, we decided to adapt this technique for use in PlanetP. In this section, we first briefly provide some background on vector space based document ranking, then we present our heuristics to adapt this technique to PlanetP's environment.

3.1   Vector Space Ranking

In a vector space ranking model, each document and query is abstractly represented as a vector, where each dimension is associated with a distinct term (word); the space would have k dimensions if there were k possible distinct terms. The value of each component of the vector represents the importance of that word (typically referred to as the *weight* of the word) to that document or query. Then, given a query, we rank the relevance of documents to that query by measuring the similarity between the query's vector and each of the candidate document's vectors. The similarity between two vectors is generally measured as the cosine of the angle between them, computable using the following equation:

$$Sim(Q, D) = \frac{\sum_{t \epsilon Q} w_{Q,t} \times w_{D,t}}{\sqrt{|Q| \times |D|}} \tag{1}$$

where $w_{Q,t}$ represents the weight of term t for query Q and $w_{D,t}$ the weight of term t for document D. Observe that $Sim(Q, D) = 0$ means that D does not have any term that is in Q. A $Sim(Q, D) = 1$, on the other hand, means that D has every term that is in Q. Typically, $|Q|$ is dropped from the denominator of equation 1 since it is constant for all the documents.

A popular method for assigning term weights is called the TFxIDF rule. The basic idea behind TFxIDF is that by using some combination of term frequency (TF) in a document with the inverse of how often that term shows up in documents in the collection (IDF), we can balance: (a) the fact that terms frequently used in a document are likely important to describe its meaning, and (b) terms that appear in many documents in a collection are not useful for differentiating between these documents for a particular query. For example, if we look at a collection of papers published in an Operating Systems conference, we will find that the terms *Operating System* appears in every document and therefore cannot be used to differentiate between the relevance of these documents.

Existing literature includes several ways of implementing the TFxIDF rule [22]. In our work, we adopt the following system of equations as suggested by Witten et al. [25]:

$$IDF_t = \log(1 + N/f_t) \qquad w_{D,t} = 1 + \log(f_{D,t}) \qquad w_{Q,t} = IDF_t$$

where N is the number of documents in the collection, f_t is the number of times that term t appears in the collection, and $f_{D,t}$ is the number of times term t appears in document D.

The resulting similarity measure is

$$Sim(Q, D) = \frac{\sum_{t \epsilon Q} w_{D,t} \times IDF_t}{|D|} \tag{2}$$

where $|D|$ = the number of terms in document D.

Given a collection of documents, current search engines implement this ranking algorithm by constructing an inverted index over the collection [25]. This index associates a list of documents with each term, the weight of the term for each document, and the positions where the terms appear. Further, information like the inverse document frequency (IDF) and other useful statistics are also added to the index to speed up query processing. An engine can then use this inverted index to quickly determine the subset of documents that contain one or more terms in some query Q, and to compute the vectors needed for equation 2. Then, the engine can rank the documents according to their similarity to the query and present the results to the user.

3.2   Search and Retrieval in PlanetP

We cannot implement the above relevance ranking directly in PlanetP because we do not have all the necessary information. Instead, we approximate this function by breaking the ranking problem into two sub-problems: (1) ranking peers according to the likelihood of each peer having documents relevant to the query, and (2) deciding on the number of peers to contact and ranking the documents returned by these peers.

The node ranking problem. To rank peers, we introduce a measure called the *inverse peer frequency* (IPF). For a term t, IPF_t is computed as $\log(1 + N/N_t)$, where N is number of peers in the community and N_t is the number of peers that have one or more documents with term t in it. Similar to IDF, the idea behind this metric is that a term that is present in the index of every peer is not useful for differentiating between the peers for a particular query. Unlike IDF, IPF can conveniently be computed using the Bloom filters collected at each peer: N is the number of Bloom filters, N_t is the number of hits for term t against these Bloom filters.

Given the above definition of IPF, we then propose the following relevance measure for ranking peers:

$$R_i(Q) = \sum_{t \in Q \land t \in BF_i} IPF_t \tag{3}$$

which is simply a weighted sum over all terms in the query of whether a peer contains that term, weighted by how useful that term is to differentiate between peers; t is a term, Q is the query, BF_i is the set of terms represented by the Bloom filter of peer i, and R_i is the resulting relevance of peer i to query Q. Intuitively, this scheme gives peers that contain all terms in a query the highest ranking. Peers that contain different subsets of terms are ranked according to the power of these terms for differentiating between peers with potentially relevant documents.

The selection problem. As communities grow in size, it is neither feasible nor desirable to contact a large subset of peers for each query. Thus, once we have established a relevance ordering of peers for a query, we must then decide how many of them to contact. To address this problem, we first assume that the user specifies an upper limit k on the number of documents that should be returned in response to a query. Then, a simple solution to the selection problem would be to contact the peers one by one, in the order of their relevance ranking, until we have retrieved k documents.

As shall be seen in Section 4, however, this obvious approach leads to terrible performance as measured by the percentage of relevant documents returned. The reason behind this poor performance is that, when a peer is contacted, it may return say m documents. In most cases, not all m returned documents are highly relevant to the query. Thus, by stopping immediately once we have retrieved k documents, a large subset of the retrieved documents may have very little relevance to the query.

To address this problem, we introduce the following heuristic for adaptively determining a stopping point. Given a relevance ordering of peers, contact them one-by-one from top to bottom. Maintain a relevance ordering of the documents returned using equation 2 with IPF_t substituted for IDF_t. Stop contacting peers when the documents returned by a sequence of p peers fail to contribute to the top k ranked documents. Intuitively, the idea is to get an initial set of k documents and then keep contacting nodes only if the chance of them being able to provide documents that contribute to the top k is relatively high. Using experimental results from a number of known document collections (see Section 4), we propose the following function for p

$$ p = \left\lfloor 2 + \frac{N}{300} \right\rfloor + 2 \left\lfloor \frac{k}{50} \right\rfloor \qquad (4) $$

where N is the size of the community.

Note that while we have presented the above algorithm as contacting peers one-by-one, to reduce query response time, we might choose to contact peers in groups of m peers at a time. Such a parallel algorithm trades off potentially contacting some peers unnecessarily for shorter response time.

4   Evaluating PlanetP's Search Heuristics

We now turn to assessing the performance of TFxIPF together with our adaptive stopping heuristic as implemented in PlanetP. We measure performance using two accepted metrics, *recall* (R) and *precision* (P), which are defined as follows:

$$ R(Q) = \frac{\text{no. relevant docs. presented to the user}}{\text{total no. relevant docs. in collection}} \qquad (5) $$

$$ P(Q) = \frac{\text{no. relevant docs. presented to the user}}{\text{total no. docs. presented to the user}} \qquad (6) $$

where Q is the query posted by the user. $R(Q)$ captures the fraction of relevant documents a search and retrieval algorithm is able to identify and present to the user. $P(Q)$ describes how much irrelevant material the user may have to look through to find the relevant material. Ideal performance is given by 100% recall and 100% precision.

We assess the performance of PlanetP by comparing its achieved recall and precision against the original TFxIDF algorithm. If we can match the TFxIDF's performance, then we can be confident that PlanetP provides state-of-the-art search and retrieval capabilities[5], despite the accuracy that it gives up by gossiping Bloom filters rather than the entire inverted index.

---

[5] when only using the textual content of documents, as compared to link analysis as is done by Google and other web search engines [2]

Table 1. *Characteristics of the collections used to evaluate our search and retrieval engine.*

Trace	Queries	Documents	Number of words	Collection size (MBs)
CACM	52	3204	75493	2.1
MED	30	1033	83451	1.0
CRAN	152	1400	117718	1.6
CISI	76	1460	84957	2.4
AP89	97	84678	129603	266.0

Finally, in addition to recall and precision, we also examine the average number of peers that must be contacted per query under PlanetP. Ideally, we would want to contact as few peers as possible to minimize resource usage per query. We study the number of peers that must be contacted as a function of the number of documents the user is willing to view and the size of the community.

4.1 Experimental Environment

We use five collections of documents (and associated queries and human relevance ranking) to measure PlanetP's performance; Table 1 presents the main characteristics of these collections. Four of the collections, CACM, MED, CRAN, and CISI were previously collected and used by Buckley to evaluate Smart [3]. These collections are comprised of small fragments of text and summaries and so are relatively small in size. The last collection, AP89, was extracted from the TREC collection [13] and includes full articles from Associated Press published in 1989.

To measure PlanetP's recall and precision on the above collections, we built a simulator that first distributes documents across a set of virtual peers and then runs and evaluates different search and retrieval algorithms. To compare PlanetP with TFxIDF, we assume the following optimistic implementation of TFxIDF: each peer in the community has the full inverted index and word count needed to run TFxIDF using ranking equation 2. For each query, TFxIDF would compute the top k ranking documents and then contact the exact peers required to retrieve these documents. In both cases, TFxIDF and TFxIPF, the simulator will pre-process the traces by doing stop word removal and stemming. The former tries to eliminate frequently used words like "the", "of", etc. and the second tries to conflate words to their root (e.g. "running" becomes "run").

We study PlanetP's performance under two different distributions of documents among peers in the community: (a) uniform, and (b) Weibull. We study a uniform distribution of documents because it presents the worst case for a distributed search and retrieval algorithm. The documents relevant to a query are likely spread across a large number of peers. The distributed search algorithm must find all these peers and contact them.

The motivation for studying a Weibull distribution arises from measurements of current P2P file-sharing communities. For example, Saroiu et al. found that 7% of the users in the Gnutella community share more files than all the rest together [23]. We have also studied a community that may be representative of future communities based on PlanetP; students with access to the Rutgers's dormitory network have created a file-sharing community comprised of more than 500 users, sharing more than 6TB of data.

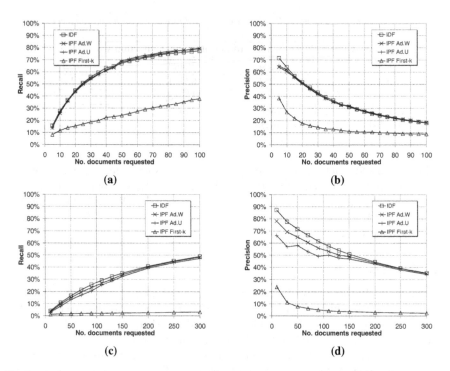

Fig. 1. *Average (a) recall and (b) precision for the MED collection distributed among 100 peers. Average (c) recall and (d) precision for the AP89 collection distributed among 400 peers. IDF is TFxIDF. IPF Ad.W is TFxIPF with the adaptive stopping heuristic on the Weibull distribution of documents. IPF Ad.U is TFxIPF with the adaptive stopping heuristic on the uniform distribution of documents. IPF First-k is TFxIPF that stops immediately after first k documents have been retrieved.*

Studying this community, we observed a data distribution that is very similar to that found by Saroiu et al., where 9% of the users are responsible for providing the majority of the files in the community. Using the collected data, we fitted a Weibull distribution with parameters ($\alpha = 0.7$, $\beta = 46$) and used it to drive the partitioning of a collection among a simulated community.

4.2   Search and Retrieval

To evaluate PlanetP's search and retrieval performance, we assume that when posting a query, the user also provides the parameter k, which is the maximum number of documents that he is willing to accept in answer to a query. Figure 1 plots TFxIDF's and PlanetP's average recall and precision over all provided queries as functions of k for the MED and AP89 collections. We only show results for the MED collection instead of all four Smart collections to save space. Results for the MED collection is representative of all four. We refer the reader to our web site, http://www.panic-lab.rutgers.edu/, for results for all collections.

We make several observations. First, using TFxIPF and our adaptive stopping condition, PlanetP tracks the performance of TFxIDF closely. For the AP89 collection, PlanetP performs slightly worse than TFxIDF for $k < 150$ but catches up for larger k's. For the MED collection, PlanetP gives nearly identical recall and precision to TFxIDF. In fact, at large k, TFxIPF slightly outperforms TFxIDF. While the performance difference is negligible, it is interesting to consider how TFxIPF can outperform TFxIDF; this is possible since TFxIDF is not always correct. In this case, TFxIPF is finding lower ranked documents that were determined to be relevant to queries, while some of the highly ranked documents returned by TFxIDF, but not TFxIPF, were not relevant.

Second, PlanetP's adaptive stopping heuristic is critical to performance. If we simply stopped retrieving documents as soon as we have gotten k documents, recall and precision would be much worse than TFxIDF, as shown by the IPF First-k curves. Finally, as expected, as k increases, recall improves at the expense of precision, although for both collections, precision was still relatively high for large k's (e.g., at $k = 40$, precision is about 40% and recall is about 60% for the MED collection.)

Figure 1 plotted the performance of PlanetP against k for a single community size: 100 peers for MED and 400 peers for AP89. In Figure 2a, we plot the recall when k is 20 against community size to study PlanetP's scalability. We only show results for the AP89 collection as the others were too small to accommodate a wide range of community sizes. We show the performance of TFxIPF with two variants of the stopping heuristic: one that is a function of both k and N, the number of peers, and one that is just a function of k.

We make two observations. First, PlanetP's recall remains constant even when the community size changes by an order of magnitude, from 100 to 1000 peers. Second, the fact that our adaptive stopping heuristic is a function of both k and community size is critical. When the adaptive stopping heuristic only accounts for varying k, recall degrades as community size grows. This is because the relevant documents become spread out more thinly among peers as the community size increase. Thus, the stopping heuristic should allow PlanetP to widen its search by contacting more peers.

4.3   Number of Peers Contacted

To better understand the effects of our adaptive stopping heuristic, we present in Figures 2c and 2d the number of nodes contacted when using TFxIDF and all variants of TFxIPF as well as the lower bound on the number of nodes that need to be contacted. To compute the lower bound, we sort the nodes according to the number of relevant documents they store (assuming global knowledge of the human ranking) and then we plot the lowest number of nodes needed to get k relevant documents (for 100% precision). Note that the lower bound is different than the number of peers contacted by TFxIDF because it is based on the provided human relevance measure (which is binary), not the TFxIDF ranking.

Again, we make several observations. First, our adaptive stopping heuristic is critical for increasing recall with increasing k because it causes more nodes to be contacted. In fact, to match TFxIDF's performance, PlanetP has to contact more peers than TFxIDF at large k's. This is because PlanetP has less information than assumed for TFxIDF, and so may contact peers that don't have highly ranked documents. On the other hand,

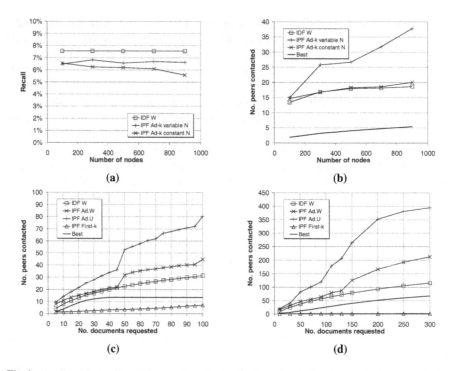

Fig. 2. *Average (a) recall and (b) number of peers contacted as a function of the community size (k=20). Number of peers contacted vs. k for (c) the MED collection distributed across 100 peers and (d) the AP89 collection distributed across 400 peers. IPF Ad-k variable N is TFxIPF with the adaptive stopping heuristic. IPF Ad-k constant N is TFxIPF with a stopping heuristic that is only a function of k and not of community size. IDF W is TFxIDF. IPF Ad.W is TFxIPF with the adaptive stopping heuristic. IPF Ad.U is TFxIPF with the adaptive stopping heuristic. IPF First-k is TFxIPF that stops immediately after first k documents have been retrieved. Best is the minimum number of nodes that must be contacted to retrieve k relevant documents. All these plots use a Weibull distribution of documents except for IPF Ad.U, which uses a uniform distribution.*

simply stopping as soon as we have retrieved k potentially relevant document gives very little growth in the number of peers contacted. As a result, it contacts many less peers than the lower bound imposed by the relevance judgments. This helps to explain the recall and precision for the various algorithms shown earlier. Second, beyond a certain k, 50 for MED and 150 for TREC, PlanetP starts to contact significantly more peers than TFxIDF. At corresponding $k's$, PlanetP's recall improves relative to TFxIDF: PlanetP outperforms TFxIDF slightly for MED and becomes essentially equal to TFxIDF. This implies that either equation 4 is too strongly dependent on k or that the relationship is not linear. We are currently working to refine our stopping heuristic to see whether we can reduce the number of peers contacted at large k without degrading performance too much. Third, PlanetP has to work much harder under the uniform distribution because relevant documents are spread out throughout the community. Thus, actual observations of Weibull-like distributions with shape parameters of 0.7 actually work in favor of a distributed search and retrieval engine such as PlanetP. Note that the results for PlanetP under the uniform distribution is not directly comparable to those for TFxIDF because we only studied TFxIDF under the Weibull distribution; we did not study TFxIDF under the uniform distribution because the distribution does not change TFxIDF's recall and precision; only the number of peers contacted. Finally, our adaptive stopping heuristic allows PlanetP to work well regardless of the distribution of relevant documents. It allows PlanetP to widen its search when documents are more spread out. It helps PlanetP to contract its search when the documents are more concentrated.

Finally, we study the effect of making our adaptive stopping heuristic a function of community size; Figure 2b plots the number of nodes contacted against community size for the AP89 collection for TFxIPF with an adaptive stopping heuristic that adapts to the community size and one that does not. Previously, we saw that adapting to community size was important to maintain a constant recall as community size increase. This figure shows the reason: if we do not adapt to community size, the stopping heuristic throttles the number of peers contacted too quickly. With increasing community size, the number of nodes contacted drops below that of TFxIDF, resulting in lower recall as previously shown.

4.4 Does PlanetP Retrieve Similar Documents to TFxIDF?

We conclude our study of PlanetP's search and retrieval algorithm by considering whether the modified TFxIPF rule finds the same set of relevant documents as TFxIDF. Comparing the sets of results returned, for the MED collection, by TFxIDF and TFxIPF at recall levels between 14% and 44%, we found intersections of 68% to 79%. We only studied the intersections for low recall values because at high recall, by definition, the intersection will approach 100%. Having, on average, an intersection close to 70%, indicates that TFxIPF finds essentially the same set of relevant documents as TFxIDF. This gives us confidence that our adaptations did not change the essential ideas behind TFxIDF's ranking.

5 Related Work

While current P2P systems such as Napster [16], Gnutella [11], and KaZaA [14] have been tremendously successful for music and video sharing communities, their search engines have been frustratingly limited. Our goal for PlanetP is to increase the power with which users can locate information in P2P communities. Also, we have focused more tightly on text-based information, which is more appropriate for collections of scientific documents, legal documents, inventory databases, etc.

In contrast to existing systems, recent research efforts in P2P seek to provide the illusion of having a global hash table shared by all members of the community. Frameworks like Tapestry [27], Pastry [21], Chord [24] and CAN [18] use different techniques to spread (key, value) pairs across the community and to route queries from any member to where the data is stored. These systems differ from PlanetP in two key design decisions. First, in PlanetP, we explicitly decided to replicate the global directory everywhere using gossiping, which limits PlanetP's scalability. The advantage that we get, however, is that we do not have to worry about what happens to parts of the global hash table if members sign off abruptly from the community. Also, the entire community collaborate to spread information about what each peer has to share, instead of putting the publishing burden entirely on the sharing peer. Second, we have focused on content search and retrieval, attempting to provide a similar service to web search engines, which none of these systems have explored.

More related to PlanetP's information retrieval goals, Cori [4] and Gloss [12] address the problems of database selection and ranking fusion on distributed collections. Recent studies done by French et al. [9] show that both scale well to 900 nodes. Although they are based on different ranking techniques, the two rely on similar collection statistics. In both cases the amount of information used to rank nodes is significantly smaller than having a global inverted index. Gloss needs only 2% of the space used by a global index. Both Gloss and Cori assume the existence of a server (or a hierarchy of servers) that will be available for users to decide which collections to contact. In PlanetP we want to empower peers to work autonomously and therefore we distribute Bloom filters widely so they can answer queries even on the presence of network and node failures.

6   Conclusions

P2P computing is a potentially powerful model for information sharing between *ad hoc* communities of users. As P2P communities grow in size, however, locating information distributed across the large number of peers becomes problematic. In this paper, we have presented a text-based ranking algorithm for content search and retrieval. Our thesis is that the search paradigm, where a small set of relevant terms is used to locate documents, is as natural as locating documents by name. To be useful, however, the search and retrieval algorithm must successfully locate the information the user is searching for, without presenting too much unrelated information.

To explore content search and retrieval in P2P communities, we have approximated a state-of-the-art text-based document ranking algorithm, the vector-space model, instantiated with the TFxIDF ranking rule, in PlanetP. A naive implementation of TFxIDF would require each peer in a community to have access to the inverted index of the entire community. Instead, we show how TFxIDF can be approximated given a compact summary (the Bloom filter) of each peer's inverted index. We make three contributions: (a) we show how the TFxIDF rule can be adapted to use the summaries of individual indexes, (b) we provide a heuristic for adaptively determining the set of peers that should be contacted for a query, and (c) we have shown that our algorithm tracks TFxIDF's performance very closely, regardless of how documents are distributed throughout the community. Finally, our algorithm preserves the main flavor of TFxIDF by returning much the same set of documents for a particular query. Our results provide evidence that distributed content search and retrieval in P2P communities can perform as well as search and retrieval algorithms based on the use of centralized servers.

Appendix A - PlanetP's Memory Usage

In this appendix, we present how we estimated the amount of memory needed by each PlanetP's member to keep track of the community's content. Note that the memory usage depends mainly on the Bloom filter size and the number of peers on the community. In our calculation we have chosen Bloom filters that are able to store each peer's set of terms with less than 5% of false positives. For example, if we spread the AP89 collection across a community of 1000 peers, each peer will receive on average 4500 terms. On this scenario a 4.6KB filter will store a single peer's data, which means that the whole community can be summarized with 4.6MB of memory. Because nodes exchange filters in compressed form, the bandwidth required by a single node to gather the remaining 999 filters will be 3.3MB.

Table 2 shows the results obtained for different community sizes using the same calculations as presented above.

Table 2. *Amount of memory used per node to store Bloom filters summarizing the whole community on AP89.*

No. peers	Memory used (MB)	% of collection size
10	0.45	0.18%
100	1.79	0.70%
1000	4.48	1.76%

References

1. B. H. Bloom. Space/time trade-offs in hash coding with allowable errors. *Communications of the ACM*, 13(7):422–426, 1970.
2. S. Brin and L. Page. The anatomy of a large-scale hypertextual Web search engine. *Computer Networks and ISDN Systems*, 30(1–7):107–117, 1998.
3. C. Buckley. Implementation of the SMART information retrieval system. Technical Report TR85-686, Cornell University, 1985.
4. J. P. Callan, Z. Lu, and W. B. Croft. Searching Distributed Collections with Inference Networks . In *Proceedings of the 18th Annual International ACM SIGIR Conference on Research and Development in Information Retrieval*, pages 21–28, 1995.
5. I. Clarke, O. Sandberg, B. Wiley, and T. W. Hong. Freenet: A distributed anonymous information storage and retrieval system. In *Workshop on Design Issues in Anonymity and Unobservability*, pages 46–66, 2000.
6. F. M. Cuenca-Acuna, C. Peery, R. P. Martin, and T. D. Nguyen. PlanetP: Infrastructure Support for P2P Information Sharing. Technical Report DCS-TR-465, Department of Computer Science, Rutgers University, Nov. 2001.
7. A. Demers, D. Greene, C. Hauser, W. Irish, J. Larson, S. Shenker, H. Sturgis, D. Swinehart, and D. Terry. Epidemic algorithms for replicated database maintenance. In *Proceedings of the Sixth Annual ACM Symposium on Principles of Distributed Computing*, pages 1–12, 1987.
8. F. Douglis, A. Feldmann, B. Krishnamurthy, and J. C. Mogul. Rate of change and other metrics: a live study of the world wide web. In *USENIX Symposium on Internet Technologies and Systems*, 1997.

9. J. C. French, A. L. Powell, J. P. Callan, C. L. Viles, T. Emmitt, K. J. Prey, and Y. Mou. Comparing the performance of database selection algorithms. In *Research and Development in Information Retrieval*, pages 238–245, 1999.

10. D. K. Gifford, P. Jouvelot, M. A. Sheldon, and J. W. O. Jr. Semantic File Systems. In *Proceedings of the 13th ACM Symposium on Operating Systems Principles*, 1991.

11. Gnutella. http://gnutella.wego.com.

12. L. Gravano, H. Garcia-Molina, and A. Tomasic. The effectiveness of gloss for the text database discovery problem. In *Proceedings of the ACM SIGMOD Conference*, pages 126–137, 1994.

13. D. Harman. Overview of the first trec conference. In *Proceedings of the 16th Annual International ACM SIGIR Conference on Research and Development in Information Retrieval*, 1993.

14. KaZaA. http://www.kazaa.com/.

15. J. Kubiatowicz, D. Bindel, Y. Chen, P. Eaton, D. Geels, R. Gummadi, S. Rhea, H. Weatherspoon, W. Weimer, C. Wells, and B. Zhao. Oceanstore: An architecture for global-scale persistent storage. In *Proceedings of ACM ASPLOS*, 2000.

16. Napster. http://www.napster.com.

17. A. Oram, editor. *Peer-to-Peer: Harnessing the Power of Disruptive Technologies*. O'Reilly Press, 2001.

18. S. Ratnasamy, P. Francis, M. Handley, R. Karp, and S. Shenker. A scalable content addressable network. In *Proceedings of the ACM SIGCOMM '01 Conference*, 2001.

19. S. E. Robertson and K. S. Jones. Relevance weighting of search terms. In *Journal of the American Society for Information Science*, volume 27, pages 129–146, 1976.

20. D. Roselli, J. Lorch, and T. Anderson. A comparison of file system workloads. In Proceedings of the 2000 USENIX Annual Technical Conference, June 2000.

21. A. Rowstron and P. Druschel. Pastry: Scalable, distributed object location and routing for large-scale peer-to-peer systems. In *Proceedings of the IFIP/ACM International Conference on Distributed Systems Platforms (Middleware)*, 2001.

22. G. Salton, A. Wang, and C. Yang. A vector space model for information retrieval. In *Journal of the American Society for Information Science*, volume 18, pages 613–620, 1975.

23. S. Saroiu, P. K. Gummadi, and S. D. Gribble. A measurement study of peer-to-peer file sharing systems. In *Proceedings of Multimedia Computing and Networking (MMCN)*, 2002.

24. I. Stoica, R. Morris, D. Karger, M. F. Kaashoek, and H. Balakrishnan. Chord: A scalable peer-to-peer lookup service for internet applications. In *Proceedings of the ACM SIGCOMM '01 Conference*, 2001.

25. I. Witten, A. Moffat, and T. Bell. *Managing Gigabytes: Compressing and Indexing Documents and Images*. Morgan Kaufmann, San Francisco, second edition, 1999.

26. B. Yang and H. Garcia-Molina. Efficient search in peer-to-peer networks. In *Proceedings of the International Conference on Distributed Computing Systems (ICDCS)*, July 2002.

27. Y. Zhao, J. Kubiatowicz, and A. Joseph. Tapestry: An infrastructure for fault-tolerant wide-area location and routing. Technical Report UCB/CSD-01-1141, University of California, Berkeley, 2000.

Freeing Cooperation from Servers Tyranny[*]

Davide Balzarotti[1], Carlo Ghezzi[2], and Mattia Monga[2]

[1] Politecnico di Milano
Dip. di Elettronica e Informazione
Piazza Leonardo da Vinci, 32
I 20133 Milan, Italy
[2] CEFRIEL
Via Fucini,2
I 20133 Milan, Italy

Abstract. This paper deals with computer supported cooperative work in the context of untethered scenarios typical of mobile environments. The scenario envisions a number of homogeneous peers that are able to provide the same services, disconnect frequently from the net, and perform part of their work while disconnected. The application we choose is Configuration Management (CM), a critical cooperative activity occurring in software development. We discuss an implementation of a configuration management tool in a peer-to-peer setting, evaluate our solution with respect to other systems, and draw conclusions for future development.

1 Motivation

A computer aided cooperative work effort typically deals with in the production of a number of software artifacts. Artifacts are parceled among collaborators. The best application of the principle of division of labor would require that only a worker manipulates each artifact. Unfortunately, this is never true. In general, for each item we can identify the role of an *owner,* i.e., the individual who has created the artifact or who has the duty of carrying out the work on it. However, there are typically other workers who need or want to see or manipulate items that are not under their control, i.e., artifacts they do not own.

A classical solution to coordination of people work relies on the existence of a shared *repository.* Shared artifacts are stored in the repository and if one wants to work on them, one has to *check-out* the needed artifact from the repository. When the work session is over the artifact has to be *checked-in* the repository again. According to this approach the repository becomes the centralized mean of coordination among workers, thus check out and check in operations can be controlled by enforcing agreed policies that ensure consistency of the collaborative work.

---

[*] This work is supported by a grant from Microsoft Research, Cambridge (UK) and COMPAQ.

In order to meet its requirements the repository has to be accessible by all the workers, thus the traditional architecture is based on a number of servers that provide the "repository service" to the client nodes that are in charge of the work. This architecture relies on two assumptions:

1. *no off-line cooperation:* check out and check in operations are performed only while a network connection is available;
2. *servers always alive:* repository servers are always available on line when check in and check out operations are needed.

The centralized repository assumption seems to be too restrictive in several current scenarios based on mobility and continuous evolution. In fact, the recent advances in the area of wireless networks and the popularity of powerful mobile computing devices, such as laptops, PDAs, or even mobile phones, is fostering the diffusion of a new form of distributed computing usually called *mobile computing.* In this scenario, where users connect to the network from arbitrary locations and typically they are not permanently connected. In a fully nomadic scenario, no fixed network topology can be assumed. Machine disconnection is not an exceptional case, but the normal way of operating. The pure client-server paradigm, where some machines play the role of service providers for other machines, appears to be unsuitable to enable the required intrinsic dynamism. The main disadvantage of client-server systems is that they are like little "solar systems": the entire application orbits around the main server stars. When servers are not reachable, the entire system is just a dead cold set of asteroids. As far as cooperative work is concerned, this means that the entire service is blocked, until servers arise again to bring new life in the collaborators' work.

Instead we are going to propose an architecture where nodes might freely accomplish their computations *off-line.* Of course, this requires some form of reconciliation with the *on-line* part of the environment when disconnected machines later rejoin the network of nodes. To achieve this goal, we claim that the presence of two classes of computational elements, namely, clients and servers, is a weak point: a service cannot be exploited every time servers are not available. Instead, when the topology of the network environment is not known *a priori,* *peer-to-peer* settings where all nodes are peers, i.e. they are functionally equivalent and any could provide services to any other [1] may provide the following advantages:

- *absence tolerance:* the absence of a single peer, because of a fault or a voluntary disconnection, can be often compensated by the presence of other peers;
- *bandwidth economy:* network links towards servers are typically the bottlenecks of client-server environments, in particular if the number of nodes is high. In a peer-to-peer setting the network topology can be conceptually considered as a complete graph, and the traffic is more homogeneously distributed on all edges;
- *ease of configuration:* because in theory each peer acts both as a client and as a server, it can customize the services it provides according some commonly accepted protocol, without requiring a centralized supervision;

— *efficient use of resources:* popular resources (data and services) can be easily replicated on several peers. Conversely, unused or obsolete resources could be eliminated by the a decision of the subset of peers which was interested in them.

These advantages are available at the cost of the loss of the centralized control. Nonetheless, it is possible and convenient to build middleware components that provide primitives aimed at supplying a common framework where coordination and cooperation of peers is facilitated, and the changing network topology is hidden. In this paper we assume the existence of such a middleware. In particular (see Section 3.1),we base our work on PEERWARE, a middleware suitable for peer-to-peer settings developed at Politecnico di Milano [2,3].

This paper is organized as follows: in Section 2 we describe the requirements for what we want from our support tool, in Section 3 we describe the architectural structure of the tool, and finally, in Section 5 we draw some conclusions.

2   Requirements for the Support Tool

As an example of computer supported cooperative work we focus on software development. Thanks to the increasing availability of distributed computational infrastructures, software production is often dispersed among geographically distant locations, and software processes become necessarily network aware cooperative processes. Software development environments, however, are still far from supporting these new forms of virtual workgroups through specific network-aware services [4]. In particular, consider the case of configuration management (CM) tools. Software processes are typically supported by CM tools [5] that help developers to keep consistent their work, and, despite of dynamic nature of software teams, these are typically client-server applications [6]. As stated, the availability of a repository machine is critical, because without it no check-out or check-in operations are permitted. This is too restrictive because it assumes the availability of the network infrastructure even in the frequent case that no concurrent work is done on a particular item. It is perfectly reasonable and desirable that one could check in a file which is under his/her control if no other developers want to manipulate it. Similarly, check out operations can be performed also when the latest version of an artifact is available somewhere, not necessarily on repository servers, but for example on the local file system because no one has checked in a newer version. However, these operations, while performed in unthetered or even off-line mode, should be fully compliant with the cooperative system policies. Thus, an off-line check in should version the artifact and, for instance, satisfy a given set of requirements.

The main point is that in a highly mobile settings, disconnected work is no more an exceptional case. A software development team, provided with laptops and some kind of wireless connection, sets up impromptu meetings during which they can, for example, correct bugs on the fly and merge the patches in the baseline. Developers may wish to check out the modules they need also when the owners are not connected to them. This, of course, requires the system to provide support for some caching policy. Similarly, check in should be a transparent operation, which should not require knowledge of who is on-line when the operation is executed. A check in request should be executed asynchronously when the owner of the item becomes available on-line. Finally, when new versions of configuration items that are under one's control become available on-line, a notification should be submitted to all interested peers, to enable them to keep an updated view of the system.

Consider the following scenario: a developer D wants to modify a source file f owned by Z, but Z is currently off-line. However, this is not a problem, because X, who is available on-line, has a recent version of f that can be downloaded by D. In the meanwhile, Z is working (off-line) on f and she checks in a new version f' of it. When Z reconnects herself with the rest of the system, a notification of the existence of f' is submitted to the peers. If X now asks to check out f, the new version f' is downloaded, since the previously locally cached copy is no more valid. If D decides to check in his modified version of f, a conflict arises, which may be solved by a manual merge of the two independently developed modifications of the same module.

Summing up our requirements, the configuration management tool should provide the following features:

1. check-out: every work session starts with this operation. Configuration items should be accessible also when owners are not connected, thanks to suitable caching policies;
2. check-in: every work session ends with this operation. It should be possible to check in items at any moment. However, the actual check-in is physically carried out only when the owner is available. Since concurrent changes of a configuration item are possible, this may generate conflicts. Conflict resolutions, which may imply some manual merge, is performed when the owner is on-line. Off-line and on-line check in operations are subjected to the same policy rules.
3. change notification: when a peer joins the network, it notifies the changes made to its own items since it last left off to all interested peers. In this way, any cached copies kept by such peers become invalid.

3   An Architectural View

In order to implement the requirements described in Section 2, the configuration items repository must be distributed among all process participants, as showed in Figure 1. In a process with n participants, the global repository R is composed by the union of the local repositories R_i

$$R = \bigcup_{i=1}^{n} R_i$$

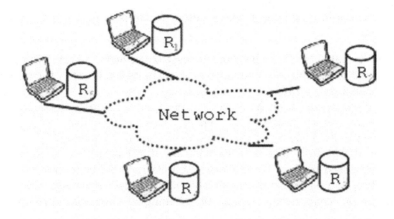

Fig. 1. Distributed repository of configuration items

Two different architectural choices are feasible:

$$\bigcap_{i=1}^{n} R_i = \emptyset \tag{1}$$

$$\bigcap_{i=1}^{n} R_i \neq \emptyset \tag{2}$$

The choice (1) gives a system with no replicated information. This solution allows efficient implementations (see for example DVS [7,8,9,6]) and does not introduce the risk of getting inconsistent replicated information. However, items can be accessed only if the unique host that provides them is on-line, and this does not satisfy our requirements about check-out.

In our system we preferred the choice (2) because by replicating information, it enables cooperation also when some nodes are not available on-line. However, more machinery to compose conflicts among different versions of configuration items is needed. In order to settle conflicts we adopt a strategy similar to the one used in the management of the distributed database of the Domain Name System [10], in which the data regarding associations between IP numbers and host names are replicated on several DNS servers. Each DNS server records some associations known with certainty (*authoritative* associations) and some others simply as remembered form previous accesses (*cached* associations). Whenever a DNS server gets a request for a host for which it cannot give an authoritative answer or that is not contained in its cache, it queries the network, possibly ending up asking the authoritative server, who knows the correct answer.

In our system each peer is *authoritative* for the configuration items it owns, and its copy of such items is the "master" copy. Every check-in of a new version becomes definitive only if it is authorized by the authoritative peer. If a peer X

wants to check-in a document whose authoritative peer is A ($\neq X$) two cases may occur:

1. A is reachable by X: a check-in proposal is notified to A. A can reject the proposal or commit to making it persistent in its local part of the repository as a new master copy;
2. A is disconnected from X: a check-in proposal is recorded in the local part of the repository hosted by X. When A becomes available, the proposal is notified to it. A can reject the proposal or commit to making it persistent in its local repository as a new master copy. If A has an item newer than the one proposed by X, a conflict arises. Similarly, other concurrently pending check-in requests generate conflicts. Conflicts must be managed by merging the various change requests, and then issuing a new check-in proposal.

When a peer X wants to check-out a document d whose authoritative peer is A ($\neq X$) two cases may occur:

1. d is present in X's the local repository and the copy is *valid,* that is, no newer versions were notified to X. The check-out operation boils down to getting a copy of d;
2. d is not present in the local part of repository under control of X: a network search is issued to retrieve a valid copy. If no valid copy is found, the check-out operation fails. Notice, however, that it may also happen that an invalid copy is found, but the authoritative peer for the searched item is off-line. This may happen when the authoritative peer gets on-line, notifies all interested peer that a new version is available for a given item, and then immediately gets disconnected from the network. In such a case, the cached versions of the item become invalid, but at the same time the most recent version of the item is unaccessible. We decided that, in this case, the check-out operation retries the invalid copy.

Finally, when a peer enters the community of peers, a reconciliation step is performed. More specifically, when X gets connected, for each item i for which X is the authority, X notifies all interested peers if a newer version of i is made available. In such a case, the locally cached copies of peers that are not authoritative for the item become *invalid.*

In the next Section we sketch the middleware we used to implement the operations we described here to support distributed configuration management.

3.1   The Underlying Middleware

PEERWARE [2,3] provides the abstraction of a *global virtual data structure* (GVDS), built out of the local data structures contributed by each peer. PEERWARE takes care of reconfiguring dynamically the view of the global data structure as perceived by a given user, according to the connectivity state. The data structure managed by PEERWARE is organized as a graph composed of nodes and documents, collectively referred to as items. Nodes are essentially containers of items,

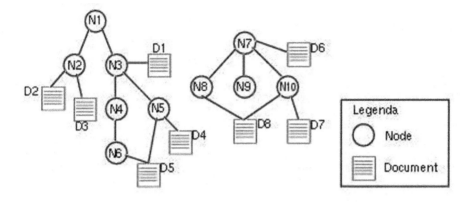

Fig. 2. An example of the PEERWARE data structure managed by a peer

and are meant to be used to structure and classify the documents managed through the middleware.

This means that nodes are structured in a forest of trees, with distinct roots, which most likely represent different perspectives on the documents contained into the data structure. For instance, one could have an "GNU/Linux projects" tree, a "Latex papers" tree, and so on. Within this graph, each node is linked to at most one parent node and may contain different children nodes (see for example Figure 2). Conversely, stand-alone documents are forbidden; documents are linked to at least one parent node and do not have children. Hence, a document may be contained in multiple nodes. As for labels, two nodes may have the same label, as long as they are not both roots and are not directly contained into the same node.

At any time, the local data structures held by the peers connected to PEER-WARE are made available to the other peers as part of the global virtual data structure managed (GVDS) by PEERWARE. This GVDS has the same structure of the local data structure and its content is obtained by "superimposing" all the local data structures belonging to the peers currently connected, as shown in Figure 3.

Changes in connectivity among peers determine changes in the content of the global data structure constituting the GVDS, as new local data structures may become available or disappear. Nevertheless, the reconfiguration taking place behind the scenes is completely hidden to the peers accessing the GVDS, which need only to be aware of the fact that its content and structure is allowed to change over time.

There is a clear distinction between operations performed on the PEERWARE local data structure and on the whole GVDS. While hiding this difference would provide an elegant uniformity to the model, it may also hide the fundamental difference between local and remote effects of the operations [11]. In particular the operations for creating or destroying a node ($createNode(node, parent)$,

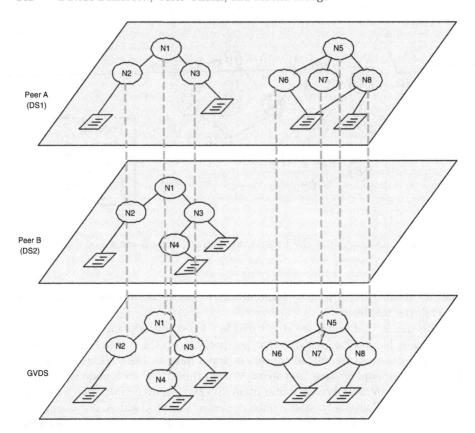

Fig. 3. An example of the global virtual data structure managed by PEERWARE

removeNode(node)), for inserting or removing a document (*placeIn(node, document)*, *removeFrom(node, document)*), and for publishing an event occurred on an item (*publish(event, item)*) are defined only on the local data structure. PEERWARE provides three operations that can be performed both on the local and the global data structures:

1. $I = execute(F_N, F_D, a)$. An action a is performed on all documents – contained in nodes whose name matches the filter F_N – that match the filter F_D. The matching set of documents I, affected by a is returned to the caller.
2. $subscribe(F_N, F_D, F_E, a)$. Allows a peer to subscribe to the occurrence of an event matching the event filter F_E and being published within the projection of the data structure identified by the filters F_N and F_D. When the event occurs the action a is executed locally to the caller.
3. $I = execSubscribe(F_N, F_D, F_E, a_e, a_s)$. Executes an arbitrary action a_e on the projection of the data structure identified by F_N and F_D, similarly to *execute*. Also, in the same atomic step, it subscribes for events that match

F_E, and occur within the same projection, by specifying the action a_s that must be executed locally to the caller, when one of such events occurs.

The semantics of a global operation can be regarded as being equivalent to a distributed execution of the corresponding operation on the local data structures of the peers currently connected. While as far as concerns local operations atomicity can be assumed, this is an impractical assumption in a distributed setting. Hence, the global operations do not provide any guarantee about global atomicity, and they guarantee only that the execution of the corresponding operations on each local data structure is correctly serialized (i.e., it is executed atomically on each local data structure).

The operations provided by PEERWARE together with a publish/subscribe engine on which PEERWARE itself relies on (the distributed event dispatcher JEDI, see [12]) build the framework needed to implement the configuration management operations described in Section 3. In particular, by using PEERWARE we can abstract from the actual network topology and perform actions on *on-line* items.

4 Related Work

Despite the recent evolution of Software Configuration Management systems, most CM systems are still founded on a centralized architecture where both the application and the repository are stored in the same physical location.
Figure 4(a) shows the traditional Client-Server architecture that is used in most conventional CM systems (CVS [13] is probably the best known). Nowadays, software production is becoming a more and more distributed activity where the project teams are physically dispersed over a great number of locations. This has fostered the design of systems that provide the distribution of the repository over

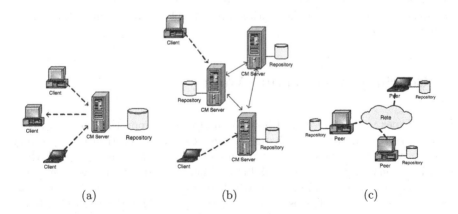

(a)   (b)   (c)

Fig. 4. CM system architectures

multiple sites. The solution usually adopted in the distributed CM systems is shown in Figure 4(b): the repository is broken up among geographically distinct servers, allowing the distribution of the data next to the actors of the software process. However, from the user point of view not much is changed because, like in the previous architecture, they must connect to a server to perform either a check-in or a check-out operation. As examples of systems built over this architecture we consider two different products : ClearCase Multisite and DVS.

Rational ClearCase Multisite [14] is a commercial product that supports parallel software development with automated replication of project database. With Multisite, each location has a copy (*replica*) of the repository and, at any time, a site can propagate the changes made in its particular replica to other sites. Nevertheless, each object is assigned a master replica and in general an object can be modified only at its master replica. To avoid this restriction Multisite uses branches. Each branch can have a different master and since the branches of an element are independent, changes made in different sites do not conflict. The concept of master is like our concept of authority; however, the access policy provided by Multisite is too restrictive for our scenario.

DVS [7] is a simple research system that allows one to distribute the CM repository over the network, but it does not allow the replication of the information. Even though the absence of replication contrasts with our assumptions, it is interesting to make an architectural comparison with DVS because it also makes a clear distinction between the CM application and the underlying middleware. In fact, DVS has been implemented on top of NUCM [8] (Network-Unified Configuration Management), whereas our system is built on top of PeerWare. NUCM defines a generic distributed repository and provides a policy-neutral interface to realize CM systems. PeerWare is a general-purpose peer-to-peer middleware, whereas NUCM is focused on the CM system creation and provides ad hoc functionalities.

To make the comparison clear, our solution is sketched in Figure 4(c). It is a pure peer-to-peer architecture where there are no servers and the whole repository is directly distributed over the users' devices. We claim that such an architecture is a more suitable solution for evolvable scenarios where topology is highly dynamic.

5   Conclusions and Future Work

In this paper we have discussed how to build a tool supporting cooperation to a networked team, without relying on the existence of centralized repository servers. We do not want to restrict the use of the system to the scenarios where repository servers are always available on line. Instead, we propose the use of a suitable peer-to-peer middleware which provides the abstraction of a global virtual data structure. This is a data structure parceled among all peers, but it can be searched and modified transparently, without knowing the actual network topology.

The use of this abstraction enabled us to design a configuration management tool which is especially oriented to supporting scenarios in which users' connectivity to the network can change dynamically. This is achieved by exploiting the global virtual data structure as the artifact repository. Our solution overcomes the intrinsic problems of client-server architectures, which are clearly not suitable for scenarios where the absence of a host is not an exceptional case, but rather the normal case. Along the same line, repositories based on distributed file systems expose the system to failures when a server is unavailable.

Our solution is based on caching copies, and then making them available for use even if the hosts that own them are disconnected. The outcome is a genuine peer-to-peer architecture, where any on-line machine can in principle replicate the unavailable resources. We pay, of course, for this advantage in terms of a harder coordination effort.

The approach we described in this paper is currently being implemented as part of our current efforts in the provision of a suite of software process support tools well suited for educational environments in which students are equipped with mobile devices.

References

1. A. Oram, ed., *Peer-to-Peer: Harnessing the Benefits of a Disruptive Technology*. O'Reilly & Associates, first ed., Mar. 2001.
2. G. Cugola and G. P. Picco, "Peerware: Core middleware support for peer-to-peer and mobile systems." submitted for publication, 2001.
3. F. Bardelli and M. Cesarini, "Peerware: un middleware per applicazioni mobili e peer-to-peer," Master's thesis, Politecnico di Milano, 2001.
4. J. Estublier, "Software configuration management: A road map," in *The Future of Software Engineering* (A. Finkelstein, ed.), ACM Press, May 2000.
5. E. H. Bersoff, "Elements of software configuration management," *Software Engineering*, vol. 10, no. 1, pp. 79–87, 1984.
6. A. van der Hoek, A. Carzaniga, D. Heimbigner, and A. L. Wolf, "A testbed for configuration management policy programming," *Transaction on Software Engineering*, vol. 28, pp. 79–99, Jan. 2002.
7. A. Carzaniga, "Design and implementation of a distributed versioning system," tech. rep., Politecnico di Milano, Oct. 1998.
8. A. van der Hoek, A. Carzaniga, D. Heimbigner, and A. L. Wolf, "A reusable, distributed repository for configuration management policy programming," tech. rep., University of Colorado, Boulder CO 80309 USA, Oct. 1998.
9. A. van der Hoek, D. Heimbigner, and A. L. Wolf, "A generic, peer-to-peer repository for distributed configuration managemenet," in *18th International Conference on Software Engineering*, (Berlin - Heidelberg - New York), p. 308, Springer, Mar. 1996.
10. P. Mockapetris, "Rfc 1035 (standard: Std 13) domain names–implementation and specification," tech. rep., Internet Engineering Task Force, November 1987.
11. J. Waldo, G. Wyant, A. Wollrath, and S. Kendall, "A note on distributed computing," in *Mobile Object Systems*, vol. 1222 of *Lecture Notes in Computer Science*, pp. 49–64, Springer-Verlag, Berlin, 1997.

12. G. Cugola, E. Di Nitto, and A. Fuggetta, "Exploiting an event-based infrastructure to develop complex distributed systems," in *ICSE98 proceedings*, (Kyoto (Japan)), April 1998.
13. "Concurrent versions system." `http://www.cvshome.org/`.
14. Rational Software Corporation, Maguire Road Lexington, Massachusetts 02421, *ClearCase MultiSite Manual (release 4.0 or later)*, 2000.

BuddyWeb: A P2P-Based Collaborative Web Caching System

XiaoYu Wang[1], WeeSiong Ng[2], BengChin Ooi[2],
Kian-Lee Tan[2], and AoYing Zhou[1]

[1] Department of Computer Science, Fudan University, China.
{xiaoyuwang,ayzhou}@fudan.edu.cn
[2] Department of Computer Science, National University of Singapore, Singapore.
{ngws,tankl,ooibc}@comp.nus.edu.sg

1 Introduction

The peer-to-peer (P2P) computing model has been increasingly deployed for a wide variety of applications, including data mining, replica placement, resource trading, data management and file sharing (see [1,2]). In this paper, we look at yet another application - that of collaborative web caching. Unlike existing web caching techniques that are typically managed at the proxies, we look at how to exploit local caches of nodes (or rather PCs) within an enterprise network.

To illustrate, consider the campus network at the Fudan University, where there are thousands of PCs, each with a web browser installed. Here, the network is not only protected from the "outside world" by firewall, any incoming and outgoing requests must go through a central proxy. In addition, there is a quota policy to restrict the amount of bandwidth each member of the university community can utilize, and every bit of external data transferred will be charged! Since there is no cache sharing among different users in current web browser architecture, even if the requested information is available in a node within the campus network, the request may be sent out, incurring both long response time and cost. By sharing the local caches, we can expect to save cost as well as reduce the response time.

To this end, we have designed the BuddyWeb, a P2P-based collaborative web caching system. In BuddyWeb, all the local cache of participating nodes are sharable, and nodes within the enterprise network will be searched first before remote external accesses are invoked. BuddyWeb accepts two kind of search queries; URL-based and keywords-based. In the first case, user who would simply enter the desired URL and BuddyWeb would download the page of a peer node if there is a cache hit. Later case, BuddyWeb in which appears to be a general search-engine-like, e.g., Google, system, returning abstracts of the pages found. BuddyWeb is unique in several way. First, the peer network can dynamically reconfigure itself based on the similarity of its interests. In other words, over time, we expect to see communities of different interests formed. Second, we propose a novel routing strategy, which based on the idea of similarity of peers' contents. Query will be routed from a peer to its neighbor that has the highest similarity value. Third, BuddyWeb adopts a self-adaptable hopping strategy

E. Gregori et al. (Eds.): Networking 2002 Workshops, LNCS 2376, pp. 247–251, 2002.

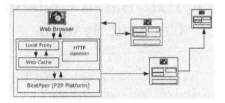

Fig. 1. BuddyWeb Architecture

in which the TTL will self adjust to achieve the objectives of maximizing the positive search results and minimizing the bandwidth usage. Finally, BuddyWeb combines the power of mobile agents into P2P systems to perform operations at peers' sites. This facilitates content-based searching easily.

We are implementing BuddyWeb on top of BestPeer[3], a agent-based P2P system. The BestPeer network consists of two types of entities: a large number of computers (nodes) and a relatively fewer number of *Location Independent Global Names Lookup* (LIGLO) servers. Each participant node must register with a LIGLO and can communicate or share resources with other nodes (i.e. peers) in the network. A LIGLO server, which has a fixed IP address, provides two main functions. It generates a BestPeer Global Identity (BPID) for a node so that nodes with varying IP addresses can be "recognized" as a single unique entity. It also maintains peer's current status, such as whether it is online or offline. Agents are extensively used in searching and to perform tasks at remote peer site.

2   BuddyWeb Node

Figure 1 depicts the architecture of an autonomous peer in BuddyWeb. The web browser, e.g., Netscape, serves as the front-end interface to user. Users will not notice any difference between a BuddyWeb-enabled browser and the original browser. In a BuddyWeb-enabled browser, there is a local proxy that works with the local cache, and a HTTP daemon to support HTTP requests. The cache in collaboration with the BestPeer platform, is responsible for sharing cache data with other peers in the BuddyWeb network. The low level communication between peers are managed by the BestPeer platform.

Whenever the web browser submits a URL request or keyword queries, the local proxy will receive and rewrite the query into the input format of the Best-Peer platform. The query will then be passed to BestPeer platform. BestPeer generates a mobile agent and dispatches it to the BuddyWeb network to search for matching documents. Upon receiving a match, BestPeer passes the information, i.e., document location, back to the local proxy. In this way, the local proxy will issue HTTP request directly to the peer that has the documents. The peer, upon receiving the HTTP request, will process it by the HTTP daemon, and sends the requested documents to the requester.

3   Similarity-Based Reconfiguration

Dynamic reconfiguration is facilitated so that a peer is always directly connected
to peers that provide the best service. BuddyWeb uses LIGLOs to facilitate the
dynamic reconfiguration. Each registered peer is responsible for sending to the
LIGLO its IP address and extra surfing information. Such surfing information
will reasonably reflect the peer's interests.

Getting the peer's interested tendency could be deployed by use of its browsed
pages. The information must be both representative and brief. Different policies
might be employed from IR (Information Retrieval) field. One simple way is to
send some useful meta-data (say, <TITLE> </TITLE>) in the browsed pages
to the associated LIGLO. Alternatively, user can provide feedback in the form
of highlighting some keywords in the browsed pages.

Peers interest tendencies will be represented as word lists in LIGLO. Dynamic
reconfiguration could be facilitated on the basis of those word lists, which we call
Peer-Tendency. Keeping reconfiguration in mind, we could see all the words in
Peer-tendencies as a word bag, which could be used to construct a vector space.
Each *Peer-Tendency* will be transformed to a corresponding vector in such a
vector space according to some weighting schemes. Note that each LIGLO only
holds information of the peers registering to it. Thus, a negotiation must be
held among all the LIGLOs, and thereby determines which LIGLO receive the
Peer-Tendencies. An alternative approach to this problem is to use hash method,
which could avoid vector computation in a single server. However, in our context,
there are relatively fewer LIGLO severs in the BuddyWeb network. Besides, the
Peer-Tendencies are "light-weight" files. Therefore, we decide to implement the
vector computation with the former approach.

A proper similarity function, e.g., cosine function, could be defined using
VSM (Vector Space Model). To keep the most beneficial peers as directly connected neighbors, each peer should maintain those peers with which it has the
highest similarity values. However, the computation of all pair-wise peers is a
time-consuming task. A simple way to solve this problem is to distribute the
similarity computation to every peer, i.e., the responsible LIGLO computes only
all the vectors in VSM. After that, those vectors will be sent to every LIGLO
server. The reconfiguration policy works as follows.

- In a certain period (say, every midnight), the LIGLOs will negotiate to compute the vectors of all the peers. After that, each LIGLO will hold the computed vectors of all the peers.
- When a peer is online, it will communicate with its registering LIGLO to send
  its current IP address and request all the other peers' vectors. Similarities
  with all the other peers will be computed by the peer locally. Those with the
  higher similarity will be ranked higher.
- The k peers with the highest value of similarity will be kept as the directly
  connected neighbors, where k is a system parameter that can be set by
  participant peers.

It is necessary to point out that effective clustering algorithms could be easily employed to group peers with common interests into clusters. This gives us a way to discover the peer communities appearing in the BuddyWeb network.

4   Similarity-Based Routing and Self-adaptive Hopping

In BuddyWeb, the dynamic reconfiguration is facilitated by use of a similarity computation, which provides a reasonable measure of the relationships between peers. Considering the situation, in which a query agent is to be forwarded to the directly connected neighbors, the peer forwarding the query agent maintains the similarity values with its neighbors. Instead of forwarding an agent to all its direct neighbors, the peer could select the neighbor with the highest similarity value. Note that the query agent from the initial node will be propagated to all its directly neighbors and similarity-based routing policy will be adopted for further forwarding.

Another benefit from using similarity measure is that query agents could self-determine its spreading hops. To our knowledge, previous P2P systems have to pre-determine the number of hops of queries, such as TTL value. If the number of hops is set too low, the search process will be limited to a small scope. However, if it is set too high, the traffic over the peer network can become heavy. An ideal trade-off is hard to be achieved because the TTL value of queries is set one-size for all.

With agent technology, the query agent could "remember" its history information in the routing path. To more visually demonstrate our strategy of self-adaptive hop, we'd like to take distance as the measure of peers' relationships. Based on the distance of pair-wise peers, the longest distance between peers could be seen as the diameter[1] of the peer network in a concept space.

The self-adaptive hopping strategy works as follows

- A peer initiates a query agent with a parameter s instead of TTL value, where s is pre-defined by the P2P network. The diameter of the peer network is denoted by D, which will be obtained in the process of facilitating the dynamic reconfiguration.
- When a query agent is forwarded to the directly connected neighbor by a peer, the agent "remembers" the distance value between the peer and its neighbor. The value is summed with the previous remembered distance values in the routing path.
- If the sum value exceeds the value of $s \cdot D$, the hopping will stop. Otherwise, the peer will forward the query agent to its neighbor further.

As such, the system need not have a fixed hop number for all the queries. With the parameter s given by the system, the number of hops of each query will be self-determined according to its searching scope in the concept space. The

---

[1] Note that the "diameter" here is just to measure the knowledge scope that all peers' interests cover

parameter s reflects the extent of scope the system likes its peers to search in the concept space, and thereby enables our system to find a proper trade-off between network traffic and search completeness in a dynamic way.

5 Agent-Based Self-adaptive Search

Applying mobile agents in P2P collaboration cache has several advantages: (a) it allows individual requester to filter the content according to what (s)he desires. (b) It facilitates extensibility - new algorithm or program can be used without affecting other parts of the system. (c) It optimizes network bandwidth utilization as only the necessary data is transmitted to the requester.

Considering the current application, the user interface allows many candidate results to be displayed. This demands that matched pages in the remote peers must be processed at the remote site and only abstracts of the pages be returned to the query peer. Thus, the search algorithm is encapsulated in the query agent and performs its operation in each destination peer. More importantly, this mechanism distributes the search operations over the peers in the BuddyWeb network. This is a reasonable approach as it exploits parallelism by enabling all peers to operate on their data simultaneously, thereby providing a potential improvement in the search performance.

Agent-based technology also enables search algorithm to self-adapt its parameters or even strategies according to the search results in the prior peers. In particular, if the given query results in few matching pages during the search process in the previous peer's cache, the algorithm could change its search policy in order to avoid final scanty results returned to the query peer. On the contrary, if the search ends up with abundant candidate pages from prior peer, it could increase some associated values of threshold parameters or even change the search strategy.

6 Conclusion

This position paper outlines some underlying ideas in our developing system, which provides the services of web caching and searching on the basis of P2P technology. The ideas mentioned in above sections will be more and more concrete in the future development of the system. We have begun implementing BuddyWeb, and expect to deploy it in the Fudan campus network very soon.

References

1. International Workshop on P2P Systems.
   http://www.cs.rice.edu/Conferences/IPTPS02/. 2002.
2. Panos Kalnis, Wee Siong Ng, Beng Chin Ooi, Dimitris Papadias, and Kian Lee Tan. An adaptive peer-to-peer network for distributed caching of olap results. In *ACM Sigmod*, 2002.
3. Wee Siong Ng, Beng Chin Ooi, and Kian-Lee Tan. Bestpeer: A self-configurable peer-to-peer system. In *ICDE 2002*.

Reliable Unicast Streaming
with Multiple Peers in IP Networks

Florian Unterkircher and Michael Welzl

University of Innsbruck, Computer Science Dept.
Technikerstr. 25, A-6020 Innsbruck, Austria
florian@unterkircher.com
michael.welzl@uibk.ac.at

Abstract. The traditional client/server model with its single point of failure and centralized administration has turned out to be a poor fit for file downloads for some applications; the same may apply to streaming media services in the near future. We propose an architecture for streaming media in a peer-to-peer network scenario that is robust and efficient, and expected to be advantageous even if links are asymmetric.

1 Introduction

It is widely expected that the live streaming of media content such as digital music and video will form a significant fraction of internet traffic in the near future[1]. Multimedia data streaming in IP networks is currently mostly implemented as a client/server or multicast architecture. A variety of problems has been identified with this traditional approach; we believe the most important ones to be:

1. *Flash crowds:* Established streaming solutions have shown not to hold up well against a flash crowd of users who request multimedia feeds from the same source; this was particularly evident on September 11th, 2001. Architecturally, it is common knowledge that single points of failure and bottlenecks should be avoided. Peer-to-peer based caching and forwarding schemes have been demonstrated that effectivively alleviate the effects of flash crowds [2] [3].
2. *Bandwidth costs:* Bandwidth costs can pose a huge problem to the content provider if he cannot charge for each stream. A prominent example of a business that failed because of high bandwidth costs[1] is AdCritic, once a popular site that offered streaming video versions of the best rated television commercials [4]. The view that streaming of data from a central source is too costly is also supported by CNN's recent decision to charge for access to its video content on their website [5]. It would be beneficial if the bandwidth

---

[1] During Super Bowl in the year 2000, for example, more than 12 terabytes of data were downloaded from the company's streaming host by 1.8 million users, at an estimated cost of USD 120,000 to the company.

E. Gregori et al. (Eds.): Networking 2002 Workshops, LNCS 2376, pp. 252–259, 2002.

cost could be at least partly shifted towards the content consumer. A peer-to-peer network can make a business proposition for streaming content more attractive compared relying on a hosted streaming service.

Generally, a peer-to-peer network that prefers local peers to such many hops away leads to better utilization of the total bandwidth capacity of the Internet and relieves the backbone. Comparing transports between random hosts in real-life networks to streams originating from servers in well-controlled environments, one, however, quickly realizes that a number of obstacles need to be overcome. In the next section, we give an overview of these obstacles. As a possible solution, we propose a novel architecture in section 3; section 4 concludes.

2   Peer-to-Peer Streaming Media Problems

2.1   Node Transience

Typically, the computers of which a peer-to-peer network is comprised are in different administrative domains; thus, they might enter or leave the network at any given time. The worst case of a user shutting down his computer while it is serving data occurs quite frequently and provides the person consuming the stream with a very bad user experience if not addressed appropriately. According to [6], roughly half of all sessions (i.e. from the time when a node registers in a network until the time it leaves it) in popular peer-to-peer networks are of 60 minutes and less.

2.2   Uplink Restrictions

Available uplink bandwidth of the computers serving content is of great importance because the stream will be interrupted if a certain data rate cannot be achieved. While an Internet user in a corporate or academic environment may not experience significant service degradation when the uplink is used by a peer-to-peer application, many users connect to the Internet through a consumer broadband connection such as cable or DSL. These connections are problematic because they are typically characterized by an assymetry in their respective uplink and downlink bandwidth capacity.

As our goal is to provide the user with the best possible experience, we want to use as much of the available downlink capacity as possible for better quality of the media stream. One could consider streaming only from computers with sufficient uplink capacity, but this would severely limit the number of possible streaming sources and be considered unfair as well: a large number of users would leech bandwidth from a relatively small set of high-bandwidth users. In addition to that, traffic shaping is on the rise with ISPs, limiting individual connections to a certain rate that is less than the maximum available link bandwidth.

2.3   Firewalls and NAT

Another problem that is not particular to streaming applications, but to peer-to-peer networks in general are firewalls and network address translation (NAT) which block some connections[2].

A trivial algorithm that keeps trying until a connection can be established and initiates push requests, such as implemented in some peer-to-peer file sharing applications [7], will not lead to a good user experience because of the large delays associated with this method (moreover, it make synchronisation exceedingly difficult – we will show later why this is important). As a possible solution to address these issues we propose a topologically aware multi-source streaming network for content delivery.

3   Proposed Architecture

Our goal was to design an efficient architecture for feeding nodes with a particular multimedia stream from a set of nodes in a peer-to-peer network, and to make that stream reliable enough to achieve satisfactory QoS in real-life public networks. In our scenario, good QoS is characterized by fast connection setup and a minimization of stream interruptions. Our architecture encompasses the following set of features:

3.1   Local Caching

In order to provide a large number of client nodes with content streams, a large enough number of nodes needs to have the data available locally in order to provide a transport stream for another node. This is achieved by retaining the data of received streams in a local cache (comparable to caches in web browsers) for a given minimum time-span. As a result, the total capacity of the peer-to-peer network to stream a particular file grows with the number of nodes that host that file [8].

3.2   Multiple Sources

The first serious obstacle to overcome is that of limited uplink bandwidth of peers. The obvious approach to this is to combine multiple transport streams

---

[2] Corporate firewalls are typically configured to allow inbound connections to a certain set of defined hosts only. In most cases, these hosts will be mail servers or web servers and not machines which are part of a peer-to-peer network. The same applies for personal firewalls which are installed at the end user's computer or even a part of its operating system. Most importantly for streaming applications which typically rely on UDP based transport, the vast majority of firewalls are configured to block incoming UDP traffic. Certain types of NAT make machines that are behind the gateway completely inaccessible from the public routing infrastructure for inbound connections.

from several peers to one content stream to be received at the client. A trivial algorithm would be to interleave bytes or fixed-size segments from the sending peers, i.e. sending byte $X \ mod \ N + I$ where N is the number of sending peers and X is the byte index in the stream from the sender identified by the index $0 \leq I < N$. This by itself would, however, just make the resulting content stream very unreliable, since the failure of any sending node would lead to a breakdown of the content stream. Due to the properties of nodes described earlier, such as transience, one would be rather lucky to experience an uninterrupted streaming session for an extended time.

3.3   Forward Error Correction

We propose to introduce redundancy into the data stream to make the resulting stream more reliably across multiple sending nodes. While forward error correction (FEC) is more frequently found at the data link layer, we believe that closely interleaving our data streams may enable us to advantageously use FEC algorithms based on block codes (e.g. Reed-Solomon) at the application layer. The media stream is first encoded at each sending node with the chosen FEC code and the resulting stream is then transmitted interleaved as described above. This should result in a reliable media stream that is not interrupted even if one or several (depending on the choice of FEC code) of the sources fail. For instance, a $(5, 1)$ Reed-Solomon code would allow one source from six to fail at a given time without breaking the media stream, at a cost of 20 per cent excess bandwidth.

The optimum code to choose for our scenario depends on a variety of factors, such as the number of sending peers, the nature of network connections, the available bandwidth at each peer, node transience and the amount of redundancy required to offset resulting transport failures (this, in turn, depends on the protocol used for transport and its behaviour with regard to session handling, congestion behavior, jitter, and so on). Another critical factor is the amount of extra data, as there exists a trade-off between FEC effectiveness and wasted bandwidth. We believe that we will be able to fine tune this parameter on-the-fly by feeding back the perceived quality of the codec the sending peers.

3.4   Recovery and Lookup Service

The content stream would still break, however, if more sending nodes failed than accounted for in the chosen FEC code. This can be prevented by substituting the data stream of a failed source node with another source during the lifetime of the streaming session. A low-latency lookup mechanism is required for this to rapidly identify other nodes that have the required data available. Candidates for such a service include refering to a central index of nodes and locally kept files at each node, a set of "SuperNodes" that keep this information for neighbor nodes (as implemented in the FastTrack peer-to-peer stack [3]), broadcasting a query and purely non-hierarchical lookup mechanisms such as in Gnutella [12].

For the purpose of good QoS with respect to the time required to set up a stream, a centrally kept index yields satisfactory response times for the setup of a streaming session or the quick substitution of a failed source while the session is in progress. Since such an index needs to accurately reflect the current state of the peer-to-peer network, a central instance should periodically check whether nodes have expired with a heartbeat mechanism, and nodes should report changes to the data in their local cache when they occur.

On the other hand, introducing a central index (yet another single point of failure) is clearly an architectural disadvantage. We are presently considering whether a hierarchical non-central network such as implemented in the FastTrack stack would be feasible for this purpose.

3.5 Locality and Breadth First Search in the Network Graph

The fewer hops there are between two nodes, the fewer things there are that can fail on the path between them. It has been documented that locality provides for more reliable transport in peer-to-peer networks and in fact many such network stacks implement some sort of locality (mostly measured by packet round trip times, i.e. ping, as in Gnutella, and some by hop counting, such as reportedly in Kontiki). This matters not only for reliability, but also for link bandwidth – the slowest link on the path determines the maximum bandwidth and the total network bandwidth capacity that can be utilized, since fewer connections will share the same paths such as backbone connections. It is particularly important to avoid bandwidth congestion at backbone connections when flash crowds demand popular content.

On the other hand, if the peers selected for a session share a common network link then the failure or congestion of that link will lead to the failure of several transport streams and probably break the content stream. This could probably be avoided by mapping the peer network and building a network graph [13] and using a breadth-first algorithm originating from the receiving node to search for suitable peers, or to avoid peers from the same subnet or autonomous system.

3.6 Copyright Management

The commercial application of the proposed architecture for the distribution of copyrighted works can requires effective access control to content distributed through it. In the traditional server-based streaming scenario, this is trivial, because each request for a streaming session can be easily authorized or denied by a central authority and content is not stored at the client side like in the

---

[3] Unfortunately, little public information exists about the FastTrack stack due to its proprietary nature – even though it is the basis for the most widely used file sharing applications at the time of this writing [9] [10]; a related concept is described as "proxylets" in [11].

local cache. The proposed architecture, however, requires that a given file is stored in other nodes' local caches and that all copies of a particular multimedia asset are identical. Therefore, where this is a concern, digital rights management technology needs to be embedded in the file format and playback client since there would otherwise be nothing preventing a user from extracting the file from the local cache and, for instance, to watch a pay-per-view movie again without payment or to distribute that movie to other users.

3.7 Protection Against Content Spoofing

Issues of content and/or node spoofing are of particular concern in peer-to-peer networks as they rely on the collaboration of nodes to work. For instance, it would clearly not be desirous that a malicious user could feeding a video stream with pornographic content to kids expecting to see the latest Disney movie trailer. Similarly, a group of attackers could perform a logical denial-of-service attack on the content delivery network by responding with bad data to each request. This is more of a problem in streaming applications than download applications because in the latter context is feasible to verify the downloaded file against a cryptographically secure hash (such as SHA-1) from a trusted source. This method can only be applied once large file segments have been completely downloaded, requiring a very small amount of known good data to verify the authenticity of a large file. In a streaming application, this is not possible because one would have to verify each video frame or segments of audio of a certain length against a known good hash value that would need to be transferred in advance from a trusted source.

If multiple transport stream sources are introduced into the architecture, however, the attacker would need to control all source nodes to successfully introduce bad content into the network, and more than one node in a particular transmission for an effective denial of service attack for that session. Therefore, a multi-source streaming architecture is likely more secure compared to a peer-to-peer streaming network with a single source peer only.

4   Conclusions and Future Work

There are many issues left open by this proposed architecture. A very important one is the optimum transport protocol between the nodes. Candidates we are considering are RTP/RTSP, TCP-RTM ([14]), TCP, and HTTP – the last two primarily to enable streams to pass through common firewall configurations. We believe that a fallback mechanism should be implemented to discover the best possible protocol allowed by a particular configuration. More research is needed on selecting a FEC algorithm and the best suited code for combining multiple streams. A protocol needs to be designed for negotiate FEC encoding and to synchronize multiple transport streams. Lastly, some empirical research is needed to assess the real-life performance and benefits of this architecture that we hope for. We also believe it would be interesting to apply the multiple-source concept to application-level multicasting for improved reliability.

Related projects include the SpreadIt architecture developed in [15], which distributes bandwidth requirements across the network for application-level multicast. The Content-Addressable Web concept seeks to create a foundation for ad-hoc content delivery with certain extensions to HTTP, as described in [16], and could serve as a mechanism to identify peers with specific content. A different, self-organizing content-addressable network is described in [17]. General approaches to efficient content distribution are discussed in [18] and [19]. Finally, a variety of commercial applications has been developed to distribute multimedia content over peer-to-peer networks [20] [21], underlining the increasing demand for such services.

References

1. Sally Floyd and Kevin Fall, *Promoting the Use of End-to-End Congestion Control in the Internet*, IEEE/ACM Transactions on Networking, August 1999.
2. Tyron Stading, Petros Maniatis, Mary Baker, *Peer-to-Peer Caching Schemes to Address Flash Crowds*, 1st International Peer To Peer Systems Workshop (IPTPS) 2002.
3. Mojo Nation, http://www.mojonation.net/, June 2001.
4. *Adcritic.com: A Victim of Its Own Success?*, NY Times, December 20, 2001.
5. *CNN's video fees add to the Net's growing price tag*, USA Today, March 18, 2002.
6. Stefan Saroui, P. Krishna Gummadi, Steven D. Gribble, *A Measurement Study of Peer-to-Peer File Sharing Systems*, Technical Report UW-CSE-01-06-02, University of Washington, July 2001.
7. P. Backx, B. Duysburgh, T. Lambrecht, L. Peters, T. Wauters, P. Demeester, B. Dhoedt, *Enhanced applications through active networking*, 2nd FTW PHD Symposium, Interactive poster session, paper 99 (Proceedings available on CD-Rom), 12 December 2001, Gent, Belgium 2001.
8. *Kontiki Technology: The Mojo*, available at http://www.kontiki.com/technology/, 2002.
9. *Napster Shutdown Feeds Dutch Peer-To-Peer Startup*, InformationWeek, July 16, 2001.
10. Joe St. Sauver, *Percentage of Total Internet2 Traffic Consisting of Kazaa/ Morpheus/ FastTrack*, available at http://darkwing.uoregon.edu/~joe/kazaa.html, 2002.
11. Atanu Ghosh, Michael Fry, Jon Crowcroft, *An Architecture for Application Layer Routing*, Yasuda, H. (Ed), Active Networks, LNCS 1942, Springer, pp 71-86. ISBN 3-540-41179-8 Springer-Verlag.
12. Evangelos P. Markatos, *Tracing a large-scale Peer to Peer System: an hour in the life of Gnutella*, 2nd IEEE/ACM International Symposium on Cluster Computing and the Grid, 2002.
13. Bradley Huffaker, Daniel Plummer, David Moore, and k claffy, *Topology Discovery by Active Probing*, available at
    http://www.caida.org/outreach/papers/2002/SkitterOverview/
14. Sam Liang and David Cheriton: *TCP-SMO: Extending TCP for Medium Scale Multicast Applications*, IEEE Infocom 2002, June 23-27 2002, New York.
15. Hrishikesh Deshpande, Mayank Bawa and Hector Garcia-Molina, *Streaming Live Media over a Peer-to-Peer Network*, Stanford Technical Report 2001-30.

16. Justin Chapweske, *HTTP Extensions for a Content-Addressable Web*, available at http://onionnetworks.com/caw/, 2001.
17. Sylvia Ratnasamy, Paul Francis, Mark Handley, Richard Karp, Scott Schenker, *A Scalable Content-Addressable Network*, ACM SIGCOMM 2001, San Diego, CA, August 2001.
18. Sylvia Ratnasamy, Mark Handley, Richard Karp, Scott Shenker, *Topologically-Aware Overlay Construction and Server Selection*, IEEE Infocom 2002, New York, June 23-27 2002.
19. Y. Chawathe, S. McCanne, and E. Brewer, *An Architecture for Internet Content Distribution as an Infrastructure Service*, Technical report, available at http://www.research.att.com/~yatin/publications/, 2000.
20. *Peer-to-Peer Streaming Finds Friends*, Streaming Media, August 28, 2001.
21. *AllCast Increases Profits for Streaming Media* (Press Release), August 16, 2001.

The Client Utility as a Peer-to-Peer System

Alan Karp and Vana Kalogeraki

Hewlett-Packard Labs
Palo Alto, California
alan_karp@hp.com, vana@hpl.hp.com

Abstract. The Client Utility system developed at HP Labs in the mid 1990s was designed to address the problems inherent in distributed computing. This paper shows that the architecture we developed solves some of the problems faced by designers of Peer-to-Peer systems, particularly those of discovery, trust, and naming. We show how elements of the Client Utility architecture can be used to address the problems found in some existing Peer-to-Peer systems.

1 Introduction

The goal of the Client Utility (CU) [14] project at HP Labs was to find a way to hide the complexity of the Internet from developers of application and users of those applications. With the increasing importance of peer-to-peer (P2P) environments [17], it has become clear that many of the issues addressed by CU are critical to the success of peer-to-peer (P2P) systems, such as Napster [19], Gnutella [8], Morpheus [18], and Freenet[7].

The most immediate problem a P2P system needs to deal with is finding out what is available or finding a specific item, be it a resource, such as a file, disk or machine, or a service of some sort, such as a backup service. A less obvious, but no less important problem, is that of trust. To what machines should you connect, and what should you allow each one to do? A third problem that is only now being recognized is that of naming things in a P2P system.

Section 2 contains a brief overview of the CU architecture, and Section 3 shows how the CU architecture addresses some of the problems common to P2P systems. Specific examples of how the approaches developed for CU can be used to address problems in P2P systems are presented in Section 4.

2 Client Utility Architecture

Although the Client Utility project started in the beginning of 1996 with its own set of goals, we ended up with an architecture that addresses the key issues we see in today's P2P environments. This section contains a brief overview of the architecture; more detail is available elsewhere [14, 15, 6, 13].

E. Gregori et al. (Eds.): Networking 2002 Workshops, LNCS 2376, pp. 260–273, 2002.
© Springer-Verlag Berlin Heidelberg 2002

We started the Client Utility project by asking ourselves what assumptions we should make and settled on the following five.

1. Large scale. We designed for 1,000,000 machines. An environment this large means that there can be no centralized point of control and that it is impossible to maintain consistency. You must assume that any piece of data you get is out of date. If that isn't acceptable, it's up to you to synchronize.

2. Dynamic. No environment that large can be static. Machines will fail; machines will join the system. Resources, both hard, such as machines, and soft, such as files, will vanish to be replaced by new ones.

3. Heterogeneous. There is no practical way to impose a single machine architecture on the world. Not only must the system be designed to deal with different hardware and operating systems, it must accommodate devices of widely different capabilities, everything from servers to cell phones.

4. Hostile. Some people will want to wreak havoc, even if there is no gain, financial or otherwise. Given the nature of the system, the security system must be scalable. In particular, it must be able to deal with an environment consisting of an extremely large number of potential users of any resource.

5. Distributed control. The environment must be able to accommodate different ways of managing systems and expressing policies. No single standard can meet all needs nor can it be flexible enough to match the rate of change such a system will have.

It should come as no surprise that this list is identical to one we'd make today for P2P systems. To see how CU addresses each of these assumptions and how those solutions apply to P2P systems, we need to examine briefly the CU architecture.

A CU system is a federation of *logical machines*. Each logical machine consists of an active component called the *core* and a passive component called the *repository*. Several logical machines can share one piece of hardware, each can have a dedicated machine, or a single logical machine can use several physical machines. How ever it is configured, programs will run the same way.

Figure 1 shows the key components of a logical machine. Entities that interact with the core are called *clients*. The basic unit of control is a *resource*. If a client wishes to make a resource or service available, it registers it with the core, which assigns the resource a repository handle. The corresponding repository entry designates the client acting as handler for the resource.

A mailbox metaphor is used for resource access. Each request consists of an *envelope* containing information used by the core and a *payload* containing the application related data. The message forwarded to the resource handler by the core has an envelope generated by the core and the original payload, unmodified and unexamined. This partitioning of the message means that the application API does not need modification.

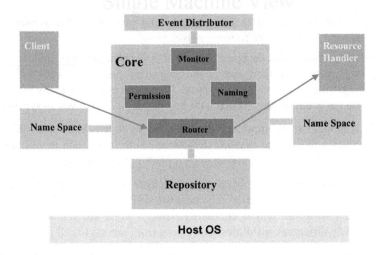

Fig. 1. Message flow within a logical machine

The core maintains in its address space a name space on behalf of each client. This name space contains mappings between strings, representing the client's names for resources, and repository handles. Name spaces are populated in one of three ways. Some names are present when the client process first connects to the core. These names are typically bound to system resources and allow the client to bootstrap its way into the system. A second way to get a name binding is to have one sent from another client. Clients can also get name bindings by finding resources as described below.

The client message names the resource of interest. The core looks up this name in the client's name space to find the associated repository handle. The corresponding repository entry is used for permission checking and to identify the client acting as the handler for a resource. The core bundles up the original payload with a new envelope and deposits the message in the handler's inbox. Any reply is sent the same way, by naming a resource associated with the target of the message.

When a client wants to obtain access to a resource on another logical machine, it sends a request to its machine's *connection manager*. This client of the core is responsible for enforcing any policies between machines. If the connection is approved, the connection manager contacts its counterpart on the other machine, and each spawns a client to act as a proxy for the other, as shown in Figure 2. These proxies use information provided by their respective connection managers to authenticate each other and exchange encryption keys. Each then *exports* metadata of the resources it will make available to the other machine. These exported resources get registered in the repository of the importing logical machine.

When a client accesses a remote resource, the core does exactly what it does for a local resource. The only difference is that the handler is a proxy that forwards the request to its counterpart on the machine that exported the resource metadata. That proxy repeats the request exactly as issued. The request passes through the proxy's core to the resource handler. The message flow is shown in Figure 3.

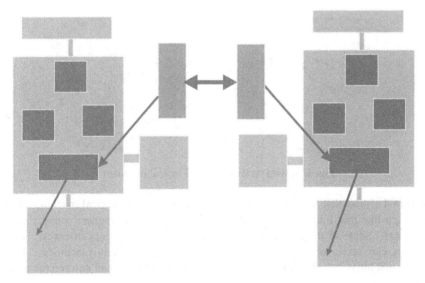

Fig. 2. Connecting two logical machines

Note that neither the client, nor the handler, nor either core does anything different than it does for a local request. Only the proxies are aware that there is another machine involved. Note, too that the machine on the right of the figure may not be the resource handler, only an intermediary. Or, the machine on the left may be forwarding a request that originated elsewhere. No special code is needed to do this kind of forwarding. It is a natural consequence of the basic architecture.

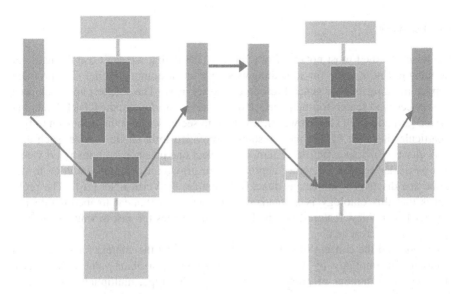

Fig. 3. Message flow when accessing a remote resource

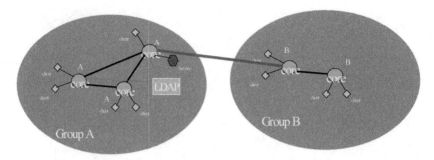

Fig. 4. Scaling up the number of logical machines

Figure 4 shows that the pattern of connections among CU logical machines looks very much like that found in P2P systems. Clients of a core request connections to other cores. Some of these cores act as gateways into other groups of cores. Server machines can serve as intermediaries for resources from many machines. These gateway machines can also limit what connections are allowed and enforce the access control policies.

3   Issues and Solutions

Designers of P2P systems need to deal with a number of issues. In this section, we'll examine questions of discovery, trust, and naming, and show how the CU architecture addresses them.

3.1 Discovery

The lesson learned most notably from Napster [19] is that we can't use the name of the thing to find it, even for something as simple as an immutable file. The problem is much more serious for general resources and services. The simplest approach used for services is to search for the interface of the service as done in the CORBA naming service [20] and Jini [11]. However, it is hard to see how to use this approach to find a particular instance of the many resources provided by a single service, such as a particular file in a specific file system, or to select one instance from many providers of a particular service. Another approach is to provide a common ontology to describe and discover resources as done, for example, by VerticalNet [26]. The problem is that this ontology is a standard that requires agreement to incorporate improvements and new features, but the P2P world changes too fast to wait for such an agreement to be reached.

CU adopted the concept of definable ontologies to set the context for searches. It represents an ontology by a *vocabulary* consisting of attribute-value pairs. Each attribute has a number of properties, including value type, multiplicity, and a rule defining what constitutes a match, as illustrated in Figure 5. Each repository entry has a field for describing the resource in one or more vocabularies. Look-ups are performed by submitting a constraint expression of attributes from one or more vocabularies. The core matches these look-up requests with the descriptions registered in the repository.

Each attribute in a vocabulary represents an agreement of its meaning among the vocabulary designer, via the matching rule, the owner of a resource, via its description in the repository, and the person seeking the resource, via a constraint expression. Hence, attributes don't contain semantic information, but they do give a convenient way to represent shared meanings.

The specific attributes and their properties are determined by the vocabulary designer. Hence, standards bodies can produce vocabularies appropriate for their industries. If we need to do a look-up in a different vocabulary, we can use a vocabulary translating service that converts a constraint expression from one vocabulary to another one.

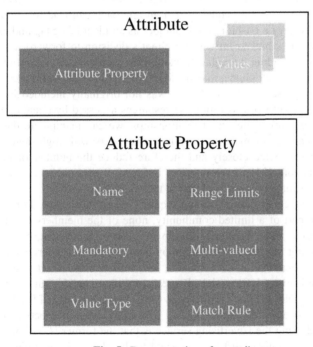

Fig. 5. Representation of an attribute

Vocabularies in CU are first class objects that can be described in other vocabularies. This feature means that extensions to standard vocabularies can be added by describing a new vocabulary in a standard one. For example, if you want to find a pair of shoes, you would look up shopping vocabularies in the base vocabulary defined to bootstrap the process, shoe vocabularies in the shopping vocabularies that you find, and so on. Any of the searches can return a list containing more vocabularies and other resources that match the description. So, if you've done a lookup in a men's shoe vocabulary, you may have found listings for wingtips and a vocabulary for tennis shoes. Since anyone can create a new vocabulary, someone who wanted to advertise special tennis shoes for playing on clay courts could advertise that vocabulary in the tennis shoe vocabulary; no global coordination is needed. RDF [22] can be used to provide a similar level of flexibility, but it lacks CU's definable matching rules.

The basic lookup mechanism starts with a search of the local repository. Part of the metadata stored when the resource is registered with the core is a description in one or more vocabularies. The core provides an engine for matching constraint expressions with these descriptions. If a match is found, a name binding is placed in the client's name space.

If a match is not found, the client can arrange for the search to be extended to the machines its core is connected to, much the way Gnutella [8] propagates searches. However, CU recognizes that one machine can only ask another to do something, not force it to. Hence, the CU *extended look-up request* does not specify a horizon; that's up to the machine receiving the request. Such an approach can lead to flooding the network, so requests carry a 64-bit random number as an identifying tag and an aging tag that can be used as a hint to influence a client's decision to forward the request further. This tag is only a hint, though. No matter how many hops a request has gone, a small device, such as a cell phone, may decide to forward the request if the next hop is known to be a large server. Although this was not originally included in the CU architecture, by taking into consideration the resources accessed by clients on different machines and exploiting their trust relationships, we can manipulate the logical connections between the machines to guarantee that peers with high degree of resource sharing are connected closely and therefore reduce the number of messages broadcast in the network [21]. If the resource is found, it is exported to the client's machine, and a name mapping to it is placed in the client's name space.

There are times when extended look-up requests aren't sufficient. For example, the client might be part of a limited community, none of the members of which has the requested resource. The extended look-up can also be inefficient, requiring too many hops and putting too much of a burden on the network and other machines. In such situations, the client can contact one of a few, well-known *advertising services*, very much like the Napster [19] model. E-speak provided one [5], but clients could use others, such as UDDI [25] or even Yahoo! [28]. Each box labeled LDAP in Figure 4 represents such an advertising service. The main difference between an extended look-up and using the advertising service is that the former is on-line, *i.e.*, the machine owning the resource must be connected to the client by some path, but the latter is off-line. If the item is found in the advertising service, the client is told what machine to connect to.

3.2 Trust

A second issue that has not been given sufficient attention in the past but that is becoming more apparent of late is that of trust. Members of a P2P system connect their machines to each other and agree to provide certain services to peers. Each direct connection conveys a measure of trust. If this trust is misplaced, bad things happen. Note that mechanisms based on encryption, such as SSL, only prevent snooping or tampering with messages. They don't prevent one peer from attacking another over a legitimate connection.

The CU architecture was designed based on an understanding of this kind of trust. Connections are initiated and/or accepted by a connection manager, a trusted process running on each machine. The connection manager is able to associate a set of permissions with any other machine based on policies specified by the owner of the connection manager's machine. Ultimately, such policies must be set by a human, but automated tools can reduce the administrative burden. In particular, an unknown machine will only be granted a small set of privileges. CU controls these privileges so that even a rogue process, perhaps started by a virus, cannot grant excessive privileges to an attacker.

In CU, all communication with the outside world is done through a proxy running on the local machine. This policy recognizes that you trust software you install on your own machine, the proxy, more than software on machines out of your control. That doesn't mean you trust this software completely. Every CU client has a name space that limits what resources it can access and a set of permissions that limit what actions it can take on the resources it names.

The proxy serves a number of purposes. Since it is a client of the core, it has a name space. No matter what the remote user attempts to do, the proxy can only access those resources that appear in its name space and can perform only those actions allowed by its permissions. This sandboxing provides a level of control on active services similar to that provided by web servers for files. The proxy also protects against some denial of service attacks. For example, an attack that causes the proxy to crash or hang has the desirable effect of cutting off the attacker.

The transparent brokering of the CU architecture also addresses a number of trust issues. Say that Alice exports some resources to Bob, and Bob exports some of them to Carol. As far as Carol is concerned, Bob is providing the resource; as far as Alice is concerned, Bob is using the resource. Each connection represents a trust relation. Alice and Bob share one; Bob and Carol share another. There is no such relationship between Alice and Carol. Should Carol contact Alice directly and ask for the same resource, Alice is likely to refuse. Of course, Bob could choose to introduce Carol to Alice so they can establish their own trust relation. The advantage of the introduction process is that Bob can tell Alice exactly which of Alice's services Bob is willing to forward to Carol. That information gives Alice an idea of what level of trust she should put in Carol.

3.3 Naming

Another problem, one that P2P systems share with all distributed systems, is that of naming [16,1]. Most distributed systems rely on a global name space, the most familiar of which is based on URLs. However, there are problems. One component of a

URL is the location if a machine, either an IP address or a domain name. The wide-spread use of dynamically assigned IP addresses makes their use problematic. Domain names are better, but the presence of Network Address Translation (NAT) fire-walls introduces private name spaces. Hence, it is difficult to avoid name collisions and to share names across firewalls. Changing ISPs is also a problem, since a machine's domain name must be changed. Since a global name points to a specific machine, using high availability solutions based on redundancy is hard.

CU names are purely local to each process. A translation table is maintained between each pair of entities, client-core, core-client, proxy-proxy. When a handler needs to change the name of a resource, perhaps because it was moved to a new disk, it need only inform the core, not every potential user of the resource. While this approach sounds strange, it is a system we use every day. We don't commonly use globally unique names for people and things; we use relative names. For example, instead of specifying the VIN for a vehicle, we refer to Alice's husband's car. Should Alice's husband trade in his Honda for a BMW, he may tell Alice to refer to it as his Beemer. Everyone else can still refer to Alice's husband's car. Alice can even change husbands without invalidating uses of the name.

This form of naming reflects the trust relations embodied in the connections between machines. Each hop on the path between requester and handler implies that an agreement has been reached on the meaning of the name shared by the two parties. Thus, when the handler gets a request, it knows that a "path of trust" exists; it's embodied in the name system. That assurance doesn't exist in naming systems that allow names to be communicated out of band, such as those using URLs. Those systems require an additional level of authentication before access can be granted. Path dependent names also have the advantage that the permissions are attached to the request through the names as they pass through the system. Other naming systems require a separate mechanism for access control.

Another advantage of CU's naming system has to do with the dynamic nature of large systems. There may be times when the named resource is not available, either because it has been moved, removed, or is temporarily unreachable. If the name of the object specified by the application includes location information, as it does with URLs, the resulting exception must be handled at the application level. The level of indirection provided by CU allows the name to be remapped to an alternate provider of the same or an equivalent resource. In particular, a client's name may be bound to a list of repository handles and a lookup request. Doing so allows the core to deal with unreachable resources without involving the application.

The CU approach to naming has some limitations, of course. First of all, these names have no meaning outside of the CU system. You can't tell a friend the name of a resource over the telephone since the name has meaning only within your name space. Instead, you send a message to your friend containing the name mapping. Another problem is knowing if two names obtained from different sources refer to the same object, a problem that exists today for URLs. Most of the time it doesn't matter, say for immutable files, but when it does, CU defines a protocol that lets you find out. Clients are also free to include a large, random number in the metadata stored in the repository, allowing a high degree of certainty to the identification of any resource.

Finally, there is the problem of knowing if this resource is the same one you used last time. Again, it rarely matters, but when it does, the authentication information used to establish a trust relation provides sufficient information.

4 Related Work

A great deal of work has been done in P2P systems. In this section, we'll discuss problems identified in a few of them, and show how solutions developed for CU address them.

4.1 JXTA

The JXTA project from Sun [12,27] is a "general-purpose" network programming and computing infrastructure that supports a wide range of distributed computing applications and runs on any device with a digital heartbeat. The JXTA architecture provides core functionality in multiple layers, including basic mechanisms and concepts (such as protocols for peer discovery, monitoring and group membership), higher-level services that expand these capabilities (e.g., authentication, discovery and management) and a wide range of applications (such as instant messaging and chat capabilities). There are many similarities in the goals of JXTA and Client Utility including interoperability, platform independence, discovery and security. However, JXTA focuses more on the peer groups, while in the Client Utility system the basic unit of control is the resource.

JXTA uses user-generated identifiers (UUIDs) to refer to entities and resources, such as a peer or a service. An entity has a unique UUID within the group in which it is created. This poses the important problem that the resource identities are based on human-generated names and therefore, there is no way to predict the name of a particular service. In the Client Utility, resource identities are based on attributes rather than names, which makes it suitable for searching for more general resources and services. Also, JXTA realizes the need for security and uses the resource UUIDs for implementing access control mechanisms. However, there is no guarantee that a particular UUID won't be reused, which means that a privilege granted on the old resource may be exercised on the new one.

Client Utility, on the other hand, uses split capabilities [15], and therefore the users do not need a separate capability for each of the services or resources they invoke. Overall, the Client Utility system has developed more sophisticated and extensible mechanisms for resource identity, description and discovery based on attributes, resource access based on capabilities, and inter-machine interactions based on the use of proxies.

4.2 Oceanstore

The OceanStore system (from the University of California, Berkeley) [16] is a utility infrastructure designed to provide secure, highly available access to persistent objects in a large-scale environment. It has many attractive features including persistence storage, fault tolerance, distributed search and routing and conflict resolution. Its main design goals are: (1) to be constructed from an untrusted infrastructure and (2) to support nomadic data. There are a number of similarities in the goals of Client Utility and OceanStore - persistence storage, distribution, resource management, and secure access to resources. However, OceanStore is geared towards file sharing applications, such as groupware and repositories for scientific data. The Client Utility is not restricted to file sharing applications, but also includes legacy applications, enterprise applications, and Internet web services.

Each object in OceanStore is named by a globally unique identifier (GUID). An object GUID is the secure hash of the owner's private key and some human-readable name. The search messages are labeled with a destination GUID and routed directly to the closest node that matches the search predicate and has the desired GUID. One problem with this strategy is that objects live longer than private keys, which are often configured to expire after a year. When a private key must be changed, the names of all objects must either be changed, in which case outstanding references become invalid, or the names lose the authentication provided by using the private key in the first place.

CU on the other hand, provides a flexible and extensible naming scheme; each resource is named in the context of the local name space and uses vocabularies consisting of attribute-value pairs to match the attributes of the corresponding resources. The advantage is that the client does not need to know the exact name when searching for a resource and that not all the clients have to be informed when the name (such as the local path) of the resource changes. The OceanStore system supports primitive types of access control, the reader restriction and the writer restriction. Reads are restricted at clients via key distribution, while writes are restricted at servers using access control lists. The split capabilities used in Client Utility are more flexible and make some attacks more difficult.

Ideas from the Client Utility system (such as authentication of both users and machines, privacy and access control) could be used in a system that is fundamentally untrusted. For example, CU employs a trust model with different levels of trust to grant privileges to other machines. This is superior to systems such as OceanStore that use only cryptographic techniques to protect the data.

4.3 Farsite

The Farsite project at Microsoft research [3] is a serverless, distributed file system that exploits the underutilized storage and communication resources distributed among the networked desktop computers in a large organization. Its distinguishing characteristic is that it can be deployed on an existing desktop infrastructure and does not assume careful administration or mutual trust among the client machines. Its goals are to provide high availability and reliability for file storage, security and resistance to Byzantine threats and automatic configuration and re-configuration mechanisms to respond to component failures and usage variations.

The Client Utility architecture uses a resource abstraction to encapsulate any functionality or service ranging from a file to a complex combination of services. Farsite, on the other hand, is restricted only to file systems. Each file in Farsite is encrypted (using cryptographic file hash), replicated and stored on multiple machines. The system provides security and availability by distributing multiple encrypted replicas of each file among the client machines. In terms of security, Farsite uses a directory host, which is a group of machines that interact using a Byzantine fault- tolerant protocol. This preserves the integrity of the group as long as fewer than one third of the machines misbehave in a malicious or arbitrary manner. The Client Utility started with the assumption of a malicious environment and implemented a sophisticated capability-based protection scheme. Farsite provides a good solution for the environment of a large company or university, but could take advantage of the CU mechanisms for creating, discovering and managing services across multiple organizations in a large-scale distributed system.

4.4 Collaborative P2P Platforms

Collaborative P2P platforms such as Groove [9] and Magi (Endeavors) [4] are increasingly becoming popular as they create secure shared spaces and interactive tools for real-time and asynchronous collaboration among multiple users. They use distributed state-management mechanisms that allow multiple users to share and concurrently operate application programs, while each member of the space maintains its own view. All transactions between the members of a shared space are encrypted through the use of public and private key infrastructures.

The Client Utility system, although it was not designed as a collaborative infrastructure, it is fully decentralized and has very attractive features (such as personalizable name-spaces, scalable lookup and brokering services, access control mechanisms) that make it ideal for building large-scale P2P collaborative spaces. On the other hand, both Groove and Magi use a hybrid centralized-decentralized approach (centralized management for discovering the peers, securing access of resources and automatically updating the data, while the data is obtained directly from the peers). These are best optimized for small-group interactions.

5 Summary

Although the development of the Client Utility architecture was independent of the development of today's familiar peer-to-peer systems, CU addresses many of the problems those systems face. Some of the ideas introduced by the Client Utility have found their way into the world of Web services. These include messages consisting of envelopes and opaque payloads (SOAP [24]), mediation of requests (Biztalk [24], J2EE[24]), and extensible vocabulary structures (RDF [24]). In the peer-to-peer space, JXTA [12] has adopted many of the concepts introduced by the Client Utility. Other parts of the architecture, such as its naming system, await adoption.

The CU design, being centered on a resource abstraction, makes it an attractive platform for developing web services. In fact, its embodiment as the e-speak product [13] provided exactly such a platform. However, the basic design goals of CU are closer to those of P2P systems. Hence, as P2P developers adopt and adapt the ongoing work in web services, they may find components of the Client Utility to be useful.

Acknowledgements

Many thanks to Dejan Milojicic for suggesting numerous improvements to the presentation.

References

1. Karl Aberer, Magdalena Punceva, Manfred Hauswirth and Roman Schmidt, "Improving Data Access in P2P Systems", IEEE Internet Computing 6(1):58-67, January-February.
2. Biztalk, The Biztalk home page, http://www.biztalk.org
3. John R. Douceur and Roger P. Wattenhofer, "Optimizing File Availability in a Secure Serverless Distributed File System", Proceedings of the 20th IEEE Symposium on Reliable Distributed Systems, New Orleans, LA (October 2001), pp. 4-13.
4. Endeavors Technology 2001, The Endeavors home page, http://www.endeavors.com
5. "E-speak Architectural Specification: Beta 2.2", http://www.e-speak.net/library/pdfs/E-speakArch.pdf (1999)
6. http://www.e-speak.net/library/pdfs/a.0/Architecture.pdf (2001)
7. Freenet 2001, The Freenet home page, http://freenet.sourceforge.net
8. Gnutella 2001, The Gnutella home page, http://Gnutella.wego.com
9. Groove Networks, 2000, The Groove home page, http://www.groove.net
10. J2EE, The Java 2 Platform Enterprise Edition home page, http://java.sun.com/j2ee
11. Jini Network Technology, http://www.sun.com/jini
12. JXTA 2001, The JXTA home page, http://www.JXTA.org
13. Alan H. Karp, "E-speak E-xplained", HP Lab Technical Report, HPL-2000-101, http://www.hpl.hp.com/techreports/2000/HPL-2000-101.html (2000)
14. Alan H. Karp, Rajiv Gupta, Guillermo Rozas, Arindam Banerji, "The Client Utility Architecture: The Precursor to E-speak", HP Labs Technical Report, HPL-2001-136, (2001) available at http://www.hpl.hp.com/techreports/2001/HPL-2001-136.html

15. A. H. Karp, R. Gupta, G. Rozas, and A. Banerji, "Split Capabilities for Access Control", HP Labs Tech Report, HPL-2001-164, June (2001), http://www.hpl.hp.com/techreports/2001/HPL-2001-164.html
16. John Kubiatowicz, David Bindel, Yan Chen, Steven Czerwinski, Patrick Eaton, Dennis Geels, R. Gummadi, Sean Rhea, Hakim Weatherspoon, Westley Weimer, Chris Wells, and Ben Zhao "OceanStore: An Architecture for Global-Scale Persistent Storage", Proceedings of the 9th International Conference on Architectural Support for Programming Languages and Operating Systems, Cambridge, MA (November 2000).
17. Dejan Milojicic, Vana Kalogeraki, Rajan Lukose, Kiran Nagaraja, Jim Pruyne, Bruno Richard, Sami Rollins and Zhichen Xu "Peer-to-Peer Computing, HP Labs Technical Report, HPL-2002-57 available at http://www.hpl.hp.com/techreports/2002
18. Morpheus 2001, The Morpheus home page, http://www.musiccity.com
19. Napster 2000, The Napster home page, http://www.Napster.com
20. Object Management Group, "The Common Object Request Broker Architecture", formal/99-10-07, Version 2.3.1, October 1999.
21. Murali K. Ramanathan, Vana Kalogeraki and Jim Pruyne, "Finding Good Peers in Peer-to-Peer Networks", International Parallel and Distributed Computing Symposium, Fort Lauderdale, Florida (April 2002).
22. Resource Description Framework (RDF), http://www.w3.org/RDF
23. Simple Object Access Protocol (SOAP), http://www.w3.org/TR/SOAP
24. http://www.e-speak.net/community/esv-about.html
25. UDDI, The UDDI home page, http://www.uddi.org
26. VerticalNet, http://www.verticalnet.com/
27. Steve Waterhouse, David M. Doolin, Gene Kan and Yaroslav Faybishenko, "Distributed Search in P2P Networks", IEEE Internet Computing 6(1):68-72, January-February.
28. Yahoo, The Yahoo home page, http://www.yahoo.com

P³: Parallel Peer to Peer

An Internet Parallel Programming Environment

Licínio Oliveira, Luís Lopes, and Fernando Silva

Departamento de Ciência de Computadores & LIACC
Faculdade de Ciências - Universidade do Porto
Rua do Campo Alegre, 823
4150 Porto, Portugal
{lsoliveira,lblopes,fds}@ncc.up.pt

Abstract. P³ is a next-generation Internet computing platform, building upon other experiments and implementing new ideas for high-performance parallel computing in the Internet environment. This paper describes its run-time system, programming model and how it compares to current state-of-the-art systems.

Keywords: Peer to Peer, Distributed Computing, Parallel Computing, High Performance Computing.

1 Introduction and Motivation

In recent years there has been a growing interest in *High Performance Computing* using distributed systems, namely the Internet itself, as the resource provider [10, 17]. This focus on current distributed systems stems from the observation that individual machines in such systems spend most of their time either idle or with very modest workloads, and that their otherwise wasted computing cycles may be gathered and used to perform large scale computations [17, 7, 8].

Grid Computing establishes the foundations for an infrastructure capable of transparently providing computational cycles over wide area networks. Such systems behave much like service providers and the first implementations are very recent and subject to discussion namely on standardization [9, 11].

Peer-to-Peer Computing is often associated with Grid Computing as it provides a fundamental change in paradigm for programming distributed systems. It provides highly efficient communication by making nodes exchange data directly, without intermediate routing servers. It also improves service availability as these are not concentrated in a few servers with higher failure rates. Several such systems have been proposed to date, mostly focusing on the sharing of computational cycles or data-storage [17, 8, 7, 10, 12].

So far the work on Peer-to-Peer systems has been focusing on infrastructure for Grid systems, stand alone parallel distributed systems and file-sharing systems. Our main interest in Peer-to-Peer computing is in using it as a basis for

E. Gregori et al. (Eds.): Networking 2002 Workshops, LNCS 2376, pp. 274–288, 2002.

the development of an efficient, highly available, parallel programming system which we named P³ (Parallel Peer-to-Peer). In this perspective we argue that current implementations lack adequate solutions on two fundamental issues.

First, to our knowledge, there is no system that integrates features such as: dynamic discovery and management of resources, scalability, accessibility, availability, portability and fault-tolerance, into an integrated environment optimized for parallel computing. In P³ we aim to provide for these features by carefully designing the run-time system. In short, our proposal is as follows:

- dynamic discovery and management of resources is supported by dynamically changing sets of nodes that monitor the network for resources and manage the computational workload;
- the portability issue is solved by using an hardware independent format for the run-time system implementation, in this case Java;
- scalability is supported by the use of dynamic workload balancing between computing nodes, peer-to-peer communication and dynamically changing sets of resource manager nodes;
- fault-tolerance is supported by keeping redundant copies of the run-time system state and using checkpoint/rollback mechanisms;
- availability of resources is guaranteed by allowing any node who has the run-time system installed to join a computation dynamically;
- finally, accessibility, by not requiring any specific properties for a node to belong to the P³ community.

A second, and most important, point is the lack of integration of an adequate parallel programming model into existing systems, as most of them deal with independent tasks. In our proposal, such a model must feature:

- builtin dynamic work balance, given the variable number of the computational resources;
- the specifications for the problem's computation and for data partitioning should be orthogonal; this allows a far cleaner and intuitive programming style;
- a shared object-space that provides a network-wide, dynamically changing, virtual shared memory.

The shared object-space, actually a Peer-to-Peer distributed file system, provides all the support required for interprocess communication and synchronization. The programmer must provide the code that solves the problem without thinking of data partition. The work partition strategy is specified independently by the programmer in a P³ application and describes the behavior of a node when a dynamic work request comes from a node joining the computation.This model hides the architectural complexity from the programmer at the expense of additional run-time system complexity. The implementation of the P³ framework is ongoing research work.

The remainder of the paper is organized as follows. Section 2 describes the software architecture of the P^3 system and its proposed implementation. Section 3 follows with a description of the programming model with an example. Finally, in section 4 we issue some conclusions and discuss future work.

2 P^3 System Overview

P^3 is a Java run-time system that uses user specified resources to provide support for a distributed programming environment in a Peer-to-Peer network. P^3 provides transparent access to network peers, persistence using shared disk storage, fault-tolerance, high availability, portability, support for parallel computations according to a specific programming model and an extensible framework.

The P^3 network is fully autonomous and self-healing in the sense that it does not need any administration nor centralized control procedures and provides the means for fault-tolerance and high availability. More specifically, peers can join and leave the network at any time and nodes do not need permanent Internet connections (although this is preferential).

The P^3 run-time tries to be as unobtrusive as possible to the host peer system, running in the background while possible and mandating child computations to have minimum operating system priority. If such restrictions should still be insufficient, the kernel scheduler could easily be adapted to include any other priority queueing policy, based, for example, on standard uptime information or collected statistical information of the runtime execution.

Although security is not a priority in the current implementation of the P^3 run-time, it is an obvious concern, especially in the Internet environment. As such, P^3 tries to be as confidential as possible by not transmitting any personal or unspecified system information through the network. As a policy, the previous is obviously unsatisfactory, but future work will address this problem more adequately.

2.1   Conceptual Organization

The P^3 network is organized in two distinct sets of nodes – *manager* nodes and *compute* nodes (fig. 1). The idea is borrowed from previous work in [10] and [14], where complete decentralization of the Peer-to-Peer network was proven, in practice, not to scale well. As such, a balance must be met between Peer-to-Peer common practice of complete decentralization of control and standard client-server techniques. P^3 uses the hybrid approach of maintaining volatile nodes marked as manager nodes[1], which perform coordination operations, maintaining quality of service. By volatile we mean that the set of manager nodes may dynamically change, expand or even contract (though it can never be empty), given the state of the current manager node set. Also, those changes are completely controlled by the run-time system, without user intervention.

---

[1] Similar, in concept, to *Gnutella*'s notion of *ultra-peer*.

Peers are known in the system by their PeerID. They are assigned by the responsible manager nodes at first login and are persistent through all sessions.

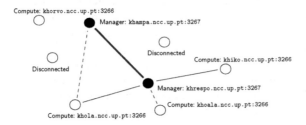

Fig. 1. Example of a possible P^3 network topology

P^3 provides an *object-space* abstraction that resembles the concept of a distributed, shared file-system. In this object-space, objects can be stored and retrieved (by name) with atomic run-time system operations and name-spaces can be created or deleted. Other operations are possible using the standard tools provided by the P^3 run-time, which include object meta-search (e.g. search by object type/contents) or storage of arbitrarily complex objects.

The shared file-system is stored across all compute nodes, thus providing almost as much disk storage as the sum of free space of all nodes in the network[2].

Manager Nodes. The manager node set is the collection of P^3 nodes that, at a given time, hold the responsibility of maintaining state coordination across the P^3 network. The state of the P^3 run-time is the union of the following:

- Peer routing and meta-data information
- File-system data, meta-data and caching information
- Global application status

Given the responsibilities of such nodes, their allocation scheme should be efficient and, by precedence, respect the following:

1. Permanent Internet connection
2. Low latency and high bandwidth connection
3. Availability of disk space
4. Good overall system performance

Nonetheless, as it is not necessarily possible to allocate peers that fulfill all of the specified goals, the choice should fall on the best rated nodes according to the requirements given above.

P^3 uses redundancy in the manager node set to provide high availability and fault-tolerance. For each manager node there is one or more shadow manager

---

[2] In reality, each node can configure the amount of disk space devoted to shared storage and the high availability kernel features use more space for data backup.

nodes. These nodes are considered secondary, in the sense that they do not hold authoritative data. They maintain consistency with the primary manager node through a round-robin differential state copy. Several primary manager nodes may exist but, in that case, they should be responsible for exclusive partitions of the system's state. Shadow manager nodes, however, need not comply to the later, to avoid allocation of excessive manager nodes. The primary and its shadow nodes must, at all times, know of each other's existence.

The manager node set grows as soon as each primary manager node determines that it cannot keep up with peer connections or runs out of disk space; the set can also grow if shadow manager nodes run out of available disk space but in this case another shadow manager node can help and the set does not need to increase in size.

Compute Nodes. All nodes that do not have manager capabilities[3] are called compute nodes and contribute to the system with usable resources. The resources that a compute peer may bring to the system are, in the current run-time implementation, of two kinds: processor time and disk storage. Several other resources may be harnessed in the future, by using the run-time system extensibility properties.

Each compute node may only be contributing to a single P^3 application at any given instant, thus avoiding local resource competition and simplifying the run-time system. The amount of work each compute node has currently in hand is dictated by the manager node that was responsible for its assignment. Compute nodes expect to receive work from the manager nodes, upon request. It is the manager's responsibility to correctly select the application that each compute node receives work from.

The Shared File-System. P^3 has builtin support for a Peer-to-Peer file-system, much in the style of current Peer-to-Peer file-sharing networks [10, 14]. The distinction between those systems and P^3 is the ability to search and store arbitrarily complex Java objects by reference, transforming the file-system into a shared associative memory or object-space. The file-system also supports the existence of arbitrary name-spaces, where objects can be independently stored. A name-space is a subset of the object-space where objects can be stored without name clashing problems. This means that object "A" living in name-space "X" is not the same as "A" in name-space "Y". Name-spaces are identified with reference keys, NamespaceIDs, which are strings.

The proposed standard for P^3, imposes the presence of at least one, global, name-space, named "global", and a local name-space for each P^3 application. This ensures that each application has, at least, one absolutely safe name-space in which to store its objects (accessible through the p3lspc method). This local name-space identifier is assigned at application startup time, by an adequate manager node. Additional management of name-spaces can be done at any time,

---

[3] The role of a node may change at any time, given the needs of the system.

using name-space creation (p3create) and deletion (p3destroy) methods of the appropriate P3NameSpace Java class.

Each object in the file-system has an associated key, ObjectID, and name-space tag, through which it is referenced. Optional meta-data can be specified for each object, through appropriate methods (p3metadata) in the main Java shared object class, P3Object. Several methods are also devoted to basic object sharing: synchronous read/write (p3get/p3set), asynchronous read/write (p3bind/p3send) and object search (p3search). The synchronous read/write methods are multiplexed into the basic Java data-types to provide commodity to the application developer, just like many other parallel programming libraries.

Objects are stored in a Peer-to-Peer fashion, across P^3's network nodes. Every P^3 node may store objects and objects can be stored in any P^3 node. Object access information is stored and kept consistent by the manager node set. Synchronization is needed when updating the state of an object in the object-space and as such, manager nodes have the ability to block access to objects during the time frame in which such actions occur. The principle is simple, as each manager node must be informed of state changes for each object it is responsible for, object locking is just a matter of disallowing or blocking the operation if a given flag is set. Certain applications might be interested in using such synchronization primitives and for that purpose one provides synchronization methods, such as p3readLock, p3readUnlock, p3writeLock and p3writeUnlock within the P3Object class.

In this context, file-system caching is of vital importance to provide higher system performance, high availability, fault-tolerance and avoiding resource deadlocking. Caching is implemented through redundancy, in a hierarchical two level scheme. Nodes are able to store local, non authoritative, object copies and asynchronously verify its consistency (local caching). Manager nodes may at any time propagate copies of objects for which request rates rise above a given threshold or for which the storage nodes disconnect from the network (global caching).

2.2 P^3 Run-Time System

The P^3 run-time system is being implemented in Java. Java was chosen due to its portability, extensibility and amazing number of features already present in the language, and not readily available in other programming languages, like C or C++. Besides, Java is the acknowledged standard for portable high performance computing projects and, as such, lessons can be learned from the implementation of those projects.

Java presents the possibility of implementing the run-time system as an applet. However, the run-time system could not have been implemented with its current features, due to the security policy enforced by the environment where applet based applications run. For example: peers could not communicate directly and a high performance persistent shared file-system could not be implemented. As such, P^3's run-time system is implemented as a Java application. Other Internet parallel computing systems follow the opposite (applet) path [3, 6].

Every machine wishing to participate in running computations must install the Java application which encapsulates the run-time system. Once installed, the run-time will need no additional setup, apart from configuration tuning.

In P^3 there is support for off-line computations; the run-time engine does not need to have network access at all time. In fact, all P^3 computations occur off-line. It is only in the presence of a blocking operation that network access must be obtained. This would be the case, for example, of a blocking read/write operation.

Futhermore, when network access is first obtained, in each session, a network login procedure is executed. This procedure is important for several reasons, the first being to refresh the manager node tables with peer information, avoiding probing every node in the network for available resources. Another reason is checking the status of the current node in respect to the task it is running.

When dealing with distributed applications, good resource management and allocation policies are vital to system performance. In the Internet environment, such concerns must be even stronger, because volatile resources are extremely common. P^3 uses a meta-data approach to the problem; manager nodes are responsible for collecting and storing relevant meta-data information for every compute node. However, as each manager node has to store information for each compute node it is responsible for, collected meta-data must be kept to a bare minimum. Usually, the interesting information to retrieve from each compute node includes: the executing P^3 application and its state, the available disk space, machine load and additional routing information.

As already stated, P^3's main goal is to reuse computing cycles of Internet connected machines. However, the P^3 run-time does not limit itself to that network environment, it is possible to use P^3 to harness the computing cycles of institutional intranets, for example. It should be emphasized that P^3 is not only a run-time system for parallel computation; it is easy to envision several non-parallel applications that could be implemented in P^3. A large scale multimedia database constructed as a P^3 application that interacts with several non P^3 client applications is an interesting example.

Run-Time System Organization. Internally, the run-time system subdivides itself into two layers: the kernel module layer, which includes the most important and necessary features like communication, fault-tolerance, persistence, resource management and discovery; and the service layer, which are all non-basic standard features of the P^3 run-time that use the kernel to access the P^3 network resources. The parallel programming model is an example of such a service. Dividing the run-time in two layers, induces a three-tier model for a P^3 application (fig. 2). This widely used paradigm allows a higher degree of control and specialization of each layer, while making project development easier. The P^3 three-tier model is not opaque, in the sense that it allows the top layer (applications) to access both lower layers (kernel and services) of the run-time system.

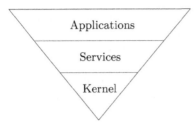

Fig. 2. P^3's three-tier model

Kernel. The P^3 run-time system kernel is the set of basic system features, like communication support, object-space access libraries and so on. The implementation tries to be expandable and modular, permitting quick and easy implementation of new replacement modules. The modules present in the current run-time implementation are those in table 1.

Table 1. Current run-time system kernel modules

Name	Description
Configuration	Permits static and dynamic kernel configuration
Communication	Communication interface and default TCP/IP backend
Object-space	Name-space management and object search/storage/retrieval procedures
Management	Manager node sub-system
Kernel	Kernel management and entry point

Although modular, the run-time engine expects some intercommunication between modules to take place, e.g. the communication module works with the management module to permit interaction compute/manager and manager/manager communications to take place.

Services. The three tier-model already explained, has the interesting property of permitting disconnected development paths to the three layers of project development, namely the kernel, the services and all applications wishing to use the system, because once a kernel/services interface becomes stable, there is no need to make any change to an existing service (or application), for each kernel (or services) update.

All a P^3 service needs, in order to be considered as such, is to subclass the P3Service class. From that point on, apart from defining some obligatory methods, the service can interact with the kernel layer to access P^3's facilities and provide whatever functionality it desires.

Service libraries should be distributed with the run-time system due to their static registration within the kernel. A useful P^3 feature would be to permit services to register within the kernel dynamically, providing a plug-in based approach as in [12]. However, at current development stage, the run-time system is not capable of doing so; registration must be statically configured and known at run-time startup time.

As an example, the parallel programming model proposed in the following section is implemented as a run-time system service.

3   Programming Model

In P^3 we want to introduce a programming model for the distributed environment that both hides the underlying architectural complexity of the system and, that is intuitive for the programmer. The first major task for a programmer in a parallel system is that of implementing the partition of data among a statically defined set of computing nodes. Given this partition the computational task for each node is then coded and this usually includes frequent interprocess communication for synchronization purposes or to share intermediate results. The implementation of this computation is usually highly dependent on the data partition chosen and thus not appropriate for environments where availability of computational resources changes dynamically.

In P^3 we solve this problem by asking the programmer to code a solution for the problem (method p3compute) and to specify a work partition procedure (method p3divide), orthogonally. For a matrix multiplication, for example, p3compute would compute the result matrix from available input matrices. On the other hand, p3divide describes how to divide the current matrix into smaller slices to assign to other nodes joining the computation. Thus, our P^3 computation involves a set of nodes calculating a number of sub-matrices of the result matrix, possibly of distinct sizes. It is the programmer that indicates the way in which a node's work is split and sent to a new node (method p3divide). This is similar to the task of implementing data partition in parallel programming except that in P^3 this procedure is invoked dynamically and adapts to the evolution of the computation.

Process synchronization and, in general, message passing are written as read and write operations on a shared object-space.

Fault-tolerance is introduced in the programming model by using system primitives supporting computation checkpointing (method p3checkpoint). These primitives create a full dump of the computing object into a standard Java format that then gets marshaled into a persistent medium. If at any time during the computation, a node failure is detected, a copy of the node's previous checkpointed computing object is fetched and the computation resumes (method p3restart).

3.1   The Execution Model

The programming model is implemented in the P^3 run-time as a service. We shall now describe the associated execution model encapsulated in the p3.services.parallel Java package.

First of all, application startup is done through a standard programming model service component, defined in the Java class P3ParallelUploader. This small application uploads the pre-compiled Java class (which must be a subclass of P3Parallel) onto the manager, making it aware of its existence. The first time the manager decides to allocate a node for this application, it will flag the node's run-time that it must start the application by running the p3main method. After doing so, the allocated node's run-time system begins to compute, executing the method p3compute. All these actions are invoked asynchronously and automatically by the service.

The programming model service is built on top of the following, simple, loop of execution:

This means that when a node's run-time is not computing a P³ task, it is probing the managers for more work. Examining fig. 3 we can see the main algorithm for work subdivision in P³. A node (node A, in the figure) requests work, not directly from another node, but through a manager node, which may query other manager nodes, and will notify the node it determines to be the most suitable (B) to share some work with the first.

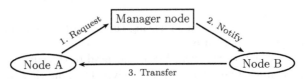

Fig. 3. Work request and attribution scheme

The work subdivision strategy is implemented by the programmer under the p3divide method. It could be as simple or as complex as one may desire. The events that follow the invocation of p3divide are depicted in fig. 4.

The division starts when a node (the nodes are the same as those in figure 3) receives a notify message from a manager node, saying it must send a work task to another node.

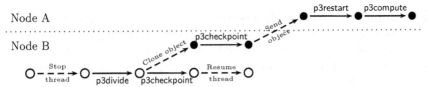

Fig. 4. Simplified execution flow after node B receives a work request from node A

During this process a clone of the current node's compute object is produced and the first object is left almost intact. The difference between the two final compute objects is that one runs p3restart while the other does not. Besides that, the objects are identical, as their state was preserved by using Java serialization facilities. They are also different in the sense that they resume computation in different locations; in node B, execution resumes from the point where it first stopped and node A restarts by invoking p3restart and then p3compute.

This behavior allows the use of save/restore variables that permit the partitioning of the problem, by carefully coding p3compute. It should be noted that all interaction is implicit and hidden from the application programmer, by the run-time system control logic.

3.2   The Programming Interface

The programming interface for P³'s parallel programming model is implemented in one major class named P3Parallel. All P³ parallel applications are instances of extensions to this class.

The P3Parallel Class The application programmer has to provide an implementation for the following methods of the P3Parallel class:

- p3main, is the method that sets up the P³ computation. It can be used to perform some I/O or for the initialization of data-structures before the actual computation begins;
- p3compute, is the method implementing the unit of parallel work in the P³ system for a given application;
- p3divide, describes how the work block allocated to the current computation is divided when a request for work is received from another node;
- p3restart, is invoked whenever a branch of the computation is resuming after a node failure or on the arrival of new work. In general, the computation must have been previously checkpointed at some point in the past, and execution will resume from that point (note that, a checkpoint is automatically created right after p3divide is invoked).

The P3Parallel superclass implements other methods, such as p3checkpoint, which may be used as a default action or re-implemented by the programmer in case some application specific needs must be fulfilled.

An Example: Matrix Multiplication In the following we describe an implementation of the usual matrix multiplication operation. To implement a solution, we define a class for the application, P3MatrixMultiply, that extends P3Parallel. The implementation of the application simply requires the definition of its attributes and methods.

In this example written in P³, we compute the matrix C, from A and B, parameterized on a few attributes. The code for the computation has no reference whatsoever to data-partition among cooperating nodes. It is apparently a sequential code. The program then provides a procedure that describes how to obtain sub-matrices for C, dynamically, when a request for work arrives.

- global class attributes: a shared object n for the size of the matrix, shared objects a, b and c to contain, respectively, matrix A lines, matrix B columns and each cell of matrix C. Additional attributes include line, column, 1, m and max which are integers used to keep track of the evolution of the computation.
- method p3main() is used to perform the initial matrix setup:

```
void p3main() {
    try {
        n.p3bind(p3lspc(), "n");
    } catch(P3BindException e) { p3abort(); }

    n.setInt(10000);    // Set matrix size to 10000x10000
    for ( int i = 0 ; i < 10000 ; i++ ) {
        // Code for initializing line i of matrix A
        // Code for initializing column i of matrix B
    }
}
```

- method p3compute() computes the matrix C. Before computing the new entry at row line and column column, it binds line line for A, column column for B and c for the resulting cell. Then, a cycle computes the value for the cell. Finally, a check is made to verify whether it is time to advance to the next line in the current work block.

```
void p3compute() {
    try {
        n.p3bind(p3lspc(), "n");
    } catch(P3BindException e) { p3abort(); }

    while ( line < max && column < n.getInt() ) {
        try {
            a.p3bind(p3lspc(), "A"+line);
            b.p3bind(p3lspc(), "B"+column);
            c.p3bind(p3lspc(), "C"+line+"_"+column);
        } catch(P3BindException e) { p3abort(); }

        for ( int i = 0 ; i < n.getInt() ; i++ )
            c.setInt(c.getInt()+a.getIntPos(i)*b.getIntPos(i));
        if ( ++column > n.getInt() ) { line++; column = 0; }
    }
}
```

- method p3divide() defines the way the computation reacts to a request for work from a coordinator node. The method is invoked synchronously and, in this case, it divides the work into two similar blocks of size (max-line+1)/2. The block to be given away will compute from line line+(max-line+1)/2 to line max. The current computation will continue from line to the new value of `max`.

```
boolean p3divide() {
    l = line + (max − line + 1) / 2;
    m = max;
    max = line − 1;
    return(true);
}
```

- method p3restart() describes the computation restart procedure. We initialize the attributes `line` and `max` to the previously checkpointed values:

```
void p3restart() {
    line = l;
    column = 0;
    max = m;
}
```

As seen, the main task for the programmer lies in the code for p3compute and p3divide. These define work partition and computation for the problem orthogonally. The big advantage of this programming model relative to the usual models used in current parallel distributed systems stems from the following features:

- we allow the computing node pool to grow dinamically. The way work is partitioned among compute nodes is controlled by the programmer at the application level;
- by implementing a solution for the problem abstracting away from data partitioning among nodes we make the code for the problem more explicit and intuitive.

While matrix multiplication is a fairly common programming example, allowing very regular data partition strategies we feel that our model provides adequate programming support for more complex applications, namely grid-based or hierarchical algorithms. In fact, the mappings used to construct the data partition in these systems may be easily adapted to produce an implementation for method p3divide. Also, the object-space may be used to store arbitrarily complex datastructures by assuming some adequate naming convention (e.g., directory style as in file-systems, or URL style as in web documents).

4   Conclusions and Future Work

We have described a development platform for high performance parallel computing in the Internet environment, based on recent and open research areas. Our belief is that the Internet and large, fast, intranets will, in the near future, be the *de facto* standard for high performance computing. Grid computing [11, 9] is an effort to take this idea even further, providing on demand computing power from high performance computers with fast interconnections.

Systems like HARNESS [12], Charlotte [3] and Javelin [6] also try to provide parallel programming environments for the Internet. However all these systems fall into the same computational and organizational model; they use the master/worker computation model and the client/server communication paradigm. P³ is distinct for it uses none of these concepts; P³ proposes a more intuitive and adaptive parallel programming model and uses Peer-to-Peer techniques to guard against common problems in those systems (server failures and connection bottlenecks), while providing a wide range of additional functionalities. The result should be a much more scalable, easier and richer parallel programming environment.

The P³ run-time system is currently being implemented and major work is underway for creating a capable run-time system with all the features exposed in this document. Our concerns, at present, are in building a high performance, stable kernel with support for parallel computations according to the proposed model. The programming model was our first priority while kernel scalability, fault tolerance, high availability and object-system performance are now the most important concerns. Active research points are scalability issues and tolerance to volatile resources in extreme conditions.

In the future, P³ will address topics such as security or dynamic system reconfiguration, but these are not short term objectives. Finally, profound tests will be conducted in three major areas: performance, scalability and fault-tolerance.

Acknowledgments

The authors are partially supported by FCT's projects MIMO and APRIL (contracts POSI/CHS/39789/2001 and POSI/SRI/40749/2001, respectively).

References

1. Albert D. Alexandrov, Maximilian Ibel, Klaus E. Schauser, and Chris J. Scheiman. SuperWeb: Research issues in Java-based global computing. *Concurrency: Practice and Experience*, 9(6):535–553, 1997.
2. J. Baldeschwieler, R. Blumofe, and E. Brewer. ATLAS: An infrastructure for global computing, 1996.
3. A. Baratloo, M. Karaul, Z. M. Kedem, and P. Wyckoff. Charlotte: Metacomputing on the web. In *Proc. of the 9th Int'l Conf. on Parallel and Distributed Computing Systems (PDCS-96)*, 1996.
4. M. Beck, J. Dongarra, G. Fagg, G. Geist, P. Gray, J. Kohl, M. Migliardi, K. Moore, T. Moore, P. Papadopoulous, S. Scott, and V. Sunderam. HARNESS: A next generation distributed virtual machine, 1999.
5. A. Bricker, M. Litzkow, M. Livny, T. Summary, and V. Report. Condor Technical Summary, 1992.
6. P. Cappello, B. Christiansen, M. Ionescu, M. Neary, K. Schauser, and D. Wu. JAVELIN: Internet based parallel computing using Java, 1997.
7. *distributed.net*. http://www.distributed.net/.
8. *Entropia*. http://www.entropia.com/.
9. I. Foster and C. Kesselman. Globus: A metacomputing infrastructure toolkit. *The International Journal of Supercomputer Applications and High Performance Computing*, 11(2):115–128, Summer 1997.

10. *Gnutella.* http://www.gnutella.com/.
11. Andrew S. Grimshaw, William A. Wulf, James C. French, Alfred C. Weaver, and Paul F. Reynolds Jr. Legion: The next logical step toward a nationwide virtual computer. Technical Report CS-94-21, 8, 1994.
12. M. Migliardi and V. Sunderam. Heterogeneous distributed virtual machines in the HARNESS metacomputing framework, 1999.
13. M. Migliardi, V. Sunderam, A. Geist, and J. Dongarra. Dynamic reconfiguration and virtual machine management in the HARNESS metacomputing system, 1998.
14. *Napster.* http://www.napster.com/.
15. *Parabon.* http://www.parabon.com/.
16. A. Rowstron and P. Druschel. Storage management and caching in PAST, a large-scale, persistent peer-to-peer storage utility, 2001.
17. *SETI@Home.* http://setiathome.ssl.berkeley.edu/.
18. D. Skillicorn and D. Talia. Models and languages for parallel computation, 1998.

Peer-to-Peer Programming with Teaq

Huw Evans* and Peter Dickman

Department of Computing Science, The University of Glasgow,
Glasgow, G12 8RZ, UK,
{huw,pd}@dcs.gla.ac.uk

Abstract. This paper introduces Teaq, a new peer-to-peer programming model and implementation that places processes into a self-healing,
ordered spanning tree, across which distributed object queries are routed.
The programmer has control over where in the tree their process resides,
how their queries are routed through the tree, and how result objects
are generated and passed back to the query initiator. Default implementations are provided that the programmer may specialise. This paper
introduces the two main algorithms for maintaining the tree and routing
queries.

1 Introduction

The Teaq[1] system addresses two shortcomings in the peer-to-peer literature [3].
Firstly, processes in the network are organised according to the processing capabilities of the machine on which they are running. Secondly, programming-level
objects in the network can be easily found by propagating a dynamically up-
dateable query through the network.

Peer-to-peer systems are still in their infancy. It is currently not clear what
kinds of topologies the machines and processes of a peer-to-peer network should
be arranged into and when one topology should be favoured over another one.
Object discovery in peer-to-peer networks is also not well understood. Objects
must be found in a dynamically changing, error prone, decentralized system that
has a high degree of machine and network heterogeneity, as shown by [5].

The motivation for Teaq is to provide a run-time system that allows machines
and processes to be arranged in such a way that the system can make profitable
decisions about the shape of the underlying peer-to-peer tree topology. In addition, the system should be able to easily find programming-level objects in a
network where the frequency of object creation and destruction is high. Flood
routing (e.g., as used by early Gnutella systems) is wasteful of network bandwidth. Other systems such as Pastry [4] and FreeNet [2,3] that use hash-based
routing rely on the fact that the object being searched for is long-lived. Neither
of these kinds of solution are appropriate in the kinds of context that Teaq is
aimed at.

---

* This work is funded by the UK EPSRC under grant (GR/N38114).

[1] Teaq stands for Trees, Evolution and Queries and the word is pronounced the same as teak.

E. Gregori et al. (Eds.): Networking 2002 Workshops, LNCS 2376, pp. 289–294, 2002.

The rest of this paper is organised as follows: section 2 describes how processes are placed into a spanning-tree; section 3 discusses the dynamically updatable, distributed object query mechanism; section 4 concludes the paper.

2   Constructing a Teaq Tree

Teaq processes communicate events to other Teaq processes and events carry code with them. When an event is received by an object, a reference to the receiving object is passed to the event. This means that the destination object can respond to an open-ended, evolvable set of events which is not hard-wired into the receiving object. With this mechanism it is possible to dynamically update the run-time system (code and state), by replacing one object with another.

A Teaq process is an instance of a Java virtual machine and each process has within it three main objects: the first is the `Capacity` object that is used to decide where the process should be placed in the tree; secondly is the `ProcessDescriptor` object that provides a unique identifier for the process and which also abstracts over the IP address of the machine and the port number on which the `ST` object is listening; and lastly is the Spanning Tree object (`ST`) that provides management for the process once in a tree, e.g., this object receives requests from other processes that may wish to become children of this process. The `ST` object has references to the `Capacity` and `ProcessDescriptor` objects.

The `Capacity` object tells Teaq how much processing capability that process has. A process running on a machine that has a large amount of physical memory, a fast CPU, and which is attached to a fast network with a lot of bandwidth, is going to have a `Capacity` object which reflects the capabilities of this machine. The capacity object is also used to control the number of children any one process is willing to support. The `Capacity` object currently contains a single integer value which is defined on a per machine basis. The more powerful the machine, the larger the integer value will be[2].

Spanning Trees. Processes form a spanning tree [1] and so have at most one parent and up to M children, where M is bounded by the capacity object. In such a tree, all processes except one (the root process) have a parent. All processes are members of the one tree and it is possible to route a message from one node to any other, assuming a route between the two is available in the face of failure (see **Failure** below). There are therefore N-1 connections between processes in the tree, where N is the number of currently involved processes. Queries are routed across this tree at run-time and the initiator of the query is seen as the root of the tree.

Connecting to a Tree. In the current implementation of Teaq, the tree attachment algorithm consists of two parts: a check is first made to see if there are

---

[2] Capturing the different aspects of a machine's capabilities (e.g., the amount of memory available, the available bandwidth and even aspects such as the observed error rate) in a multi-dimensional value space, together with a more powerful comparison mechanism (that does not rely on the current total ordering of capabilities) would give Teaq more power in deciding how to adapt the tree at run-time to make best use of the available resources. This is an area for future work.

any local processes that may be attached to; if not, a remote process is searched for to act as the parent. In this paper, only the protocol for remote attachment is discussed in detail. Briefly, local attachment consists of one process acting as the parent for all other local processes and that parent connects to the remote tree. If the local parent fails, a leader election protocol is executed. If, when a process is started it can find no local processes, it must find its rightful place in the remote tree. To connect to the remote tree, the initiating process joins a multicast[3] group that can be seen by other processes on other machines. A datagram packet is sent to it, announcing the presence of the new process. Processes that respond send back their `ProcessDescriptor` objects. From this list, the initiating process selects a process with a capacity higher than its own. This ensures that the processes with a higher capacity, i.e., those that are capable of supporting more children, are placed closer to the root. The initiating process then sends this selected process a `ConnectionRequestEvent` that will be processed in the target process. If there is no such process, e.g., there are only two processes and the one with the lower capacity started first, the process with the highest capacity in the list is returned.

Attachment Algorithm. The initiator's `ConnectionRequestEvent` is received by the target process and the attachment algorithm in listing 1.1 is then executed.

The first two if-statements of this algorithm add new processes to the tree at the first process that asserts can handle it. This may involve some manipulation of a process' children. The second two if-statements cause the tree to be extended, so that one process does not become the parent of too many children.

```
connecting = true

lock(st) {
    if (target process has available capacity)
        attach new process
    else {
        if (target process is full and new process has less capacity) {
            move some children of target process to new process
            attach new process to target process
        }
        else {
            if (capacity of new process >= capacity of target process) {
                if (target process has no parent)
                    make new process the parent of the target process
                else
                    forward request to the parent of the target process
            }
        }
    }
}

connecting = false
```

Listing 1.1. Pseudo Code for the Process Attachment Algorithm

---

[3] In the current prototype implementation of Teaq the availability of multicast is assumed. This has implications for scale as IP-multicast is not widely supported on the Internet backbone. In future versions it will be possible for the programmer to specify a set of well-known processes to connect to.

Maintaining the tree property is an important aspect of this algorithm and two important parts are the prevention of cycles and dealing with capacity ties. To prevent a cycle between two nodes that attempt to connect to each other at the same time, the attachment algorithm sets a boolean variable `connecting` to true before attempting to connect to the tree. When the two nodes try to connect to each other, they notice their `connecting` is true and so back off for an amount of time that is drawn randomly from an exponentially increasing value. `connecting` is also used to prevent cycles between more than two nodes. If one node attempts to connect to another node when both nodes have the same capacity (i.e., there is a capacity tie), the process that initiated the connection becomes the parent. In future it may be necessary to temporarily tolerate the tree property being false, e.g., in the face of multiple process failure cycles may develop. Further analysis of the tree property is an area for future work.

Failure. Processes can fail as they may crash or the machine that is hosting them may be shutdown. If a parent process fails, all its children are temporarily disconnected from the tree. Should this happen, when a process next needs to communicate with its parent, an error will be received and the tree attachment algorithm, given above, is re-run.

3   Teaq Queries

Objects are found in Teaq by running queries across the tree. A query is an OQL-like statement of this form: `select t from T where t.m() == true;`. All object of type T whose method m returns true become part of the query result. A programmer makes an object available for local or remote query by registering it (and implicitly, all objects reachable from the registered object) with ST. The registration code builds a data structure for fast lookups based on an instance's class. When running a local query, the array of objects is returned immediately. However, in the remote case, it may not be feasible to send back to the query initiator a serialized copy of the matching instance. Instead we may want to send back an object that refers to the remote matched object. Teaq supports this by allowing a programmer to pass back a proxy to the matched object as part of the query result.

Sending a Query into the Tree. To initiate a remote query, a programmer first of all creates a listener object that will be called-back whenever a query result has been found. This object is passed to the Teaq run-time system, together with a class object that indicates the type of the instances the query is interested in. The run-time system then sends out a default query object into the tree. The programmer receives an object of type `QueryToken` that represents the remote query and which defines a method called `close`. `close` is typically called by the programmer when they have received the result they require and they, therefore, want the propagation of the query to be stopped in the system (see Query Termination below).

Routing a Query through the Tree. Query routing in Teaq is flexible. A programmer is able to define how this routing is performed through a tree and what actions are performed at each process. A default query routing object is provided which, currently, visits every process, thus for a system consisting of N machines, there will be at least N messages sent out per query.

The role of the `QueryToken` object is to manage the initiating end of the query, such as receiving results and passing them to the listener. The query event that is sent into the system has three main objects that control the actions of the query as it is replicated throughout the tree: `Distance`, `Reply` and `QueryId`.

`Distance` controls how far the query will travel in the system. Currently, it ensures that the query will visit every process in the system (visiting children nodes in parallel). The `Reply` object passes results back to the initiating process. `QueryId` is a probabilistically[4] unique query identifier. It is retained on the initiating side and a copy is kept in the query event that sent into the system.

When query results are passed back from the remote query, a copy of the `QueryId` is sent back as well. This is compared with the local copy to check the identity of the remote query. This comparison is necessary as the query could be locally shutdown and another started that just happened to be listening on the same local server-socket. In this way, the initiating side can be probabilistically sure that query results are from the query that it sent into the system.

Query Termination. When the programmer has the result they desire, they call the `close` method. This shuts down the initiating side of the query. When the remote query event arrives at its next process, it will execute the query and attempt to pass the results back. However, this will not work as the initiating side has closed its side down. The remote query will receive an error message. In the current implementation, it is assumed that seeing such a message means that the initiating side has been closed down. Therefore, the event does not send itself to any parent or children processes. In this way, we prevent the remote query event from propagating itself. This removes the need to run a costly distributed query termination algorithm. However, this assumes that errors are not transient. If the query was propagated, by the time a new query result was ready to be passed back, the error situation may have passed. This approach also reduces the parallelism of remote queries but in the current prototype implementation this is felt to be preferable to having to run a distributed query-termination algorithm. The programmer can choose how to program this aspect of the system; an alternative mechanism would be to allow the query to propagate to children without having to send the result back first and to check back with the initiating site every n hops where n was configurable.

4   Conclusions

This paper has introduced the Teaq system for programming peer-to-peer systems via a self-healing, ordered spanning tree, that supports flexible routing

---

[4] It is currently a Java integer assigned at random using `java.util.Random`. This shall be changed in a future version to more accurately reflect the process that initiated the query.

of object queries across it. The contribution of this paper is the use of the self-healing, machine-capability-aware spanning tree to dynamically organise the underlying peer-to-peer topology and the promotion of the query-based model of programming. This paper has shown that short-lived objects and peer-to-peer programming can mix.

References

1. Mikhail J. Atallah, editor. *Algorithms and theory of computation handbook.* CRC Press, 2000 N.W. Corporate Blvd., Boca Raton, FL 33431-9868, USA, 1999.
2. Ian Clarke, Oskar Sandberg, Brandon Wiley, and Theodore W. Hongang. Freenet: A distributed anonymous information storage and retrieval system in designing privacy enhancing technologie. In Hannes Federrath, editor, *Designing Privacy Enhancing Technologies*, volume 2009 of *Lecture Notes in Computer Science*, Berkeley, CA, USA, July 2000. Springer-Verlag, Berlin Germany.
3. Andy Oram (ed). *Peer-to-Peer: Harnessing the Power of Disruptive Technologies.* O'Reilly, 2001.
4. A. Rowstron and P. Druschel. Pastry: Scalable, distributed object location and routing for large-scale peer-to-peer systems. In *IFIP/ACM International Conference on Distributed Systems Platforms (Middleware)*, pages 329–350, Heidelberg, Germany, November 2001.
5. Stefan Saroiu, P. Krishna Gummadi, and Steven D Gribble. A measurement study of peer-to-peer file sharing systems. Technical report, Department of Computer Science and Engineering, University of Washington, 2002.

Towards a Data-Driven Coordination Infrastructure for Peer-to-Peer Systems

Nadia Busi, Cristian Manfredini, Alberto Montresor, and Gianluigi Zavattaro

Dipartimento di Scienze dell'Informazione, Università di Bologna, Mura A.Zamboni
7, I-40127 Bologna, Italy,
{busi,manfredi,montresor,zavattar}@cs.unibo.it

Abstract. Shared dataspaces, initiated by Linda since the beginning of the 80s, has been successfully adopted as a coordination model in a huge variety of systems and applications, going from parallel computing to web-based collaborative work. We point out several scalability problems which arise when trying to exploit the original Linda coordination model in peer-to-peer systems. The objective of this analysis is to produce some guidelines for the design of a data-driven coordination infrastructure suitable for the peer-to-peer scenario.

1 Introduction

The rapid evolution of computers and networks is calling for the development of middleware platforms responsible for the management of dynamically reconfigurable federations of devices, where processes cooperate and compete for the use of shared resources. In this scenario one of the most challenging topics is concerned with the coordination of the activities performed by the federated components.

Generative communication, realized by means of the insertion and withdrawal of elements from a shared multiset, is the peculiar feature of a family of coordination languages, of which Linda [Gel85] is the most prominent representative. Generative communication is based on the following principles: a sender communicates with a receiver through a shared data space (called *tuple space*, TS for short), where emitted messages are collected; the receiver can consume the message from TS; a message generated by a process has an independent existence in the tuple space until it is explicitly withdrawn by a receiver; in fact, after its insertion in TS, a message becomes equally accessible to all processes, but it is bound to none.

In the last decades, the shared dataspace approach has been successfully adopted in a huge variety of systems and applications, going from parallel computing to Web–based collaboration system. Recently, this communication mechanism has been adopted also by several proposals of coordination platforms (see, e.g., Sun Microsystems JavaSpaces [W+98] or the IBM T Spaces [WMLF98]) for the management of dynamically reconfigurable federations of devices, where processes cooperate and compete for the use of shared resources.

E. Gregori et al. (Eds.): Networking 2002 Workshops, LNCS 2376, pp. 295–299, 2002.

In this paper we investigate the scalability of this coordination approach to the realm of peer-to-peer systems.

Informally, *peer-to-peer* (P2P) systems are distributed systems based on the concept of resource sharing by direct exchange between *peer* nodes (i.e., nodes having the same role and responsibility). Exchanged resources include content, as in popular P2P file sharing applications [Shi01, Kan01, Lan01], and storage capacity or CPU cycles, as, for example, in computational and storage grid systems [And01, RD01, K+00].

Distributed computing was intended to be synonymous with P2P computing long before the term was invented, but this initial desire was subverted by the advent of client-server computing popularized by the World Wide Web. The modern use of the term P2P and distributed computing as intended by its pioneers, however, differ in several important aspects. First, P2P applications reach out to harness the outer edges of the Internet and consequently involve scales that were previously unimaginable. Second, P2P by definition, excludes any form of centralized structure, requiring control to be completely decentralized. Finally, and most importantly, the environments in which P2P applications are deployed exhibit extreme dynamism in structure, content and load. The topology of the system typically changes rapidly due to nodes voluntarily coming and going or due to involuntary events such as crashes and partitions. The load in the system may also shift rapidly from one region to another, for example, as certain files become "hot" in a file sharing system; or the computing needs of a node suddenly increase in a grid computing system.

2   Shared Dataspaces in Mobile Systems

The pervasiveness of the client-server architecture also affected the design of shared dataspace based coordination infrastructures. Indeed, in most of the currently available implementations of Linda-like systems, the dataspace metaphor is intended as a (centralized) repository service.

An interesting proposal breaking the client-server bias is represented by the *transiently shared dataspace* metaphor introduced in Lime [PMR99].

Lime [PMR99] (Linda in a Mobile Environment) is a coordination middleware supporting both logical and physical mobility. It provides programmers with a Linda-like dataspace, whose content is determined by the connectivity among mobile hosts.

It is reasonable to investigate the scalability of Lime to a peer-to-peer context, characterized by dynamically changing connectivity, significant autonomy for the processes and direct communication between them.

The following discussion takes into consideration three different aspects of coordination models: *coordinables* (what is coordinated), *coordination rules*, *coordination medium*.

As far as coordinables are concerned, in a Linda-like system, the coordinated entities are usually active programs called agents. In Lime, agents with their own local dataspace reside on hosts and are able to logically move from a host to another one; the hosts themselves can physically move. In a peer-to-peer scenario, the involved entities (peers) are dynamic, i.e., they can frequently connect and disconnect, but they are not necessarily mobile. Mobility is not a peer-to-peer requirement in general.

With regard to the coordination rules, we can distinguish between two different programming styles: *context aware programming* and *context transparent programming*. Context aware applications are those which access both the system configuration context and the data context explicitly. For example a piece of new data may be stored on a specific mobile host. In contrast, context transparent applications can be developed without explicit knowledge of the current context. Peer-to-peer applications do not need to know where a resource is located, they only need to know if the resource is available. From this point of view, it is advisable to avoid context aware programming and replicate resources in order to improve their availability.

In Lime, the coordination medium is accomplished via a *transiently shared dataspace*. The dataspace content is determined by the connectivity among the mobile hosts. This kind of coordination medium supports physical and logical mobility of host and agents, respectively, and guarantees the consistency of the global data structure. As already discussed in [BZ01, BCV01], the consistency assumptions taken in Lime require an agreement among the involved entities regarding the set of federated hosts. For this reason, the system does not scale satisfactorily to a peer-to-peer scenario in which a clear partition of the peers in distinct clusters is unavailable and, moreover, the connection topology may be highly dynamically reconfigurable.

3 Shared Dataspaces in Peer-to-peer Systems

In this section we present some guidelines permitting to solve the scalability problems envisaged in the previous section. To be as general as possible, in this analysis we abstract away from the internal structure of the shared data. In this way, the proposed model can be instantiated to deal with any form of data, such as, e.g., Linda-like tuples, XML documents or JavaSpaces-like entries. Regarding the structure of the global dataspace, we assume that data are not correlated one to each other, i.e., the dataspace can be considered as a bag of independent items. This features differentiate our vision from other approaches, such as PeerWare [CP02], in which an overall tree-like structure is imposed on the collection of data.

The guidelines proposed in this work can be classified into two groups: those concerned with the production of data and those related to data retrieval.

As far as the nature of shared data in a P2P context is concerned, we single out two new classes of data that a peer can produce, besides the typical Lime-like, location aware form of datum.

As in Lime, also in P2P systems it may be useful to locate a new datum on a specified peer. This feature is useful to model resources or information which are strictly connected to an entity of the system, hence they must disappear when the entity becomes disconnected. As an example, consider data which represent resources or services provided by a peer.

As discussed in the previous section, we think that in this setting it is useful to provide abstractions for context transparent data sharing. We characterize at least two forms of such data.

The first step towards context independence is represented by *generic data*. In the spirit of the generative communication approach, a datum belonging to this class has an existence which is completely independent from its producer. Hence, the coordination infrastructure may decide to locate this datum in any of the available storages, as well as to move the datum according to some system or application specific needs. As an example, consider load balancing or accessibility improvement. An interesting aspect related to this form of datum is the so called time- and space-uncoupling: data are accessed independently of both the time when they are produced and the peer which created them. This kind of datum can be useful, e.g., to achieve a form of disconnected master-worker interaction, in which the involved entities connect to the P2P system only when they need to produce or consume job requests, which are processed while disconnected.

A further step towards context transparency can be performed in the case the datum represents an information or a resource that cannot be consumed. Clearly, these data can never be explicitly removed from the repository. Because of this feature, the coordination infrastructure can transparently replicate the datum in order to improve its availability to the peer community, as well as fault tolerance. We refer to this class as *replicable data*. A typical application which surely benefits from this kind of data is represented by file sharing systems.

Concerning data retrieval mechanisms, we observe that it is useful to provide the peers the possibility to define their own visibility horizon of the system, instead of forcing a predefined scope, as it happens, e.g., in Linda and in Lime. In fact, in the first case the scope coincides with the whole dataspace, while in the second one the scope is formed by the union of the contents of the repositories of the currently federated hosts. This idea may be realized by equipping each retrieval operation with an extra parameter, specifying the actual scope to be used. A reasonable metric for scope definition is the Time To Live (TTL), corresponding to the relative distance between the peer hosting the datum and the peer performing the operation in the current topology. This feature adds both inter- and intra-peer flexibility. More precisely: two different peers may have different visions of the global dataspace and the same peer may change its own scope in different retrieval operations.

4   Conclusion and Future Work

In this paper we initiate the design of a data-driven coordination infrastructure suitable for P2P systems; more precisely, we discuss some useful guidelines we intend to follow in the design of this infrastructure.

We plan to continue this line of work along two tightly related directions. On the one hand, we plan to develop a formal specification of the infrastructure, useful to clarify possible design ambiguities as well as to provide a formal framework for property verification.

On the other hand, we intend to verify the feasibility of the proposed model by implementing a prototype based on JXTA [jxt], an open-source P2P project promoted by Sun Microsystems. JXTA is aimed at establishing network programming platform for P2P systems by identifying a small set of basic facilities necessary to support P2P applications and providing them as a building block for high-level functions.

The choice of basing our implementation on JXTA has several benefits. First of all, the JXTA core provides the possibility of using different transport layers for communication, including TCP/IP and HTTP, and is capable of handling firewall- and NAT-related problems. Furthermore, the peer discovery mechanism included in JXTA will be used to enable peers to discover each other in the network and merge their dataspaces. Finally, we will exploit the complex security architecture that is being developed for JXTA, in order to add security mechanisms to our implementation.

References

[And01]   D. Anderson. SETI@home. chapter 5. March 2001.

[BCV01]   M. T. Valente B. Carbunar and J. Vitek. Lime Revisited. Reverse Engneering an Agent Communication Model. In *Proc. of MA'01*, Lectures Notes in Computer Science. Springer-Verlag, Berlin, 2001.

[BZ01]   N. Busi and G. Zavattaro. Some Thoughts on Transiently Shared Dataspaces. In *Proc. on the Workshop on Software Engineering and Mobility (at ICSE 2001)*, 2001.

[CP02]   G. Cugola and G.P. Picco. Peerware: Core middleware support for peer-to-peer and mobile systems. Draft - 2002.

[Gel85]   D. Gelernter. Generative Communication in Linda. *ACM Transactions on Programming Languages and Systems*, 7(1):80–112, 1985.

[jxt]   Project JXTA. http://www.jxta.org.

[K+00]   J. Kubiatowicz et al. OceanStore: An Architecture for Global-Scale Persistent Storage. In *9th International Conference on Architectural support for Programming Languages and Operating Systems*, Cambridge, MA, November 2000.

[Kan01]   G. Kan. Gnutella. chapter 8. March 2001.

[Lan01]   A. Langley. Freenet. chapter 8. March 2001.

[PMR99]   G.P. Picco, A. Murphy, and GC. Roman. Lime: Linda Meets Mobility. In *Proc. 21th IEEE Int. Conf. on Software Engineering (ICSE)*, pages 368–377, 1999.

[RD01]   A. Rowstron and P. Druschel. Storage Management and Caching in PAST, a Large-Scale, Persistent Peer-to-Peer Storage Utility. In *18th*, Canada, November 2001.

[Shi01]   C. Shirky. Listening to Napster. chapter 2. March 2001.

[W+98]   J. Waldo et al. Javaspace specification - 1.0. Technical report, Sun Microsystems, March 1998.

[WMLF98]   P. Wyckoff, S. McLaughry, T. Lehman, and D. Ford. T spaces. *IBM Systems Journal*, 37(3):454–474, 1998.

Towards Adaptive, Resilient and Self-organizing Peer-to-Peer Systems

Alberto Montresor[1], Hein Meling[2], and Özalp Babaoğlu[1]

[1] Department of Computer Science, University of Bologna, Mura Anteo Zamboni 7,
40127 Bologna, (Italy),
{montresor,babaoglu}@CS.UniBO.IT

[2] Department of Telematics, Norwegian University of Science and Technology,
O.S. Bragstadsplass 2A, N-7491 Trondheim (Norway),
meling@item.ntnu.no

Abstract. Peer-to-peer (P2P) systems are characterized by decentralized control, large scale and extreme dynamism of their operating environment. Developing applications that can cope with these characteristics requires a paradigm shift, placing adaptation, resilience and self-organization as primary concerns. In this note, we argue that *complex adaptive systems* (CAS), which have been used to explain certain biological, social and economical phenomena, can be the basis of a programming paradigm for P2P applications. In order to pursue this idea, we are developing Anthill, a framework to support the *design*, *implementation* and *evaluation* of P2P applications based on ideas such as multi-agent and evolutionary programming borrowed from CAS.

1   Introduction

Informally, peer-to-peer systems are distributed systems where all nodes are *peers* in the sense that they have equal role and responsibility. In fact, distributed computing was intended to be synonymous with peer-to-peer computing long before the term was invented, but this initial desire was subverted by the advent of client-server computing popularized by the World Wide Web.

The modern use of the term peer-to-peer (P2P) and distributed computing as intended by its pioneers, however, differ in several important aspects. First, P2P applications reach out to harness the outer edges of the Internet and consequently involve scales that were previously unimaginable. Second, P2P by definition, excludes any form of centralized structure, requiring control to be completely decentralized. Finally, and most importantly, the environments in which P2P applications are deployed exhibit extreme dynamism in structure, content and load. The topology of the system typically changes rapidly due to nodes voluntarily coming and going or due to involuntary events such as crashes and partitions. The load in the system may also shift rapidly from one region to another, for example, as certain files become "hot" in a file sharing system; or the computing needs of a node suddenly increase in a grid computing system.

E. Gregori et al. (Eds.): Networking 2002 Workshops, LNCS 2376, pp. 300–305, 2002.

2   Contribution

In order to deal with the scale and dynamism that characterize P2P systems, a paradigm shift is required that includes self-organization, adaptation and resilience as intrinsic properties rather than as afterthought. In this note, we suggest that *complex adaptive systems* (CAS) commonly used to explain the behavior of certain biological and social systems can be the basis of a programming paradigm for P2P applications. In the CAS framework, a system consists of a large number of relatively simple autonomous computing units, or *agents*. CAS typically exhibit what is called *emergent behavior*: the behavior of the agents, taken individually, may be easily understood, while the behavior of the system as a whole defies simple explanation. In other words, the interactions among agents, in spite of their simplicity, can give rise to richer and more complex patterns than those generated by single agents viewed in isolation.

As an instance of CAS drawn from nature, consider an ant colony. Several species of ants are known to group objects in their environment (e.g., dead corpses) into piles so as to clean up their nests. Observing this behavior, one could be mislead into thinking that the cleanup operation is being coordinated by some "leader" ants. Resnick [7] describes an artificial ant colony exhibiting this very same behavior in a simulated environment. Resnick's artificial ant follows three simple rules: (i) wander around randomly, until it encounters an object; (ii) if it was carrying an object, it drops the object and continues to wander randomly; (iii) if it was not carrying an object, it picks the object up and continues to wander. Despite their simplicity, a colony of these "unintelligent" ants is able to group objects into large clusters, independent of their initial distribution.

What renders CAS particularly attractive from a P2P perspective is the fact that global properties like adaptation, self-organization and resilience are achieved without explicitly embedding them into the individual agents. In the above example, there are no rules specific to initial conditions, unforeseen scenarios, variations in the environment or presence of failures. Yet, given large enough colonies, the global behavior is surprisingly adaptive and resilient.

In order to pursue these ideas, we are developing *Anthill*, a novel framework for P2P application development, based on ideas such as multi-agent systems and evolutionary programming borrowed from CAS [10,6]. The goals of Anthill are to provide an environment that simplifies the design and deployment of P2P systems based on these paradigms, and to provide a "testbed" for studying and experimenting with CAS-based P2P systems in order to understand their properties and evaluate their performance.

In the next sections, we provide an overview of Anthill and we present the first results obtained through it, by presenting a load-balancing algorithm called *Messor*. Messor is a simple variant of the above artificial ant algorithm: ants drop an object they may be carrying only after having wandered about randomly "for a while" without encountering other objects. Colonies of such ants try to disperse objects (in the case of Messor, computational tasks) uniformly over their environment rather than clustering them. As such, they form the basis for a completely decentralized load balancing algorithm.

3   Anthill

Anthill uses terminology derived from the ant colony metaphor. An Anthill distributed system is composed of a self-organizing overlay network of interconnected *nests*. Each nest is a peer entity sharing its computational and storage resources. The network is characterized by the absence of a fixed structure, as nests come and go and discover each other on top of a communication substrate. Nests handle requests originated by local users, by generating one or more *ants* – autonomous agents that travel across the nest network trying to satisfy the request. Ants communicate indirectly by observing and modifying their environment, through information stored in the visited nests. For example, an ant-based implementation of a distributed lookup service could store routing information to guide subsequent ants towards a region of the network where the searched key is more likely to be found.

The aim of Anthill is to simplify P2P application development and deployment by freeing the programmer of all low-level details including communication, security and ant scheduling. Developers wishing to experiment with new protocols need to focus on designing appropriate ant algorithms using the Anthill API and defining the structure of the P2P system. When writing their protocols, developers may exploit a set of library components and services provided by nests. Examples of such services include failure detection, document downloading and ant scheduling for distributed computing applications.

A Java prototype of the Anthill runtime environment has been developed. The runtime environment is based on JXTA [4], an open-source P2P project promoted by Sun Microsystems. JXTA is aimed at establishing a network programming platform for P2P systems by identifying a small set of basic facilities necessary to support P2P applications and providing them as building blocks for higher-level services. The benefits of basing our implementation on JXTA are several. For example, JXTA allows the use of different transport layers for communication, including TCP/IP and HTTP, and deals with issues related to firewalls and NAT.

In addition to the runtime environment, Anthill includes a simulation environment to help developers analyze and evaluate the behavior of P2P systems. All simulation parameters, such as the structure of the network, the ant algorithms to be deployed, characteristics of the workload presented to the system, and properties to be measured, are specified using XML. Unlike other toolkits for multi-agent simulation [5], Anthill uses a single ant implementation in both the simulation and actual run-time environments, thus avoiding the cost of re-implementing ant algorithms before deploying them. This important feature has been achieved by a careful design of the Anthill API and by providing two distinct implementations of it for simulation and deployment.

In Anthill, we further exploit the "nature" metaphor through the use of evolutionary techniques for improving various characteristics of a P2P system. In particular, we make use of genetic algorithms [6] in tuning the ant algorithms used by the P2P system, by specifying optimization criteria and constraints for the parameters of the operating environment and ant algorithms.

4 Messor

The aim of Messor is to support highly parallel computations, such as the one performed by the Seti@Home [9] project, in which the workload may be subdivided in a large number of independent tasks. Unlike Seti@Home [9], however, Messor is not based on the master-slave paradigm, in which a well-known centralized master is responsible for supplying slave machines with computational tasks. In Messor, every node of the network is enabled to produce new tasks and introduce them in the network for computation. A swarm of Messor ants is responsible for exploring the network and balancing the workload by dispersing the tasks among all reachable nodes. Once computed, task results are sent back to the originator node, that may use appropriate mechanisms based on lease techniques to keep track of task assignments, in order to re-insert tasks that have been lost because they were assigned to crashed or partitioned nodes.

The Messor algorithm is a variation of the artificial ant algorithm illustrated in Section 2. Each ant can assume three different states: SearchMax, SearchMin and Transfer. While in the SearchMax state, the ant wanders across the network, looking for overloaded nodes. When a sufficient number of nodes has been visited, the ant switch to SearchMin state, during which the ant wanders across the network looking for underloaded nodes. Again, after a sufficient number of steps, the ant switch to the Transfer state, during which it transfers tasks from the most overloaded node to the most underloaded one, selected among those visited during the SearchMax and SearchMin phases. When the transfer state is completed, the ants switch to SearchMax and the process repeats itself.

The SearchMax and SearchMin walks are not performed completely at random. When wandering, ants collect information about the load of the last visited nodes. This information is stored in the nodes themselves and is used by ants to drive the SearchMax and SearchMin phases: at each step, the ant randomly selects the next node to visit among those that are believed to be more overloaded (in SearchMax) or underloaded (in SearchMin). In this way, ants move faster towards those regions of the network in which they are more interested.

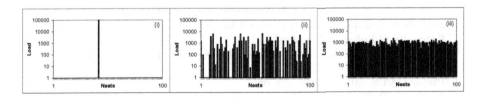

Fig. 1. Load distribution after (i) 0, (ii) 20, (iii) 40 iterations in the simulation.

Figure 1 shows some preliminary results obtained by Messor. More details about the algorithm and its performance can be found in a companion paper [2]. These results were obtained in a network of 100 idle nodes, by generating 100,000 tasks from a single node. At each iteration, all ants perform a single step by executing their algorithm and moving to the next node. As shown in the figure, after only 40 iterations, the workload is evenly balanced among all nodes.

5 Conclusions and Future Work

We have argued that ideas and techniques borrowed from CAS could form the basis for a new paradigm for building P2P systems that are adaptive, resilient and self-organizing. The approach we are advocating is quite different from those adopted in recent P2P routing algorithms [8,11,3] where complex protocols are required to reconfigure the routing tables in the event of nodes joining or leaving (voluntarily or due to crashes) the system. The adaptiveness and resilience of Anthill applications may be traced back to several sources. First, complex systems are composed of large number of entities, each of them interchangeable for another. Moreover, interconnections between entities are flexible, allowing transfer of tasks between entities, and communication throughout the system. Finally, the differences between entities enables a diversity of responses in a changing environment.

Algorithms developed in Anthill are often based on a probabilistic approach, and thus it is difficult to provide guarantees on their behavior. Nevertheless, our preliminary results are indeed interesting; using Anthill, we have implemented the load-balancing application briefly introduced in this paper, and we have realized a file sharing application called *Gnutant*, that again is inspired to the behavior of ants [1]. Gnutant ants builds a distributed index consisting of URLs to documents, by traversing the network looking for documents and leaving information trails to be followed in future searches.

References

1. O. Babaoğlu, H. Meling, and A. Montresor. Anthill: A Framework for the Development of Agent-Based Peer-to-Peer Systems. In *Proc. of the 22th Int. Conf. on Distributed Computing Systems*, Wien, Austria, July 2002.
2. O. Babaoğlu, H. Meling, and A. Montresor. Implementing a Load-Balancing Algorithm in Anthill. Technical Report UBLCS-02-9, Dept. of Computer Science, University of Bologna, Apr. 2002.
3. S. R. et al. A Scalable Content-Addressable Network. In *Proc. of the ACM SIGCOMM'01*, San Diego, CA, 2001.
4. Project JXTA. http://www.jxta.org.
5. N. Minar, R. Burkhart, C. Langton, and M. Askenazi. The Swarm Simulation System, A Toolkit for Building Multi-Agent Simulations. Technical report, Swarm Development Group, June 1996. http://www.swarm.org.
6. M. Mitchell. *An Introduction to Genetic Algorithms*. MIT Press, Apr. 1998.
7. M. Resnick. *Turtles, Termites, and Traffic Jams: Explorations in Massively Parallel Microworlds*. MIT Press, 1994.
8. A. Rowstron and P. Druschel. Pastry: Scalable, Decentralized Object Location and Routing for Large-Scale Peer-to-Peer Systems. In *Proc. of the 18th International Conference on Distributed Systems Platforms*, Heidelberg, Germany, Nov. 2001.

9. SETI@Home Home Page. http://setiathome.ssl.berkeley.edu.
10. G. Weiss. *Multiagent Systems: A Modern Approach to Distributed Artificial Intelligence.* MIT Press, 1999.
11. B. Y. Zhao, J. Kubiatowicz, and A. D. Joseph. Tapestry: An Infrastructure for Fault-Tolerant Wide-Area Location and Routing. Technical Report UCB/CSD-01-1141, U.C. Berkeley, Apr. 2001.

Peer Pressure: Distributed Recovery from Attacks in Peer-to-Peer Systems

Pedram Keyani, Brian Larson, and Muthukumar Senthil

Computer Science Department
Stanford University
Stanford, CA 94305
{pkeyani, balarson, msenthil}@stanford.edu

Abstract. Peer-to-peer systems such as Gnutella are resilient to failures at a single point in the network because of their decentralized nature. However an attack resulting in the removal of a small percentage of highly connected nodes could cripple such systems. We believe that distributed attack recovery is not simply a reactive process but requires proactive measures by the nodes in the system. We propose a distributed recovery method, where clients proactively detect attacks by monitoring the rate at which their first and second-degree neighbors leave the network and reconfigure themselves to form a topology that is more resilient to attacks when one has been detected. This topology is created and maintained through a new type of node discovery mechanism that is used during normal network operations. The recovery method is able to reconnect the network and deal with any ongoing attacks once one has started.

1. Introduction

P2P systems are becoming more prevalent in our lives as the Internet has gained widespread acceptance. Clearly, before we become more reliant on such systems, they must be shown to be secure, and the next generation of P2P applications must be able to survive malicious attacks to the network. Currently, P2P systems are not the subject of widespread attacks, but it is not difficult to envision scenarios where attacks could occur. As an example, it would not be out of line for a major record label to attack Gnutella because one of their songs becomes freely available.

Gnutella is one of the most widely used peer-to-peer (P2P) protocols for file sharing on the Internet. It is a simple protocol for communication between peers (*servants* in Gnutella) to form an overlay network on top of the Internet topology. This protocol does not specify a recovery mechanism, only a format for clients to communicate [7, 9].

The current topology of Gnutella adheres to a power law distribution in which most nodes have few connections, while a small fraction of the nodes have many connections and hold the entire network together [12]. It is this property that makes the Gnutella topology particularly susceptible to malicious attacks on highly connected nodes. By merely removing a small portion of these highly connected nodes, it is possible to fragment the entire network into many isolated pieces [12].

To make matters worse, current clients do not even attempt to detect attacks on the network. Most clients can and do detect failures of neighboring nodes, but

E. Gregori et al. (Eds.): Networking 2002 Workshops, LNCS 2376, pp. 306–320, 2002.

surviving an isolated failure is different from surviving an attack. Furthermore, clients do not have a backup plan that is resistant to attack. This leads to a system extremely vulnerable to malicious attacks and unsuitable for critical applications.

The first step to surviving an attack is detection. It is our position that nodes must be able to detect an attack quickly and without knowledge of the global network topology. Our method for detecting attacks requires nodes to keep track of the rate at which their first-degree-neighbors (direct neighbors) and second-degree-neighbors (neighbors of first-degree-neighbors) leave the network.

It is also our position that nodes must plan for an attack before it happens. Each node needs to discover backup connections during normal network operations and maintain a list of them in case of an attack. Our proposed technique for this requires the addition of a *random discovery ping (RDP)* to the Gnutella protocol. In order to form a more resilient network during an attack, failed neighbors are replaced with the backups discovered using the random node discovery ping during normal operations.

Our results show that this technique reduces fragmentation by more than a factor of 25 times from the standard approach. In addition, our results also show an improvement in querying effectiveness both during and after the attack. Finally, we show that only a small increase in traffic on the network is required to implement our technique.

In section 2 we describe the background to the problem more fully. We describe our proposed solution in section 3. In section 4 we describe the experimental model we used to validate our solution. In section 5 we describe our simulator and show the results of the experiments we ran. Finally, in section 6 we conclude and talk about future work.

2. Problem Background

There are currently a wide variety of decentralized P2P schemes that are highly resilient to failures of random components [15, 17, 18]. Because these systems expand with no centralized planning, they often result in a type of topology that can be severely fragmented by attacking a few nodes that hold the entire network together [2]. Several programs exist that "crawl" the Gnutella network and report its topology, allowing a person to isolate and attack the nodes that keep the network together [16]. Mounting a distributed denial of service attack against these nodes could effectively kill them in a time-span of a few minutes [11, 13].

It has been shown that if 4% of the most highly connected nodes are removed from Gnutella, the network will severely fragment, rendering it useless [12]. Gnutella's robustness to random failure and vulnerability to malicious attack is not unique. Indeed, the Internet has similar characteristics; an attack on 5% of nodes would result in the total collapse of the Internet [14].

2.1 Gnutella Network Topology

Many real-world networks fall into a class of inhomogeneous networks called *scale-free networks*, where a few nodes have many connections, but most nodes have only a few connections [3]. Scale-free networks abide by the power-law relationship, $P(k) \sim k^{-a}$, where $P(k)$ gives the probability that a node is connected to k other nodes [2]. It has been shown that networks such as the Internet, the WWW, and Gnutella tend to self-organize into scale-free topologies that abide by the power law [1, 3, 8, 10, 12].

There are two mechanisms that cause the formation of scale-free topologies. First, networks expand continuously by the addition of new vertices, and second, new vertices attach preferentially to vertices that are already well connected [3]. In Gnutella, the first mechanism can be seen by the fact that new nodes are continuously entering and leaving the system, meaning the topology is undergoing constant change and growth. The second mechanism can be seen by the fact that there are only a few hosts that clients initially connect to, due to the way bootstrapping is handled (further discussed in section 4.1). Furthermore, clients preferentially attach to stable, high bandwidth nodes. Hence, the topology of the Gnutella network is scale-free because of its adherence to these two mechanisms.

Failures in P2P systems are viewed as nodes suddenly and unexpectedly dropping out of the network. Scale-free networks such as Gnutella are very robust to failures of random nodes. This robustness is rooted in the inhomogeneous nature of the network. Nodes with few connections will fail with much greater probability than nodes with many connections [2]. Unfortunately, the same inhomogeneous nature of scale-free networks that makes them robust to random failures makes them vulnerable to an attack resulting in the removal of the most highly connected nodes.

2.2 Failure and Attack Detection

Failure detection is the process of detecting isolated random failures of peers on the network. Current Gnutella clients detect a failure when one of their neighbors stops responding to them unexpectedly. The only information that can be derived from this process of detection is that a neighbor has died. There is no indication of how significant the neighbor was in terms of connections to other nodes and how important it was in holding the graph together.

Attack detection, on the other hand, is the process of detecting an attack on the network as a whole. Methods for attack detection could take into account the importance of nodes being lost in the system or the frequency of node loss. Attack detection is necessary for any system where mounting an attack is a relatively easy and inexpensive task.

Responding to failures is very different from responding to attacks because of the nature of the nodes that are lost. If a small percentage of nodes at the core of a network were attacked, clients responding only to the failure of these nodes would not address the severity of the problem. A system that cannot detect an attack has little chance of surviving it.

2.3 Attack Backup Plans

Most Gnutella clients maintain a "cache" of host names, which they have communicated with within a certain time period. These cached hosts are often used as replacements for failures, but they make poor replacements for attacked nodes. If a client does detect an attack in progress, and connects to hosts in the cache as a response, hosts that most recently sent queries through the network would appear in thousands of caches. This means they could be overwhelmed by connection requests, or even become targets of the attack themselves. It becomes very clear that a backup plan must be picked that is resistant to further attacks.

One network topology that is more resilient to attacks is an exponential network [2]. An exponential network is a homogenous network where each node has roughly the same number of links k. Instead of following the power law, $P(k)$ peaks at k and decays exponentially, following the Poisson distribution [2]. Exponential networks are built by connecting random neighbors together with no preference of one node over another. In this configuration, it is improbable that any one node is holding the network together. The homogeneous nature of exponential networks makes them much less vulnerable to attacks on a small number of nodes than scale-free networks.

3. Recovery Method

We would like to have a recovery method that prevents the network from becoming fragmented by an attack and prevents the decrease in querying effectiveness during the attack. By querying effectiveness, we mean the number of neighbors that can be reached with a query.

We would like to be able to reconfigure the topology of the network from scale-free to exponential in order to survive an attack, since exponential networks fare much better than scale free networks under attack on a small percentage of nodes [2]. Our solution is to maintain a virtual exponential overlay network in addition to the active scale free overlay network used by the system. We refer to the network as virtual since connections between nodes on the network will not be made and no query traffic will be sent over the network.

Reconfiguration of the topology to exponential requires nodes to discover other nodes randomly, but this reconfiguration must be done before the network becomes fragmented from the attack. Each node will maintain a list of virtual neighbors in addition to the node's active neighbors, and they will be selected using a process for random node discovery that we have developed. Because there are no preferential connections, these random connections will constitute an exponential network.

The virtual exponential network will be used in place of the active scale-free network during an attack, which each node in the network is responsible for detecting. When a node detects an attack, the node will begin replacing its dead neighbors with nodes from its virtual neighbor list, thus making the exponential network active as the scale free network disintegrates as a result of the attack. By combining these two types of network topologies, we will have the robustness of scale-free networks to failure coupled with the robustness of exponential networks to attack.

3.1 Random Node Discovery

Our recovery mechanism requires that nodes be able to discover random nodes in the system with little or no preference in order to construct an exponential network. An optimal solution would allow for any node in the network to be chosen with equal probability, a task that could be accomplished by a centralized name authority. In a decentralized system such as Gnutella, maintaining a database of all active nodes in the system would be difficult, if not impossible.

Our solution is for nodes to forward a message randomly through the network for a certain number of hops. This message, which we will call a random discovery ping, will be similar to a Gnutella ping. An RDP contains an originating node, a hop count, and is forwarded from node to node through the network. The final node that receives the RDP, determined when the hop count is decremented to one, will respond with a pong and is thus discovered. This node will then be added to the virtual neighbor list maintained by the originating node.

While standard Gnutella pings are forwarded by a node to all of its neighbors, an RDP is only forwarded to one of the node's neighbors. This will allow us to use a much larger time to live (TTL), thus getting deeper into the network without overwhelming the network with ping traffic. In our implementation, random discovery pings are created with a TTL of 20. This number is a good approximation of the diameter of the Gnutella network [6], so this will enable a ping to reach any node in the network. Acknowledgment messages are used to ensure that an RDP is not lost.

Initially a node forwards an RDP to a neighbor N selected randomly with probability scaling linearly with the number of neighbors that N has. This means that a node with 6 neighbors is 3 times as likely to have the ping forwarded to it than a node with 2 neighbors. This strategy is used for the first 10 hops in order to get the ping as far away from the originating node as possible (we want to have the node connect outside its immediate vicinity). If this strategy is not used, in most cases the ping is only forwarded within the immediate vicinity of the originating node, cycling around the originating node's most connected neighbor many times.

For the next 10 hops, the opposite strategy is used. The ping is forwarded to nodes with lower number of neighbors, meaning that a node with 6 neighbors is 1/3 times as likely to have the ping forwarded to it than a node with 2 neighbors. If this strategy is not used, then the nodes with the most neighbors will be selected with a frequency scaling with their connectivity. This is not what we desire because it replicates the preferential attachment property of the scale-free active network.

3.2 Maintenance of Virtual Exponential Network

The process by which each node discovers and maintains a certain number of virtual neighbors globally maintains an exponential network. Nodes are discovered by creating and forwarding an RDP, as outlined in section 3.1. Although this is not specified in the Gnutella protocol, all clients have a range of neighbors <X, Y> and must maintain at least X neighbors. Similar to active neighbors, virtual neighbors are maintained through periodic pings, or heartbeats, which must be responded with a pong by the neighbor if it is alive [7, 9]. This allows nodes to detect the liveliness of their virtual neighbors. If a node's virtual neighbor is found to be dead or a node has less than the minimum number of virtual neighbors, then the node discovers a new random node.

3.3 Attack Detection

One of our goals in creating an attack detection mechanism was to minimize the amount of coordination between nodes. Our attack detection scheme leverages the information that a node has of its immediate neighbors (1st degree) and their neighbors (2nd degree), and is based on measuring changes in this local topology.

From the viewpoint of a node in the network, an attack will most likely result in the removal of the most highly connected of its 1st degree neighbors. The removal of highly connected neighbors will be the most detrimental to the node because they contain a disproportionate amount of its 2nd degree neighbors.

For example, consider the node shown in black in figure 1A. This node has three 1st degree neighbors, which are show in gray. One of the neighbors has 3 connections (not counting the node itself), one has 5, and one has 12. This means the node has a total of 20 2nd degree neighbors, which are shown in white. Figure 1B shows what would happen if the neighbor with 12 connections is removed, such as might happen during an attack on the network. The node will lose 12 of its 20 2nd degree neighbors, or 60%. However, the node only lost 33% of its 1st degree neighbors.

Now consider what happens if one of the neighbors is removed at random, such as in the case of a failure. The average number of 2nd degree neighbors the node will lose is 6.67, or 33%. This is the same as the percentage of 1st degree neighbors lost. Clearly, in an attack a node will lose a greater percentage of its 2nd degree neighbors than 1st degree neighbors. This is different from random failures, where the percentage of 1st and 2nd degree neighbors lost will be roughly equal.

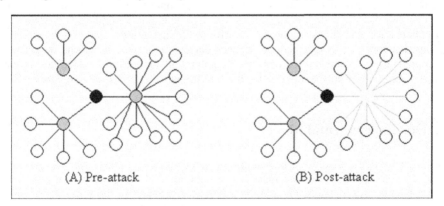

(A) Pre-attack   (B) Post-attack

Fig. 1. Attack detection example

Our attack detection mechanism requires nodes to maintain the number of 1st and 2nd degree neighbors lost during a specified time period T. These losses will be used to calculate the percentage of 1st and 2nd degree neighbors lost during this period. If the percentage of 2nd degree neighbors lost is greater than the percentage of 1st degree neighbors lost, and greater than a threshold P, an attack is detected. The threshold P is used to filter out false positives where some of a node's neighbors fail at random, but the total percentage of 2nd degree neighbors lost is very small. In our implementation, we used a value of 30 seconds for T and a value of 50% for P.

We have performed some initial experiments varying T and P in order to find optimal values for them but surprisingly have not seen much variation in behavior. We have explored values for P ranging from 90% to 10%. Attack detection rates increase as P decreases, but the detection rate increase is very slight. Varying P anywhere from 80% to 20% makes only about a 5% difference in detection rate, while dropping P below 20% results in increasing amounts of false positives. We have also explored values for T ranging between 10 seconds and 2 minutes. Increasing T from 10 seconds to 1 minute tends to increase attack detection rate a small amount, but increasing T above 1 minute makes nodes increasingly "paranoid" and increases the amounts of false positives. Our initial results show that our values for T and P may not be optimal, but they are within 5% of the best attack detection rates we have been able to generate without seeing false positives.

3.4 Reacting to Attacks

The virtual exponential network will be used in place of the active scale free network during an attack. Upon detecting a malicious attack, a node will begin replacing its dead neighbors with nodes from its virtual neighbor list, thus making the exponential network active as the scale free network disintegrates due to the attack. Also after detection, the node counts the number of neighbors that have failed recently and replaces each of these with a virtual neighbor. The node creates an active connection with the virtual neighbor and removes it from the list of virtual neighbors. During the attack, the node replaces each neighbor that dies with another virtual neighbor, until the node determines that the attack is over, or it runs out of virtual neighbors. Also, it is important that the node not seek out new virtual neighbors to replace its lost virtual neighbors during an attack, as the extra traffic would increase the stress on the already failing network. Once a node no longer detects an attack, it returns to normal operations using its current list of active neighbors, including those added during the attack. As a part of normal operations, it rebuilds a new list of virtual neighbors.

4. Our Experimental Model

Before we propose a solution to making the protocol more robust, it is necessary to describe some assumptions we make about Gnutella and the corresponding models that we built. As it stands, Gnutella is a very free protocol in the sense that it only prescribes the types of messages sent between nodes and leaves the remainder up to the client [7]. Some of the open properties of Gnutella include bootstrapping, the number of neighbors maintained be each node, the up-time distributions of nodes, and the initial topology. We model the first two properties (bootstrapping and number of neighbors maintained by each node) by adopting the method used by the most common Gnutella client, Bearshare [4]. For the up and down time distributions we use a power law relationship fitted to measurements of node uptimes, and for the initial topology we use data collected through crawling the network [12].

4.1 Bootstrapping

There are many ways that Gnutella clients handle bootstrapping. This used to be done by connecting to a well-known point, Gnutellahosts.com, which maintained a list of servants with high availabilities that were likely to accept incoming connections [12]. On a connection from a newcomer, gnutellahosts.com returned one of these available servers. Bearshare works similarly in the sense that clients connect to a well-known Bearshare server (public.bearshare.net) and receive a list of servants from it [4]. Clients then directly connect to these servants.   This preferential connection mechanism is responsible for the construction of a scale-free topology.

4.2 Number of Connections

The number of connections that a node maintains is not specified by the Gnutella protocol, so it is entirely left up to the specific client. Also finding out which client a node is running is not a trivial problem. We believe that a reasonable thing to do here is adopt the default value used by one of the most popular clients, BearShare. This client is set with a default max of 10 and min of 3 neighbors to maintain. We use these max and min values in modeling our nodes in our experiments.

4.3 Initial Topology

All of our experiments are based on a measured Gnutella topology that contains nodes that have been up for a 12-hour period [12]. This data contains roughly 3,000 active nodes and the edges between them.   We built an initial topology by adding 17,000 nodes to this base topology using the bootstrapping and uptime models discussed above, resulting in a network with roughly 20,000 nodes alive at any given time.

4.4 Up and Down Time Distributions

A study of Gnutella shows that there are somewhere between 10,000 and 30,000 nodes that are alive at any given time slice [6]. Our initial topology contains 3,000 nodes that are alive during the course of a 12-hour period. We model the uptime distribution using the power law

$$P(t) = t^{-a} \, , \tag{1}$$

where $P(t)$ is the probability that a node is up for time t. The power law is an accurate model to use, because the majority of Gnutella nodes are up momentarily while fewer and fewer are up progressively longer. We conservatively estimate that the shortest period of time a node can be up is 1 minute, since our experience shows this to be the time required to sign on and off from the system.

4.5 Simulation and Data Collection

The results we use to measure the effectiveness of our recovery method were generated using a general P2P network simulator that we have created. The simulator provides a framework for maintaining peers and delivering messages between them. It includes support for peers joining the network, peers leaving the network, and removing peers suddenly from the network. This last feature allows us to simulate an attack by removing the most highly connected peers. To simulate Gnutella, we created two Gnutella clients compatible with the simulator: one based on Bearshare with the base caching and failure recover methods, and another with the additional attack detection and recovery method built into it. We ran our experiments using the models and topology information described above to generate the results presented in the following sections.

4.6 Experiments

We ran two versions of our experiment: a control case with the base recovery method, and a test case with the attack recovery method enabled. Each version was run 10 times and plotted on a 95% confidence interval. In our experiment, we simulate an attack on the network as removal of 5% of the most highly connected nodes. We removed these nodes over a period of 5 minutes, a period measured as a common length for denial of service attacks [11]. Experiments were run for 10 minutes, with the attack starting at 2 minutes.

5. Results

We chose metrics that would represent the fragmentation of the system, and end-to-end performance of the system from the point of view of a user. To measure fragmentation in the system, we calculated the percentage of living nodes in the largest connected component. A connected component is a set of nodes where a path exists between all pairs of nodes [5]. This measure shows whether the majority of nodes are in one connected component, or fragmenting off into other clusters of nodes. Another measure of fragmentation is the number of connected components, which measures the difficulty of rebuilding the network after the attack has done its damage. To measure end user performance, we calculated the average number of nodes reachable within 6 hops of any node as a percentage of the total number of living nodes. We chose 6 hops, because it is roughly the maximum hop count used when performing a search [6]. Because Gnutella is mainly used for searching and downloading files, this metric gives us an end-to-end measurement of the average number of nodes a user will be able reach with a query.

5.1 Connected Component Results

Figure 2 shows the percentage of living nodes that are in the largest connected component. These results show that without our recovery method, this percentage drops significantly from nearly 100% to below 30% in less than 30 seconds after the attack begins. With our recovery method in place, this metric stays almost constant, initially dipping to just above 98% before quickly returning to the 99.9% range. This initial dip is due to the delay between the beginning of the attack and the detection of the attack by individual nodes. Once nodes start detecting the attack, they are able to keep the network from fragmenting and maintain a very high percentage of nodes in the most highly connected component.

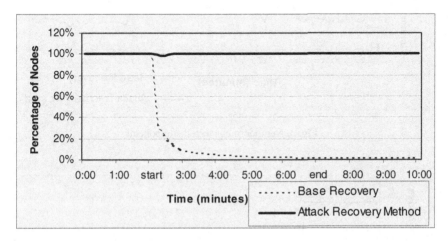

Fig. 2. Percentage of nodes in the largest connected component

Figure 3 shows the number of connected components in the system over time. The steady state value measured is close to 5 before the attack, counting the largest connected component and a few nodes that have just come online but have not bootstrapped onto the network yet. These results show that without our recovery method the number of connected components increases very rapidly as soon as the attack begins, yielding hundreds of network fragments. With our recovery method, there is an increase in the number of connected components during the attack as more nodes are temporarily split from the network, but it returns to the initial steady state after the attack.

5.2 Average Percentage of Neighbors Reachable in 6 Hops

Figure 4 shows the average percentage of nodes reachable within 6 hops in the network. Again, the results show that without our recovery method this percentage drops off significantly from roughly 25% before the attack to under 1% in just 30 seconds. With our recovery method, this percentage drops below 4% initially but begins to recover immediately. The initial drop in nodes reachable within 6 hops is still severe as a result of the most connected parts of the network being removed, but the recovery method is able to increase this measurement to 12% over the length of the attack. Our method shows a return to roughly half of the pre-attack performance of the system in terms of query effectiveness.

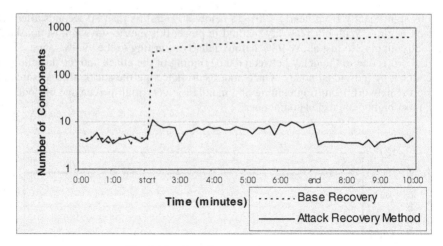

Fig. 3. Number of connected components

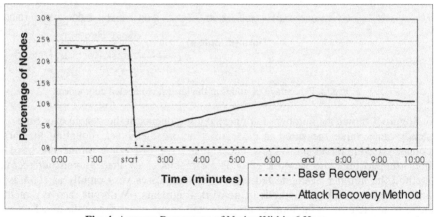

Fig. 4. Average Percentage of Nodes Within 6 Hops

5.3 Random Node Discovery

Figure 5 shows the effectiveness of RDPs in discovering nodes in a non-preferential way. The number of times a node is selected, or frequency, is plotted against the percentage of nodes having this frequency. The binomial distribution, showing the results for node selection by random independent trials, is plotted against the distribution measured using RDPs. These results show that our node discovery technique succeeds in selecting nodes in a non-preferential way in order to form an exponential network.

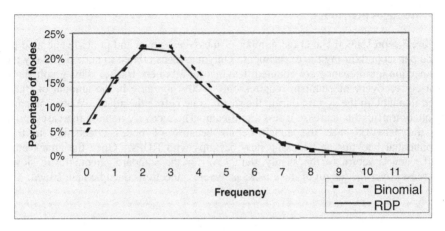

Fig. 5. Frequency distribution for number of connections

5.4 Attack Detection Mechanism

Figure 6 shows the effectiveness of our attack detection mechanism at differentiating random failures in the network from true attacks. In this experiment, 5% of the nodes were removed over a period of 5 minutes as discussed in our experimental setup, but the way in which nodes were selected was varied. The solid line shows the attack detection rates if the most highly connected nodes are removed, while the dotted line shows the rates if random nodes are removed. Less than 1% of the nodes detect an attack when removing random nodes, compared to as many as 14% when removing highly connected nodes. Also, it is noteworthy to mention that no attack is detected outside of the attack interval, despite nodes entering and leaving the system constantly.

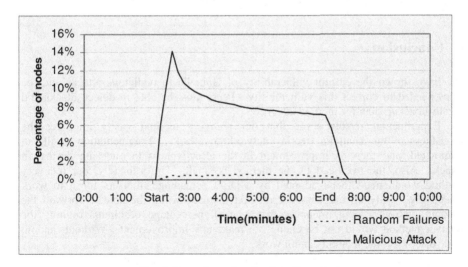

Fig. 6. Percentage of nodes detecting attacks

5.5 Messages per Node

Figure 7 represents the average number of messages (pings and pongs) generated per node per second during the experiment. Only messages related to node discovery and connection maintenance are counted, leaving out all query traffic. This graph shows that our recovery mechanism requires only a 20% increase in the amount of traffic used to maintain the system during the steady state before the attack. When compared to query traffic, this increase is less significant. The recovery method increases traffic on the network once the attack begins because of nodes connecting to their exponential backups and seeking new backups with RDPs. Once the attack ends, traffic levels return to the steady state. As for the standard client, traffic slowly decreases over the length of the attack, as fewer connections must be maintained.

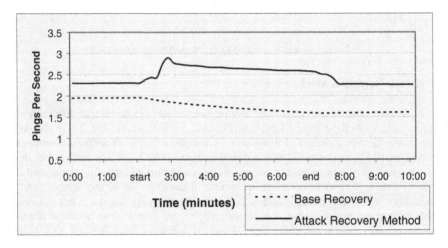

Fig. 7. Average number of pings

6. Conclusions

We have shown the current vulnerability of Gnutella to malicious attacks and the steps needed to correct this vulnerability. Peers must be able to detect attacks and create a backup plan for them in advance.

Experimental results show that our recovery method vastly improves the robustness of the Gnutella overlay network to attacks. Fragmentation is all but eliminated, and there is improvement in the effectiveness in querying during an attack. Also, the overhead of the method is small. Unfortunately, our recovery method would need to be adopted by a large percentage of users for it to work effectively. Only clients with our method in place would be able to forward the random discovery ping, meaning that a small percentage of clients running the recover method would not be enough to make any improvement. Without random node discovery, the method cannot work.

Our recovery method has an advantage that there is very little incentive to lie, an important quality given that peers tend to deliberately misrepresent themselves if there is any incentive to do so [12]. The only additional information that peers need to report is the number of connections they have. Reporting this as too high would lessen the likelihood of a peer being connected to a backup neighbor during an attack, while reporting this as too low would give the peer too many backups during an attack and potentially make it a target. Also, this information is something that peers can easily measure if an incentive to lie existed.

7. Future Work

We believe there are certain aspects of our recovery method that can be studied in greater detail. For example, we would like to investigate other techniques for random node discovery. Another area that we would like to look into is bringing the network back to a scale-free topology after an attack is over. Our initial premise was that exponential networks are better at surviving attacks, but a scale-free topology is ideal for handling normal operation including query forwarding and surviving random failures. Finally, we would like to finish our experiments, varying the parameters of the attack detection mechanism in order to find their optimal values.

A potential limitation of our recovery method is that it fails to take into account how suitable a given peer is for the task assigned to it [12]. In our method, this relates to the suitability of a peer selected as a backup to hold the network together during an attack. Much of the recovery work is done by the least highly connected nodes, which may be dialup users who are unable to handle the added stress during attacks, or users who are unwilling to handle the added stress. This limitation is lessened given the high redundancy of the exponential backups but is still a potential problem that we did not model.

Acknowledgments

We would like to thank Stefan Saroiu and Steven Gribble for providing us with topological data they collected on Gnutella. Armando Fox and George Candea are our advisors on this project, and without their advice our work would have been much harder. Finally, we would like to thank Jim Gray and Brendan Murphy for their advice on this project.

References

1   W. Aiello, F. Chung, and L Lu. "A Random Graph Model for Massive Graphs." Symposium of Theory of Computing, 2000.
2   R. Albert, H. Jeong, and A. Barabási, "Error and attack tolerance in complex networks," Nature 406
3   A. Barabási and R. Albert, "Emergence of scaling in random networks," *Science*, 286
4   http://www.bearshare.com/
5   F. Buckley and F. Harary, *Distance in Graphs*. Addison-Wesley, New York, 1990.

6   www.clip2.com, Gnutella Measurement Project
7   http://www.clip2.com/GnutellaProtocol04.pdf
8   C. Faloutsos, M. Faloutsos and P. Faloutsos, "On power-law relationships of the Internet Topology," Proc. of ACM SIGCOMM, Aug. 1999.
9   http://www.gnutelliums.com/linux_unix/gnut/doc/gnutella-prot.html
10 A. Medina, I. Matta and J. Byers, "On the Origin of Power Laws in Internet Topologies," ACM Computer Communication Review, vol. 30, no. 2 , Apr. 2000
11 D. Moore, G. Voelker, and S. Savage, "Inferring Internet Denial-of-Service Activity," in Proceedings of the 2001 USENIX Security Symposium.
12 S. Saroiu, P. Krishna Gummadi, and S. Gribble, "A measurement study of peer-to-peer file sharing systems," Technical Report UW-CSE-01-06-02, University of Washington, June 2001.
13 http://www.denialinfo.com/
14 R. Cohen, K. Erez, D. ben-Avraham and S. Havlin, "Breakdown of the Internet under intentional attack," Phys. Rev. Lett. 86, 3682 (2001)
15 B. Yang and H. Garcia-Molina, "Comparing hybrid peer-to-peer systems," In Proceedings of the 27th International Conference on Very Large Databases, September 2001.
16 M. Ripeanu, I. Foster and A. Iamnitchi, "Mapping the Gnutella Network: Properties of Large-Scale Peer-to-Peer Systems and Implications for System", IEEE Internet Computing Journal special issue on peer-to-peer networking, vol. 6(1) 2002.
17 B. Y. Zhao, J. D. Kubiatowicz, and A. D. Joseph, "Tapestry: An infrastructure for fault-resilient wide-area location and routing", Technical Report U. C. Berkeley, April 2001.
18 A. Rowstone, P. Druschel, "Pastry: Scalable, distributed object location and routing for large-scale peer-to-peer systems", in Middleware, 2001

Implementing a Reputation-Aware Gnutella Servent

Fabrizio Cornelli[1], Ernesto Damiani[1], Sabrina De Capitani di Vimercati[2], Stefano Paraboschi[3], and Pierangela Samarati[1]

[1] Dipartimento di Tecnologie dell'Informazione, Università di Milano, Via Bramante 65, 26013 Crema (CR), Italy, fcornelli@crema.unimi.it, {damiani,samarati}@dti.unimi.it
[2] Dipartimento di Elettronica per l'Automazione, Università di Brescia, Via Branze 38, 25123 Brescia (BS), Italy, decapita@ing.unibs.it
[3] Dipartimento di Elettronica e Informazione, Politecnico di Milano, Via Ponzio 34/5, 20133 Milano, Italy, parabosc@elet.polimi.it

Abstract. We describe the design and implementation of a reputation-aware servent for Gnutella-like peer-to-peer systems.

1 Introduction

Peer-to-peer (P2P) architectures have recently become the subject of considerable interest, both in the population of Internet users and in the research community [4,6,7,8,9,10,11,17]. Internet users find in P2P applications a convenient solution for the anonymous exchange of resources. The research community has looked with interest to the huge success that these applications were achieving and it has started to investigate many issues that arise in this context, like performance, usability, and robustness [2,6,12,13]. These architectures appear as an interesting paradigm for the development of many novel network applications.

One of the urgent issues to be investigated is the definition of security mechanisms that would permit to reduce the risks that are currently faced by users of these applications [1]. Anonymity of the interaction is one of the major reasons of the success of these solutions, but it usually implies that no guarantee can be assumed on the quality of resources available on the network. In previous work we have designed a protocol [3] that focused on this issue and offered a mechanism that, even in the presence of anonymous participants, permits to ask the user community an opinion on a particular node. The *reputation* [10] of the node can then be the basis on which a user can assess the risk of using a resource retrieved by the network. The protocol is designed following traditional guidelines for secure protocols and is robust against attacks by malicious users, who can badmouth reputable nodes or try to build a good reputation for a tampered with resource.

In [3] we presented the main features of the protocol. In this paper we discuss the implementation of the protocol and its integration with a P2P application.

E. Gregori et al. (Eds.): Networking 2002 Workshops, LNCS 2376, pp. 321–334, 2002.

2   P2PRep **Protocol**

In a traditional Gnutella interchange, a servent p looking for a resource broadcasts to all its neighbors a `Query` message reporting the search keywords. Each servent receiving the `Query` and with resources matching the request, responds with a `QueryHit` message. The `QueryHit` message includes the number of files *num_hits* that matched the keywords, a set of triples *Result* containing the files' names and related information, the *speed* in Kb/second of the responder, the *servent_id* of the responder, a *trailer* with application-specific data, and the pair ⟨IP,port⟩ to be used to download the files. Based on the offers' quality (e.g., number of hits and declared connection speed), as well as on possible preference criteria, p then chooses the servent from which to execute the download and directly contacts it for the download.

Our proposal, called P2PRep, enhances this process by providing a *reputation-based* protocol by which p can assess the reliability of an offerer before actually downloading a resource from it. The basic idea is very simple. After a servent downloads a resource from another servent, it can record whether or not the download has completed to its satisfaction. Before downloading a resource from another servent, a servent can poll its peers about their knowledge of the offerer, thus assessing its reputation. If that offerer is then chosen, the downloading servent can update its local recording of both the offerer (recording whether the downloaded resource was satisfactory or not) and the peers that expressed an opinion on it (recording whether their opinion on the offerer matched the final outcome – *credibility*).

The realization of the protocol requires some considerations. First, in order to keep track of a servent's reputation and credibility, identifiers' persistency must be assumed. In traditional Gnutella, the identifier with which a servent presents itself can, in principle, change at every session. However, a servent wishing to establish some reputation as offerer or voter is encouraged to maintain its identifier persistent. Note that this does not imply that the servent's identity is disclosed, as the declared identifier works only as a pseudonym (opaque identifier).[1] Second, care must be taken to ensure confidentiality and integrity of the messages being exchanged. To this purpose, our protocol uses public key encryption. In particular, a servent's identifier is assumed to be the digest of a public key, obtained using a secure hash function, and for which the servent knows the corresponding private key. Exchanged messages are assumed to be signed with a secret key established by the sender (when integrity must be ensured) and encrypted with a public key established by the recipient (when message confidentiality must be ensured). The key ring used to these purposes can be the pair associated with a servent's identifier or can be generated ad-hoc for the exchange (if the identifier of the involved servent is not to be disclosed).

---

[1] The ability of changing pseudonyms at any time, makes it possible for malicious peers to not be recognized from one interaction to another simply by changing their identifier. This is not a problem as by changing their identifiers, such peers will start as new, with no reputation at all, and they are therefore unlikely to be chosen.

Protocol 1 P2PRep *protocol*

Initiator: Servent p
Peers: Participants in the message broadcasting, among which a set O of offerers and a set V of voters

INITIATOR
Phase 1: Resource searching
(G)   1.1 Start a search request by broadcasting a `Query` message
            `Query`($min\_speed, search\_string$)
(G)   1.2 Receive a set of offers from offerers O
            `QueryHit`($num\_hits, port, IP, speed, Result, trailer, servent\_id_i$)
Phase 2: Polling
        2.1 Select top list $T \subseteq O$ of offerers
        2.2 Generate a pair of public, secret keys (PK_{poll}, SK_{poll})
        2.3 Poll peers about the reputations of offerers T
            `Poll`(T, PK_{poll})
        2.4 Receive a set of votes from voters V
            `PollReply`($\{([(IP, port, Votes, servent\_id_i)]_{SK_i}, PK_i)\}_{PK_{poll}}$)
Phase 3: Vote evaluation
        3.1 Remove from V voters that appear suspicious (e.g., checking IP addresses)
        3.2 Select a random set $V' \subseteq V$ of voters and check their identity by sending message
            `AreYou`($servent\_id_j$)
        3.3 Expect back confirmation messages from each selected voter
            `AreYouReply`($response$)
Phase 4: Resource downloading
        4.1 Select servent s from which download files
        4.2 Generate a random string r
        4.3 Send a `challenge` message to s
            `challenge`(r)
        4.4 Receive a `response` message from s containing its public key PK_s and the challenge signed with its private key SK_s
            `response`($[r]_{SK_s}, PK_s$)
        4.5 If the challenge-response exchange fails terminate the process
(G)   4.6 Download the files
        4.7 Update experience and credibility repository

PEERS
        Q.1 Upon receiving a search request (`Query` message), check if any locally stored files match the query and if so send a `QueryHit` message
        Q.2 Broadcast the query through the P2P network

        P.1 Upon receiving a poll request (`Poll` message), check if know any of the servents listed in the poll request and express an opinion on them by sending a `PollReply` message
        P.2 Broadcast the poll request through the P2P network
        P.3 Upon receiving an `AreYou` message, confirm the identity by sending an `AreYouReply`

Fig. 1. Sequence of messages and operations in the P2PRep protocol

Figure 1 illustrates the operations executed and the messages exchanged in the context of a P2PRep enhanced interaction. In the figure, a "**(G)**" at the beginning of a step indicates that the step pertains to traditional Gnutella interchange; unmarked steps are peculiar to our protocol. The application of encryption is indicated with notations $[text]_{SK}$, when *text* is signed with private key SK, and $\{text\}_{PK}$, when *text* is encrypted with public key PK.

From the point of view of the servent looking for the resource, the protocol can be separated in four phases: *1) resource searching, 2) polling, 3) vote evaluation*, and *4) resource downloading*. Resource searching works like in a traditional Gnutella interchange. Then, in phase 2, p determines, based on some preference criteria, a top list of offerers and broadcasts a `Poll` message requesting peers to vote on them. In the message, p also includes a public key PK_{poll} with which voters are requested to encrypt their replies to the poll (so to maintain the confidentiality of the votes when transiting on the network). Before encrypting their votes with PK_{poll} for transmission, voters will sign them with their secret key. This allows p to assess the authenticity of the votes and also that they have not been modified in transit. Phase 3 evaluates collected votes identifying possible cliques under the control of individual servents, discards suspicious votes, and selects a random set of voters which are contacted directly, via the pair ⟨IP,port⟩ they declared, to assess the correct origin of votes. Based on the election outcome, p can decide the servent from which download the resources. The actual download is preceded by a challenge-response handshake between p and the selected servent. In this way p makes sure that it is actually talking to the servent corresponding to the declared identity. (The challenge-response exchange exploits the fact that a servent's identifier is a digest of its public key). After the download completes, and based on its outcome, p updates its local repositories where it maintains its own view of peers' reputation and credibility.

Figure 1 also reports the operations of the other peers in the network. Peers, beside flooding the messages to others according to the Gnutella protocol, can originate responses by responding to queries as resource offerers (step Q.1) or to polls as voters (steps P.1 and P.2).

P2PRep was designed to be robust against most well-known security threats posed to reputation-based systems on anonymous P2P networks. *Pseudospoofing* and *shilling* are two typical attacks to reputations [10], both exploiting the fact that on a P2P network peers' identities are not certified by any global authority. In pseudo-spoofing attacks, a malicious peer alleges that many witnesses are ready to vouch for its reputation, and produces a false witness list by forging the witness identities. In shilling attacks, a malicious peer actually creates and activates a number of false witnesses, ready to vouch for it. Recently, the term *sybil attacks* [5] has been proposed to designate all attacks of this kind. Our approach does not try to prevent all sybil attacks completely; rather, P2PRep tries to prevent pseudospoofing and increase the cost of shilling. Pseudospoofing prevention is obtained by checking the IP addresses of part of the peers that voted in favor of a servent: if a voter is not on line, its vote is eliminated from the poll. On the other hand, the choice of the IP addresses to be checked is not random, but relies on an evaluation of their heterogeneity [16]. While our technique can indeed be beaten, doing so would require a malicious peer to incur in the cost of setting up false witnesses having highly heterogeneous IP addresses. Increases in IP address reliability may make this task potentially very difficult.

3   Design and Implementation of a P2PRep Enhanced Servent

Component-based techniques are widely used for designing and implementing distributed software systems. We relied on component-based design both to re-

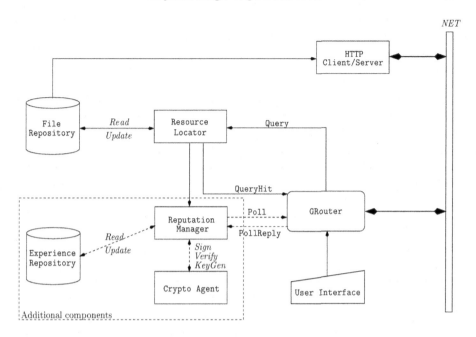

Fig. 2. Typical component-based structure of a Gnutella servent

verse engineer and complement the internal structure of a Gnutella servent to support reputations.

3.1 P2PRep Extensions to Gnutella Servents

Figure 2 shows the modular structure of a Gnutella servent; the dotted line encloses three additional components that are not present in ordinary servents but are needed to support the P2PRep protocol.

- The **Reputation Manager** manages all the new messages needed to send and receive reputation values.
- The **Experience Repository** is a repository (see Section 3.2) storing the experience values accumulated during past interactions with respect to reputations and credibilities.
- The **Crypto Agent** implements all encryption functions used in the protocol. This component must generate the key pair used in the asymmetric protocol.[2]

Besides adding the auxiliary software components listed above, some minor changes to existing components must be introduced in order to manage

---

[2] In our current prototype we use RSA with 512 bits keys. This key can be encoded in 128 bytes, substituting 8 bits with two bytes in the set: $(0 - 9, A - F)$. This substitution is done whenever the field is a null-terminated string. The MD5 digest algorithm is used, producing signatures of 128 bits, encodable in 16 or 32 bytes.

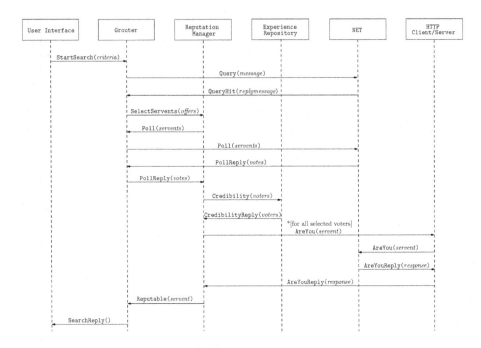

Fig. 3. UML Sequence diagram of a search session

reputation-related messages. Message routing in itself requires no changes: reputation-related messages can be routed as usual, because they are piggybacked on currently defined messages (Section 3.3). However, the part of GRouter that unpacks incoming messages should now recognize new unicast and multicast messages. This modification can be done quite easily in most current implementations.

The method invocations' sequence of a file search is summarized in Figure 3. The User Interface sends a Query message to the GRouter containing the search criteria. The GRouter recognizes the incoming message as a multicast one and spreads it on the Gnutella network. When replies arrive, a standard Gnutella servent would pass them on to the User Interface component, which is responsible to show them to the user. In our prototype, the Reputation Manager selects a subset of the servents listed in the reply set; choice criteria are the servents' connection speeds, the extra information included in some version of the protocol,[3] and, possibly, the content of Experience Repository, which is queried using the servent identifier *servent_id* as key. In such a case, the Reputation Manager uses the record extracted from the Experience Repository to decide whether to trust the corresponding servent or not. After a set of reliable servents

---

[3] For instance, the open data field [16] allows servent to specify if they have successfully uploaded at least one file, if the servent's upload slots are currently full, and also if their connection is firewalled.

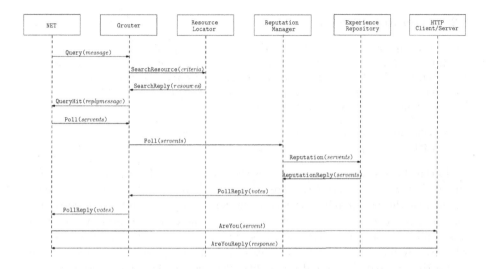

Fig. 4. UML Sequence diagram of a reply session

has been chosen, a poll message is broadcast by the GRouter. Replies to the poll request are forwarded to the Reputation Manager. The last step of P2PRep requires this component to verify votes through a direct connection. The percentage of servents that are actually contacted is a configuration parameter that is set by the user.

Once verification has been completed, the Reputation Manager can associate, with each servent, the sum of all positive votes about it.[4] Votes given by servents that are considered not trustable according to the credibility information stored in the Experience Repositoryare ignored, and the best servent is chosen for download via HTTP Client/Server.

After downloading, the user may cast a vote about the resource. This binary vote is used to update Experience Repository, and properly changing the reputation of the servent that provided the resource and those who voted for it.

At the receiving end, the method invocation sequence is summarized in Figure 4. Incoming queries are unpacked by the GRouter and sent to the Resource Locator, which is responsible of checking in the file repository if there are files that match that criteria. The information on these files is sent to the GRouter that just send it back, in a QueryHit message. When a Poll message arrives, it is sent to the Reputation Manager which checks if the Experience Repositoryincludes information about the servents listed in the message. If this is the case, it passes the encrypted information about them to the GRouter. The latter then sends a PollReply message. Note that IP verification messages (AreYou messages) come directly to the HTTP Client/Server component, that is able to reply correctly.

---

[4] Our current implementation considers binary votes, where 1 represents a positive vote (in favor of the servent) and 0 a negative vote.

3.2   Repository Schema

Several schema and data model solutions can be adopted for the reputation and credibility information managed by the **Experience Repository** component. In our current implementation, the **Experience Repository** consists of two tables, namely **reputation_repository** and **credibility_repository**. The tables' schemata are summarized below:

- **reputation_repository**: (*servent_id,num_plus,num_minus,timestamp*)
- **credibility_repository**: (*servent_id,num_agree,num_notagree,timestamp*)

In the above schemata, *servent_id* is the primary key of both tables, *num_plus* and *num_minus*, respectively, store the servent's positive and negative experiences with the peer having servent identifier *servent_id*, while *num_agree* and *num_notagree* contain the number of times that the vote expressed by *servent_id* was confirmed or not by the servent's experience. *servent_id* is 16 bytes long while the remaining fields are 4 bytes each. The purpose of the timestamp is supporting an experience and credibility lifecycle, allowing for filtering out entries unused for a long time. Each entry of the experience table is 28 bytes long, this means that less than 700Kb are needed for 25.000 servents; therefore, a relatively limited amount of storage should be enough to keep trace of both experience and credibility of all relevant servents. It is worth noticing that P2P applications are typically used to exchange resources of considerable size and the space required, even by an extensive repository, should be quite manageable.

3.3   Additional Protocol Messages

The implementation of P2PRep requires two additional protocol messages: **Poll** and **PollReply**. Since interoperability with the existing Gnutella network is of paramount importance, new messages introduced by our extension should be routable via standard servents. Our implementation satisfies this requirement by piggybacking the additional messages on standard **Query** and **QueryHit** Gnutella messages. Namely, **Poll** messages are implemented using the field **search criteria** of standard **Query** messages. As described before, **Poll** messages carry a servent list and a session public key. In order to identify the message and its encoding correctly, the payload starts with the string **REP:poll:HEX** as shown in Figure 5, followed by a list of the *servent_ids* of all servents whose reputation is being checked. At the end of the message there is the public key of the polling session. Standard Gnutella servents will process piggybacked queries as ordinary ones that do not match any file. In turn, **PollReply** messages are realized piggybacking **QueryHit** Gnutella messages. The first file entry contains zeros both as index and size, and the string **REP:prep:HEX** is specified as filename. We use the *private data* field in the trailer (introduced by version v1.3.0 of the **BearShare** servent), to store the encrypted payload and its signature. The payload, encrypted with RSA(512), begins with the servent's **IP** and **Port**. A sequence of **index-vote** pairs follows, where **index** is a two bytes field specifying the position of the *servent_id* in the **Poll** message, while **vote** is encoded

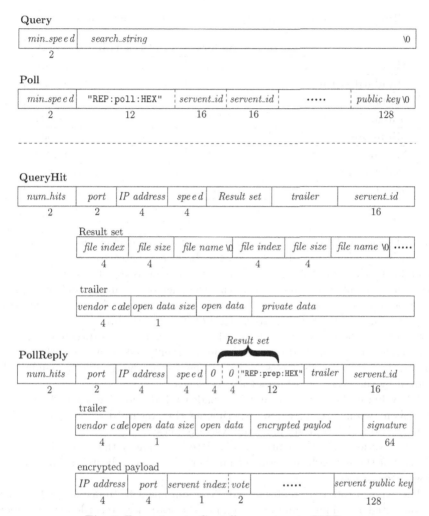

Fig. 5. Extensions to Gnutella messages in P2PRep

in one byte. The payload ends with the `Servent public key`. A 64 bytes long
signature for the whole message is appended. It is computed as follows: a digest
of the plain text payload (MD5) is encrypted (using RSA) with the private key
associated to the servent public key. Finally, some of the incoming `PollReply`
messages are chosen for vote checking and IP addresses listed in the messages
are checked via a direct connection. The message used to this purpose has the
form `AreYou`*servent_id*, where *servent_id* is encoded in 16 bytes.

3.4   Performance

The P2PRep protocol requires additional message exchanges for every successful
request. A limited impact on the performance of the P2P network is a critical

Table 1. Statistical measures obtained by 100 experimental sessions

	# of responders	# of reachable servents
Mean	785.7	343474.2
Standard Error	45.0	21095.6
Median	679	342000
Range	2213	946000
Minimum	71	16000
Maximum	2284	962000
95% CI min	696.3	301599.7
95% CI max	875.1	385348.7

success factor for the protocol. The protocol additional exchanges can be distinguished in broadcast and direct messages. It is reasonable to assume that the major load of the protocol on network performance is due to broadcast messages. Direct communication requires the exchange of a limited number of quick messages. For instance, direct connections are used to implement the AreYou message, which is a call to the HTTP Client/Server module. This exchange is very quick, as the message contains only few bytes and it is directed to a few of the nodes that expressed their votes on a servent. Indeed, most performance models of P2P networks stress as a limiting factor the aggregate bandwidth required by the exchange of broadcast messages.

To evaluate the impact that the broadcast Poll messages could have on the P2P network, we ran a few experiments that returned a few quantitative measures, on which a preliminary analysis was based.

A first series of experiments was dedicated to identify the regularity on the behavior of the network, in terms of number of reachable hosts and number of answers to a query.

The experiments were realized connecting our client to 10 fast servents. Each session lasted 10 minutes and at the end of the session we recorded the number of hosts that were signaled as reachable by the protocol. We repeated this experiment 100 times in two days and the results are shown in Table 1. After 5 minutes in each session we started a search for a common file (5 minutes are in our experience sufficient to reach a stable horizon, with a fast Internet connection as the one we were using). The node waited for results of the search for 5 minutes, until the end of the session.

The results we obtained indicate a relative stability of the network configuration. Both the number of reachable hosts and the number of replies to the search request exhibit a limited variation interval for the 95% of the measures. Also, the number of hosts that are reachable is relatively high and this guarantees that a sizable portion of the Gnutella network is within the horizon. It is then reasonable to assume that the protocol will be able to find an adequate reputation support for the nodes which have offered, for a period, quality resources on the network.

Table 2. Speed of servents that responded to queries

Class	Speed	# of servents	% over total
Cell	0	361,804	3.32%
14	14	55,293	0.51%
28	28	715,546	6.56%
56K	53	460,544	4.22%
ISDN	128	1,665,283	15.27%
Cable	384	3,351,010	30.73%
DSL	768	1,151,967	10.56%
T1	1500	1,508,287	13.83%
T3	>1500	1,634,979	14.99%
Total		**10,904,713**	**100%**

We now estimate the size of the messages required to evaluate the reputation of servents offering a resource. First, we observe that many servents can be polled with a single `Poll` message. The size of a `Poll` message is proportional to the number of servents to inquire. As most implementations drop messages bigger than 64Kb [15], a `Poll` message can carry up to around 4,000 different *servent_id*. We assume that it will not be necessary to ask on the reputation of so many servents. Instead, we assume that when a resource is offered by many servents, the client could select a subset of the servents to inquire, using as selection parameters the bandwidth that servents offer (faster is better) and heterogeneity in the IP address. Assuming to choose only 10 to 20 servents, the impact of the polling phase becomes comparable to an additional query delivered onto the network. To evaluate the distribution of network bandwidth among the servents, we ran another series of experiments. For a total of 32 hours a Gnutella node logged all the `QueryHit` traffic. The speed of the servents is distributed as shown in Table 2. We can see that most of the servents declare a high bandwidth, it is then reasonable to assume that a restriction only to servents offering a high bandwidth will not pose a limit on the number of servents that could offer the resource.

Several optimizations can reduce the impact of P2PRep on network performance. For instance, reputations can be cached on the nodes, and servents that have already been voted as reliable following a search, can keep the reputation for the remainder of the session. Reputations may be kept across sessions, further reducing the number of polling requests (at the expense of an increase in the storage requirements and a decrease in the responsiveness of the network to node misbehavior).

4   Handling Resource-Based Reputation

The solution described in this paper considered reputations associated with servents. An alternative (or complementary) solution consists in associating reputations with resources themselves. Intuitively, each resource can be associated

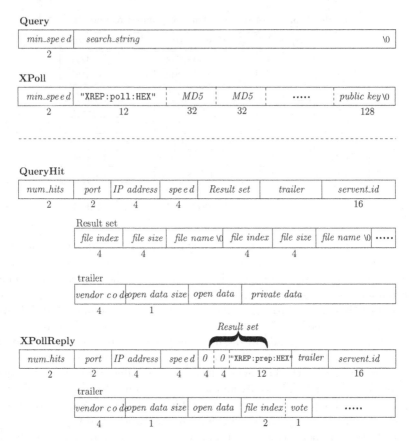

Fig. 6. Extensions to Gnutella messages in XP2PRep

with a digest computed applying a secure hash function to the resource's content. When a servent downloads a resource, it can record whether the resource (identified by its digest) is satisfactory or not. Then, it can share this opinion with others by responding to `Poll` requests broadcasted by a protocol's initiator to inquire about resource reputations (in contrast to servent's reputations). With respect to message exchanges, the resource-based reputation solution works essentially in the same way as the servent-based one. The messages content is adapted to support references to resources as illustrated in Figure 6.

Also, experience repository will need to refer to resources. Unlike with servents it is sufficient to maintain just a record stating whether the resource is reliable or not (there is no need to maintain good and bad records). The repository has then three fields: `digest`, `vote`, and `timestamp`. With a digest 16-bytes long, a vote 1-byte long, and timestamp 4-bytes long, we can store up to 50,000 entries in 1 Mb. Therefore, while the number of resources is expected to be much greater than the number of servents, the storage requirements appear not to be a problem.

5   Conclusions and Future Work

We have presented the design and implementation of a reputation-aware Gnutella servent. The overall rationale and some specific choices of our design were discussed. Our experience shows that introducing reputations does not require extensive re-engineering either of existing clients or of the Gnutella protocol itself. The additional performance burden of managing and exchanging reputation data does not seem to significantly degrade Gnutella's performance. The piggybacking technique adopted in our implementation allows our reputation-aware servents to take advantage of the evolution of the standard Gnutella protocol.[5] In our opinion, P2PRep performance impact is potentially well counterbalanced by the overall increase in P2P network security that could result from its large scale adoption.

In the long run, reputation-based protocols may even allow P2P systems to preserve anonymity without the need of costly central agencies for managing identities [5]. We are well aware that servent self-regulation alone cannot guarantee identity persistence; however, cooperative solutions like P2PRep encourage servents that want to act as distribution points to keep a single, trusted identity.

P2P applications are evolving very quickly and many of the results we present in the paper will have to be adapted to the architectures that are now going to be implemented (e.g., architectures with ultra-peers, as the architecture on which the last version of the Gnutella protocol is based). Also, our future implementations will rely on richer query support provided by sophisticated Gnutella servents. LimeWire, for instance, implements a new XML-based encoding for Gnutella queries [14]. With respect to Gnutella 0.4 queries [16], the LimeWire format uses an additional section, located after the ordinary query, to contain the extended query. A valid extended query has to comply with an XML schema specified via a Uniform Resource Identifier (URI). Several standard URIs have already been defined, but other XML schemata can be added. By defining a suitable XML schema, meta-information could be added to our protocol messages, enabling P2PRep aware servents to exchange semantically richer information about other servents and resources.

References

1. S. Bellovin. Security aspects of Napster and Gnutella. In *Proc. of USENIX 2001*, Boston, June 2001.
2. I. Clarke, O. Sandberg, B. Wiley, and T. Hong. Freenet: A distributed anonymous information storage and retrieval system. In *Proc. of the ICSI Workshop on Design Issues in Anonymity and Unobservability*, Berkeley, CA, July 2000.
3. F. Cornelli, E. Damiani, S. De Capitani di Vimercati, S. Paraboschi, and P. Samarati. Choosing reputable servents in a P2P network. In *Proc. of the Eleventh International World Wide Web Conference*, Honolulu, Hawaii, May 2002.

---

[5] For example, LimeWire's Ping messages are not routed as usual multicast messages, but cached. This solution could be used also for *servent_id*, fostering reduction of the length of PollReply messages.

4. R. Dingledine, M.J. Freedman, and D. Molnar. The Free Haven project: Distributed anonymous storage service. In *Proc. of the Workshop on Design Issues in Anonymity and Unobservability*, Berkeley, California, USA, July 2000.

5. J.R. Douceur. The sybil attack. In *Proc. of the IPTPS02 Workshop*, Cambridge, MA (USA), March 2002.

6. P. Druschel and A. Rowstron. Past: A large-scale persistent peer-to-peer storage utility. In *Proc. of the Eight IEEE Workshop on Hot Topics in Operating Systems (HotOS-VIII)*, Schoss Elmau, Germany, May 2001.

7. P. Golle and K. Leyton-Brown. Incentives for sharing in peer-to-peer networks. In *Proc. of the Third ACM Conference on Electronic Commerce*, Tampa, Florida, USA, October 2001.

8. L. Gong. JXTA: A network programming environment. *IEEE Internet Computing*, 5(3):88–95, May/June 2001.

9. Openprivacy. http://www.openprivacy.org.

10. A. Oram, editor. *Peer-to-Peer: Harnessing the Power of Disruptive Technologies*. O'Reilly & Associates, March 2001.

11. M. Parameswaran, A. Susarla, and A.B. Whinston. P2P networking: An information-sharing alternative. *IEEE Computer*, 34(7):31–38, July 2001.

12. M. Ripeanu. Peer-to-peer architecture case study: Gnutella network. Technical Report TR-2001-26, University of Chicago, Department of Computer Science, July 2001.

13. S. Saroiu, P.K. Gummadi, and S.D. Gribble. A measurement study of peer-to-peer file sharing systems. In *Proc. of the Multimedia Computing and Networking*, San Jose, CA, January 2002.

14. S. Thadani. Meta information searches on the Gnutella network. http://rfc-gnutella.sourceforge.net/Proposals/MetaData/meta_information_searches.htm.

15. S. Thadani. Free riding on Gnutella. Technical report, LimeWire LLC, 2001. http://www.limewire.org.

16. *The Gnutella Protocol Specification v0.4 (Document Revision 1.2)*, June 2001. http://www.clip2.com/GnutellaProtocol04.pdf.

17. B. Yang and H. Garcia-Molina. Comparing hybrid peer-to-peer systems. In *Proc. of the 27th International Conference on Very Large Data Bases*, Rome, Italy, September 2001.

Transaction-Based Charging in Mnemosyne: A Peer-to-Peer Steganographic Storage System

Timothy Roscoe[1] and Steven Hand[2]

[1] Intel Research, 2150 Shattuck Ave Suite 1300, Berkeley, CA 94704, USA,
troscoe@intel-research.net
[2] University of Cambridge Computer Laboratory, Cambridge, CB3 0FD, UK,
steven.hand@cl.cam.ac.uk

Abstract. Mnemosyne is a peer-to-peer steganographic storage system: one in which the existence of a user's files cannot be verified without a key. This paper applies the techniques used in Mnemosyne – erasure codes and anonymous block writing – to move most of the administrative overhead of a commercial storage service over to the client, resulting in cost savings for the service provider.

The contribution of this paper is to present a radically alternative way of charging for storage services. In place of renting some amount of space for some period of time, systems like Mnemosyne allow more flexible billing models closer to those proposed for network bandwidth, including versions of congestion pricing. We show how a reliable, commercial storage service using is feasible, and examine the details of the tradeoff it offers compared with conventional storage services.

1 Introduction

This paper describes a novel paradigm for a distributed storage service built over a peer-to-peer network. The benefits of the approach are extreme simplicity of operation with compared with traditional storage services.

Several current research efforts are building Internet-scale object storage systems by addressing the problem of distributing the functionality of an object store over a peer-to-peer network. This results in self-organising distributed object storage that provides high availability in the face of node failure or network partition. However, such systems share with traditional, more centralised storage systems the complexity that comes from keeping track of large numbers of users and multiplexing storage space among them. Billing for storage adds even more complexity (and administrative overhead) to the system.

The original goal for Mnemosyne[1], described in [1], was to provide extremely high levels of privacy for low-volume, high-value data. As part of this, instead of maintaining space allocation at the server, Mnemosyne holds *no* information at the servers as to which blocks are in use or by whom, and instead relies solely on erasure codes to prevent each user's data being destroyed by the others' activities.

---

[1] Pronounced *ne moz'nē*.

E. Gregori et al. (Eds.): Networking 2002 Workshops, LNCS 2376, pp. 335–349, 2002.
© Springer-Verlag Berlin Heidelberg 2002

In this paper, we investigate the feasibility of this approach applied to general distributed storage. In particular we are interested in the costs and benefits of the Mnemosyne approach over traditional storage service models. We show that Mnemosyne in combination with charging for write transactions, rather than storage space *per se*, moves most of the complexity of storage service into the client software, resulting in extreme simplicity (and therefore low administrative overhead) for service providers.

The rest of this paper is structured as follows. In section 2 we briefly review the peer-to-peer application space and position Mnemosyne in this space, both as a highly secure system and as the commercial storage and messaging service we describe here. This latter application of Mnemosyne sidesteps a number of serious design challenges that have recently come to light with peer-to-peer systems.

In section 3 we give a functional overview of Mnemosyne, including a brief description of the current implementation.

In section 4 we use simulation to investigate what kinds of integrity guarantees Mnemosyne is capable of delivering, and what this integrity costs in extra disk storage over conventional systems. In particular, we derive a measure of the "effective capacity" of a Mnemosyne system, which we use to motivate the next section.

Section 5 explores the implications of the findings in section 4 for running a commercial peer-to-peer storage service based on Mnemosyne. We give several different models of charging, and show how what calculations clients must make to use the system, and how service providers decide how much to provision their system for a given effective capacity.

Finally, section 6 concludes with a summary of the tradeoff that Mnemosyne offers.

2   Context and Related Work

Perhaps the defining characteristic of peer-to-peer systems is their ability to self-organize – new nodes can join and leave the network without disruption or the need for central coordination or control.

This self-organisation and absence of central control has been exploited to produce systems with strong properties of anonymity and resistance to censorship, such as Freenet [2], FreeHaven [3], and Publius [4].

Research peer-to-peer systems have also appeared which address the scalability problems with early file sharing networks like Gnutella [5]. Projects like Tapestry [6], CAN [7], Chord [8] and Pastry [9] aim to provide robust and highly available generic *distributed hash table* (DHT) functionality; that is, they logically provide an operation lookup(key) which maps from an opaque bit string to a node address. In practice, most implementations provide "route message to key" functionality which can then be used to build a variety of applications, for example Oceanstore [10], Bayeux [11], CFS [12], PAST [13], and SCRIBE [14].

The original motivation for Mnemosyne involved a combination of privacy and storage service. Mnemosyne is a distributed *steganographic* file system.

A steganographic file system [15] has the property that it gives a user strong protection against being compelled to disclose (all) its contents. Whereas in a cryptographic file system, attackers not in possession of the secret are unable to acquire the contents of files, in a steganographic system they cannot even gain information about whether a given file is present or not. Mnemosyne achieves this property by spreading data pseudo-randomly throughout a peer-to-peer network.

Recently, a combination of deployment experience and research has pointed out a number of vulnerabilities of peer-to-peer systems, both the adversarial attacks and pathological (but common) traffic and usage patterns. For example:

- Load Skew: most P2P schemes assume all participants are equal (i.e. peers) yet studies have shown that node capabilities and user behaviour vary greatly [16,17]. This negates the basic design assumptions and requires new, non-uniform solutions, such as supernodes in Gnutella [18].
- Untrustworthy Peers: since anyone can join at any time, these schemes are vulnerable to certain denial of service attacks: a 'bad' peer can interfere with the lookup or search processes yet typically cannot easily be identified or avoided. Recent schemes acknowledge this problem and hope to address it by using byzantine fault-tolerant schemes.
- 'Sybil' Attacks: identity replication attacks [19] illustrate that even byzantine fault-tolerant protocols cannot adequately operate in a completely free-for-all environment.

We observe that these problems can be avoided by limiting those who may participate in the peer-to-peer network, either by limiting the system to a closed environment (such as Google's search engine implementation) or by system design (such as Farsite [19] or Oceanstore's inner ring [10]).

This paper discusses the issues in using Mnemosyne to provide a commercial distributed storage service, for both long-term applications (such as archival storage) and short-term storage needs (such as secure messaging applications). For this scenario, we consider Mnemosyne nodes to be "servers" and under the control of either one service provider, or a group of reputable, federated providers (as is the case with BGP peers in the Internet, for example). In contrast, Mnemosyne "clients" are users of the system and do not participate in the peer-to-peer network.

This division is useful for many reasons: servers are readily identifiable (e.g. via a certificate) and so Sybil attacks are avoided; servers are at least somewhat trusted, and so byzantine fault tolerance techniques can be applied, and servers are stable and can be dimensioned so that load skew and server "churn" is not an issue.

Clients are still part of the overall system, and may use the same or similar protocols as servers. In general, clients contact any server and ask it to perform the relevant operation (lookup, routing, etc) as its proxy. The results, if any, are returned by the same server. Clients do not directly communicate with each other.

This generalised many-clients/many-servers model also allows us to draw a clear trust boundary within the system: the point of client-server interaction.

As we discuss in section 5, it is where one can use micropayment schemes (e.g. Chaumian digital cash [20]) to not only pay for the service on a per-transaction basis but also mitigate denial of service attacks (by making them expensive).

3   A Functional Overview of Mnemosyne

Mnemosyne [1] is a peer-to-peer steganographic storage system built at Sprint Labs. The principle of steganographic storage, proposed in [15], is that users of the system who do not have the required key not only are unable to read the contents of files stored under that key (as with a conventional encrypting file system), but furthermore are unable to determine the existence of files stored under that key.

In a multiuser distributed system such as Mnemosyne, this leads to an interesting property: since users cannot know anything about the location of file blocks stored by other users, it is always possible for them to unwittingly overwrite them; the existence of a file allocation table or list of in-use blocks defeats the steganographic properties of the system. Instead, Mnemosyne uses redundancy in the form of erasure codes to prevent file data being lost due to the write activity of other users.

The process by which a user of Mnemosyne stores a vector of bytes in the system can be broken down into four phases: dispersal, encryption, location, and distribution, which we describe in turn.

Dispersal: In the dispersal phase, the data is encoded to make it robust in the face of losses of blocks. Our implementation uses Rabin's Information Dispersal Algorithm [21] in the field $GF(2^{16})$ to transform n blocks of data into $m > n$ blocks, any n of which suffice to recover the original data. In our implementation, m is typically $5n$ for file data (as opposed to directories and inodes), the block size is 1000 bytes, and n is no greater than 32. Files of larger than 32,000 bytes are handled by chunking. We discuss choices of m and n later on in this paper.

Encryption: The dispersed blocks from the previous step are now encrypted under the user's key K. The purpose of this is twofold: firstly for security and privacy, but secondly for authenticity. This is especially important in a system like Mnemosyne where we expect significant numbers of blocks to be overwritten by other users in normal usage. Thus we need a mechanism by which a user can determine whether a block subsequently retrieved from the network is really the one originally written. Since this check must be made before the data is reconstituted by reversing the dispersal step, encryption is done after dispersal.

Mnemosyne as currently implemented uses the AES algorithm in Offset Code Book (OCB) mode [22] to provide security and a 16-byte Message Authentication Check in one step. An alternative would be two-pass generic composition approaches, but OCB makes for easier key management. AES-OCB encryption of the (padded) dispersed blocks adds 16 bytes of MAC to the message for a total of 1024 bytes per block.

Location: Mnemosyne achieves its security properties by storing encrypted data blocks in pseudo-random (and to an adversary, unpredictable) places in a large virtual network store, which is then mapped onto distributed physical storage devices. The locations of the encrypted blocks making up a data set are determined by a sequence of 256-bit values obtained by successively hashing (using SHA256 in the current implementation) an initial value h_0.

The initial value h_0 depends ultimately on the user's key K. For file data itself, h_0 is generated randomly and stored in an inode; for inodes and directory blocks, h_0 is computed by encrypting the pathname or directory name with the key K and hashing the result.

Distribution: The sequence of 256-bit location identifiers from the previous step is finally mapped onto physical storage using a peer-to-peer network of storage nodes, each of which holds a fixed-size physical block store.

For each block to be stored, both the node identifier and the block offset within the block store are derived from the corresponding location identifier. In the current implementation of Mnemosyne, the top 160 bits of this identifier are used to as a node identifier in a Tapestry [6] network. A block to be written is sent to a randomly selected Tapestry node, which routes the block to the "surrogate" node for the 160-bit node identifier. The next 20 bits of the location id are then used as a block number in a 1GB block store.

The node location component of distribution is relatively independent of the underlying peer-to-peer lookup service employed; while Mnemosyne currently uses Tapestry [6], any of [7,8,9] would work just as well. Indeed, since the Mnemosyne client is not itself a Tapestry node, but communicates with a randomly chosen node using a simple UDP-based protocol, a client could conceivably use several P2P networks from different storage providers simultaneously. What we require of the P2P network is deterministic routing of messages tagged with arbitrary n-bit identifiers to nodes.

The block store at each peer-to-peer node supports only the following two operations:

- **putBlock**(*blockid, data*)
- **getBlock**(*blockid*) → *data*

Note that the block storage nodes themselves need perform no authentication, encryption, access checking, or block allocation to ensure correct functioning of the system, though they might for billing purposes. Indeed, a block store may ignore the above operations entirely: as long as sufficiently many block stores implement the operations faithfully, users' data can be recovered.

Retrieval: Data is retrieved from Mnemosyne by the reverse process: given an initial hash value for the data, a user computes the sequence of location identifiers and uses it to retrieve at least n "good" blocks (i.e. blocks which pass the MAC check). Given these, the original data can be recovered by inverting the IDA. Requests for blocks can proceed in parallel to reduce the effects of network latency.

3.1 Filing System Structures

In [1] we describe one implementation of a per-user filing system over the data storage and retrieval procedures described above. The filing system uses directories and inodes to simplify the management of keys and initial hash values, and also handles versioning of files, a necessity since it data is never actually deleted from Mnemosyne, but rather decays over time. When retrieving blocks for a file it is essential that the blocks retrieved all correspond to the latest version of the file.

3.2 Implementation

A working implementation of Mnemosyne for Linux exists. The client is written in C and C++, using freely available reference implementations of SHA-256 and AES-OCB. It provides a command-line interface with operations for key management, creating and listing directories, and copying files between Mnemosyne and the Unix file system. A simple block protocol over UDP is used for communication with block servers. The block server is implemented in Java and runs on Tapestry [6] nodes. Performance is plausible - we can copy files into Mnemosyne at 80 kilobytes per second, and read them at 160 kilobytes per second. A principal limiting factor in both cases is our (unoptimised) $GF(2^{16})$ arithmetic implementation.

We hope to make the source code for our implementation available in the near future.

4 Experimental Results: Measuring File Resiliency

In this section we use simulation to investigate the feasibility of Mnemosyne as a serious storage service. While analytical results are obtainable for most of what follows, the simulation results are more useful for giving a feel of how the system works. Since Mnemosyne relies on extensive redundancy in data encoding, and overwrites of blocks are part of the normal operation of the system, we define here two quantities which are of obvious interest when considering whether the system is practical: *efficiency* and *life expectancy*.

4.1 Asymptotic Efficiency and Capacity

We define *capacity* of a Mnemosyne system as the quantity of (undispersed) data that can be stored. The *efficiency* is this capacity, expressed as a fraction of the total raw disk space available in the system. Since we are dealing with a multiuser system in which users are generally unaware of each others' activities, efficiency is primarily of interest to service providers as part of their provisioning process: it gives them a handle on how much raw disk space they need to provide.

We first present a naive but intuitive notion of efficiency that we call *asymptotic* efficiency E_{asym}. Figure 1 shows the results of repeatedly writing fixed-size files into a store under different coding schemes. In this, as in all the other results in this section, files are 5 blocks in size before dispersal and the total size

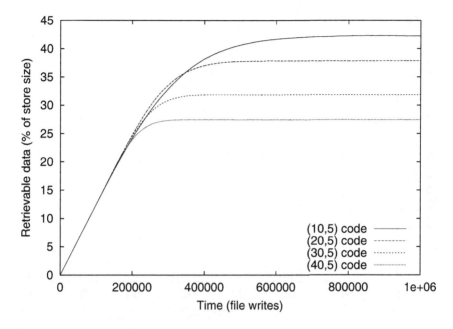

Fig. 1. Writing files into a simulated 4Mblock store.

of the store is 4,000,000 blocks. The simulation keeps track of which files are still recoverable from the store, that is, those files that still have 5 blocks of their original data in the store.

Figure 1 shows the total number of accessible files, starting with an empty store. As more files are written, the system reaches a steady state in which writing each new file, on average, renders one existing file unreadable (by overwriting one of the five remaining blocks of the victim file). The total amount of data in accessible files at this limit is the asymptotic capacity C_{asym} of the store. The asymptotic efficiency E_{asym} is this divided by the capacity of the store (4M blocks).

We can see that E_{asym} varies with the redundancy used: for a redundancy factor of 2 – a (10,5) code – we can store data equal in size to about 42% of the store. As we increase the redundancy of the coding, this figure drops to about 27% for a redundancy factor of 8 with a (40,5) code.

Figure 2 shows how E_{asym} varies with a larger number of coding schemes. While there is a maximum at around (12,5), a more important result is that for redundancy factors between 3 and 8, the asymptotic efficiency of the store remains at over 25%, a remarkably high figure. This suggests that we have, from an efficiency standpoint, a fair degree of freedom in choosing our coding scheme.

While E_{asym} is relatively intuitive measure of store utilisation, it doesn't capture anything about how long files can be expected to survive after being initially written. More precisely, it contains no notion of the distribution of file lifetimes.

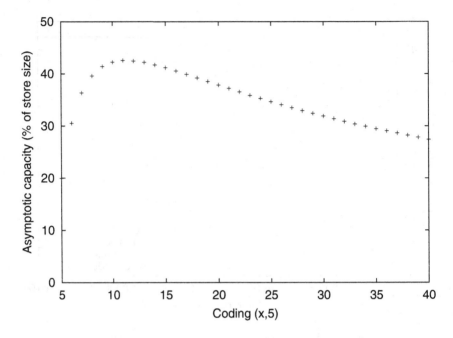

Fig. 2. Asymptotic efficiency E_{asym} of a simulated 4Mblock store.

4.2   Life Expectancy

Figure 3 shows the cumulative distribution of file lifetimes. We run the experiment as before, but now each time a file becomes inaccessible, we record the number of files written between the time when the victim file was first written, and the time it is lost. This distribution of file lifetimes is important to Mnemosyne users because it gives them realistic expectations of how long their data is likely to be around if it isn't "refreshed" (rewritten to the store).

For comparison, we have included the (5,5) code in this graph, that is, the results of writing files with no redundancy at all. This clearly doesn't constitute a useful file service: a significant number of files written under this scheme are completely lost within a small number of subsequent file writes.

For redundant coding schemes, the median file lifetime decreases as the redundancy of the coding increases - the halfway point of the curve moves left towards the origin. However, the variation in file lifetimes also decreases.

Of primary concern to a client of Mnemosyne is the region of these curves very close to the x-axis, which is the region where the proportion of files lost is very low. Figure 4 shows the region between 0 and 0.01% of files. We can see that for (25,5) and (35,5) coding schemes, the chance that a file will have been lost from this store after 80,000 other files have been written is less than 0.00001. In other words, the chances that a file is accessible after 80,000 other files have been written is better than 99.999%.

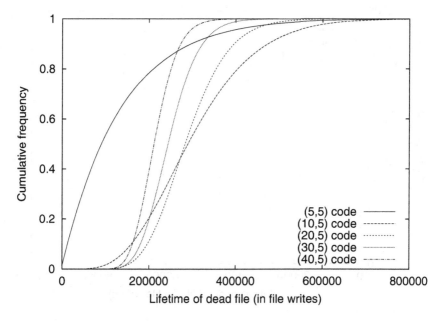

Fig. 3. File lifetimes in a simulated 4Mblock store.

Recall that in this simulation we used a store with 4 million blocks, and files were all 5 blocks in size. 80,000 files therefore corresponds to 400,000 blocks, or 10% of the store size in *undispersed* data.

It's clear that this figure of 10% in blocks (rather than files) is valid for other file sizes and store sizes, as long as files are much smaller than the total store size (a reasonable assumption in a distributed storage system of this kind). The implication is that, using a redundancy factor of 5, users can retrieve their files with 99.999% certainty provided they do it before 10% of the total store capacity in raw data has been written by other users.

This probability is likely to be better than the probability of disks or machines failing during a reasonable period, and is unlikely to be a dominant factor in determining the resilience of a storage service. We discuss below some options for allowing users to determine how long it takes for 10% of the store size in real data to be written or, in this case, 50% of the store size in dispersed data to be overwritten. This latter measure is more significant since this is independent of any client's coding scheme, can be directly observed by a service provider, and also estimated by a 3rd party using sampling techniques, as we discuss below.

4.3   Effective Capacity and Efficiency

The preceding observations lead to more useful corresponding measures of capacity and efficiency. For a particular probability of retrieval (say 99.999%), a file must be retrieved before some amount of the store k blocks of the store have

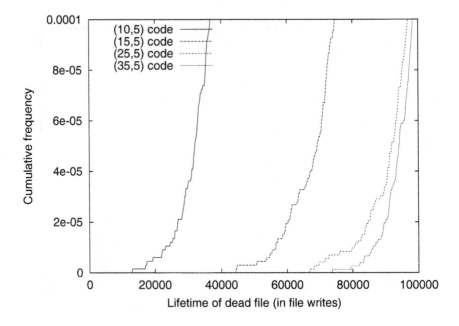

Fig. 4. Enlarged area of figure 3.

been has been written to (in our example, 50% of it or 2M blocks). For long term storage, a given file will need to be rewritten ("refreshed") each time this point is reached.

If we consider a store of fixed size where no files are ever discarded, it is clear that no more than k blocks may be used to store data – when k have been used, all further writes must be to refresh existing files in the store.

This gives us the notions of *effective* capacity and efficiency: for a given redundancy of encoding and retrieval probability, the effective capacity C_{eff} is the maximum quantity of raw data that can be written to the store before all subsequent writes must be refreshes. C_{eff} is equal to k divided by the redundancy of the coding scheme used (5 in our example).

The effective efficiency E_{eff} of the store is the ratio of C_{eff} to the total store size. On the basis of our simulations, we can say that the effective efficiency of a Mnemosyne store with 5:1 redundancy and retrieval probability of 99.999% is about 10%. Our current work includes reproducing this result analytically.

10% effective efficiency (i.e. we need 10 times as much disk as the amount of data to be stored) is a plausible degree of overprovisioning. Whether this makes economic sense in practice depends on the ever-changing cost tradeoffs between disk drives, network bandwidth, maintenance, etc. However, in the next section we formulate arguments as to why this extra cost in disk space might be more than compensated for by cost savings in areas like administrative complexity and billing infrastructure.

5   Economics of Steganographic Storage

In this section, we discuss charging for steganographic storage (understood now as storage where clients write blocks arbitrarily in a large distributed store). Mnemosyne as described has a number of important characteristics in this regard.

In Mnemosyne, all filing system structures and policy have been moved into the client. While our inode-based filing system works well in practice, each user is free to implement whatever structure they like over the basic block store. Furthermore, tradeoffs involved in how to encode a file, how often to refresh it, etc. are decided by the client and not the server. The server in fact doesn't really know how much capacity a client is using.

The upside of this is that all the complexity associated with traditional storage services (whether network-attached storage systems providing CIFS and NFS, or storage-area networks providing raw SCSI logical units, or object-based storage like Oceanstore) is removed from the server and transferred to the client. Steganographic storage providers *only* need to be concerned about overall capacity planning.

However, charging for such a service cannot therefore be done on the basis of space used, or time periods over which such space is used, since the servers do not have access to this information. It is ultimately unreasonable in Mnemosyne to charge based on the presence of a user's data block on the system, since no guarantees are made as to the life expectancy of a single block.

Instead, the natural charging model for Mnemosyne and other steganographic storage services is to charge *individually per write transaction* (and, possibly, read transactions as well). This several additional advantages: there is no longer any need for a centrally coordinated accounting system to be involved in individual writes: since each transaction can be treated independently, billing records can be aggregated and processed later, off-line.

Indeed, note that in Mnemosyne the service provider has no direct need to know the identity of any client executing a write, as long as their money is good. Consequently, a digital cash scheme such as [20] not only has potentially desirable anonymity properties, but can also result in even lower billing overhead.

5.1   The Mnemosyne Tradeoff

Of course, it is hard to obtain accurate information for how much of the cost of running a storage service is due to maintaining file system metadata, user account details, enforcing space quotas, and billing. This will also vary between different providers and the different types of storage service offered, and will also change over time as technology and demand evolve.

However, there does seem to be agreement that this complexity is a significant cost factor, and this overhead increases if we consider large numbers of users with (relatively) small storage requirements, rather than the large, corporate-wide data warehousing applications that current storage providers target.

This is the crucial tradeoff that Mnemosyne offers: additional requirements in raw disk space, in return for extreme operational simplicity. Whether a Mnemosyne service makes commercial sense depends on the nature of this tradeoff in each particular instance. Our contribution in this paper is to present the Mnemosyne model as a radical alternative to traditional approaches to storage service.

We observe that RAID as a technology for increasing reliability and performance offer very little benefit in our case, since Mnemosyne is already spreading load and redundant data over a much larger set of disks. Using raw disks without RAID controllers will, on a large scale, offer better global optimisation of both performance and reliability.

As an additional comment, we would point out that in scenarios where much disk space would normally be unused (for example, due to static allocation between users), the tradeoff tips more in Mnemosyne's favour.

5.2   The Time Constant of a Store

For clients to be able to make effective use of a Mnemosyne store, they need to know the rate (over time) at which writes to the store happen, expressed as a fraction of the total size of the store. This allows them to calculate, for their own desired encoding scheme and retrieval probability, the refresh interval they need to work to. Providers also need this value in order to perform provisioning, discussed below.

This value is the *time constant*, τ of the store. It can be understood intuitively as the time period over which $1/e$ of the store is written to. In reality τ is not constant over time, but changes both as load on the store changes and capacity is added.

Given this notion of a time constant, we can now discuss how storage providers and clients make decisions over the service.

5.3   The Provider's Standpoint

How does a provider of steganographic storage provision and charge for their storage capacity? The problem is somewhat flexible due to the extra variable of write rate: if the capacity is small, clients will need to refresh their files more often, which increases the write rate, which increases the cost to clients of storing data for long periods. This of course assumes in turn that clients know the rate of block writes expressed as a fraction of the store capacity.

It will become clear that there are parallels between this problem, and that of charging and traffic engineering in data networks. We point out some of these connections below. Several approaches suggest themselves. We outline three (non-exclusive) options here; they are the subject of ongoing research:

Fixed advertised time constant: The provider advertises a particular time constant τ'. This τ' then becomes the basis of the contract (explicit or implied) between clients and provider. The provider needs to ensure that enough disk space is added to the system to ensure that the "real" time constant τ is always greater than τ'. While very simple, this approach has some parallels with how IP backbone capacity is provisioned today.

Measurement-based provisioning: 3rd-party measurement services can verify or discover the time constant of a particular storage provider. They would do this by writing known data into a randomly chosen collection of blocks, and then observing how rapidly this data becomes overwritten. This market-based approach allows clients to select storage providers with appropriate capacity and also encourages storage providers to provision adequately to remain competitive. Naturally such a scheme requires that unscrupulous providers cannot or do not give preferential treatment to measurement services in an attempt to appear to have better time constants than they really do. A similar issue exists today with web latency measurement services like Keynote and content distribution networks.

Congestion pricing for storage: Rather than a fixed charge per transaction, a provider might charge for a write transaction based on the current instantaneous write rate seen by that provider. This has obvious parallels with the congestion pricing approach to network provisioning [23]. Most of the proposals related to congestion pricing (such as 3rd party aggregators who charge a premium in return for carrying the risk of price fluctuations) carry over to storage in this case.

5.4   The Client's Standpoint

A client using a Mnemosyne service is interested in ensuring a particular level of resilience for their data while minimising cost. The time constant τ of the store gives, for any encoding scheme, the longest period after which data must be refreshed to be retrievable with the appropriate probability. Assuming a fixed transaction cost, the client should then pick an encoding scheme which minimises the number of writes over a long period within these constraints.

If there are multiple storage services to choose from, the situation becomes a little more complex. Each will have different time constants and charges, and so the client should perform the optimisation described above for each service and pick the cheapest.

6   Conclusions

We have presented Mnemosyne, a distributed storage system based on a peer-to-peer lookup service. The system holds no metadata whatsoever at storage nodes (including information about users). Mnemosyne therefore presents a novel tradeoff: simplicity of operations, maintenance and management in exchange for disk space. Mnemosyne has been implemented and demonstrated using the Tapestry routing layer as its lookup service.

This paper has examined the practical considerations for both service providers and users: service providers must provision their service and charge for it, clients must implement their desired resiliency tradeoffs, minimise their costs, and calculate when to periodically refresh files. We have shown that for both players, optimal behaviour depends on the time constant of the store: a measure of how quickly new data is written to it.

References

1. Steven Hand and Timothy Roscoe. Mnemosyne: Peer-to-Peer Steganographic Storage. In *Proceedings of the 1st International Workshop on Peer-to-Peer Systems, Boston, MA*, March 2002.
2. Ian Clarke, Oskar Sandberg, Brandon Wiley, and Theodore W. Hong. Freenet: A Distributed Anonymous Information Storage and Retrieval System. In *Workshop on Design Issues in Anonymity and Unobservability*, pages 46–66, July 2000.
3. Roger Dingledine, Michael J. Freedman, and David Molnar. The Free Haven Project: Distributed Anonymous Storage Service. In *Workshop on Design Issues in Anonymity and Unobservability*, pages 67–95, July 2000.
4. Marc Waldman, Aviel D. Rubin, and Lorrie Faith Cranor. Publius: A robust, tamper-evident, censorship-resistant, web publishing system. In *Proceeding of the 9th USENIX Security Symposium*, pages 59–72, August 2000.
5. F.S. Annexstein, K.A. Berman, and M. Jovanovic. Latency Effects on Reachability in Large-scale Peer-to-Peer Networks. In *Proceedings Thirteenth ACM Symposium on Parallel Algorithms and Architectures (SPAA)*, 2001.
6. Ben Y. Zhao, John D. Kubiatowicz, and Anthony D. Joseph. Tapestry: An Infrastructure for Fault-tolerant Wide-area Location and Routing. Technical Report UCB//CSD-01-1141, U. C. Berkeley, April 2000.
7. S Ratnasamy, P. Francis, M. Handley, R. Karp, and S. Shenker. A Scalable Content-Addressable Network. In *Proceedings of ACM SIGCOMM 2001, San Diego, California, USA.*, August 2001.
8. I. Stoica, R. Morris, D. Karger, F. Kaashoek, and H. Balakrishnan. Chord: A Scalable Peer-to-peer Lookup Service for Internet Applications. In *Proceedings of ACM SIGCOMM 2001, San Diego, California, USA.*, August 2001.
9. Antony Rowstron and Peter Druschel. Pastry: Scalable, decentralized object location and routing for large-scale peer-to-peer systems. In *Proceedings of the 18th IFIP/ACM Internation Conference on Distributed Systems Platforms (Middleware 2001), Heidelberg, Germany*, November 2001.
10. John Kubiatowicz, David Bindel, Yan Chen, Steven Czerwinski, Patrick Eaton, Dennis Geels, Ramakrishna Gummadi, Sean Rhea, Hakim Weatherspoon, Westley Weimer, Chris Wells, and Ben Zhao. OceanStore: An Architecture for Global-Scale Persistent Storage. In *Proceedings of the Ninth international Conference on Architectural Support for Programming Languages and Operating Systems (ASPLOS 2000)*, November 2000.
11. S. Zhuang, B. Zhao, A. Joseph, R. Katz, and J. Kubiatowicz. Bayeux: An Architecture for Scalable and Fault-tolerant Wide-area Data Dissemination. In *Proceedings of the Eleventh International Workshop on Network and Operating System Support for Digital Audio and Video (NOSSDAV 2001)*, June 2001.
12. F. Dabek, M. Kaashoek, D. Karger, R. Morris, and I. Stoica. Wide-area cooperative storage with CFS. In *Proceedings of the 18th ACM Symposium on Operating Systems Principles, Banff, Canada.*, October 2001.

13. Anthony Rowstron and Peter Druschel. Storage management and caching in PAST, a large scale persistent peer-to-peer storage utility. In *Proceedings of the 18th ACM Symposium on Operating Systems Principles, Banff, Canada.*, October 2001.

14. Antony Rowstron, Anne-Marie Kermarrec, Miguel Castro, and Peter Druschel. SCRIBE: The design of a large-scale event notification infrastructure. In *Proceedings of the Third International Workshop on Networked Group Communications (NGC2001), London, UK*, November 2001.

15. Ross Anderson, Roger Needham, and Adi Shamir. The Steganographic File System. In *IWIH: International Workshop on Information Hiding*, 1998.

16. Matei Ripeanu and Ian Foster. Mapping the Gnutella Network: Macroscopic Properties of Large-Scale Peer-to-Peer Systems. In *Proceedings of the 1st International Workshop on Peer-to-Peer Systems, Boston, MA*, March 2002.

17. Bryce Wilcox-O'Hearn. Experiences Deploying a Large-Scale Emergent Network. In *Proceedings of the 1st International Workshop on Peer-to-Peer Systems, Boston, MA*, March 2002.

18. Qin Lv, Sylvia Ratnasamy, and Scott Shenker. Can Heterogeneity Make Gnutella Scalable? In *Proceedings of the 1st International Workshop on Peer-to-Peer Systems, Boston, MA*, March 2002.

19. John R. Douceur. The Sybil Attack. In *Proceedings of the 1st International Workshop on Peer-to-Peer Systems, Boston, MA*, March 2002.

20. D. Chaum, A. Fiat, and M. Naor. Untraceable Electronic Cash. In *Advances in Cryptology - CRYPTO '88 Proceedings*, pages 319–327, 1989.

21. M. Rabin. Efficient dispersal of information for security, load balancing, and fault tolerance. *Communications of the ACM*, 36(2):335–348, April 1989.

22. Phillip Rogaway, Mihir Bellare, John Black, and Ted Krovetz. OCB: A Block-Cipher Mode of Operation for Efficient Authenticated Encryption. In *Eighth ACM Conference on Computer and Communications Security (CCS-8)*. ACM Press, August 2001.

23. Peter Key. Service differentiation: Congestion pricing, brokers and bandwidth futures. In *Proceedings of the Ninth International Workshop on Network and Operating System Support for Digital Audio and Video (NOSSDAV 1999)*, June 1999.

Author Index

Lecture Notes in Computer Science

For information about Vols. 1–2387
please contact your bookseller or Springer-Verlag